The Complete Idiot's Reference Card

The Eleven Most Common Woods and Their Characteristics

➤ **Soft maple.** The vanilla of woods, soft maple is often called broad leaf maple. It is light in color, relatively easy to work, and fairly stable. It has a nonporous, subtle grain pattern. It's also moderately inexpensive for a hardwood. Most curly maple is of the soft variety.

➤ **Hard maple.** Similar to soft maple, hard maple is—surprise!—harder. Often called rock maple, it is a real workhorse and is often the choice for butcher blocks, truck beds, and anywhere toughness is important. Hard maple is rarely curly, but it has greater visual depth to its grain when it is curly, which makes it spectacular.

➤ **Cherry.** This wood has a light, but rich, reddish color. Moderately hard and easy to work, cherry is very beautiful, especially when it's figured. Moderately priced and relatively stable, cherry is one of my favorite woods.

➤ **Walnut.** Rich, variegated dark brown and very sought after, walnut has become rare and expensive. Boards today frequently have defects and are narrow. Good quality walnut is a joy to work, relatively stable, and full of beautiful greens and purples among the browns.

➤ **Poplar.** Cheap and soft for a hardwood, poplar is not very distinctive-looking, but it is used as a secondary wood for drawer sides, internal parts, and painted projects, because it is workable, stable, and tightly grained.

➤ **Birch.** A step above poplar, birch is used as a secondary wood, and sometimes as a cheaper stand-in for maple, which it resembles. It is workable but takes stain unevenly. Birch is most commonly found as the face veneer on inexpensive plywood cabinets.

➤ **Pine.** Soft, cheap, and plentiful, pine also works and sands easily and can be quite beautiful. Prone to warping, knots, and other defects, pine does not take stain evenly, but it is often used for projects that are to be painted.

➤ **White oak.** Porous, light colored, and dramatically grained, it is moderately expensive, workable, and available. Like all oaks, it is both hard and strong. It also has a high rate of expansion and contraction.

➤ **Red oak.** Like white oak, but with a redder color, red oak does not generally work quite as easily, but it depends on the boards. These days, it's cheaper because it is not as desirable, but tastes and prices change.

➤ **Ash.** Ash is similar in appearance to white oak, but it is lighter in color. Although ash is often mistaken for white oak, it is not as popular or available. It is moderately priced.

➤ **Honduran mahogany.** All South American mahogany is now sold as Honduran. It is a great furniture wood that grows in huge trees, which means that 30-inch-wide boards are often available. It is very stable and workable. It's a bit expensive, although you save money on labor because it's so easy to work. It's also available in thick boards; four inches and thicker is not unusual.

alpha books

The Tools You Can't Live Without

- Workbench with vise
- Measuring tape (I like a $3/4$-inch × 12- to 25-foot-long blade)
- Combination square with 12-inch blade
- Set of four or five good butt chisels ($1/8$- to $1/4$-inch wide)
- Maul or mallet
- Screwdrivers (a #2 Phillips and a #2 slot head to start)
- Pliers
- Finish hammer
- Small back saw or Japanese Dozuki-style saw
- Cork sanding block
- Safety glasses
- Sharpening stones
- Marking knife
- Bevel gauge
- Smoothing plane
- A rasp or two
- File
- Marking gauge
- Drill with $1/2$-inch capacity and drill index
- Toolbox (an inexpensive plastic one is fine)

The Big Six Finishes

1. **Oil.** Simple to apply, oil requires lots of elbow grease. It can be very beautiful, but it offers little protection from moisture, humidity, or abrasion because it penetrates rather than building up a film on the surface.

2. **Shellac.** An ancient finish made from the secretions of the lac bug, shellac comes in both clear and orange or yellow color. It is easy to apply with a brush and builds a film in several coats. It offers great sealing properties against stains and airborne humidity, but it offers little protection against water. It is susceptible to heat and solvents such as alcohol as well. It can be touched up easily.

3. **Varnish.** Modern varnishes come in three main varieties: polyurethane, phenolic, and alkyd. Varnish is one tough finish, especially phenolic and polyurethane, and is perfect for tabletops and any other high-wear surfaces. It offers excellent protection against moisture, solvents, and abrasion. Varnishes are relatively hard to apply and take a long time to cure, but they build a thick film in few coats.

4. **Lacquer.** Most lacquers have to be sprayed, although some can be brushed or padded on. Lacquer dries easily, and you can apply a lacquer finish quickly. It offers moderate resistance to moisture, solvents, and abrasion. It also has great visual clarity and comes in colors.

5. **Water-based finishes.** Vastly improved in recent years, water-based finishes offer the benefits of low toxicity and less harm to the environment. They are getting tougher, and most offer decent protection from moisture, solvents, and abrasion. Clarity varies greatly from finish to finish. Most are easy to apply.

6. **Wax.** It does not offer much protection when used alone, but wax can be used to revive another finish that has gotten dull or scratched from use. It helps protect against abrasion by helping objects slide instead of digging in.

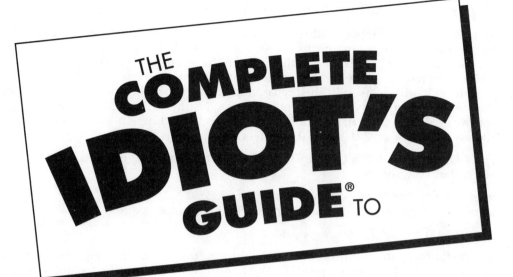

THE COMPLETE IDIOT'S GUIDE® TO

Woodworking

by Reed Karen

alpha books

Macmillan USA, Inc.
201 West 103rd Street
Indianapolis, IN 46290

A Pearson Education Company

Copyright © 2000 by Reed Karen

THE COMPLETE IDIOT'S GUIDE TO and Design are registered trademarks of Macmillan USA, Inc.

International Standard Book Number: 0-02-863237-0
Library of Congress Catalog Card Number: Available upon request.

02   01   00   8   7   6   5   4   3   2   1

Interpretation of the printing code: The rightmost number of the first series of numbers is the year of the book's printing; the rightmost number of the second series of numbers is the number of the book's printing. For example, a printing code of 00-1 shows that the first printing occurred in 2000.

Printed in the United States of America

Publisher
Marie Butler-Knight

Product Manager
Phil Kitchel

Managing Editor
Cari Luna

Acquisitions Editor
Randy Ladenheim-Gil

Development Editor
Doris Cross

Production Editor
Christy Wagner

Copy Editor
Heather Stith

Illustrator
Jody P. Schaeffer

Cover Designers
Mike Freeland
Kevin Spear

Book Designers
Scott Cook and Amy Adams of DesignLab

Indexer
Lisa Wilson

Layout/Proofreading
Angela Calvert
Mary Hunt
Paula Lowell
Jeannette McKay

Contents at a Glance

Part 1: Getting Real About Woodworking   **1**

1 Basics: The Shop, the Shopping, and the Skills   3
Figure out your goals, priorities, budget, and where to set up shop. Here's what you need and what you can live without.

2 I Need My Space: Setting Up Shop   11
We'd all like more space; here's how to make the most of what you have, including three strategies for organizing your work area.

3 A Workshop That Works   21
Before the machines arrive, you need to furnish your shop by picking out a workbench, sorting out a tool cabinet, and stabling the sawhorses.

Part 2: The Tools: The Work They Do and How to Work Them   **33**

4 Your Hand Tool Arsenal: The Cutters   35
This guide to chisels, planes, rasps, and files explains how to tell them apart, use them, and care for them.

5 Hand Tools for Measuring, Marking, and Other Basics   47
Carrying on where Chapter 4 left off, this chapter explains the other tools in your kit.

6 Feel the Power: Portable Power Tools   59
This introduction to the wonderful world of drills, circular saws, sanders, and routers explains how to handle the power safely.

7 The Big Machines: Stationary Power Tools   73
Graduate to the big leagues with this guide to the tools that really make a shop a shop. These machines turn rough lumber into finely milled legs and stretchers.

8 Keeping Your Edge   87
Get your tools razor sharp and keep them that way.

Part 3: The Word on Wood   **99**

9 Wood's Wild Ways   101
Wood is a natural material and must be treated accordingly. Learn how its natural origins affect you in the workshop.

10 The Subtle Art of Buying Solid Wood   111
Learn what it takes to navigate the lumberyard with confidence in this guide to picking boards.

11 The Sawmill: Where Trees Become Lumber   121
The sawmill determines what your lumber will look like, and the drying process can make or ruin your day.

12 Plywood: The Engineered Natural Material 129
Plywood can make your life a lot easier. Here's why.

13 Words to the Wise About Storing Wood 139
*You can easily ruin good lumber and plywood by storing it badly.
Here's a guide to keeping your wood high and dry.*

Part 4: Putting It All Together: Means and Methods **147**

14 All About Adhesives 149
Get your parts together and keep them that way.

15 Frame Joints: The Skeleton as a Model 157
*Nothing defines woodworking like a well-cut joint. This chapter
looks at mortise-and-tenon joints, spline joints, dowel joints, and
other frame joints.*

16 Carcass Joinery: The Box as a Model 167
*This chapter picks up joinery where the last left off and explains
the other category of joinery: box joints.*

17 Nails, Screws, and Bolts: When It's Okay to Use
Fasteners 181
*So many screws, so little time. This chapter looks at the myriad
types of screws, nails, and bolts and explains how to choose and
use them.*

18 Doors and More Doors 191
*Doors and drawers are the trickiest characters in woodworking
because they work mechanically. This chapter shows you the
ropes.*

19 The Ins and Outs of Drawer-Making 203
*This chapter explains how to make drawers that close as effort-
lessly as they open.*

20 Edgings and Moldings: The Last Details 213
*These simple details can make your project come alive. Here's
how they work, how to buy them, and how to make your own.*

Part 5: **From Principles to Practice** **223**

21 Plan It on Paper: Drawings, Cut-Lists, and Procedure Lists 225
*These simple organizational tools keep your head above the
maze and prevent problems and mistakes before they mate-
rialize.*

22 Milling: How to Make Parts That Fit 235
*This step-by-step guide to the parts-making process explains how
to cut out your parts so they resemble the ones on the drawing.*

23 How the Parts Become a Carcass 245
*Now it's time to round up those parts, get them ready, and glue
them together. This chapter will help you keep your glue-up from
becoming a fiasco.*

24 Woodworking Art: Tabletops and Other Flat Surfaces   257
    Grain patterns can make or break a tabletop or panel. This chap-
    ter walks you through the aesthetic and technical steps to mak-
    ing a tabletop.

25 The Well-Hung Frame-and-Panel Door   267
    A detailed guide to every stage of making and hanging a frame-
    and-panel door. You learn about hinges, panel profiles, and how
    to use grain patterns to give your door a sense of unity.

Part 6: The Finishing Touch   277

26 A Fill-In on Finishing   279
    This short history of finishing introduces the cast of players and
    explains their characteristics.

27 Choosing Finishes: Knowing Fact from Fiction   289
    This in-depth look at the pros and cons of the various finishes
    explains how to choose the right one for the job at hand. It also
    looks at stains and fillers.

28 Surface Prep: Groundwork for a Great Finish   303
    If the surface isn't right, the finish won't be. Learn about the
    different sandpapers and other abrasives and how to get this
    onerous task over and done with quickly.

29 Let's Get It On!: Applying Finish Step by Step   313
    There are different strokes for different folks. Each finish is ap-
    plied differently; here's a guide to all of them.

Appendixes

A Glossary of Woodworking Terms   323
B Resources   335
C Organizing Your Project   343
   Index   349

Contents

Part 1: Getting Real About Woodworking   **1**

1 Basics: The Shop, the Shopping, and the Skills   **3**

What Do You Want from Woodworking? 4
Inch by Inch 5
Basic Buys and Budget-Busters 5
Space—the Final Frontier 6
The Tools of the Trade 7
   Tool Lust: The Woodworker's Waterloo 9
   Tools on the Cheap: Flea Markets, Auctions, and Want Ads 10

2 I Need My Space: Setting Up Shop   **11**

Apartment Woodworking: The Big Squeeze 12
   Think Small 12
   The Stowed-Away Shop 13
Stretching Out: The Garage or Basement Shop 15
   Enter the Machine Age 15
   Freedom of Storage 15
   Flexing Your Space 16
Movin' Up and Out: The Rented Shop 17
   Scouting a Space 17
   Setting Up Housekeeping 18

3 A Workshop That Works   **21**

The Supporting Cast: Workbenches, Sawhorses, and Other
   Shop Fixtures 22
Home Base: The Workbench 22
   Working Your Workbench 23
   Trust Me 24
Horsing Around 25
Beam Me Up 26
The Tool Cabinet 27
On a Roll 28
Push It with Push Sticks 29
Tooling Around 29
The Jig's Up 30
Storage Savvy 30

**Part 2: The Tools: The Work They Do and How
to Work Them**   **33**

4 Your Hand Tool Arsenal: The Cutters   **35**

Who's a Chiseler? 36
   Butt Chisels: The Cabinetmaker's Workhorse 36
   Paring Down: Paring Chisels 38
   Choosing Your Chisels Wisely 39
Grasping Rasps and Files 39
Handy Handsaws 40
The Plane Truth 42
Push Me, Pull You: Japanese Tools 43
Safety Rules for Hand Tools 44

5   Hand Tools for Measuring, Marking, and Other Basics   47

Taking the Measure of Measuring Tools 47
  The Six-Inch Rule 48
  The Combination Square 48
  The Six-Inch Engineer's Square 49
  The Framing Square 49
  The Bevel Gauge 49
  The Tape Measure 50
  The Folding Rule 50
  The Long Straightedge 50
Hit the Mark with Marking Tools 50
  Make Your Mark with a Marking Knife 50
  Keep Your Distance with the Marking Gauge 51
  Drop a Chalk Line 52
Driving Things Home: Striking Tools 52
  The Classic Claw Hammer 53
  The Mighty Wooden Maul 53
  Synthetic Mallets for Safe Strikes 54
The Old Bunch: Tools You May Have Met Before 54
  How About a Screwdriver? 54
  Hex Keys 55
  Ratchet Socket Wrench Sets 55
  Pliers, Vise Grips, Adjustable Wrenches, and Tweezers 55
  On the Level 56
Tackling Tool Storage 56

6   Feel the Power: Portable Power Tools   59

Ladies and Gentlemen, Start Your Engines 60
Start with Safety 60
The Drill on Drills 61
  Your Friend Chuck 61
  Drill Speed 62
  A Bit About Drill Bits 62
  Screw Guns 62
Portable Power Saws 63
  The Circular Saw 63
  The Jigsaw 64
Power Sanders 65
  Disk Sanders 65
  Belt Sanders 65
  Orbital Pad Sanders 66
  Random Orbit Sanders 67
Power Planes 67
Routers 67
Biscuit Joiners 68
Nail Guns and Other Pneumatic Tools 69
  Just a Lot of Hot Air 69
  Nail Guns 70

7   The Big Machines: Stationary Power Tools   73

Why Stationary Machines? 74
Safety First (and Last!) 75
The Jointer 76

The Thickness Planer 77
The Table Saw 78
   Ripping on the Table Saw *78*
   Crosscutting *79*
   Sorting Out Saw Blades *80*
   Table Saw Safety *80*
The Band Saw 81
The Radial Arm Saw and Portable Chop Saw 82
Router Tables 83
The Drill Press 84
The Stationary Belt and Disk Sander 84
Dust Collectors 85

8   Keeping Your Edge   87
The Geometry of an Edge 88
   Your Aim Is True *88*
   Look Sharp *89*
   The Sharpening Angle *90*
The Stone Cold Truth About Abrasives 91
Sharpening the Easy Way 92
   First, a Good Grinding *92*
   Burning the Blade *94*
   Using the Stones *95*
   The Finishing Touch *96*
   When Do I Sharpen? *97*
   So You Have a New Chisel *97*
Sharpening Gadgets and Gizmos 98
Sharpening Saws: Leave It to the Pros 98

Part 3:   The Word on Wood   99

9   Wood's Wild Ways   101
The Call of the Wild 102
Tree Life 101 102
   The Trunk, the Whole Trunk, and Nothing but the Trunk *102*
   Reading Rings and Following Fibers *103*
   Sapwood vs. Heartwood *104*
   Fathoming Fibers *104*
Grain's Beautiful Ways 106
   Name That Grain *106*
   Curly, Bird's Eye, and Other Oddities *108*
Water, Water, Everywhere 109
   Wood and Weather *109*

10   The Subtle Art of Buying Solid Wood   111
Mother Nature's 37 Flavors 112
   The Domestic Woods *113*
   The Imports *113*
The Lowdown on Lumberyards 114
   Lumber-on-the-Side Stores *115*
   The Builder's One-Stop Lumberyard *115*
   The Hardwood Yard *115*
   Buying Hardwood: Surfaced vs. Rough-Milled *116*

Buying by the Board/Foot 117
More Measuring Madness 118
Getting Your Wood Home 119
Skip the Middleman: Find a Mill 120

11   The Sawmill: Where Trees Become Lumber   121

From Log to Board 122
The Cuts: Flat-Sawn, Quarter-Sawn, and Mixed-Sawn 123
Drying Lumber 124
  Air-Drying *124*
  Kiln-Drying *125*
Making the Grade 125
The Planing Mill 126
The Veneer Mill: Where the Best Logs Land 127
  Rotary-Cut Veneer *127*
  Sliced Veneer *128*

12   Plywood: The Engineered Natural Material   129

How Plywood Works 130
Cores: It's What's Inside That Counts 130
  Lasting Lumber-Core Plywood *131*
  Flake Board and Fiberboard *131*
  Core-Veneer Variables *132*
  Playing with Platform Stock *133*
Face Veneers: Book-Matching vs. Slip-Matching 133
  Book-Matching *134*
  Slip-Matching *134*
  Playing the Matching Panels Game *134*
Sizing Up Plywood 134
Grading Plywood Grading 136
Pointers on Buying Plywood 136
Wrestling with Edges 137

13   Words to the Wise About Storing Wood   139

Why Store Solid Wood? 139
Store Smart 140
  Taking It Outside *142*
  Letting Your Lumber Adapt *142*
Make Sure with a Moisture Meter 142
Storing Precut Lumber 143
Building a Lumber Rack 144
Sensible Plywood Storage 145

Part 4:   Putting It All Together: Means and Methods   147

14   All About Adhesives   149

Bond: Chemical vs. Mechanical 149
Long Grain: Yes! End Grain: No! 151
Choosing the Glue for the Job 151
  White Glue *152*
  Yellow Glue *152*
  Plastic Resin Glues *152*
  Epoxy Resins *153*

    Hide Glue 154
    Contact Cement 154
    Other Glues 155
  Too Much of a Good Thing? 155

15 Frame Joints: The Skeleton as a Model   **157**
  Joinery: Who Needs It? 158
  Joinery: Frame vs. Carcass 158
  Classic Frame Joints and Not-So-Classic Variations 159
    The Mortise and Tenon 160
    The Bridal Joint 161
    Lap Joints 161
    Spline Joints 161
    The Dowel Debate 161
    Biscuit Joints 162
    Miter Management 163
  Frame Structures: Joints in Context 164
    The Dining Table 164
    The Side Chair 165

16 Carcass Joinery: The Box as a Model   **167**
  Old Carcasses and New 167
    Going with the Grain 168
    The Practical Plywood Carcass 169
  So Many Carcass Joints ... .169
    The Single Spline 170
    The Tongue-and-Groove Joint 171
    The Biscuit Joint 171
    The Finger Joint 172
    The Multiple Spline 173
    The Lovely Dovetail 174
    The Lowly Screw 176
  Some Classic Carcass Types 177
    The Modern Kitchen Cabinet 177
    Chest of Drawers 177
    The Blanket Chest 179

17 Nails, Screws, and Bolts: When It's Okay to Use Fasteners   **181**
  The Wonderful World of Wood Screws 182
    Head Types (Screw Heads, That Is) 182
    Drive Types 184
    What's Your Screw Made Of? 184
    Screw Sizes 185
    Placing Your Order 185
  Getting It Together 186
  The Nuts and Bolts 187
  Welcome to Washers 188
  Getting Nailed 188
    Nailing Pneumatically 189
    The Power Nailers 189

18 Doors and More Doors   **191**

Doorology 101 191
Those Swinging Doors! 193
Choose Your Panel: Solid Wood, Plywood, or Glass 193
Cabinet Doors: Closing the Box 194
Full-Overlay, Half-Overlay, and Inset Doors 195
Sliding Cabinet Doors 196
Hinges: The Usual (and Unusual) Suspects 197
Butt Hinges: The Old Standby 197
European Cabinet Hinges 198
Other Hinge Options 199
Knobs, Pulls, Catches, and Other Door Hardware 200
Pulls and Knobs 200
Catches and Locks 200

19 The Ins and Outs of Drawer-Making   **203**

Crafting Traditional Drawers 204
Sliding Dovetails 205
The Dovetail Machine 206
Traditional Drawers: Fitting Words 206
Contemporary Drawer Construction 208
Surveying Drawer Slides 208
Drawer Slide Extensions 210
Drawer Slide Finishes 211
Applied Drawer Fronts 211
Drawer Bottoms, Then and Now 211

20 Edgings and Moldings: The Last Details   **213**

Whose Whim Were Moldings? 213
Interior Architectural Moldings 214
The Majestic Crown Molding 215
Picture Moldings 216
Chair Rail 216
Basic Baseboard 217
Coping with Corners 218
Furniture and Cabinet Moldings 219
Buying Basic Molding 220
Rolling Your Own 220

Part 5: From Principles to Practice   **223**

21 Plan It on Paper: Drawings, Cut-Lists, and Procedure Lists   **225**

What Drawings Will Do for You 226
Nail Down the Details 226
When Memory Fails 226
A Drawing Is Worth a Thousand Words 227
I Have a Pencil, Now What? 227
Will a Sketch Do? 230
Good Old Graph Paper 230
Trace It and Save Time 230
The Cut-List: Hallmark of a Pro 231
The Procedure List: The Project's Rudder 232

22 Milling: How to Make Parts That Fit   **235**
Cut It Out! 235
Avoid Warping: Premill 237
Flat's Where It's At! 238
Pick Your Thickness 238
Another Jaunt to the Jointer 239
Let 'Er Rip! 239
Crosscutting Cautiously 240
  Smooth Sledding 240
  Milling (Continued) 241
  Rabbets, Grooves, and Chamfers 242
A Shapely Form 243
Milling Plywood 243

23 How the Parts Become a Carcass   **245**
On Your Marks 246
Time to Clean Up! 247
Gluing Up in Sections 248
Setting Up the Glue-Up 248
  A Solid Foundation 248
  Hey, Back Off! 249
  Other Accoutrements 249
The Dry Run 249
Show Time! 250
  The Pressure's On 251
  Be Square, Be Flat 252
The Colossal Cleanup 253
The Morning After 253
Royal Flush 254
Miter Matters 254

24 Woodworking Art: Tabletops and Other Flat Surfaces   **257**
Not Just Another Pretty Tabletop 258
Matchmaker, Matchmaker 258
Picking the Winners 259
  On-the-Job Planing 260
  Cleaving to a Tree 260
Milling About 261
Gone Clamping 262
The Final Surface 263
Getting an Edge 264
Attachment Anxiety 265

25 The Well-Hung Frame-and-Panel Door   **267**
Choosing the Best Boards 267
It's Milling Time! 269
The Joints Are Jumping 270
Raised Panel Picks 271
Flat Is Where It's At 271
But I'm Not Finished Yet! 272
Getting a Snug Fit 273
Fit for Hanging 274

A Touch of Glass 274
Mission Control: We Have a Problem 274

Part 6: The Finishing Touch — 277

26 A Fill-In on Finishing — 279

Finishing: A Woodworker's Story 279
What's Finish for, Anyway? 280
Essential Oils 281
Shellac: Beetlemania 282
  French Polishing (Ooo La La!) 282
  Shellac 2000 283
Traditional Varnishes: Finishing's Best Friends 283
The Lacquers of the East 284
Spray Lacquer for Speed 284
The Complex Conversion Finishes 285
Water-Based Finishes: Wave of the Future 286
The Name Game 286

27 Choosing Finishes: Knowing Fact from Fiction — 289

Finishing Mythology 289
You Think It's Easy? 290
To Spray or Not To Spray 291
But Will It Last? 292
You've Struck Oil 292
  The Linseed Oil Legend 292
  The Buzz on Tung 293
  Is Danish Oil Really Oil? 293
  Caution: Flammable! 293
  A Word on Waxes 294
  Oil's Pluses and Minuses 294
Getting a Shellacking 294
The Varnish Vista 296
Nitrocellulose Lacquer 297
Water-Based Finishes 297
It's Raining Stains 298
  Where Colors Come From 298
  Binders and Solvents 299
  Wonderful Water-Based Stain 299
  NGR: Non-Grain-Raising Stains 300
  Effortless Oil-Based Stain 300
  Alcohol-Based Aniline Dye Stains 300
  Enter the Gel Stains 300

28 Surface Prep: Groundwork for a Great Finish — 303

Different Facts for Different Finishes 303
The Gritty World of Abrasives 304
  Is There Sand in Your Sandpaper? 305
  Sandpaper's Mysteries Solved 305
Other Abrasive Characters 306
  Steel Wool: A Staple 306
  Variations on the Steel Wool Theme 306

Sanding Made Simple 307
    The Basic Moves 307
    Smoothing Things Out, Grit by Grit 308
    Breaking Edges 309
Power Up! 309
Getting Out of a Scrape 309
The Goods: Figured Woods 311
So You Want to Be a Stripper 311

29 Let's Get It On!: Applying Finish Step by Step   **313**

Finally! The Finish Line 314
    Dissing the Dust 314
    A Little Atmosphere 314
    The Brush-Off 315
    Different Strokes 316
Applying an Oil Finish 317
Step On It with Shellac 317
Varnish: Hurry Up and Wait 318
Water-Based Finishes: Stirred, Not Shaken 319
The Many Ways to Stain 320
Filling the Pores 320

Appendixes

A Glossary of Woodworking Terms   **323**

B Resources   **335**

C Organizing Your Project   **343**

Index   **349**

Foreword

Remember ninth-grade woodshop class—the sweet smell of sawdust … spilled glue … funny-looking safety glasses, sanding until you thought your arm would drop off (only to have your shop teacher point out a whole new batch of scratches)? Fun, wasn't it? A great counterpoint to English and social studies. And now you're in a position to get back into the craft. But where to start?

Well, if you're like me, your first move might be to check out your local bookstore to see what they have on the subject. You're not likely to be disappointed. Bewildered, yes, but not disappointed. The current boom in woodworking has led to a ton of woodworking books being available—I should know, I've helped to write and edit a bunch of them. The problem will be choosing which one to buy.

If you're new to the craft (ninth grade not withstanding) it's easy to become a little overwhelmed with the sheer volume of information available, especially because much of it is so specialized. There are books out there on every facet of the craft, from cutting joints to spraying on a final finish. But all these books seem to assume you have a complete shop set up and a few projects under your belt. Where do you go to learn the basics?

Well, until now, there wasn't a really good book out there that laid out the fundamentals of woodworking. But thanks to Reed Karen and *The Complete Idiot's Guide to Woodworking,* all that information is now available in one place. And it really is all there: choosing tools and machinery, setting up shop (even in a limited amount of space), deciding what kind of woodworking you want to pursue, even learning how to talk to a plywood vendor so you won't sound stupid.

Reed has written a book that blends hard facts with well-grounded opinion, all tempered with a little humor (just wait until you meet Bruce, the engineering hammer). He draws from his formal training with Tage Frid (one of America's premiere woodworkers and teachers) as well as his diverse woodworking experiences. He is willing to share his mistakes to keep others from making the same ones, and he has a wealth of "war" stories to help illustrate his points. If you are looking for one woodworking book that will set you well on your way to a satisfying pastime, this is the book to buy.

Ken Burton

Ken Burton is a studio furniture maker operating Windy Ridge Woodworks in New Tripoli, Pennsylvania. He has been teaching woodworking at the Yestermorrow Design/Build School in Warren, Vermont, since 1995. He is a former editor of Rodale Press's woodworking books and is co-author of *Jigs, Fixtures, and Setups* (Rodale Press, 1993) and author of *Knots* (Running Press, 1998).

Introduction

No one activity can be all things to all people, but woodworking comes close. It's a hobby to some and a profession to others; some use it as an excuse to buy vast collections of tools and machinery, yet it can be practiced with a small box of hand tools. Some people get into it because they have some projects around the house or just want to fix up and refinish some antiques; for others, it is an almost mystical quest for perfection in physical form. You can focus on construction, carving, hand tool techniques, modern technology, or finishing. The one thing, however, that seems to seduce everyone who gets involved with woodworking is the beauty and richness of the material itself. Unlike carpentry, which is a construction trade, woodworking plunges deeply into this amazing material and explores both technical and aesthetic issues.

The thing that makes wood such a remarkable material is that not that long ago it was a living thing. Like people, trees are individual characters; some are wild and interesting; others are a little on the plain side. Wood has grain patterns, flaws, and always a surprise or two. One way or another, you have to tune in to the quirks of the particular boards you have in front of you; you have to read them and respond accordingly. Eventually you get good at it, and you learn to read subtle clues. For example, if you give me a peek at the cut end of an oak board, I can tell you whether it's going to be hard or soft, heavy or light, or easy or difficult to work, and I can tell you approximately what the faces of the board will look like. It's like meeting someone at a cocktail party; you read the clues.

There is also a technical side to woodwork. You need to learn how to handle tools and work with machines. You need to learn certain processes and how to put them together into a flow of work where one step prepares you for the next. You have to learn how wood, as a material, goes from the forest to workable lumber. There's a lot to know, and you have to develop a learning strategy that is a combination of reading, hands-on training, and practice.

This book attempts to give you a view of the maze from above. It breaks woodworking into different areas and examines the components. It explores aesthetic issues and the nature of this rich and difficult material, as well as the technical aspects of the craft. One thing that I also go into extensively is how to organize your work in a professional way, because good quality craftsmanship requires control and that comes from discipline and order, something that had to be beaten into your author with a stick. Only when the technical becomes automatic can you explore the artistic side of a craft.

How to Use This Book

I recommend that you read this book through from start to finish to acquaint yourself with all the aspects involved. There are many different stages and steps to a project, and they are all interrelated. You have to know where you are going to understand where you are now. You also need to learn about the nature of the materials. Later, you can go back and focus on individual chapters, and they'll make more sense in the context of the book as a whole.

The Sum of the Parts

This book is divided up into six parts. Each one covers a series of related topics. This organization allows you to focus on one general aspect of woodworking at a time. The parts are as follows:

Part 1, "Getting Real About Woodworking," shows you how your goals, priorities, available space, and budget all determine how you will set up your work area. You may have a closet, a basement, or a garage available; you may have room for big machines, or you may want to stick with hand tools. Either way, your workspace should be efficient and allow you to make the most of what you have available. Part 1 looks at the possibilities.

Part 2, "The Tools: The Work They Do and How to Work Them," is a long, hard look at the arsenal of tools and machinery used in woodworking. Tools are a big part of the craft, and this part lists the tools and machines you can't live without, the ones that would be handy down the road, and the ones that make good fishing weights. It explains how they're used, points out safety considerations, and gives you advice on what to look for in a tool and how to maintain the tools you buy.

Part 3, "The Word on Wood," looks at the material itself. It covers how wood grows, how trees become useable lumber and plywood products, how to buy wood, and how to store it. It examines aesthetic issues as well as technical, exploring the mysteries along with the mundane. By the time you're done reading this part, you'll be able to strut around a lumberyard with confidence.

Part 4, "Putting It All Together: Means and Methods," gets to the nitty-gritty of construction. This part looks at joinery, adhesives, fasteners, and all the principles involved in getting a project to come together. It also explains how doors and drawers, the mechanical wonders of woodworking, work. This is the seat-of-your-pants engineering section.

Part 5, "From Principles to Practice," goes from the abstract to the nuts and bolts of cabinetmaking, exploring the logistics of building a project. It looks at processes and how to go from point A to point B in a efficient step-by-step manner.

Part 6, "The Finishing Touch," covers the slightly separate craft of finishing. Many woodworkers try to skirt the finishing aspect of their projects, partly because there is less accurate information about the topic than there is about the mechanical aspects of woodworking. This part teaches you to look finishing fearlessly in the face. It cuts through the myths and old wives' tales and provides the straight dope on finishing.

Extras

You will also find sidebars sprinkled liberally throughout the book. They are there to emphasize or clarify certain points or nomenclature and give you safety warnings, tips to make things go smoother, and shaggy dog stories. Each type has its own icon:

Tricks of the Trade

These hints and special advice make the job at hand go more smoothly.

I Woodn't Do That!

These are warnings about things to avoid, either for safety reasons or because it's just a bad idea.

Wood Words

Woodworking has a lot of special terminology, and these sidebars clue you in to the lingo.

Woodlore

These are historical tidbits and woodworking stories from your author's repertoire.

Acknowledgments

We are all the product of our teachers, and I wouldn't know any of this stuff without mine. There are my real-world past masters such as Hank Gilpin, who whipped me into shape over a three-year apprenticeship and still whips me from time to time. There's Tage Frid, also known as the Great Dane, who I was fortunate to both study and work with, and the late Stan Jameson and Dana Haggerty. There are colleagues whom I worked alongside of who taught me a lot, most notably Glen Johnson, Nicolo Biert, Horuo Sato, and Phillip Ponvert. Then there are my professors at Rhode Island School of Design, besides Tage, such as Seth Stem, Rosanne Sommerson, and Ken Hunnibel. There's also Mr. Kroft, my grade-school shop teacher who saw my interest and started this whole thing.

I also want to thank my wife, Kyle, who makes living with a woodworker look easy and who did the drawings herein to boot, and my son Ray for cheering me up when writing made me wish I were woodworking.

I especially want to thank my editor Doris Cross for her great patience in putting up with me. Doris, I'm better with wood than I am with words, I swear.

Trademarks

Part 1
Getting Real About Woodworking

The first thing you have to do before embarking upon your woodworking career is to set up your work area. This requires some planning and some soul searching. First of all, you need to allocate space. Do you have a basement? A garage? How about a closet? What can you spare without aggravating a spouse? Remember, woodworking gets a little messy from time to time.

Second, you have to figure out your goals and interests. Will you be working on small or large projects? Are hand tools your thing, or will large machinery be involved? Will you be doing carving or refinishing? These choices affect your decisions. And then there's your budget. Most of us have a limited amount of cash to spend at any given time and want to spend it wisely. You need to plan what you can afford now and what you can put off until later. These first three chapters deal with setting up your shop, so you don't blow your wad right away on the wrong stuff.

Chapter 1

Basics: The Shop, the Shopping, and the Skills

In This Chapter

➤ Planning your work, working your plan

➤ Defining your goals and priorities

➤ Evaluating your available budget and space

➤ Developing your skills progressively

➤ Using a sensible approach to buying tools

If your only tool is a hammer, the world starts to look like ... a nail?

Okay, you've decided to try your hand at woodworking. Maybe you just want to build some bookcases and get your library off the floor. Or perhaps your heart beats faster every time you see that Goddard and Townsend highboy with its mile-deep French polish finish at the Metropolitan Museum. Or maybe you're going through a midlife crisis, and you want to quit your job in sales and drag the family off to Vermont to open a woodshop. Whatever your reason, whether practical or romantic, you need to start by learning the basics and setting up your workspace, which is where this book comes in. It's designed to give you the information you need and help you move toward where you want to go.

Woodworking is fun and enormously satisfying when everything is going right and you're getting things done. The process is enjoyable, and you end up with something tangible to show for your work. What could be better? But without a plan and some guidance, woodworking can get frustrating fast. It's labor intensive, and you have to use your time well or you'll get lost in tedium and mistakes. So the first thing you want to do is establish a game plan.

What Do You Want from Woodworking?

People get into woodworking for different reasons. These reasons may be purely practical: You may have some specific projects you want to get done around the house, such as building a bathroom vanity or restoring some antiques. In that case, you may want to concentrate your energies on acquiring easy-to-learn, serviceable skills that will get the job done. Or you may just want a constructive hobby, where the point is to have fun and not stress out. In this case, you may gravitate toward smaller projects that involve problem-solving and developing progressively challenging techniques. On the other hand, you may be a romantic, a "Zen and the art of woodwork" type who wants to develop samurai-like hand-tool technique and bond with the materials.

Whatever the reason, evaluating your aims when setting up shop, buying tools, or choosing projects is important. If you're a romantic perfectionist, you may not want to start building that Godzilla-sized home-entertainment center, because you're likely to get bogged down fussing with the details. A jewelry box would probably be a better scale, especially at first, so you can concentrate on meticulously fitting the hinges and rubbing out the finish. Consequently, a small work area emphasizing hand tools would be appropriate. If home improvement is the name of your game, you will likely need more space and an arsenal of power tools. If you're thinking of an eventual career in the field, you may want to rent some workspace in a professional shop—some shops will rent bench space and machine use, often during off-hours—so you can get a firsthand feel for the profession of woodworking.

The point is that a clear understanding of what you want to do with woodwork will expedite the learning process and keep you from spinning your wheels, because it will help limit the scope of your study. It will also help you avoid buying tools and shop equipment that is ill-suited for the type of work you'll be doing.

Tricks of the Trade

Everyone has a physical scale they are most comfortable working in. It's a personal thing, and a psychologist would probably have something to say about it. Some people like to build houses, and others like to make toys. People who like to work large become frustrated with working small and vice versa. The sooner you find the scale that's right for you, the happier you'll be.

Inch by Inch

Woodwork is a craft, and developing your skills takes time. Don't try to learn everything in one project. You'll learn faster if you start small and simple and then progress in clear steps. Remember, the big payoff is the finished product. It feels great to make a beautiful, useful object. I find that people work harder, learn faster, and have more fun if they get the frequent gratification that comes with producing smaller, shorter projects. Every time you make something, it gives you a little kick and encourages you to keep forging ahead. If you get bogged down in some long-term, overly ambitious project, morale and productivity tend to wane.

Choose projects that build on the skills you already have by giving you experience in one or two new techniques, not five or six. You want the work to be challenging, not overwhelming. It's like learning to drive: If you're learning how to handle a stick shift, you go to an empty parking lot and focus on the basics; you don't try to learn to drive a stick on an alpine road. That's too many things at once.

You should also plan work that is within the parameters of your workspace and tool collection. Don't start a project that requires you to buy too many new tools; again, you shouldn't have to buy more than one or two new tools. If you're working in your apartment, make sure the project is of a size that can be put away when you're not working on it. More than one marriage has been strained by imposing projects left for weeks in high-traffic areas. Also make sure that the finished project will have somewhere to go. A hobbyist woodworker I taught some years back built a lovely mahogany breakfront in his basement only to discover that it wouldn't fit up the stairs. Oops!

Basic Buys and Budget-Busters

Your budget plays a key role in your choice of tools, materials, and projects. If you spend all your tool money on one of those ebony-handled, bronze-bodied, usually useless tools that tool dealers love to push at us tool junkies, you won't be able to afford the genuinely useful items you need to get your work done. Buying fancy tools and exotic materials is a form of self-indulgence that woodworkers are especially prone to (see the following section on tool lust). The thing to remember is that skill, not cash outlay, determines the quality of the finished piece. You don't need fancy tools, merely decent ones. Some tools are worth spending money on, a good square for instance, and I've noted those on the tool lists that follow; others are not worth spending a lot of money on, and I've noted those, too.

I Woodn't Do That!

Don't think you have to spend a fortune on expensive, exotic materials. Beginners tend to become intoxicated by ebonies and rosewoods. These woods are alarmingly expensive and very hard to work with. Think like Japanese woodworkers, who make the finest work out of the simplest materials. Finesse, not cash, makes the project.

Woodlore

As a young cabinetmaker, I once stopped at a fancy New York tool dealer with four weeks' back pay in cash in my wallet (after several celebratory drinks with my fellow workers). I woke from a nap some time later to find myself the proud owner of a set of 12 ebony-handled Japanese teahouse maker's chisels, which had cost a little more than the car I was then driving. At the time I could have used a circular saw and some other more prosaic tools, but it was some time before I could afford them—or a decent lunch for that matter. The chisels are certainly beautiful, but they are awkward and fragile and have spent the last 20 years or so in one drawer or another. Remember: Tools and drinking don't mix.

The trick is to plan your purchases ahead of time. If you go to the tool dealer or lumber store without a plan and with cash burning a hole in your pocket, chances are you're going to buy impulsively and regret it later. Buy the basic tools you absolutely need, and then buy others as the need arises. The more experience you have, the wiser your choices will be. Your faithful author, who has always had a sweet tooth for tools, lives above a basement full of quirky oddities that I thought I needed at some point or another. On this particular topic, do as I say, not as I do.

Space—the Final Frontier

Available workspace is an important factor in your plan. If you live in a studio apartment, the size and scope of both your work and your equipment will likely be more modest than if you live in the country with an outbuilding or two. It's generally a good idea to discuss with your spouse the appropriation of valuable garage or basement real estate before you sink money into a batch of stationary machines and back the delivery truck up to the door.

If space is limited, you may have to forgo the big machines and buy your lumber already *milled* to size, either from a lumberyard or from a local woodworker willing to do that sort of thing. I periodically mill lumber to size for a friend who builds musical instruments as a hobby. He has rigged a pull-out workbench and tool and lumber storage in a 3 × 4-foot closet in his one-bedroom Brooklyn apartment. He lays down a drop cloth, sets up his small bench, and works on his guitars and mandolins. It's simple, neat, and perfect for small projects. He has a decent selection of hand tools and trades favors for machine work.

If your ambitions outgrow your living quarters, you can look into renting space elsewhere. Most cities have industrial space available somewhere, and rural areas have barns and sheds. If you're not ready to lay out the money to buy stationary machines, see whether there's a woodworking cooperative in your area—many towns have them—or a local woodworker who is looking to defray overhead by renting shop space. Many areas have woodworking clubs with members willing to share their machines.

You'd be surprised what you can do in a small space with a little ingenuity. The trick is to be efficient. In Chapter 3, "A Workshop That Works," I provide some sample shop layouts of varying size that should be adaptable to a variety of circumstances.

Wood Words

Milling is the process of taking rough-surfaced lumber that's likely a bit warped and twisted from the sawing and drying processes, machining the surfaces flat and clean, and cutting the thickness and width of the boards down to the dimensions required by the project. Although milling can be done with hand planes and handsaws, that's a laborious process; milling is now generally done by machine.

The Tools of the Trade

The three tool lists that follow should help you plan your setup. The first list is the essentials, the next list is the handy tools, and the last list is for you investment bankers who are having a midlife crisis. These tools may be familiar to you; you may have some of them clanking around your toolkit, or you may remember them from grandpa's toolkit. You can look up any that are not familiar in the chapters in Part 2, "The Tools: The Work They Do and How to Work Them," where I give detailed descriptions of their operation.

These are the basic tools you need to get started:

➤ Workbench with vise.

➤ Measuring tape with a $3/4$-inch wide blade (tape) that is 12 to 25 feet long.

➤ Combination square with a 12-inch blade. Get the best you can reasonably afford; the accuracy is worth it.

➤ Set of four or five good butt chisels: $1/8$-inch, $1/4$-inch, $1/2$-inch, $3/4$-inch, and $1 1/4$-inch.

➤ Mallet or maul.

➤ Screwdrivers: A #2 Phillips head and a #2 slotted are a good start.

➤ Pliers.

➤ Finish hammer.

➤ Smallish crosscut saw (approximately a 12-inch blade): Either a Western back saw or a Japanese Dozuki style are fine.

➤ Cork sanding block.

➤ Safety glasses.

➤ Sharpening stones.

➤ Marking knife.

➤ Bevel gauge: Cheap ones work just as well as good ones.

➤ Block plane.

➤ Smoothing plane.

➤ Rasp.

➤ File.

➤ Drill with $1/2$-inch capacity chuck and basic $1/16$- to $1/2$-inch drill index.

➤ Toolbox: An inexpensive plastic one is fine; you just want to protect your tools and keep them organized.

When you're solvent again, buy these tools:

➤ Marking gauge: Cheap ones tend to be just as good as expensive ones.

➤ Chalk line.

➤ Six- or eight-foot folding rule with extending blade for inside measurements.

➤ Framing square.

➤ Six-inch rule.

➤ Jack plane.

➤ Rabbet plane.

➤ Vise grips.

➤ Miter box: You can make your own.

➤ Broader range of butt chisels.

➤ One or two paring chisels.

➤ Engineer square.

➤ Level.

➤ Jigsaw.

➤ Keyhole saw.

➤ Cabinet scraper.

➤ Random orbit sander.

➤ Router.

➤ Handheld circular saw.

➤ Cordless screw gun with bit holder.

➤ Set of countersinks.

➤ Set of spade bits.

➤ Plumb bob.

➤ Biscuit joiner.

The following specialized and luxury tools are items to get for a specific project as needed or if you have some extra cash. They're useful, but they're generally not required:

➤ Belt sander

➤ Carving gouges

➤ Dead blow mallet

➤ Pneumatic nail gun with compressor

➤ Moisture meter

➤ Compass plane

➤ Eighteen- or 24-inch graduated straightedge

➤ Dial calipers

➤ Compound miter saw

➤ Bullnose plane

Tricks of the Trade

Tool companies play on the woodworker's inherent weakness for the well-made object; catalogs describe tools as "the Rolls Royce of hand planes" or describe a tool as being the result of "old-world craftsmanship." As often as not, these descriptions are malarkey. Don't believe that just because a tool was made overseas it's necessarily better than a cheaper American model. This is especially true of chisels, planes, and measuring tools; the cheaper model is likely to be just as good.

Tool Lust: The Woodworker's Waterloo

If you spend any time with woodworkers, you begin to suspect that many of them just use woodworking as an excuse to buy tools. They collect shelves full of highly specialized tools made of exotic materials, whose primary function is to collect dust. I myself am a member of Toolaholics Anonymous. I can often be found fingering the catalogs my wife refers to as "tool porn" or cruising flea markets, haggling over some 1930s delicacy. For some reason, the tool bug seems to strike men worse than women. It's some hormonal thing no doubt, which might be why my wife has threatened to have me gelded after some of my more extravagant purchases.

Now there's nothing wrong with collecting tools, but don't kid yourself that it will improve your woodworking. It's a related but separate hobby. Just be sure you don't start blowing your budget on esoterica before you get the useful stuff.

Tricks of the Trade

When woodshops go out of business, their contents are often sold at auction on the premises. There is a viewing, when you can examine the tools, followed by the sale. Auctions can be fun even if you don't buy anything, and there are often bargains. Just decide what you're willing to spend for an item and stick to it; don't get carried away with the thrill of bidding.

Tools on the Cheap: Flea Markets, Auctions, and Want Ads

Scores of catalogs and companies (some of which you will find listed in Appendix B, "Resources") are out there selling high-quality woodworking tools, but if you have the time and patience, the used-tool market is a cheaper alternative. Check your local papers and want ads for auctions, flea markets, and individuals selling tools. Bargains abound. The only tools I would not buy used are measuring tools such as squares, levels, and measuring tapes, because they're fragile and once they're damaged, they're pretty much worthless. On the other hand, chisels, planes, and so forth can be great buys; just avoid tools with welds and other repairs or too much wear. Older tools are often better made than newer versions, and I personally find their patina irresistible.

So now you have some idea of how to start gearing up and planning your work. Maybe you've started to think about how your work can reflect your personality and preferences. Next, I'll break things down and delve into the specifics of laying out your workspace and how all these woodworking tools work.

The Least You Need to Know

➤ Have a game plan before you start setting up shop.

➤ Clarify your goals before you formulate your plan.

➤ Your budget and available space will determine the scope of your projects and setup.

➤ Resist the urge to indulge your tool lust; don't spend money on tools you really don't need.

➤ Buying used tools can help make setting up your workspace affordable.

Chapter 2

I Need My Space: Setting Up Shop

In This Chapter

➤ Planning workspaces of every size

➤ Working within your space and budgetary limits

➤ Creating an efficient layout

➤ Working in your apartment, basement, garage, or rented shop

➤ Considering alternatives to building your own shop

Woodworking is messy business: There's dust and finish spills, and it involves so many accoutrements. It's important to find a place to work where it won't be a catastrophe if you make a mess and where you have storage for tools, unfinished projects, materials, and scrap. You also need a work surface with a vise and maybe even some stationary machines. And then there's electricity …

A lot of the planning that goes into your workspace is just common sense, something woodworkers often seem to be short on. They start out with a reasonable plan, but then they get some itch, some compulsion to buy a preposterous piece of equipment. A hobby woodworker I knew who lived in a New York walk-up apartment was offered a lathe really cheap. It was just too good an offer to pass up; it was almost free, for crying out loud. Did I mention that it was a column-turning lathe over 10 feet long? He lived on the top floor, and he convinced himself he could keep it in the hallway and run it off an extension cord. Well, he's a single man now, and, after his wife couldn't make him get rid of the thing, his neighbors did. True story.

This chapter explores the possibilities of three shop scenarios: the apartment shop, the garage or basement shop, and the rented shop space. It lays out the considerations involved and offers sample floor plans. Read it so you don't end up latheless and spouseless.

Apartment Woodworking: The Big Squeeze

If you live in an apartment and don't want it to look like a frat house after St. Patrick's Day, you're going to have to plan your work area ruthlessly. It will have to be as efficiently set up as the space shuttle crew quarters. Minimizing mess, making adequate storage, having a good work surface, and limiting the size and scope of your projects are the key considerations. You'll also have to think long and hard about where you set up.

I actually have a little experience with this. When my classmates and I graduated from the furniture program at the Rhode Island School of Design, we dragged the benches and tool cabinets we had made from the 8,000-square-foot school shop back to our dinky little student apartments and set to work. We'd been eating and sleeping in the shop, so working in our apartments didn't seem strange. We were also young and foolish, so we put up with some things that might seem less than civilized, but eventually most of us got things squared away.

One thing I like about the apartment shop is that it separates the people who really want to make things from the people who just want an excuse to buy gobs of tools and machines. There isn't much room for tool fetishism in an apartment.

Tricks of the Trade

Woodworking kits often supply parts with the machine work done, and you just do the handwork. You can always customize them if you're feeling creative. From birdhouses to mandolins, everything is available in kit form from woodworking catalogs.

Think Small

If you're working in an apartment, you're going to have to limit your scope a bit. Ultimately, you'll be happier if you set some boundaries and don't even start down certain paths. Tool selection and scale are going to be major considerations as you plan your setup.

You'll probably want to stick with hand tools and a few conservatively chosen portable power tools. Stationary machines aren't an option in an apartment; even if you can put up with the noise and the dust, your neighbors can't: The vibrations will have the eviction notice hurtling through the mail in no time. I am an advocate of developing your chops with hand tools, and this is the perfect opportunity to do it.

Because you won't have a jointer or planer, you'll have two choices for milling lumber to thickness: Either buy the lumber from a dealer who will mill it for you or make friends with someone with a shop and either barter or pay him or her to do it for you. The first choice is easier, but the second choice allows you to cultivate a relationship with a more experienced woodworker and get advice, training, and shop use.

As for portable power tools, drills and screw guns are probably fine. You can possibly use a jigsaw and maybe a biscuit joiner if it's hooked up to a vacuum, but the other stuff is probably too noisy and/or dusty. Power sanders, even when hooked up to a vacuum, will have everything, including the inside of your electronic equipment, coated with a fine layer of dust. Forgoing the power sanders probably won't be such an inconvenience, though, because another thing you're going to have to limit is the size of your projects, so you won't have vast expanses of real estate to sand.

Work small. I recommend this for beginners anyway, but especially if you're limited by space and are using only hand tools. You might be able to do some larger cabinet work if it's for your own space, but you don't want to slice 4 × 8-foot sheets of plywood in your apartment. Finding a place to store lumber, parts, and projects in progress is going to be a dilemma, so keeping things small will preclude real problems.

Accessibility is another issue. Always measure all doorways between your work area and the street, as well as stairways, elevators, or anything else that might be a limitation. You don't want the "ship in the bottle syndrome." I can't tell you how many professionals neglect to measure the entranceways to their clients' homes, only to get jammed up at delivery (here in New York City it can be a major problem).

You'll also want to limit the finishing products you use. I wouldn't want a lot of toxic finishes where I eat and sleep. Stick with shellac, some safer oil finishes, or even wax. And invest in a good vacuum; the dust is not only a nuisance, it's also a safety hazard. Another safety hint: Pack edged tools away where children can't get at them.

I Woodn't Do That!

Don't strip furniture in your home! Chemical strippers are extremely toxic. Methylene chloride, the active ingredient in most good strippers, was recently rated the most toxic chemical commonly available to the public. Stripping should be done outside or in an area outside your living space with a good exhaust fan and lots of ventilation.

The Stowed-Away Shop

If possible, commandeer a closet in your apartment for your wood shop. This will allow you to hide your paraphernalia from the civilized world and still have easy access to it. Remove any closet rods and wrap the three walls of the closet with shallow shelves so that you still have room in the middle for a rolling tool cabinet. If you can't allocate a closet, grab a corner and fill it with tall, shelved cabinets. The cabinets should have doors so the area looks neat.

Pack the shelves according to category:

➤ Tools

➤ Lumber

➤ Adhesives

➤ Finishing products

➤ Safety equipment

➤ Abrasives

➤ Sharpening equipment

I would build or buy a workbench with a vise or two that can be fit against the wall when not in use and is good-looking enough to leave out. It should have a storage shelf for unfinished projects. I suggest keeping the tools you use regularly in the rolling tool cabinet and bringing it over to the bench when you are working. Keep the top clear so you can place tools or parts on it as you work. I would also recommend a tarp or some other floor covering to protect against spills and dropped tools. The following figure shows a sample floor plan for an apartment work area.

When the apartment work area is not in use, the workbench slides to the wall, the tarp folds up, and the tool cabinet rolls into the closet.

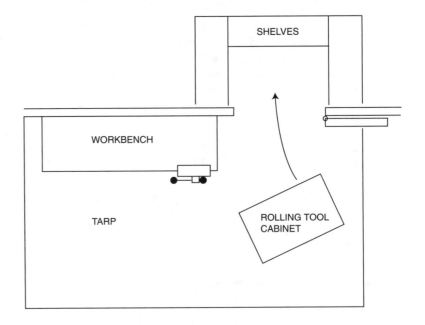

Stretching Out: The Garage or Basement Shop

A garage or basement—now we're talking!—more space and the freedom to make a mess and noise without it being a tragedy. It's a workshop, not a section of your home, so organization, not appearance, is the goal. Get some machines, some sloppy finishes and open shelving, and have a party.

Enter the Machine Age

In a basement or garage, you can make some noise. So what machines should you get first? The machines you need depend on what kind of projects you're planning, but for general work, this is the order I would choose for most usefulness:

1. Drill press
2. Band saw
3. Table saw
4. Jointer
5. Planer
6. Router
7. Lathe

You can also start buying all those noisy power hand tools you've been wanting. You should consider buying a small dust collector as well, one that can be easily hooked and unhooked to any machine, so you don't have to install ductwork for ventilation purposes. You may also find that you have to install some sound-dampening material if the room is acoustically "hard."

Freedom of Storage

For storage, think about open shelving, either cantilevered off the wall or resting on the floor. It's not as pretty as closed cabinets, but it's more convenient. If you have open rafters, they're a great place to store lumber; the air is drier up there, which is good for the wood. Flammable finishing materials are best stored in an explosion-proof cabinet that's ducted to the outside. This sort of cabinet is expensive, but so is your house.

I Woodn't Do That!

Many finishing products, notably linseed and Danish oils, will cause soaked rags to spontaneously combust if they are left sitting around. So don't leave your finish-soaked rags around! Figure out a plan for getting rid of them. They should be taken outside and spread flat to dry or thrown in a bucket of water. I've worked in two shops that had bad fires because someone threw oily rags in the garbage.

15

If you have concrete floors, moisture may be a problem. Never leave lumber lying on a cement floor; it will warp from the moisture. It's better to stand the lumber up and lean it against the wall. Your tools, too, may rust if you don't take precautions. If your shop is damp, consider using closed shelving and a dehumidifier. Woodwork and moisture don't mix.

Flexing Your Space

Whether you're in a basement, attic, or garage, you probably don't have as much space as you'd like. The key is to keep the space flexible. For example, you can put your woodworking machines on wheels. Wheels allow you to keep the machines out of the way when they are not in use. Some companies make special rolling systems, or you can just mount lockable casters or a dolly to the machines yourself. Alternatively, a number of companies are making bench-top machines that can be stored on a shelf and taken down when needed.

And there are also combination machines that run several different power tools off a single motor. Using nesting sawhorses to support a piece of plywood for a temporary work surface keeps space available, too. You still need a good, strong workbench, but for glue-ups and finishing, it's nice to have something you can stow away when you don't need it.

Light is an issue, too. You need good overhead light. If you're lucky you'll have lots of windows for natural light in the daytime, but you should also keep movable task lighting around. Good light is critical to clean work.

The following figure shows a layout for a basement/garage shop.

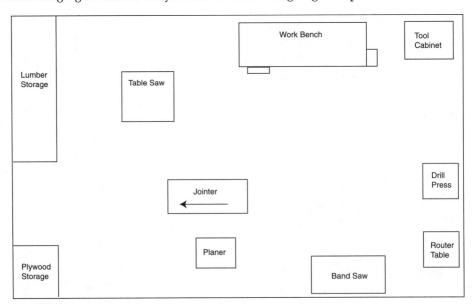

In a basement or garage shop, it's important to keep a flexible, open space for the task at hand. Equipment that is not being used should stow out of the way.

Movin' Up and Out: The Rented Shop

If you really start to get serious about woodworking, are going professional, or cannot find a place in your home to set up a shop, you may want to find a commercial space. There are several ways to do this:

➤ You can rent a shop space and set it up yourself.

➤ You can look for a cooperative in your area where a group of woodworkers have already set up a shop and buy a share (like a co-op apartment), dividing up expenses.

➤ You can look for a woodworking club that has its own shop.

➤ You can find an existing shop that will rent you bench space and machine time.

Setting up your own space allows you the most freedom, but it is also the most expensive option. Plus, it can take a long time to get the shop rolling. I've set up two shops in my life: one on a 78-acre island in the Caribbean (now that's a story) and one in Brooklyn. There's inevitably more work and more money involved than you expect. On the other hand, it's good to be the king or queen of your own castle.

Joining a cooperative is a more affordable compromise. I worked in a co-op for a few months once, and I liked it. You don't have the same independence, and sometimes you have to wait for a machine, but the stakes are lower. Being in close proximity to other woodworkers is also worthwhile; you can get advice, help, moral support, and even work that overflows from a busy shop. My only warning is to make sure that the cooperative is solvent and that no major personality conflicts are simmering. You'll find co-ops in many cities.

Joining a woodworking club with a shop is an option if you're not planning to work professionally but just want to enjoy your hobby in the bonhomie of fellow wood-workers. Clubs sometimes bring in experts for seminars and demonstrations and can be helpful when you're starting out. There are often members with real skills who can offer hands-on training to complement your readings.

Renting space in a professional shop has a lot going for it, too. You can see how the pros do it (fast and furious compared to more thoughtful, romantic amateurs), and you don't have to cough up big bucks going in. You will have to work around your land-lords, and they may restrict your hours, but you'll always have wood scraps to scrounge.

Scouting a Space

I would look for several things in a shop space. First of all, if I ever set up another shop, it's going to be on the ground floor. If I added up all the time I've spent horsing around with service elevators and moving supplies in and work out, I could have built a pyramid. Elevators are always full of someone else's stuff, broken down, or closed for the weekend. If you have ground-floor access, you bypass a major bottleneck.

Electrical service is very important. I wouldn't rent a place without *three-phase power*, which is a special type service used in industry. (You can find out about it from your electrician or your local power company.) Three-phase power is a factor for me because the beautiful, old, affordable, industrial machines that I prefer often cannot run on conventional single-phase power. Also make sure the fuse box has enough amperage to run the equipment you're planning to use. Bringing in new electrical service is expensive.

Make sure the space has good natural light and ventilation; windows are often responsible for both. Good light will improve the quality of your work, and ventilation will maintain the quality of your health. Be careful, however, that windows and doors don't provide access to burglars. If you're going to leave several thousand dollars' worth of tools lying around overnight, you'd better evaluate the security of the space.

I would see who my neighbors are going to be and find out whether they're going to be complaining about noise and fumes. As more people use industrial lofts for living space or white-collar businesses, problems arise with industrial tenants who make noise and stink up nearby lofts.

Woodlore

My penchant for working late led to near fisticuffs with a downstairs neighbor who lived in his loft on the Brooklyn waterfront. Fortunately, the landlord backed me up, and the man with the sensitive hearing moved out; some woodworkers I know have had the opposite experience.

Setting Up Housekeeping

The first thing you'll want to do is plan the location of your machines. Unlike the smaller basement/garage shop, the machinery in a rented shop is going to have fixed locations. When planning what goes where, think about the flow of work through the shop. I like to keep lumber and plywood stored near the entrance, so I don't have to drag it through a forest of projects when I get a delivery. I also like to keep the bench area separate from the machines. I keep workbenches, tools, the sharpening station, and supplies I use often in one area where the light is particularly good. I like to have the band saw and the drill press closest to the bench area because I often have to dash over and use them in the course of bench work and glue-ups. I keep the jointer and planer next to each other because I usually use them together, and I make sure they are close to the lumber rack. I keep the radial arm saw near the lumber rack for rough cutting before milling and the table saw between the milling area and the bench area.

If you set up an office area, I recommend walling it in with clear plastic or Sheetrock with windows. You want to cut down on dust but still be able to see what's going on in the work area. Air compressors and dust collectors should also be walled in and kept out of the way to cut down on noise. But make sure they're accessible for maintenance and easy dust disposal.

After you figure out where you want things, install your mechanical systems. Make sure you have enough electrical outlets and try to avoid having electrical conduit on the floor, where it will just get in the way; it's better to run conduit across the ceiling and have drops to each machine. Air lines from the compressor are best run the same way, with drops to regulators and quick disconnects where you need them. Ductwork to the dust collector should also run along the ceiling. The following figure is an idealized floor plan for a shop that I put together based on a Swiss technical manual I have. (When it comes to getting organized, I defer to the Swiss.)

Tricks of the Trade

Make sure you check local and OSHA (Occupational Safety and Health Administration) regulations for air compressors. Many municipalities require permits for air compressors that run over a certain pressure. You may also have to take certain safety precautions and have inspections.

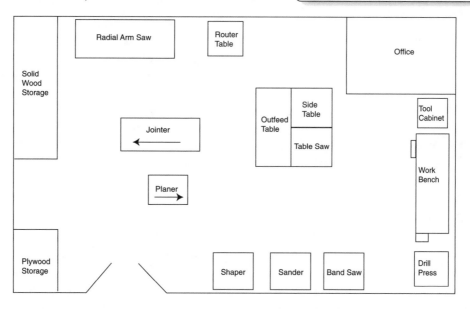

Work flow and convenience determine the layout in the professional shop.

The Least You Need to Know

➤ Working in your living space requires that you limit the scope of your work.

➤ Dust and fumes have to be controlled in the home shop.

➤ Small garage and basement shops necessitate flexible workspace.

➤ An organized plan is key to any shop.

➤ If you must rent space, consider the alternatives to building a shop from scratch.

Chapter 3

A Workshop That Works

In This Chapter

➤ Understanding the nonmechanical foundation of your shop

➤ Setting up and using fixtures

➤ Making and maintaining jigs and fixtures

➤ Being savvy about storage

➤ Buying versus making a workbench

Beginning woodworkers want to spend all their money on fancy tools, but I notice that as apprentices make the transition to journeymen, they start talking about more mundane things like workbenches and efficient tool storage—it's kind of like when women quit dating bad boys and start looking to settle down with a nice guy.

These mundane things, known as fixtures, make your work go smoothly. They help you work efficiently and turn awkward tasks into pleasant ones. To learn how to make your own fixtures or find out what to look for when you buy them, read this chapter.

The Supporting Cast: Workbenches, Sawhorses, and Other Shop Fixtures

If the machines are the stars of the workshop, the fixtures are the supporting players. Welcome to the world of jigs and sleds and workbenches and tool cabinets and all the other fixtures that are staples in a shop. These fixtures take some of the work out of woodworking and make it fun. Sawhorses may not be as glamorous as a shiny, new table saw, but you need them all the same. The right shop fixtures will help you work like the pros.

Beginners are consumed with learning the techniques; as you advance, you start looking to make the work go quickly and easily. If you watch the masters work, they always look graceful and relaxed, even when they are working fast. The main reason behind this ease is that they know how to set up their workspace efficiently.

Developing work systems is important. Becoming a good craftsperson is not all dovetails and mastering the hand plane; you have to step back and get the big picture to look at the shop itself as a machine that helps you work. One of the strong points of the European guild tradition is that it emphasizes shop setup and methodology. This is the professional approach, but it's useful for amateurs, too. Just because you're not earning a living from woodworking doesn't mean you should do it the hard way.

Home Base: The Workbench

When you aren't using the machines, the world revolves around your workbench. It's like the counter in a kitchen: As you work at it, you need easy access to the refrigerator, sink, and utensils. To save steps, your tool cabinet should be no more than a couple of paces from your workbench. So that you don't clutter up your workbench, you should also have two other surfaces, one for the parts you're working on and the other for the tools that are in use. And when you're doing a glue-up you'll need yet another space to keep your workbench clear.

I like to keep my bench freestanding in the room instead of shoved up against the wall, because this position allows me to work on something from all angles. I used to keep my tools in a tall, mahogany cabinet, but after working in a Swiss-run shop, I switched to a low cabinet on wheels. It allows me to keep my tools close but out of the way. I spread out the tools that I'm using on its top surface. I keep the parts I'm working with on a rolling cart nearby. If I need to glue something up, or want a large, flat surface for some other purpose, I pull over two sawhorses (designed so they nest together when not in use), set two lightweight, six-foot beams on top, and place a sheet of plywood over them both. Voilà! I now have a sturdy, flat work surface.

Working Your Workbench

A workbench has to have the following qualities:

➤ It needs to be heavy enough to remain still and stable when you are planing and sawing.

➤ It needs to be tall enough for close work but low enough to permit you to work on a completed piece of furniture.

➤ Its work surface needs to be flat, and its base must be sturdy.

➤ It needs versatile vises to hold all the differently shaped pieces of wood for the myriad processes you perpetrate upon them.

Wood Words

Bench dogs are square or round pegs that stick out of the surface of the bench, one in the vise and one in the bench top. They are used to hold parts, especially long ones, on top of the bench. As you tighten the vise, it moves one peg toward the other, pinching the part and holding it fast.

I favor the classic Northern European bench with all its refinement. It has a heavy shoulder vise for heartier tasks and an end vise with *bench dogs* for holding panels and long boards. If you can't afford to buy the ultimate workbench—even buying the lumber and hardware to make your own can be daunting—you can make do with a section of butcher block on a base with a decent woodworker's vise.

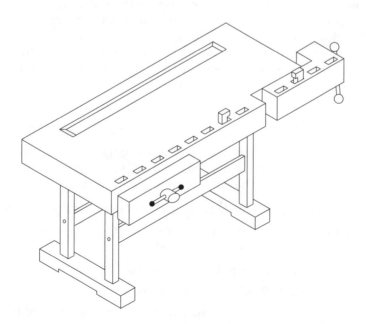

The classic European workbench, with its shoulder vise in front and its end vise with bench dogs for holding panels and long boards, is the distillation of centuries of trial-and-error research.

A good quality wood-worker's vise can be attached to a bench top.

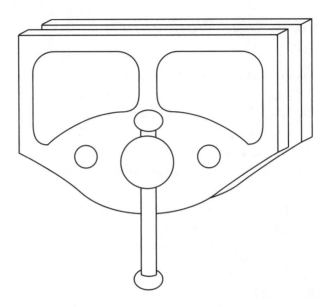

I've made several benches in my career, all based on the European model, but each a little bit different. The best way to build a workbench is to find several woodworkers who all want one and build them together as a production project. It's much more efficient to mill all the parts and cut all the joints at once. When I was studying furniture-making, we would do a run of benches every two years, and at the end of the run, everyone would get a pile of bench parts that they had to fit and assemble themselves. Some people would get their benches done right away; others would still be dragging the parts around years later. I now have a low, heavy workbench for planing and sawing, and a tall, lighter one for delicate work. You should buy or make a workbench that is geared to the type of work you do.

Trust Me

After so many years of woodworking, I've probably seen everything that can possibly go wrong on a workbench and a lot of things that can make it a more efficient fixture. Using these tips will help you make the most of your workbench:

➤ If you use a metal vise, line its jaws with pine or plywood to protect your work.

➤ Dried drops of glue on your bench will mar your work, so scrape down your workbench frequently, and wipe up glue when it spills.

➤ Oiling your bench frequently helps keep the glue from sticking.

➤ Don't eat on your bench; foodstuffs will stain your work.

➤ I keep a power strip screwed to the base of my bench so I can plug in hand tools quickly without having to hunt down an extension cord.

➤ I keep a tiny shelving unit with quarter sheets of sandpaper, each grit on a different shelf, screwed to the base of my bench. It's very handy.

➤ I keep a tall stool near my bench because I find it helps to sit down when I'm doing certain close-focus tasks such as laying out joints. Don't sit down for active tasks such as sanding, though; it's a bad habit.

One handy fixture is the bench slave, which is a device to help hold large pieces in conjunction with a vise. Some bench slaves have a base; I like mine to clamp into the tail vise. You can make one very easily.

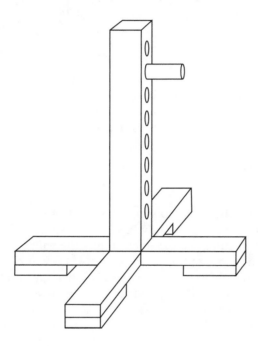

The bench slave helps hold large work in conjunction with the shoulder vise. It has an adjustable support and comes in very handy.

Horsing Around

Sometimes it seems like you can never have enough sawhorses in a shop. I use them for all sorts of things: to support boards when rough-cutting lumber with a circular saw, for gluing up tabletops, in conjunction with beams and plywood to make a work surface, at the in-feed and out-feed sides of the jointer and planer to set parts on when milling, and so on. So where do I keep my stable of sawhorses? Well, these are not your run-of-the-mill sawhorses; they nest together and take up a minimum amount of space. Again, they are a fairly traditional European design.

Traditional European-style sawhorses take up minimal shop space when nested together.

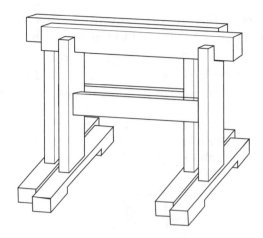

I often prefer to do glue-ups on sawhorses rather than on the bench or other flat surface because the horses allow me access to the underside of the work. For example, I may want to get a clamp under a tabletop to balance the pressure, and a flat work surface would get in the way.

Beam Me Up

Beams are used in conjunction with sawhorses to support a sheet of plywood as a temporary work surface. Let's face it: Almost nobody has enough space in his or her shop, and those of you working in a garage or basement know the value of flexible workspace. The beams and plywood store out of the way, but when you need it, you have a 4 × 8-foot table for glue-ups, finishing, or whatever. You just glue and screw together strips of plywood with internal blocking. This makes a relatively lightweight but rigid structure. Sometimes the beams come in handy without the plywood, such as when you're sanding a tabletop.

Beams are used to support a sheet of plywood to make a temporary work surface.

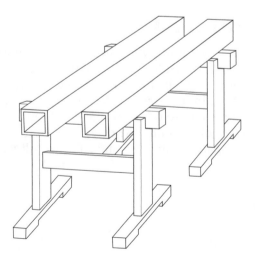

The Tool Cabinet

As I mentioned earlier in the chapter, I used to favor a large tool cabinet with room for every tool in the world. The problem with a large tool cabinet is that sometimes you want to move your tools to the other side of the shop or throw them in a truck and take them to a job site. Let's face it: Fat birds don't fly. So my closet of a tool cabinet went the way of the dodo, and now I use three low, rolling cabinets: one with tools I use all the time and two others with tools I use less frequently. The tools I'm using at the moment share the top surface with a coffee cup and a notepad.

You can make your own cabinet to fit your needs, or you can buy one from any one of several companies that cater to auto mechanics or machinists. Any good industrial supply company will have many to choose from. I've made several, but I bought my last two because I'd rather spend my time making furniture than making tool cabinets. I use one that I made to store table saw accessories, such as blades, push sticks, wrenches, and so forth. It rolls under the saw's side table and keeps things protected and organized.

I Woodn't Do That!

Make sure that all four wheels on a rolling cabinet swivel! Having even two fixed wheels makes a cabinet infuriatingly hard to maneuver around a crowded shop. Swivel casters are a little more expensive, but it's money well spent. Incidentally, rolling cabinets and carts make the shop much easier to sweep.

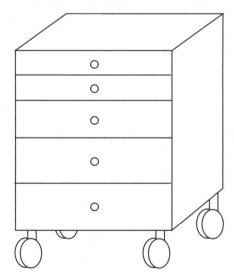

Rolling cabinets are available with nearly any combination of drawers and open space.

I keep tools separated by type: chisels, knives and other cutting tools in one drawer; files and rasps in another; measuring tools in a third; screwdrivers and pliers in a fourth; and so on. Within each drawer, I keep things laid out in subgroups. I keep sets of things, such as chisels or screwdrivers, in divided trays so I can quickly pull out the whole lot and take it to where I'm working. Don't let edged tools roll around; they'll just get dull. Use divided compartments to protect them. Many craftspeople line their drawers with felt so tools don't rattle around. It's a good idea and a nice touch, but I never seem to find the time to do it.

On a Roll

As long as we're on the subject of wheels, let's look at the rolling cart. It seems like every time you stack up a pile of parts you have to move them again to another machine or to your bench to work on them, and then you have to find someplace to store them where they won't get in the way. Enter the rolling cart. Rolling carts make it easy to go from machine to machine, and your storage space suddenly becomes flexible.

Tricks of the Trade

With anything that rolls, consider using lockable casters, especially if your floors are not level. Also make sure the wheels themselves are at least four inches in diameter (five or six inches is even better), so they will roll over debris, irregular floors, or extension cords. Large wheels roll easier, and even on flat floors, a cart heavily loaded with lumber can be hard to start rolling if the wheels are small.

Some people like complicated contraptions. I keep mine simple with just an upper and a lower surface and I make them the same height as the table saw. I also like to have different size carts: big ones for long parts and small ones that are more maneuverable.

Rolling carts are ideal for moving lumber and parts around the shop. They also make great storage because they don't tie up valuable space.

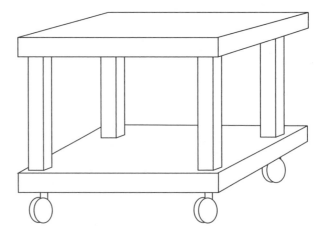

Push It with Push Sticks

Push sticks are used on some of the more danger-ous tools, such as the table saw, jointer, and router table, as extensions of the user's hand. That way, if something goes wrong, the push stick, not your fingers, hits the blade. Many styles of push sticks are available in woodworking stores. You can make your own, but you might want to copy a commer-cially made one so you know the design is tested and proven.

Push sticks can be awkward at first, so make sure you practice using them with the machine turned off until you've learned to control them. (It's a bit like learning to use chopsticks.) See what type of push stick you find comfortable; it tends to be a matter of personal taste. If you're doing the same process over and over, and your hand starts to cramp up from holding the push stick; stop, stretch, and take a break. Many times accidents happen when your hand starts to get tired and you slip. The following figure shows a common type of push stick.

I Woodn't Do That!

It's important that push sticks be accessible. Don't just leave them in one spot on your workbench or in your tool cabinet; hang them near the machine they're used with. De-velop specific habits; always put them back in the same accessible place. For example, I always keep a push stick on the table saw fence so I can get to it as I start a cut. Some people tie them to the machine so they won't absent-mindedly walk away with them.

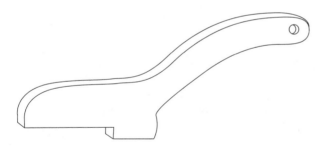

Push sticks are used as an extension of your hand so you can keep the real thing away from spinning blades.

Tooling Around

Certain machines, such as the drill press, table saw, router table, and band saw, have all sorts of blades, wrenches, and other accessories (known as *tooling*) that are frequently needed for their operation. It wastes time to walk halfway across the shop every time you need to get a new drill bit or change the table saw blade. I prefer to keep a cabinet, often wall-mounted, next to the machine to hold all its paraphernalia. Make sure there's a specific place for everything. Consider outlining that place with paint or a felt-tip pen, so you'll put things back where they belong.

Wood Words

Tooling is the term for blades, cutters, wrenches, spacers, bush-ings, and other hardware neces-sary to operate a machine. Some tooling comes with the machine; other tooling, especially blades and cutters, is bought separately.

The Jig's Up

Jigs or fixtures are generally homemade devices to help get a job done. Usually they are designed to hold a part while a machine works on it or to hold a portable tool on a particular orientation while it does a specialized task. Basically, a *jig* is a tool that holds a tool or a part for another tool. Jigs are generally developed to make a specific job more efficient. Although many jigs are made for one job and thrown away, others have an ongoing application and are saved around the shop. Some jigs have such universal application that you see them in nearly every shop, and they may even be sold commercially.

The table saw sled is a jig, and so are those contraptions that hold your chisel at the right angle on the sharpening stone. There are jigs to cut tapers on legs, jigs to cut circles with a hand router, and jigs to drill evenly spaced shelf pinholes in your cabinet sides. Jigs are made out of plywood, solid wood, aluminum, or whatever works. They embody the seat-of-your-pants problem-solving that Americans pride themselves on.

Once you get the idea, a mania can set in where you want to figure out a jig to do everything: mark holes, make angled cuts, and butter your toast. This is fine, but make sure it doesn't take longer to make the jig than it would to do a satisfactory job without one; woodworkers have a tendency to get carried away with their own cleverness. Jigs that will be useful again should be saved, perhaps in the tooling cabinet of the machine they work with.

Storage Savvy

The longer your shop has been set up, the more stuff you accumulate: scrap wood, lumber bought without a project in mind, veneer, fasteners, first-aid and safety equipment, abrasives, finishing supplies, and so on. This stuff includes things you need every day and some you'll probably never use but are too good to throw away. You have to get organized: If you can't lay your hands on the thing you need quickly, you're wasting time.

Most items can go on shelves. Make sure they're divided into categories and organized within those categories so you can find what you're looking for. For example, I keep all fasteners on one set of shelves, where they are divided up into categories: screws, pneumatic nails and staples, regular nails, anchors, brads, nuts and bolts, and so on. Those categories are divided up further into subgroups: Screws are divided into brass and steel, which are divided into Phillips head and slotted head, and then separated by size. For example, in one section, all #6 steel screws are arranged by length from shortest to longest.

Some people like doors on their cabinets; others don't. Open shelving is easier to get to, but doors keep things from getting dusty, which is an issue in a wood shop. I like doors because they hide the visual clutter, which I find distracting. My shelves are open, however, because I was too lazy to put doors on when I built them. We do what we can.

Some items have special storage considerations. Lumber needs to be absolutely flat if it's going to be stored horizontally: Any sagging leads to bowed boards. Most woodworkers just lean their lumber against the wall, which is fine. Just make sure it's nearly vertical so it won't bow and stable enough so it won't tip over. I like cantilevered steel lumber racks because they're neat and handy. Unfortunately, they're also expensive. Plywood, too, should be stored nearly vertically or dead flat horizontally.

Tricks of the Trade

The way I store my tools may sound obsessive, but it's the only way to get any work done. Digging through a bucket of miscellaneous screws to find the one you need will take you longer than going to the hardware store and buying a new box, and you'll be ready for the booby-hatch by the time you're done.

Solid wood should be stored in the driest part of the shop. Veneer is best stored where it will not get too dry, but not get so moist that it will mildew. Finishing supplies should be stored in an explosion-proof cabinet with the fumes vented to the outside. These cabinets are expensive new, but they can be found cheap, especially at auctions.

After a while, everyone's shop starts to reflect their personality and the kind of work they do. As you go along, you'll try new systems; some will work, and some will not. Check out other woodworkers' shops and get clues from them. One of the great things about woodworking today is that there is so much information around that everybody learns from one another.

Remember, though, the shop is just a means to produce beautiful work, not an end in itself. I see hobbyists who spend so much time perfecting their shops that they don't produce any work. Don't spend too much time obsessing over setting up your shop—just do it!

The Least You Need to Know

➤ Some shop accessories are just as important as your machinery and tools.

➤ A good workbench is the heart of a system that includes tool cabinets, sawhorses, and rolling carts and allows you to work efficiently.

➤ Adding wheels to your cabinets and parts storage units provides flexible space and greater efficiency.

➤ Push sticks are a shop aid crucial to safe machine use.

➤ Learning to make and use jigs will help you work faster and cleaner.

➤ Storage that is accessible and organized is essential to working smoothly.

Part 2

The Tools: The Work They Do and How to Work Them

Some woodworkers seem to use their hobby as an excuse to indulge their fetish for tools. I understand the urge; good tools have an almost spiritual allure. It's important to have the tools you need and to know how to use them. The chapters in this part lay out the basic arsenal of woodworking tools and explain what they do and how to use them. It covers hand tools, power tools, and stationary machinery, and there's a whole chapter on the all-important subject of sharpening. Obviously, no amount of written instruction can replace hands-on training, but these chapters should serve as an introduction to the tools you'll be working with and a guide to refer to when you're buying or using a new tool. Major emphasis is placed on safety, which is one of the reasons that hands-on training is so critical. These tools are dangerous, so pay attention to the safety instructions.

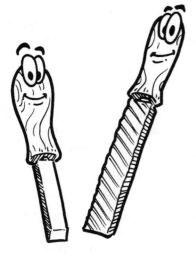

Chapter 4

Your Hand Tool Arsenal: The Cutters

In This Chapter

➤ Discovering the world of fine chisels

➤ Handling hand planes

➤ Appreciating Japanese tools

➤ Using rasps and files

➤ Taking tool safety seriously

There's something very personal about hand tools. We may get excited about a new power tool, but hand tools make us downright sentimental. Maybe it's because they're a link with the past, or perhaps it's because we know that if these tools are treated with care, they'll outlive us and be part of our legacy some day.

I have a friend whose father was a master machinist when he got Alzheimer's disease in his 80s. I was given the task of sorting through his life's collection of tools. After seeing how he'd modified this tool for his way of working or made a new handle for that one, I began to feel like I knew the old guy. There was one beautiful, bronze wrench from the 1930s on which he'd engraved the words: "Bill: This belongs to Ray. Put it back!" Seems he'd worked in a shop with some guy who kept borrowing his wrench. Every time I use it, it makes me crack a smile. Strange that something so utilitarian holds such pathos.

This chapter covers the cutting tools used in woodworking and explains how to use them. The next chapter continues the saga by covering the rest of the common hand tools. In both chapters, I talk about how to distinguish a good version from a lower-quality one. Remember: Price does not a good tool make.

Using hand tools well requires practice and patience. Certain tools, such as the hand-saw or the hand plane, can seem impossible at first, but if you stick with it, the learning curve is pretty fast. I recommend that you practice using tools you're unfamiliar with on scrap wood first, so you don't make mistakes on your precious projects. Practice often: Practicing often for a little while is better than overdoing it infrequently.

Who's a Chiseler?

The chisel is the archetypal woodworking tool, used for everything from chopping joints when timber-framing a barn to mortising for a hinge or delicately paring a plug so it's flush. Because chisels are used for such a wide range of tasks, several types are available; some are common, and some are more specialized.

Different types of chisels.

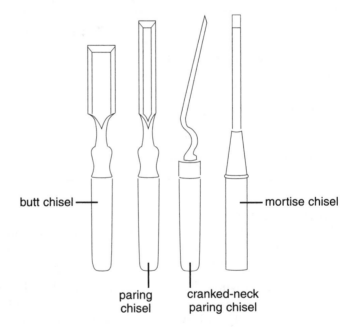

butt chisel

mortise chisel

paring chisel

cranked-neck paring chisel

Butt Chisels: The Cabinetmaker's Workhorse

Butt chisels have a short blade of medium to light thickness and a short handle, which makes them easy to handle and balance. The sides of the blade are beveled so they can get into tight corners. Butt chisels usually are available in sets or individually by blade width from $1/16$-inch to 2 or 3 inches wide, in $1/16$-inch or $1/8$-inch increments.

If you're going to buy one type of chisel, the butt chisel is it. Butt chisels are the most versatile, all-purpose chisel and can be struck with a mallet or pushed by hand. They may have a metal ring or cap at the end of the handle to protect the wood from damage.

When doing rough chopping, you can hold the handle in your fist with the blade pointing down and hit the end with a wooden mallet (don't use a hammer; hammers are for nails). The pressure of the wood on the *bevel* as it enters the wood drives the chisel in the direction of its back, so generally you should keep the bevel facing out, which helps the blade stay in the wood and makes it easier to control.

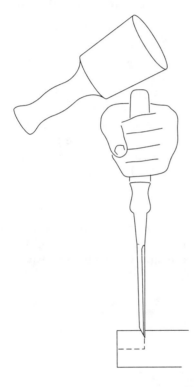

How to chop with a butt chisel.

For more delicate work, such as mortising for a hinge or cutting to a line, as you do when making dovetails, pinch the blade down near the edge between your middle finger and thumb while using your index finger to guide the handle this way or that as you tap it with your mallet. Holding the chisel this way lets you steady your hand on the workpiece and lower the blade to your mark, which imparts a deft control not possible when you're holding the chisel up on the handle. It also makes it easier to estimate the angle or squareness of the cut you're making.

Paring Down: Paring Chisels

Paring chisels are pushed by hand, not struck with a mallet, thus they're used primarily for trimming, not chopping. Examples of the kind of work they are used for are paring plugs flush, trimming the ends of dovetails flush, or delicately *chamfering* (or *beveling*) end grain. To pare or trim a plug or anything else flush to a surface, you generally lay the back of the chisel on the surface and push the edge into the object to be trimmed with a firm but gentle sideways shearing action. One hand pushes the handle while the fingers of the other hand keep the blade flat to the surface with downward pressure and simultaneously slide it sideways in the shearing motion.

Wood Words

A **bevel** is the angle that one surface or line makes with another when they are not at right angles. **Chamfering** is beveling on workpieces.

Paring chisels have long blades for more bearing surface to keep them flat as they cut and to reach farther. They also have long handles for more leverage. They are commonly used in wider widths because greater width allows a longer shearing stroke and provides more bearing surface. Like butt chisels, paring chisels have beveled-edge blades. Paring chisels are generally sharpened to a lower, sharper angle than butt chisels because they're not struck and are typically the choice for more delicate tasks that don't require such a sturdy edge.

Cranked-neck paring chisels have an offset handle that allows you to trim in the center of a large surface without the handle interfering. They can be handy, but they are exotic and generally expensive, so don't run out and buy one until you need it.

When you are paring, one hand pushes the handle while the other hand pushes the blade down and sideways in a shearing motion.

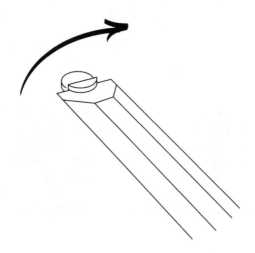

Choosing Your Chisels Wisely

Look for these characteristics in a chisel:

- ➤ Good quality steel
- ➤ Good balance and weight
- ➤ A comfortable, durable handle
- ➤ A flat, well-finished blade

The steel is impossible to judge until you've used the chisel. Don't be fooled by brands boasting Sheffield or Solingen steel. I've found the steel on less expensive American chisels, such as Stanley and Buck Bros., to be better than that used in expensive English and German ones, and this judgment has been borne out by a prominent woodworking magazine, *Fine Woodworking,* that tested them. Talk to other woodworkers to see what they like, and try their chisels.

Balance and weight are subjective, as is handle comfort. I generally prefer lighter chisels because they're easier to control, though heavier chisels might be safer for a beginner. I also keep a set of beaters (cheap, expendable chisels) that I use when I have to seriously hog off (rapidly remove) stock.

A well-finished, straight blade makes a tremendous difference. Modern chisel manufacturers tend to overbuff the blades so they're no longer flat, which is inconvenient. A bowed blade is hard to line up for a square cut (see Chapter 8, "Keeping Your Edge," to learn more about sharpening).

As for my own prejudices: I scour flea markets for 1930s, '40s, and '50s Eskiltuna chisels, a Swedish brand identifiable by the shark stamped on the blade. I love their feel, and the steel is excellent. Unfortunately, in the '60s, another company bought Eskiltuna, and the tools became mediocre, although the shark is still on them. I also like many Japanese brands, though they tend to have an overly thick blade for my taste. I like older English chisels, too. If I were starting fresh, I would probably buy an inexpensive American brand and scour flea markets for old, high-quality chisels.

Grasping Rasps and Files

Rasps and files are used for shaping irregular forms, flushing end grain, beveling small surfaces, and many other odd jobs. Rasps are tools with sharp, pointy teeth, and files have sharpened ridges that run diagonally across the tool's surface. Rasps are only for wood or soft materials, but files can be used for metal as well.

The file has grooves; the rasp has sharp, pointed teeth.

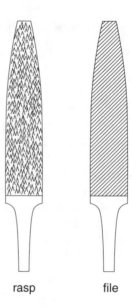

rasp   file

Both tools cut in only one direction, so you don't scrub the tool back and forth: You stroke it in the direction it cuts. The correct way to make a standard cut with either tool is to pinch the front of the tool between your thumb and index finger in one hand and hold the handle or tang the same way in your other hand, with the cutting face down. This hold affords control whether you're drawing the tool toward you or away and keeps your wrists loose if you're filing a curve.

Wood Words

Tearout is a term for what happens when a cutter tears rather than cuts the wood's fibers, leaving an ugly surface defect. A saw is said to tear out when it blows out little pieces of wood as it exits a cut. A plane tears out sometimes when it cuts against the grain.

Handy Handsaws

Traditionally, a wide range of handsaws was used in woodwork, but most sawing today is done with power saws. I still use a panel saw (the classic carpenter's saw) or a bow saw (the European equivalent) for crosscutting lumber if I don't have a power tool or am too far from electricity. But most of my handsawing is detail work with small back saws, where the handsaw's finer control makes it the better choice. I cut dovetails with them and use them to quickly cut small pieces to length. I use coping saws for ornamental work. The past few years I've been switching gradually to Japanese saws, but more on that later. You may want to practice using handsaws when you're starting out, because they are an inexpensive and space-saving alternative to power saws.

The larger saws come in two types: the ripsaw and the crosscut saw. Ripsaws have larger, straight, chisel-like teeth and are designed for cutting parallel to the wood's grain direction. Crosscut saws have offset, beveled teeth to minimize *tearout* when you use them to cut perpendicular to the grain direction.

Western handsaws cut on the push stroke, and if you don't have an even, straight stroke, the blade wants to bend against the work. A straight saw stroke keeps the cut straight, cuts down on binding (the saw's tendency to bog in the cut due to friction), and allows you to have a relaxed handgrip, which cuts down on fatigue. The trick is to position yourself comfortably over the work, with your shoulder in line with the cut, and swing your arm straight, like a pendulum. Clamp the work if necessary to keep it stable; if it slides around, your cut will stray.

Because I'm right-handed, I cut with my saw to the right of the line I've marked so the blade doesn't obscure it. I like to start my cut by placing my thumbnail on the line and bringing the blade to it, drawing it back a few inches to seat the blade, and then sawing. It's important to keep the waste supported if it's heavy, so it doesn't pinch the blade or go crashing down toward the end of the cut.

Woodlore

Sawing did not come easily to me, and I used to marvel at Tage Frid when I worked for him as he cut dovetails in several drawer sides at once with a large bow saw. He pointed out, however, that when he started his apprenticeship in Denmark in the early 1920s, all lumber was dressed by hand over a saw pit. One apprentice, the one with seniority, stood on top of the thick lumber with one end of the two-man ripsaw while another apprentice, the new guy, held the other end from the pit. Of course, it was pretty cold in that pit in the winter and pretty hot in the summer, and all that sawdust had to fall somewhere, mostly in the apprentice's eyes and down his shirt. The quicker an apprentice could master sawing, the quicker he could get out of the pit and up the ladder.

The Plane Truth

Hand planes are used for flattening, straightening, and smoothing wood and are generally used for shaving off small amounts of wood when you are fitting doors and drawers. Traditionally, they were the only means for cutting profiles in moldings and for cutting rabbets and grooves, but today this type of cutting is done with power tools because using hand planes is so labor-intensive.

Top to bottom: bench plane, block plane, and rabbet plane.

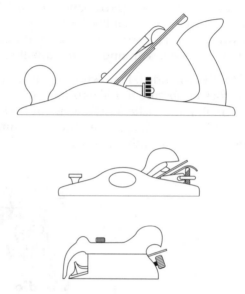

There are many types of planes out there, but the ones you need to concern yourself with in the beginning are *bench planes, block planes,* and *rabbet planes.*

Bench planes are held with two hands by a knob in front and a handle in back. They're used for general work at the workbench, hence the name. Smaller bench planes are called *smoothing planes,* medium ones are called *jack planes,* and long ones are called *jointer planes.* Smoothing planes are the most versatile, but they are designed for leveling and smoothing tabletops and other flat expanses. Jointer planes are better at straightening out narrower parts, such as table legs. Jointer planes are also used for truing long, thin glue joints dead straight, like when you're preparing the edges of boards being glued up into a tabletop. Jack planes are more general-purpose tools.

Block planes are small and are very handy for trimming stock when it can't be held in a vise; in this situation, you have to hold the part in one hand and use the plane with the other. Low-angle block planes have their blades set at a more acute angle and are used for planing the end grain of boards, which prefer their shearing cut. Rabbet planes have a blade that extends to the tool's square sides and are used for cleaning up rabbets (steps) and notches and for other delicate operations.

The bottom, or sole, of the hand plane rides on the surface you're working on, and the blade is held at just the right angle to take a thin shaving. Most modern planes have a thumbscrew that adjusts the depth of the cut, and most planes have a lateral adjusting lever that adjusts the evenness of the cut by shifting the angle of the blade side to side. The blade of most bench planes has a flat metal plate screwed to it, called a *chip-breaker,* that reduces tearout. The blade and chip-breaker are held in place by the lever cap. Block planes and rabbet planes have no chip-breaker, and the blade sits bevel-up to compensate.

Make sure your plane is properly adjusted before you try to use it. The chip breaker should be about $1/32$ inch from the edge of the blade and sit absolutely flat (hold the assembly up to the light and check to see whether any light leaks through; if it does, lap the front of the chip-breaker on a sharpening stone until it fits flush). With the blade in the body, hold the plane upside down in front of a light source and sight down the sole and adjust the blade until it's even. The blade should protrude just enough to take a paper-thin shaving. Make sure the blade is sharp. Nothing makes learning to use a plane harder than a dull blade.

It takes some practice to get the hang of hand-planing. Like learning a golf swing, you have to learn to get the right stroke when pushing a plane. To start, hold the plane in a firm, relaxed grip, with the sole flat on the work. Begin the stroke with most of the downward pressure on the front of the plane, ahead of the blade. As you push the plane, transfer the downward pressure toward its back. It helps if you drive the plane with your hips, rather than just your hands. Hand-planing is kind of like throwing a punch or hitting a tennis ball in that the power comes from your body, not just your arms and hands.

If you buy only one plane at first, it should probably be a smoothing plane, which is the best all-purpose plane. After that, in order of importance, I would get the block plane, a rabbet plane, and a jack plane.

Tricks of the Trade

The largest makers of planes are Stanley and Record, and both have fine, almost identical lines. You don't have to spend a fortune on exotic, limited production planes. In fact, I recommend checking flea markets for cheap, older planes. Just make sure they're not cracked or otherwise damaged.

Push Me, Pull You: Japanese Tools

In the past 20 years or so, Japanese tools have made quite a name for themselves in this country. The big stars are their chisels, saws, and, to some extent, their planes, which are generally made to much higher standards than Western tools. Made more along traditional lines, Japanese tools have some fundamental differences from the tools Americans are used to.

Japanese chisel and plane blades are made from steel harder than that which Americans use for their tools and are laminated to a softer steel. Used alone, the hard steel would be too brittle, but the softer steel supports it and keeps it from breaking. The hard steel takes a great edge and stays sharp longer than Western blades. Another difference between Japanese and Western planes and saws is that the Japanese models cut on the pull stroke, not the push stroke. This difference gives Japanese saws one real advantage, namely that they can use a much thinner blade because it doesn't have to resist jamming up into the work. The thinner blade means Japanese saws provide a finer cut.

Woodlore

The reason the Japanese have a tradition of producing such great tools is because during the Meiji period, when samurai were banned, many of the sword makers turned to tool-making. They brought to it the rigor and passion of the samurai tradition and highly developed metalworking techniques. In Japan, some chisel, plane, blade, and saw makers are designated national living treasures.

The Japanese also sharpen their saws differently, so, unfortunately, the saws tend to be fragile and prone to losing teeth when cutting hardwood. Japanese planes are made of wood, like traditional Western planes, and that means they also have to be tuned up every time the weather changes, which is a pain, but because Japanese tools in general are of such high quality, they also carry a high price.

Safety Rules for Hand Tools

Hand-tool safety is often overlooked, because hand tools seem so nonthreatening. But accidents do occur. Most of them are minor cuts with chisels, but I've seen a few doozies. I once set a marking knife on top of a cabinet as I was working on the base; it rolled off and buried itself to the hilt in my hand, which was outstretched and supporting all my weight on the floor. The unnerving part was that it just stuck there, handle straight up in the air, until I removed it and got patched up.

Be on the safe side and follow these basic hand-tool safety rules:

➤ Never push an edged tool into the work when there is a body part on the other side. If it slips, it will cut the body part.

➤ Never set a tool down on top of a tall cabinet or ladder. You or someone else will not remember it's there and will move the thing, and the tool will land on someone's head. Use a tool belt instead.

➤ Wear safety glasses when working above your head, or debris will fall in your eyes.

➤ Wear a dust mask when creating dust.

➤ Don't work when you're exhausted, and take breaks to prevent fatigue.

➤ Stretch your wrists frequently to help prevent repetitive stress disorders.

Finally, don't get careless; work like your mother was watching.

The Least You Need to Know

➤ Cutting tools are the aristocrats of hand tools.

➤ You don't need to spend a lot to get good tools.

➤ Scour flea markets for cheap but excellent old cutting tools.

➤ Look for tools that feel good in your hand.

➤ Keep your tools sharp and on the ready.

➤ Always follow the safety rules for using hand tools.

Chapter 5

Hand Tools for Measuring, Marking, and Other Basics

In This Chapter

➤ The measuring tools and how to use them

➤ Marking knives, marking gauges, and chalk lines

➤ Hammers and other striking tools

➤ The old favorites that fill out a toolbox

➤ Tool storage for safety and convenience

Aside from the cutting tools (covered in Chapter 4, "Your Hand Tool Arsenal: The Cutters"), woodworkers use a host of other basic tools. Because precision is essential in woodworking, measuring and layout tools are extremely important. At the other end of the spectrum are hammers, mallets, and mauls. Plus, a crowd of screwdrivers, wrenches, pliers, and other old friends are called into service on a regular basis. This chapter investigates the particulars of these tools and generally continues where Chapter 4 left off. At the end, this chapter reviews strategies for tool storage.

Taking the Measure of Measuring Tools

Without measuring tools, there is no accuracy. When you're doing fine woodwork, such as furniture or cabinets, even $1/64$ of an inch can seem like a large increment when it's a mistake. Consequently, it pays to buy the best measuring tools you can afford.

Don't waste money on fancy rosewood and brass squares (unless you want to hang them on the wall) because a marking knife will shave scallops into the soft brass blade, and wood beams aren't stable enough. The best measuring tools are made for the machinist trade. Starret makes the finest, but they're quite expensive. General makes a cheaper line that's good for beginners. With machinist's measuring tools, you do get what you pay for. The following sections describe the basic measuring tools you need.

The Six-Inch Rule

The short length and thin, narrow blade of a six-inch rule make it very easy to handle, and easier handling means greater accuracy. No matter how precise a ruler's graduations are, it's hard to measure accurately when you're trying to balance a long, awkward rule in your hand; it's like playing hopscotch on stilts. I recommend a $1/2$-inch wide, flexible rule graduated in $1/16$-inch and $1/8$-inch increments on one face and $1/32$-inch and $1/64$-inch increments on the other. Keep the rule in your shirt pocket for easy access.

The Combination Square

Arguably the most important measuring tool in the woodworker's kit, the combination square (also known as the combo square) has a metal head that measures 90 degrees on one side and 45 degrees on the other and slides up and down a removable blade (usually 12 inches long, although 6-, 18-, and 24-inch blades are available), which can be used separately. It is extremely versatile and is used for measuring depth, length, square, and 45-degree angles and laying out lines and angles on work. There are optional protractor and center-finding heads for measuring odd angles and finding the center of round stock. If you're going to splurge on a tool, splurge on this one.

The combination square is used for measuring depth.

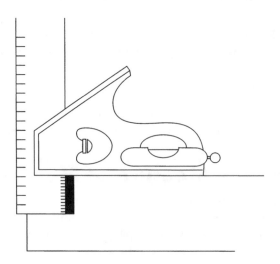

The Six-Inch Engineer's Square

A six-inch engineer's square is originally a machinist's tool, but it is great for setting jointers and table saw blades square and checking stock and small parts. It has no length graduations; it checks square only. Like the six-inch rule, its strength is its handy size and balance, which make for greater accuracy. Its all-steel construction and fixed blade make for durable accuracy.

The Framing Square

The framing square is large (18 × 24 inches) and flat (it's stamped out of sheet metal) and appears simple, but good ones have elaborate tables for doing the trigonometry involved in roof framing. I ignore the tables and use mine for doing large-scale layout where absolute precision is not necessary, such as laying out cabinet location on a floor or checking the factory edge on a piece of plywood for square.

Tricks of the Trade

When checking an object for square, hold the square by its beam in one hand and the workpiece in the other. Keep the beam tight to the reference edge and slide the blade down until it just touches the edge to be checked. Make sure there's a bright light behind the square, and look to see where the light leaks between the blade and the edge you're checking.

The Bevel Gauge

The bevel gauge is not so familiar to the average citizen, but it is indispensable to you, the woodworker. It's composed of a wooden or metal beam with a locking pivot at one end and a thin, metal blade with a slot through half its length. It does not have any angle graduations of its own, but instead is used to transfer angles from a protractor, combo square, or for example, an angled part you're working on. Its most common use is setting the table saw blade at 45 degrees: Because you can't fit the angled head of your combo square under the table saw blade, you transfer the angle to the bevel gauge and adjust the blade to that.

When you're buying a bevel gauge, go cheap. Just make sure the blade is straight and the locking thumbscrew doesn't interfere with its use. This problem is common; it's as though the manufacturers never bother to check whether the gauges work. I have an expensive rosewood German bevel gauge, but I had to file the pretty brass wing nut half off to use it.

The Tape Measure

The tape measure is probably the most commonly used measuring tool. Get a good one; Stanley, Lufkin, and Starrett are all good brands. Apply the Goldilocks rule: Get one that's just the right size. For furniture and cabinets, I use a $3/4$-inch × 12-foot tape, and I use a 1-inch × 25-foot tape measure for carpentry. A tape measure that's too big will bump into things when it's clipped to your belt and make your pants sag; one that's too small won't be long enough to measure your work and its thin blade will sag when extended.

The Folding Rule

The folding rule is handy for taking accurate inside measurements. The only brand I've found that I like is the Lufkin Red End. Make sure you get one with an extending blade at one end. Skip the ones with a hook on the end; they're never accurate enough. Folding rules come in six- and eight-foot lengths. I prefer the six-foot, but it's up to you.

The Long Straightedge

It's a good idea to have a long (36 × 48-inch) straightedge for checking straightness and flatness. It's great if it has graduations on it, too, for measuring, but a straightedge is for testing trueness, not dimension. As with the squares, when you're checking for accuracy, try to get light behind the straightedge.

Hit the Mark with Marking Tools

Clean, professional-looking woodwork is the result of dead-on accuracy, which in turn is based on careful measurement and layout. If you're cutting to a line you've laid out on your work, you want it to be a fine, sharp one, not a broad, fuzzy one. That soft, dull, no. 2 pencil you write with just won't do.

Make Your Mark with a Marking Knife

You can make a more accurate line with a small, sharp knife than you can with a pencil. The knife's cut line also serves as a groove that your chisel can find by feel. When you lower a chisel to a drawn line, it's difficult to see whether you're dead on; with a knife line, you can feel when you're dead on. When sawing to a cut line, you can find the line by feeling with your thumbnail and then use your nail to guide the saw blade.

The trick with a marking knife is to figure out where you want your line. Use your square or a straightedge to establish where the line will go and hold the square or straightedge there firmly while you gently mark a shallow, preliminary line, steering the blade so it hugs the straightedge. A marking knife steers like an ice skate, and it takes some practice to get the hang of using one. After you have your first light line where you want it, go over it with more pressure until it's as deep as you want it. The subsequent passes will stay in the already established groove and steer more easily than if you tried to mark the line in one deep pass.

The blade on a marking knife should be very thin and delicate. To start, I recommend getting an inexpensive Exacto knife with disposable blades, which can be sharpened to better than new or replaced when dull. Just make sure the knife holds the blade tightly. My all-time favorite marking knives, though, are surgeons' scalpels with replaceable blades sold by White Chapel Brasses (see Appendix B, "Resources"), and they're surprisingly affordable. You do not need to spend a lot of money on a rosewood-handled model.

I Woodn't Do That!

Don't go deeper than necessary with marking tools. The deeper you go, the wider the line becomes, and therefore the less precise the line is. Also, if the surface being marked is going to be visible later, you'll have to sand out any segments left, and the deeper the mark is, the more you have to sand. As long as the line is visible, and you can key your chisel into it, it's deep enough.

Keep Your Distance with the Marking Gauge

A marking gauge is just a device that holds a small marking knife at a set distance (which is adjustable) from a fence. It allows you to make repeated, consistent lines parallel to an edge, which is something woodworkers do a lot of, for example, when marking similar joints on several pieces of wood.

Set the marking gauge carefully to the dimension you want with a small rule. Snug the thumbscrew lightly, tap the beam holding the blade this way or that until you're on, and then tighten the thumbscrew all the way. Hold the gauge with sideward pressure to keep the fence in contact with the piece being marked. Angle the whole thing forward so the blade will cut smoothly and make a light preliminary pass, followed by a heavier pass or two to make the line legible. The trick is to keep the fence tight to the edge.

A cheap marking gauge can be just as good as an expensive one. Fancy woodworking stores are full of expensive rosewood and brass marking gauges that are absolute junk. Marking gauges need to be comfortable in the hand, have a flat fence, and have a locking system that stays put. Nearly all marking gauges these days come with a pin rather than a knife, and the pin must be filed into a knife by the user or it will leave a bouncy, scratchy line. File a tiny flat spot on the side of the pin facing away from and parallel to the fence, and a tiny bevel on the side facing the fence. The bevel will help the pin steer the fence tight to the workpiece.

Keep the marking gauge fence tight to the edge and angled forward as you draw the knife across the workpiece.

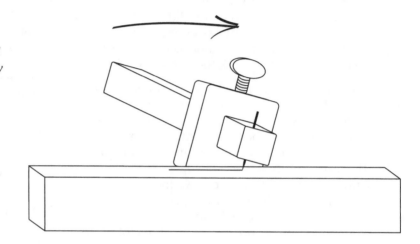

Drop a Chalk Line

The chalk line is just a string with hook on one end that reels into a reservoir of chalk dust. It's drawn tight over the surface to be marked, connecting two points, and when snapped like a bow string, it deposits a straight line of colored chalk. The line is relatively wide and fuzzy, but it is a fast way to mark a long line, especially when you don't have a straightedge off which to reference. I use a chalk line for snapping lines on rough lumber that is to be cut oversize at first and doesn't require great precision. Carpenters use chalk lines for marking layout lines on floors and walls.

Driving Things Home: Striking Tools

Woodworkers use a variety of striking tools: metal hammers for striking nails and wood; rubber or plastic hammers when striking tools, the work, or their assistants (I wrote that just to see if you were paying attention).

The Classic Claw Hammer

The claw hammer is familiar to everyone: One side drives nails; the other side removes them. Generally, the larger the nail is, the larger the hammer you need, ranging from dinky 12-ounce finish hammers for brads and small finish nails to huge 26-ounce framing hammers for driving 20-penny nails in a couple of shots. Handles come in wood, metal, and Fiberglas. I like wood, but *chacun à son goût* (everyone to his taste).

The trick to using a hammer, even on the tiniest brad, is to swing it, not push it, which takes confidence and practice. You have to let the hammer do the work. It's very Zen, really. It's like a mentor of mine, Darwin Sawyer, said when teaching me to shear the heads off large, frozen bolts with a sharp cold chisel and a 50-ounce engineer's hammer (named Bruce): "You have to swing it like there's not a chance in the world you'll miss." About 15 minutes after he said this, I broke a couple of small bones in my left hand, but eventually I got the hang of it.

You often want to use a *nail set* with a hammer, which is a metal punch that allows you to drive the nail below the surface of the wood without leaving "bear tracks," which are the imprint of a carelessly swung hammer. Nail sets come in different sizes for different-size nails. You can use a metal hammer on the workpiece, such as when you're tapping joints into place during a glue-up, but you must use a block of scrap wood as a buffer to prevent marring.

Tricks of the Trade

Clean up ("dress") the face of your hammer with sandpaper frequently to remove dents and dings, and it will hammer straighter. Small irregularities on the hammer face will deflect nails this way and that, bending them and marring your surface.

The Mighty Wooden Maul

Wooden mauls are used for driving tools like chisels and gouges, which would be damaged by a metal hammer. Their softer face absorbs impact and gives more of a pushing force than a striking force, even when swung hard. I prefer a round-turned maul because it's what I'm used to, but some, particularly those who learned in the German tradition, like square mauls.

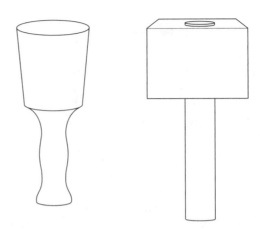

The square and the round maul.

Synthetic Mallets for Safe Strikes

I'm a big fan of both rubber and Stanley Deadblow mallets. I use them for knocking parts into place because they won't dent wood as long as you're reasonably careful. Rubber mallets are softer, but they are prone to bouncing. I wrap a piece of cotton over the head of the rubber mallet and tie it around the handle with string to prevent the black rubber from leaving skid marks. Deadblow mallets are made of plastic and are loosely filled with lead shot, which keeps them from bouncing.

Tricks of the Trade

When I have to leave the shop and drag along a toolbox, I carry a screwdriver with a battalion of replaceable tips that camp out in the handle. This type of screwdriver saves both space and weight. I can also use the same tips in my screw gun, which is handy.

The Old Bunch: Tools You May Have Met Before

A host of tools used periodically in the course of working with wood are not specifically woodworking tools. Many of them should be familiar to you. You can review them in the following sections.

How About a Screwdriver?

Screwdrivers are classified according to the type of screw head they drive. The two most common types are slotted head (which look like a minus sign) and Phillips head (which look like a plus sign). The advantage of the Phillips head is that it is self-centering; the slotted screwdriver can drift to one side during use, gouging the wood around the screw (this issue is especially crucial when using a power screw gun). Screws are sized by the diameter of their heads, and it's important to use the right size screwdriver for the screw you're installing (see Chapter 17, "Nails, Screws, and Bolts: When It's Okay to Use Fasteners").

You can buy short, stubby screwdrivers for jobs with tight clearance or extra-long screwdrivers for when you need reach. For comfort, I prefer wood handles, especially in cold weather, but plastic is more durable. The important thing is to buy screwdrivers with hardened tips; mild steel tips wear quickly and start to strip the heads of your screws.

Hex Keys

Hex or Allen keys are kissing cousins of the screwdriver. They drive the somewhat fancier socket head machine screws and set screws on power tools and machines that woodworkers commonly use. It's good to have an inexpensive *fractional* set and a *metric* set handy, especially if you plan to be a do-it-yourselfer with machine maintenance. Hex keys come L-shaped with T-handles or in a fold-up arrangement like a pocketknife. Suit yourself.

Ratchet Socket Wrench Sets

Socket wrenches are those things your car mechanic uses. You can always tell a woodshop that doesn't have a set: All the nuts and bolts on the machines are stripped from pliers being used to loosen them. Socket wrench sets can be expensive, so don't buy them until you need to, like when you're setting up a complete woodshop. But don't wait too long, either; stripping all your nuts and bolts can be expensive, too. Socket wrenches come in both fractional and metric sets. Choose the one that is appropriate for your machines.

Wood Words

Metric wrenches are sized in millimeters (7 mm, 12 mm, 25 mm, and so on) and are now the standard for every nation except the United States and, I believe, Madagascar. (Certain American industries, such as the automotive and aerospace fields, now use metric, too.) **Fractional** wrenches are sized in fractions of an inch ($^1/_4$-inch, $^3/_8$-inch, and so on). I'm not looking forward to changing to metric, but it does seem like a good idea to be on the same page as the rest of the world.

Pliers, Vise Grips, Adjustable Wrenches, and Tweezers

Pliers are great for grabbing irregularly shaped objects, and pliers come in all shapes and sizes. For example, needle-nose pliers are useful for delicate work or where clearance is a problem; linemen's pliers with built-in wire cutters for electrical work. Common pliers are good for general work; channel lock pliers can handle torquing larger parts.

Vise grips lock tight and can be used like a third hand. It's handy to have a selection of vise grips, and they're relatively inexpensive, especially at flea markets.

Remember, a pair of pliers should never touch the facets of a bolt head or nut, unless maybe (and I say maybe) your life depends on it. Using pliers on a nut or bolt will ruin the nut or bolt and invite the ridicule of your peers. If you don't have a socket set, use an adjustable wrench, which has two jaws that stay parallel so they don't ruin the facets of a bolt head.

Sometimes tweezers can be the most important tool in your toolkit, such as when you have a splinter under your fingernail. I sharpen my tweezers to a point with a file. (There will come a time when you'll think this is the best advice in this whole book and, like Aesop's lion, will be tempted to send me a thank-you letter.)

On the Level

A level is a wood or metal straightedge with vials of liquid and a bubble in each. By lining up the bubble with lines drawn on the vial, you can test the levelness, or plumbness, of surfaces; that is, whether they are perpendicular or parallel to sea level. Levels are used for installing cabinets and countertops, walls, ceilings, and so forth. You don't need one if you're building freestanding furniture.

If you buy one, look for accuracy and durability. Don't buy used levels: If they've ever been dropped, they may be worthless. I prefer cast aluminum levels or these "unbreakable" German levels that have become available recently. Some prefer mahogany levels, and they're fine, but stay away from cheap, stamped metal models. They're unreliable.

Tackling Tool Storage

It doesn't pay to buy good tools and spend time sharpening and tuning them up if you're just going to throw them in a bucket. Many different toolboxes and cabinets are available, and you should find one that fits your situation. You may be able to start with a tackle box or two and then move up as you accumulate more tools.

Here are the important criteria for choosing tool storage:

➤ It should keep tools separate, so they don't knock into and thus dull or damage each other.

➤ It should keep tools organized, so you can find what you're looking for.

➤ It should keep tools accessible, so you can lay your hands on them quickly, without a lot of fuss.

➤ It should keep tools dry.

➤ It should have a lock, so your tools don't sprout legs.

➤ If you make your own, it should be meticulously crafted, so it serves as an endorsement of your work to potential clients, and so it doesn't drive you crazy as your skills improve.

Woodlore

When I was in graduate school at the Rhode Island School of Design, my department had a longstanding first project: Design and build your own tool cabinet. Mine was an elaborate mahogany number, and I figure I built it at least twice, because I made so many mistakes. I finally gave it away to a friend because I couldn't stand to look at all my old mistakes. I've made four or five others since then, but they've been more utilitarian. I think I'm due to build a fancy one again.

Building your own tool cabinet can be a very satisfying, if advanced, project. Look at other peoples' cabinets for ideas and synthesize them into your own design.

The Least You Need to Know

➤ Measuring tools are the key to accuracy.

➤ Do not drop squares or other measuring tools, or they'll lose their accuracy.

➤ Store tools so they don't knock into each other or become exposed to the elements.

➤ A meticulously made tool cabinet is like a calling card; it demonstrates your ability as a craftsperson.

Chapter 6

Feel the Power: Portable Power Tools

In This Chapter

➤ Hand tools versus power tools

➤ The importance of safety

➤ The basic portable power tools and how to use them

➤ The pneumatic power tool group

➤ Cordless power tools

By the end of the last century, someone had developed a power tool to perform just about every task that was traditionally performed by a hand tool. Some power tools revolutionized the way we work; others have been helpful; and many have been, like the electric back scratcher, a solution looking for a problem. Some power tools, like routers, do a better job than you could do by hand; others, like sanders, just do an adequate job faster.

This chapter gives you an overview of the various power tools and how they work. It also looks at the pros and cons of using power tools as opposed to hand tools and gives you my best advice on what features to look for in a particular power tool. You'll also find a section on pneumatic power tools. These tools were once solely the province of the professional, but now they're more and more accessible to the amateur. Tool safety is critical with power tools, and I will go over that as well.

Ladies and Gentlemen, Start Your Engines

Power tools are great time savers, no question. Without them, it would be nearly impossible to compete as a professional woodworker today. But don't feel obligated to buy the complete arsenal right away. Saving time is not so critical if you're not a professional, and there can be advantages to using hand tools for a while.

Tricks of the Trade

When you get a little more advanced, you might buy a router, which is useful for a multitude of tasks, but is more complicated to use than any other power tool. If you're going to be making a lot of cabinets, then you should buy a biscuit jointer as well.

When you do buy power tools, the first one you should probably get is a drill. I can't think of much of anything you'll learn from drilling holes by hand. After that, you may want to buy a cordless screw gun because they're so handy. If you're going to be doing a lot of rough carpentry, I would go for a circular saw next. If you plan to be doing finer work, like cabinetry or furniture, consider buying a jigsaw or the sanders, because, let's face it, sanding stinks.

The market for power tools is very competitive, and you can find very good prices if you look. See Appendix B, "Resources," for ideas of good places to shop. I don't recommend buying used power tools because it's too hard to tell whether they've been abused or possibly stolen.

Start with Safety

The ante is up with power tools: You can do a lot more damage with them a lot faster than you can with hand tools. I happen to have all of my fingers; some of my colleagues do not. I don't mean to scare you off or make you panicky, which can be as dangerous as being careless, but it's important to have a healthy respect for power tools.

The most important thing, both for safety and for getting the best results from a tool, is to understand its physics. By this I mean understanding the dynamic forces that occur as the tool works. For example, when the circular saw's blade is adjusted all the way out, its cutting force wants to pull the tool down into the work as it cuts; if the blade is adjusted for a shallow cut, the geometry is different, and the force will want to kick the saw back. As the belt sander sands, it wants to run forward like a car. The drill wants to spin around. Use Sir Isaac Newton's old rule, "Every action has an equal and opposite reaction," to help you visualize the operation before you dive in. Visualization is key. Act out the operation you're planning to do beforehand with the power off, as a kind of rehearsal before you cut wood. You'll have fewer surprises.

When you work with power tools, follow these precautions:

➤ Use safety glasses with most tools.

➤ Wear a dust mask with any tool that creates dust.

➤ Wear ear protection when using noisy tools such as circular saws and routers.

➤ Don't mess with guards; they are there for a reason.

➤ Don't wear loose clothing or loose, long hair when working.

➤ If a tool has a three-prong plug, it needs to be grounded; don't remove the third prong.

➤ Unplug the tool when adjusting it or changing bits and blades.

➤ Don't talk while using a tool. Give it your full concentration.

➤ Make sure the tool is turned off before you plug it in.

The Drill on Drills

The power drill was the first portable power tool and is now so pervasive that almost no one has a hand drill in their tool box anymore. It's nearly always the first tool people buy. The two main decisions you have to make when buying a drill, besides price, are chuck size and speed range.

Your Friend Chuck

The *chuck* is the round metal apparatus that holds the drill bits. Usually, the bit is locked in place with a *chuck key* tied to the power cord with a chuck key lanyard. When the chuck key is inserted into one of three holes in the chuck, its teeth are engaged: If you turn the key clockwise, you tighten the chuck's jaws; if you turn it counterclockwise, you loosen the jaws. To be sure the jaws have fully tightened down on the bit, first tighten the chuck key in one hole as far as it will go, and then tighten the key in one of the other holes as hard as you can. It's important to fully tighten the chuck, because if the bit binds in the wood, the chuck will gall the bit (wear it away) as it spins, which is not a good thing.

Chucks come in three basic sizes: $1/4$-inch, $3/8$-inch, and $1/2$-inch. These numbers represent the maximum diameter drill shank the chuck will accept. The $1/2$-inch chuck is the most versatile because it has the greatest range, but it can be cumbersome for delicate drilling, and it may not fit where a $1/4$-inch chuck will. A $1/2$-inch chuck is also more expensive, other factors being equal. There is usually a relationship between the size of the drill body and the chuck size, although you can put any size chuck on any size drill. I recommend getting a $1/2$-inch drill to start with so that you can use any standard drill bit. You can always get a smaller, $1/4$-inch one later if you find you need it.

In the last few years, there's been a trend toward *keyless chucks*. You tighten them by grasping the chuck in one hand while turning on the drill with the other hand. My only caveat is: Cheap keyless chucks always slip, so make sure you get a good one. Jacobs is my favorite brand of chucks.

Drill Speed

Drill speed is measured in revolutions per minute (RPM). The general rule is that the larger the diameter of the drill bit is, the slower the speed; the smaller the diameter of the drill bit is, the faster the speed. Therefore, a large-diameter drill bit requires a slow, powerful drill, and a small drill bit demands a fast drill that does not have to be so powerful. In general, $1/4$-inch chuck drills are faster; $1/2$-inch chuck drills are usually slower and more powerful.

Make sure that the drill you get is variable speed. If you run a drill bit too fast it may heat up, and the steel will lose its temper, becoming discolored and dull.

A Bit About Drill Bits

The standard type of drill bit woodworkers use is the *twist drill,* so named because of the *flutes* that twist around the bit to pull waste out of the hole as it drills. Twist drills were originally designed for metal, and a variation called the *brad point bit* was designed specifically for wood. I find, however, that plain twist drills work just as well and are less expensive and less delicate than the brad point bits.

The noncutting end of the drill bit that fits into the chuck is called the *shank* and is usually the same diameter as the business end, up to $1/2$-inch. Larger drill bits usually continue to have $1/2$-inch shanks, because that is the largest of the standard chuck sizes. *Reduced shank* drill bits are also available with $1/4$-inch shanks to fit $1/4$-inch chucks.

Twist drills come in sets, arranged in increments, called *drill indexes.* You can buy indexes in various ranges of size and in bigger and smaller increments. The standard full range index goes from $1/16$-inch to $1/2$-inch in $1/64$-inch increments.

Two other types of specialized drill bits woodworkers use from time to time are the Forstner bit and the multispur bit. Both drill a flat bottom hole and are available in much larger diameters than twist drills. Hole saws are inexpensive and can cut large holes, but do not cut as cleanly these bits. The multispur bit cuts faster and is guided by a point in its center. The Forstner bit cuts slower, but you can overlap holes because the bit is guided by its rim.

Screw Guns

Screw guns are a variation of the drill. You can drive screws with a drill by inserting a screw bit, but a screw gun has a few features that make it work better. Screw guns have a clutch, so you can disengage the drive when the screw has reached the right depth. Screw guns generally don't have a chuck but rather a hex socket into which you can snap a *screw bit holder,* which is handier and lighter.

In the last 20 years, cordless tools have come into their own, and cordless screw guns and drills have led the way. They are great, and battery improvements mean that they are plenty powerful and have adequate speed. Their best feature, though, is their excellent braking, which is made possible by their DC motors. When you release the trigger, they stop instantly, which gives you much better control when trying to drive a screw to a particular depth. I use plug-in screw guns if I'm driving extra big or long screws and need the power, but most of the time I use cordless models.

Portable Power Saws

The two power hand saws used in woodwork are the circular saw and the jigsaw. Although they are both saws, they have very little in common and are used in very different ways. The circular saw is a rougher tool, used more by carpenters than for fine woodworking; the jigsaw is popular with both carpenters and woodworkers.

The Circular Saw

Circular saws are used for cutting plywood, 2×4s, rough lumber, and finishing lumber in carpentry. A circular saw can cut fairly cleanly in expert hands, but it is not a particularly fine tool. Cabinet makers and furniture makers would not use a circular saw for joinery unless they had no alternative.

Circular saws use a circular blade ($7^1/_4$-inch or $8^1/_4$-inch diameter are the standard sizes) with steel- or carbide-tipped teeth that can be lowered for deep cuts, raised for shallow cuts, or angled for bevel cuts. The blade has a spring-loaded guard that swings down to protect the section of the blade not necessary for the cut. Never disable this guard! I have witnessed three very ugly accidents that occurred when carpenters, who found the guard irritating, wedged it permanently in the open position, and then hit some part of their body with the exposed blade. I can assure you the guard is not as inconvenient as slicing through your kneecap.

To make a cut, you first mark a straight line on the work (circular saws cut only straight lines, not curved ones). With the base plate or *shoe* of the tool on the work, you turn on the saw and bring the blade into the line. Let the saw do the work; don't force it. You also can clamp a straight piece

I Woodn't Do That!

Never disable or remove guards or safety features on power tools; they are there for a reason. I frequently hear the complaint that this or that guard "gets in the way." If you ask someone who's lost a finger or two because they disabled a guard, they would invariably trade the inconvenience of the safety feature for the inconvenience of the injury.

of wood to the work and run the shoe of the saw against the piece of wood, using it as a guide or a *fence*. If you use a fence, you have to measure the distance between the edge of the shoe and the blade and clamp the fence that distance from where you want the cut.

When you buy a circular saw, look for sturdy construction, light weight, adequate power, and a *brake*. A brake, which stops the blade quickly when you release the trigger, is convenient and safe. It also pays to get a good carbide-tipped blade; carbide stays sharp longer than steel.

Circular saws are probably the most dangerous of the portable power tools, so they get their own safety checklist:

➤ Read your saw's owner's manual and all included safety information.

➤ Wear eye protection.

➤ Wear ear protection.

➤ Wear a dust mask.

➤ Keep the blade sharp; dull blades make you force the saw, and reduce control.

➤ Don't overextend the blade. The blade depth should be $1/8$-inch to $1/4$-inch greater than the thickness of the material being cut.

➤ Never lift a running saw in the cut.

➤ Make sure the work is properly supported so it won't bend and pinch the blade as you're cutting. A bend or pinch could lead to the saw kicking back suddenly.

Tricks of the Trade

Obviously, you can cut yourself on the jigsaw, but it is much less aggressive than the circular saw. Jigsaws are designed to cut on the upstroke, which pulls the tool firmly to the work (so-called **reverse cutting** blades cut on the downstroke, when you want your tearout on the bottom of the work, but they make the tool bounce around).

The Jigsaw

Jigsaws are used for cutting curves and intricate patterns. They have a thin, narrow blade about three inches long that goes up and down like the needle on a sewing machine. The narrow blade allows you to cut tight radiuses with a great deal of control. It is, however, slow and less well-suited to cutting straight lines than the circular saw. You can get blades for fast, rough cutting or smooth finish cuts, for extra tight radiuses, and for metal, plastic, and other specialty applications. Most good jigsaws allow you to angle the blade for bevel cuts. Many people find the jigsaw less intimidating than the circular saw, and I have had students who used the jigsaw for long, straight cuts that the circular saw would have handled better.

Power Sanders

Sanding is onerous. (My publisher won't let me use the word I really want to.) There may be someone out there somewhere who enjoys sanding; if that person is you, you should seek treatment for obsessive-compulsive disorder. On second thought, you should come work for me instead. One of the best applications of electricity is the power sander, because it speeds up the sanding process.

Unfortunately, power sanders can also be very destructive and are responsible for a lot of ugly work. In finesse-less hands, they round over corners, sand through veneer, turn flats into curves, and generally make a clean, sharp piece of furniture mushy. I use sanders sparingly on flat planes, for flushing up joints, and, with great caution, on wide edges. I do not use them on shaped work, narrow edges where there is not enough bearing surface to keep the tool flat, on bevels, or anywhere else where they might ruin the crispness of my work. Never sand surfaces of glue joints (the faces that will meet when the joint is glued together)! These surfaces must be absolutely flat and square.

The following sections serve as a guide to the common portable sanders and what I think of them.

Disk Sanders

Disk sanders, by which I mean sanders that spin an abrasive disk on a shaft, are a metalworking tool where grain direction is not an issue. They can be used for rough-shaping wood, but I don't use them for that because I can usually find a better way to do the job. Their problem is that the spinning leaves nasty cross-grain scratches in the wood that then have to be taken out by hand, and they dig in uncontrollably because of the rotational force. I don't recommend them.

Belt Sanders

To visualize how a belt sander works, imagine a miniature army tank with a single tread that is made of sandpaper and two handles on top. I like belt sanders, but they cut very aggressively, and it takes a lot of practice to develop a sensitive touch with one. I always dread letting a student or assistant use one for the first time, because the potential to wreck a project is so great. I always make students practice on scrap wood first for a long time, which helps.

What I like about the belt sander is that it works fast, and because the belt runs in a linear fashion, you won't get cross-grain scratches if you line up the sander properly with the grain direction. I use belt sanders only on solid wood, never on veneer or plywood, because they can sand through the surface layer in a heartbeat. They are best when you have some deep defect, such as bad planer tearout, in a solid wood surface that you have to sand out. They can also be handy for flushing up boards after a tabletop glue-up.

To sand a surface, you set the machine on the wood so that it is lined up with the grain direction and pull the trigger. As the machine comes on, you start moving it in forward and backward strokes with the grain, moving gradually to the side and overlapping each stroke. Don't press down; let the weight of the tool do the work, and remember: Keep the tool moving in broad strokes when it is turned on, or it will dig a hollow in the surface. After you've covered the entire surface like this, you change direction and go back the way you came. The tricky part is to keep the bottom of the machine that supports the sanding belt, called the *platen,* flat to the work. As the machine runs, the force of the belt makes it want to pull forward and dive when you change direction. A belt sander is especially tricky at the edges of the work, which it wants to roll over. Power sanding is like surfing; it takes time to get the feel of it.

The main safety hazards of the belt sander are the dust it creates and the danger of the belt grabbing clothing, fingers, hair, or the electric cord and pulling them into the machine. Wear a dust mask, tie your hair back, don't wear loose clothing, and keep your cotton-picking fingers away from the belt. I like to throw the cord over my shoulder to keep it out of the machine. As with any tool, read the owner's manual thoroughly.

Of the many belt sanders available I recommend one with a four-inch-wide belt because it's easier to keep flat, and variable speed for better control.

Tricks of the Trade

It's a good idea to use a vacuum with your sander. Most decent machines have optional adapters so that they can be hooked up. Vacuums not only improve safety by removing dust from the air, they also keep the sandpaper from clogging and leave a better finish. Some fancy vacuums have a relay switch, so they turn on automatically when the sander is turned on.

Orbital Pad Sanders

An orbital pad sander has a flat, rectangular pad, usually made of soft felt, that holds sandpaper ripped to size. When you turn on the sander, it moves the pad in a small circular "orbit." Orbital pad sanders are not nearly as aggressive as belt sanders; you can't do as much damage so quickly. What I don't like about them is that the orbits leave a pattern, known as *swirls,* in the wood, which often appear serious only when you put on finish. Stain, in particular, exaggerates the appearance of swirls.

Another problem is that the droning buzz orbital pad sanders make seems to hypnotize people, and lulled into a false sense of security by the nonaggressive cutting action, they oversand, rounding over edges and making things mushy with their soft pads. Another complaint I have is that I can sand faster by hand than the small inexpensive pad sanders most people buy can sand; these sanders are only for the very lazy. I much prefer random orbit sanders.

Random Orbit Sanders

Random orbit sanders are more expensive than orbital pad sanders, and they're worth it. They have a special action that makes orbits in a random pattern that doesn't read as easily as those of the simple orbital sander. They also, in general, cut more aggressively than the orbital sanders and have a hard, round pad that is less prone to rounding over corners than the soft pads. As you may have figured out, the random orbit sander is my favorite type of sander, and I recommend it highly.

As with the belt sander, you have to keep the random orbit sander moving, or it will leave a hollow. You have to use pre-cut abrasive discs with these sanders, and they come in two types: adhesive-backed and hook-and-loop–backed (like Velcro). The hook-and-loop is better because you can reuse the discs after changing grits.

Power Planes

The power plane is very much like a hand plane, but with a round, rotating cutter head that holds two or three blades instead of a fixed, flat blade. The plane is used in much the same way as a hand plane, but you don't have to drive the plane through its stroke; you just push it slowly. You can take a much heavier pass with the power plane, but you can't get as fine a surface as with a hand plane. Power planes are not used for smoothing, but rather for trimming edges or hogging off stock. A perfect use of a power plane would be fitting a door to a door opening.

Routers

Routers are used for operations that vary so much in type you would not think they were done with the same tool. They cut the elaborately profiled moldings on traditional furniture, grooves, hinge mortises, sliding dovetails, and mortises in mortise-and-tenon joints. They can be used for shaping curved planes with elaborate jigs, trimming plastic laminate and veneer flush with countertops and panels, and cutting shapes out of wood (when used with a template). The complexity of their use makes them a more advanced tool, but a great one.

The router is a deceptively simple machine. It's just a motor that holds bits at one end, somewhat like a drill, with a base attached to it that holds the bit perpendicular to the surface it sits on. However, a router differs from a drill in more ways than the base plate. The router motor spins extremely fast, 22,000 to 28,000 RPM, and the router holds the bits in a *collet,* which is more precise than a chuck, but does not hold an infinitely variable range of sizes.

I Woodn't Do That!

The power plane is more of a professional tool; it has fairly specialized uses and can be dangerous in the hands of a novice. It is certainly not one of the first tools I'd spend my money on. Carefully read the safety instructions that come with your power plane before you use one.

Router collets come in three sizes: $^1/_4$-inch, $^3/_8$-inch, and $^1/_2$-inch. Therefore, the shank of router bits has to be one of those sizes (the $^3/_8$-inch size has become somewhat obsolete, and you don't see many bits that size anymore). They are tightened with wrenches rather then a chuck key. Unlike drill bits, which cut only with their ends, router bits also cut with their sides.

Woodlore

Traditionally, routers were set at a fixed depth and cut only by moving the tool sideways into the work. The past 20 years has seen the rise of the **plunge router,** which has a tel-escopic base that allows you to plunge the bit into the work vertically and then move it sideways, permitting stopped grooves. There are also **laminate trimmers,** which are just small, easy-to-handle routers used for beveling, flush trimming, and other light duty cutting.

Left to right: fixed-base router, plunge router, and a laminate trimmer.

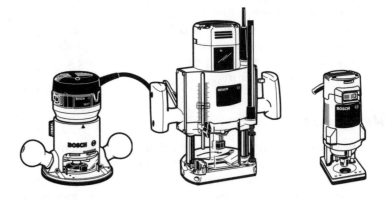

A complete explanation of how to use a router would require a separate book devoted to the subject. These books exist, and if you want to delve into the router, you should get such a book, as well as some hands-on training.

Biscuit Joiners

Biscuit joiners are a relatively new and highly specialized tool. But in the last 15 or 20 years, they have revolutionized the capabilities of amateurs and small shops. What they do is cut a circular slot that allows you to use standardized wood splines, which are manufactured by the tool companies, to join cabinet panels, doors, frames, and so forth. They have replaced dovetails, tongue-and-groove joints, and other traditional joinery. I personally think they are often used where they shouldn't be, and although they are adequate for carcass construction such as kitchen cabinets and light frame joinery, I don't think they are strong enough for, say, chair construction or entry doors. For jobs they are suited for, they are fantastic, making basic joinery fast and easy work. They can be used on miters, butt joints, and fixed shelves. They also can be used to run grooves.

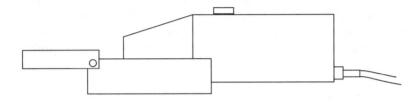

Biscuit joiners are used for miters, fixed-shelf butt joints, and frame joints.

Each company's biscuit joiner is different, so I can't give you a useful explanation of how they work. You have to choose a model and learn how to use that particular machine.

Nail Guns and Other Pneumatic Tools

Not all power tools have electric motors; a whole range of tools runs on air pressure. These *pneumatic tools* used to be reserved for large professional shops. In the last few years, however, they have become more user-friendly and have trickled down to the home shop. Whereas a large shop would have a big air compressor with an elaborately plumbed air distribution system, with regulators, air dryers, and so forth, the small home shop can use a small, portable compressor that plugs into a wall outlet, has a built-in regulator, and uses a simple rubber hose instead of plumbing.

Just a Lot of Hot Air

Compressors are just sophisticated air pumps. They are rated by horsepower (h.p.), the speed at which they will pump air measured in cubic feet per minute (c.f.m.), and air tank volume measured in gallons. Air tools are rated by how many c.f.m. they require, so it's important that the compressor can supply enough c.f.m. to run the tool or tools

Wood Words

Pneumatic tools are hooked up to the compressor or its distribution system with a $1/4$-inch air hose (like you use to fill your tires) and **quick-release couplings.** These couplings allow you to switch tools without a lot of horsing around. Pay attention when buying pneumatic tools, because there are several different systems and they are not compatible with each other. Make sure that all your tools are using the same type of couplings.

your planning on using. For example, a 12 c.f.m. compressor can run a 6 c.f.m. tool and two 3 c.f.m. tools simultaneously. Tank volume gives some indication of how often the compressor has to turn on when you are using a tool. Remember to drain the water out of your compressor tank before each use. Air compressors draw water out of the air, and water is bad for tools and will rust your tank if it sits there.

Nail Guns

Some tools are more efficient when driven by air, and because pneumatic tools don't have to have a motor, a pneumatic tool can be lighter and cheaper than standard power tools. Small pneumatic random orbit sanders can be quite handy, as can pneumatic drills. The most valuable pneumatic tool for the woodworker, however, is probably the nail gun.

A nail gun.

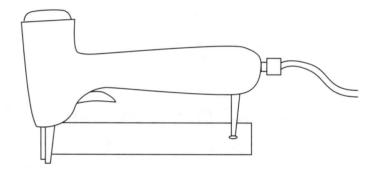

Nail guns come in many sizes and types. They shoot small brads, finish nails, large nails, staples, and so forth. Each gun has a range of size and length nails it will shoot. They have many advantages over hand nailing; they are faster, can be used one-handed, and drive the nail so fast the parts are less prone to sliding out of position during the process, as often happens when using a hammer.

The nail gun is hooked up to the compressor with a rubber hose and *quick-release couplings*. Nail guns hold a magazine full of nails, which they fire when the tool is placed against the workpiece, which depresses a safety, and the trigger is pulled. The safety is very important: It prevents the tool from being fired into thin air, where it might hit somebody. Do not disable the safety! Nail guns can be dangerous, so make sure you read the safety instructions carefully, wear eye protection, and make sure the nails you are shooting are not longer than the thickness of the material you're shooting them into.

The Least You Need to Know

➤ Portable power tools can increase your productivity.

➤ Though faster, portable power tools may not be better than hand tools.

➤ Power tools require greater attention to safety than hand tools.

➤ Drills and screw guns are woodworking staples.

➤ Power sanders can save time and tedium, but they must be used carefully if you want to keep your work looking crisp.

➤ Pneumatic tools are driven by air and require an air compressor to operate.

Chapter 7

The Big Machines: Stationary Power Tools

In This Chapter

➤ A machine safety checklist

➤ Milling lumber: the jointer and the planer

➤ Sawing: the table saw, radial arm saw, and band saw

➤ The drill press, the router, and the dust collector

Stationary machines allow you to do things faster and better. Certain tasks that would be near torture if done by hand, such as milling rough lumber into finished boards, become a walk in the park with a jointer and a planer. A table saw that is set up well can leave a much finer cut than would be possible with a hand saw or a circular saw. The downside of stationary machinery is that it is expensive and potentially dangerous. Still, the expense is worth the productivity, and with proper training, you can minimize the danger.

This chapter explains the function of the most commonly used woodworking machines: what they do and how they do it. It will examine them in the order that they're used to turn a piece of rough lumber into a fully prepared part that is ready to glue up. Evaluate the machines; you don't have to buy them all. Many woodworkers make do with two or three, especially in their home shops.

Why Stationary Machines?

Stationary machines differ from portable power tools in one critical way: You take the work to them. Portable tools move through the wood; stationary machines stay put, and the wood moves. Because the machines do not move, there is less vibration and *chatter,* which is when the tool, or cutter, bounces in and out of the cut. Vibration and chatter are responsible for tearout, cuts that are not smooth, and ugly surface texture. Generally, the heavier and more stable a machine is, the less it will vibrate, and the better the surface it will leave when it cuts. For this reason, the better stationary machines are often heavier than would seem necessary, with great cast-iron frames and *beds* or *tables.*

Cheaper machines, especially these days, are often made with sheet metal and aluminum extrusions. Some high-end machines use a special technique of filling a sheet metal exoskeleton with a special vibration-dampening cement, which some think works better than cast iron. I don't know which works better, but I prefer the feel of good old cast iron.

Another factor that affects the accuracy and finish of a machine's cutting action is the trueness and stability of its *fence.* A fence is a secondary reference surface that orients the wood being cut to both the bed and the cutter. For example, the table of a table saw allows you to make a cut square to the flat surface that runs over it; the table saw fence allows you to make that cut parallel to and a fixed distance from an edge. The fence must have a flat surface, have a stable system holding it in place, and be properly adjusted.

Wood Words

The **bed** or **table** of a stationary machine is the (usually heavy) flat surface that the wood sits on or slides over as the machine does its thing. Tables must be absolutely flat, stable, and square to the cutting action of the machine, or the machine will not work accurately. Beds and tables sometimes need to be adjusted to make them true.

The board lies on the table and runs against the fence as it is ripped to width.

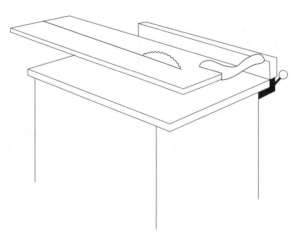

Safety First (and Last!)

Stationary machines are dangerous. They can cut woodworkers just as easily as they cut wood. This book is not intended to prepare the uninitiated to use power tools and machinery; no book can do that. It provides a theoretical understanding of how they work, so you can take the next step and get some hands-on training. There is a physical component to woodworking instruction that is crucial to your safety. Woodworking is like a sport: You can learn the rules, principles, and the plays from books, but you need the live action experience to play the game right.

Before you touch a machine or power tool, you should get some expert instruction in a real shop. Plenty of classes are available. Don't assume that just because your Uncle Bill or that well-meaning neighbor is a woodworker that they're qualified to teach you how to do it. I see professionals on job sites doing things that make me cringe; sooner or later they're going to have an accident.

There is a gender factor, too. Men tend to feel like they're supposed to know this stuff, so they dive right in without asking questions. Often, in the classes I teach, the men will start explaining how to do things to the women, when they're totally clueless themselves. My wife calls this hormonally induced stupidity, like when guys drive around in circles rather than ask directions. Remember, ignorance is easily cured by asking questions; stupidity is a state of mind.

Here is an informal safety checklist for working with machines:

➤ Wear eye protection at all times.

➤ Wear ear protection.

➤ Wear a dust mask.

➤ Read the owner's manual and safety instructions first.

➤ Make sure the machine is in proper working order and the cutters and fence are tightened down.

➤ Make sure all guards and safety devices are in place. Do not use a machine without proper guards.

➤ Don't talk to anyone while using a tool or machine.

➤ Don't have loose hair or wear loose clothing while using machines.

➤ Don't use alcohol or mind-altering drugs while using tools or machines.

➤ Don't run into a shop while someone is using a machine, and don't try to squeeze by them while they're working.

➤ Don't work when you're tired or sick.

➤ Keep your hands focused on the work, not fluttering around.

➤ Know the physics of the machine and where the cutting force wants to throw the wood. Make sure that when it throws the wood, your hand is not in a place that will get dragged into the cutter and that the wood will not hit your body.

The Jointer

When you get your wood from the lumberyard it has been rough-cut, dried, and left sitting around. This means that it will not be particularly flat, and unless it's been dressed before you bought it, it will have the rough, fuzzy surface left by the saw that cut it out of the log. The first step in making the wood a thing of beauty is to run it over the jointer, which will flatten one face and leave a smooth surface. After that's done, the jointer is used in a separate operation to make one edge straight and square to the face that was flattened initially.

The main body of the jointer holds two tables, the in-feed table and the out-feed table, which are parallel to each other. Between the tables is a round cutter head that holds two, three, or four blades called jointer knives, which turn in the direction of the in-feed table. The in-feed table raises or lowers, depending on how deep a cut you want. The wood is laid flat on the in-feed table and pushed into the spinning cutter head. If the in-feed table is set 1/16-inch below the peak of the arc made by the jointer knife, then it will remove 1/16-inch from the face of the board. The out-feed table is kept level with the peak of the blade's arc so that it will support the wood as it comes off the knives. As you make passes over the jointer, the knives progressively remove the low spots on the board until you've planed the entire surface flat.

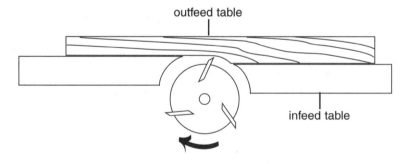

Tricks of the Trade

Don't push down on a board in an effort to keep wood in contact with the cutter. This prevents the jointer from removing just the low spots. Instead, figure out where the low spots are and keep downward pressure there. As soon as you have a few inches of lumber on the out-feed table, concentrate most of your pressure there.

outfeed table

infeed table

Side view schematic of a jointer doing its thing (the guard is removed for clarity). As the wood passes over the cutter head, the low spots are removed, and the wood moves onto the out-feed table.

The jointer also has a fence that holds the lumber square (or at a preset angle) to the tables. If you place the edge of the board on the in-feed table, press the previously flattened face against the fence, and push the board into the cutter, the jointer will now cut the edge flat and square to the face. When you are jointing an edge square, it's important to keep the face tight against the fence throughout the pass.

Always position your hands so that if they slip off the work they will not come anywhere near the cutter head. And always use a push stick where possible. Also, keep your shirt tucked in when using the jointer. I had a T-shirt catch in the cutter head when I was in graduate school, and in an instant, the jointer had ripped off all the fabric below the armpits. I was in pretty good shape at the time, but I still felt a little silly walking home with an exposed midriff.

Fortunately, the shirt had been washed about 1,000 times and was so thin that it tore easily. I shudder to think what would have happened if the jointer had reeled me in.

The Thickness Planer

I Woodn't Do That!

Never run end grain over the jointer! It is dangerous and will ruin the knives. Plywood will ruin jointer and planer knives, too, and should be kept away from both. The jointer and planer are meant to cut parallel to the grain or fibers of the wood only.

So why not just flip the board over and flatten the other side on the jointer? If you used the jointer to surface the two opposite sides of the board, they would end up flat, but not parallel to each other. Basically, you'd have a very large wedge. For this reason, we move on to another machine for the second face: the thickness planer, or planer, for short.

The planer has a single short table called the bed that serves as a reference surface for the jointed face of the board. At an adjustable height above the bed is a cutter head like the one on the jointer. There are also two spring-loaded feed rollers that hold the board down and move it into and out of the cutter head, so unlike the jointer, you do not have to push the board into the planer. Just get the board started into the machine and catch it when it comes out the other side. Another feature you'll see on most planers is a pair of bed rollers, which sit a hair above the bed and spin, reducing friction so that the board moves freely through the machine.

As the board moves through the planer, the cutter head cuts the top face parallel to the lower face. If the bottom face is bowed or not flat in some other way, the planer will cut the same irregularities in the top face; it does not make the surface flat, just smooth and parallel to the opposite one.

After both sides of the board are flat and parallel, you can continue making passes through the planer, milling the board thinner until it has reached the thickness you want. Planers have thickness gauges that measure the distance between the bed and the cutter head, but don't assume that this measurement is accurate. This is one of those times when you want your six-inch rule handy to check the board.

The reference surface left by the jointer passes over the planer's bed and bed rollers, driven by the overhead feed rollers. As the board moves through the machine, the knives in the cutter head above trim the top surface parallel to the bottom surface.

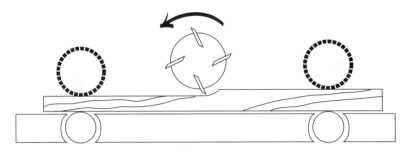

Because the cutter head of the planer is enclosed, the machine is relatively safe. Still, there are plenty of ways to hurt yourself on it. Never put your hands inside the planer while it's plugged in, and never look inside the in-feed or out-feed openings of the machine while it's turned on.

The Table Saw

The table saw is like a stationary version of the circular saw. It's used primarily for ripping and crosscutting lumber and plywood, although it also cuts dadoes, rabbets, tenons, bevels, and various other joints and detailing operations. The basic saw is just a flat table with a saw blade poking out. A fence runs parallel to the blade, and the height and angle of the blade are adjustable. The heart of the woodshop, the table saw is the most important stationary machine. Consequently, many jigs and fixtures have been developed to extend its usefulness.

Ripping on the Table Saw

As the board left the planer, it had two faces flat and parallel to each other and one edge flat and square to both. If the board were square or nearly so in section, like a table leg, you could surface the fourth side by running it through the planer with the jointed edge down. If, however, like most boards, it's thin and flat, there won't be enough bearing surface on the edge to run with any stability on the planer bed. In this case, you bring it over to the table saw and run it with a face on the table and the squared edge against the fence (see the first illustration in this chapter). The blade will rip the edge square and parallel to the three previously milled surfaces.

When you are ripping a board, be sure to use a guard and a *splitter,* which is a piece of metal that prevents the wood from closing on the back of the blade, which can lead to kickback. It also helps to prevent disaster when someone commits the number one cardinal sin on the table saw by putting his hand behind the blade. Don't ever put your hand behind the blade while the saw is on! I know it's tempting to do it when you're trying to keep the wood tight to the fence, but it is a mistake. If the blade's cutting force throws the piece to the in-feed side, and sooner or later it will, it will pull your hand into it. You may think you can react fast enough, but you can't. You should also use a push stick when cutting, which works like an extension of your hands, and practice pushing with the stick while the saw is turned off to get the hang of it.

Crosscutting

Now the board has been milled in two dimensions: thickness and width. That leaves length. To crosscut on the table saw, you need a fixture that will hold the board square to the blade. The two most common fixtures are the miter gauge and the *sled*. The miter gauge generally comes with the saw; you have to make the sled for yourself. Both slide in the two grooves machined into the surface of the table by the factory. The miter gauge is small, has a protractor for cutting angles, sits on a single rail that runs in either groove, and is suitable for short pieces of wood. Never try to crosscut a piece of wood by running the narrow end against the fence! The cutting force will throw the piece of wood, and you will be injured.

The sled is invaluable for cutting both long and short pieces square. To cut more than one piece of identical length, you can clamp a stop to the fence at the desired distance from the blade. You can also use a block clamped to the fence in conjunction with the sled or miter gauge to make identical repetitive cuts. The block sets the length of the cut, but there is space between the piece and the fence during the cutting action to prevent jamming.

Never make a cut where the workpiece is touching both the fence and the sled or miter gauge simultaneously while the blade is cutting! The piece will jam, be thrown by the blade, and you will be hurt. This is one of the most common causes of serious injury on the table saw (see the preceding illustration).

Wood Words

The **sled** consists of a plywood bed that the blade pokes through with a fence on the back end and a support on the other end. It is a simple fixture, though making it dead accurate takes careful work.

A stop clamped to the sled's fence allows you to make multiple cuts of identical length.

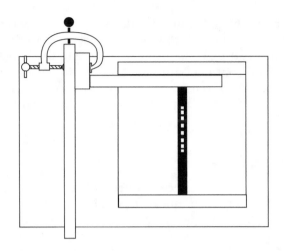

Sorting Out Saw Blades

There are blades specially designed for ripping, blades for crosscutting, and combination blades. Rip blades have the fewest teeth, and the ones they have are ground with a flat chisel edge that cuts well with the grain. Crosscut blades have the most teeth, and the teeth are angled to points alternately when viewed on edge (this is known as an ATB blade, which stands for Alternate Tooth Bevel). Combination blades tend to perform both ripping and crosscutting equally badly, so I don't recommend them. Don't think that just because a blade has lots of teeth it will cut better. Blades with 80 and 100 teeth are for relatively thin material and will overheat and burn thick stock.

Dado sets are a group of blades that are placed side by side on the arbor of the saw to cut wide grooves. By using chipping blades of different thickness in the middle and shims, you can adjust the width of the groove to suit your purpose. However, don't get greedy and try to go too wide. It's dangerous if all the threads on the arbor nut are not engaged.

Table Saw Safety

Here is a safety checklist for the table saw (see also the previous general machine safety checklist):

➤ Keep the blade as low as you can, $1/8$-inch to $1/4$-inch above the piece being cut.

➤ Never perform an unfamiliar technique without hands-on training.

➤ Always use a splitter when ripping.

➤ Use a push stick when ripping.

➤ Never place your hand behind the blade when cutting.

➤ Make sure there is sufficient bearing surface against the fence to keep the piece stable.

➤ Never crosscut with one end of the board against the fence.

➤ When you are crosscutting using the sled or miter gauge, the workpiece must never touch the saw fence and the blade at the same time.

The Band Saw

If the table saw is like a stationary circular saw, the band saw's closest relative in the portable power tool realm is the jigsaw. But instead of a straight, rigid blade that pumps up and down, its blade is an endless metal belt with teeth on one edge. The blade runs between two wheels that have rubber tires. Between the wheels is a work-table and two sets of guides to keep the blade straight. The wood is placed on the table and pushed into the blade. Unlike the table saw, the band saw can be used to cut curves and can generally cut thicker stock.

The primary functions of the band saw are cutting curves and roughing out stock before milling. Cutting curves is pretty straightforward: You mark a curved line, you cut just enough to the outside to leave the line, and then you clean up the wood with rasps and sandpaper. You leave the line so as not to lose your reference when sanding.

Most people find the band saw one of the less-threatening machines. It is less danger-ous than, say, the table saw, but this fact lulls people into a false sense of security. Consequently, I've seen more accidents on the band saw than on any other machine, albeit less catastrophic ones than jointer or table saw accidents.

In addition to the general guidelines, here is a safety checklist specific to the band saw:

➤ Keep the blade guard as low as you can, $\frac{1}{8}$- to $\frac{1}{4}$-inch above the piece being cut.

➤ Never perform an unfamiliar technique without hands-on training.

➤ Never push the wood with your fingers heading into the front of the blade. Sometimes the wood will split from tension at the end of the cut, and your fingers will go into the blade.

➤ Use a push stick or a block to push when possible.

➤ Make sure the *throat plate,* the filler plate where the blade passes through the table, is flat and tight to the blade.

➤ Make sure the guides are properly set.

Band saw blades are relatively inexpensive. Narrower blades can cut a smaller radius, but they leave a rougher finish and are more fragile. A wider blade is stronger and leaves a better finish, but it cannot cut as tight a curve. I like to keep a selection of blades between $\frac{1}{4}$-inch and 1-inch (check your machine's maximum width). As with most saw blades, the general rule is: The thicker the material you're cutting, the fewer the teeth; the thinner the material, the more teeth you need.

The Radial Arm Saw and Portable Chop Saw

The radial arm saw uses the same type of blade as the table saw, but instead of poking through the table, its blade and motor roll on a track above the table, cutting as they go. I use radial arm saws for crosscutting only. Many models can be set up for ripping lumber, but it's dangerous, and I don't recommend it.

The radial arm saw has a fixed fence attached to the back of the table. A metal arm above holds the track that the cutting mechanism rolls on. The cutting mechanism rests behind the fence and has a handle. You place lumber against the fence and pull the handle toward you, into the wood. Here's the scary part: The force of the cutting action makes the cutter want to run toward you, into the cut, which forces the workpiece tight against the fence, which can be a bit unnerving. The trick is to never have any part of your body in the path of the blade. Hold the workpiece against the fence with your hand well off to the side.

Radial arm saws are particularly useful for crosscutting long boards and rough lumber before milling. For precision work, I prefer the table saw, but many woodworkers use the radial arm saw for final cuts. Both the blade and the arm pivot for angled cuts in two axes.

The chop saw, or compound miter saw, is a little brother to the radial arm saw. Chop saws have become increasingly sophisticated and popular in the past few years. They are portable, but heavier than a power hand tool, and are stationary when in use. Carpenters use them on site for cutting moldings, studs, and trim. It is very easy to set them up to cut angles, especially compound angles, so they're great for cutting miters.

In addition to the general guidelines, here is a safety checklist specific to the radial arm saw and compound miter saw:

Tricks of the Trade

Many shops use chop saws to cut narrow stock and make angled cuts because they can be less awkward than table saws. Chop saws use many different mechanisms, but all are similar to the radial arm saw in principle. One important difference, though, is that you never pull the blade toward you; you either swing the blade down or push it away from you into the wood, depending upon the model.

➤ Make sure no part of your body, especially your hand, is in the path of the blade.

➤ Keep the workpiece tight to the bed and the fence before engaging the blade.

➤ Never pull the handle and blade of a compound miter saw toward you when the saw is on.

Router Tables

The router table is a machine you see in many shops. Traditionally, woodworkers made their own router tables, but various manufacturers wised up and started making them commercially. In essence, a router table is just a stationary table with a hole in the center and a router screwed in from the bottom so that the bit protrudes through the hole. Often a fence is clamped to the table so that straight slots can be cut parallel to an edge or a molding detail can be cut. It can also be used with a flush trim bit for routing shapes with a template or with a bearing-guided round over, beading, chamfer rabbeting, or molding bit. (See Chapter 20, "Edgings and Moldings: The Last Details," for a guide to these and other moldings that can be cut with a router table.)

Router tables have a big advantage over portable routers because they are more stable. Portable routers are versatile and allow a certain freedom, but a router table often offers greater control, especially on small parts where the handheld router would not have enough bearing surface to stay perched on the workpiece. The router table (and the portable router as well) lends itself to jigs and fixtures, and many books have been written specifically about their use. You would do well to obtain one of these books, because it will suggest a world of uses for the router table that might not have occurred to you.

The router table has two industrial siblings: the shaper and the overhead router. Both are highly sophisticated machines used in professional woodworking and are for the advanced craftsperson only.

Although the router table uses smaller cutters, which lessens the possible damage it can inflict, its cutting forces can be inscrutable to the beginner, making it hard to predict danger. Again, some hands-on training is essential. Here are some general rules to follow:

➤ Make sure no part of your body, especially a hand, is in the path of the blade.

➤ Keep the workpiece tight to the table and the fence while the router is cutting.

➤ Always cut against the force of the cutter, never in the direction that the cutter wants to pull. Always visualize where the cutting force is going to want to move the piece before you turn it on.

➤ Always hold your hands and fingers so that if the piece is thrown, they will not be pulled into the cutter, and never push the workpiece so that your hands are headed in the direction of the cutter.

➤ Make sure that the bit is properly tightened and the fence is clamped tight.

The Drill Press

The drill press is just a flat table that slides up and down on a stand with a drill suspended above it. The drill is held in a spring-loaded contraption called a *quill* that allows you to lower the drill bit into the work to a preset depth with either a lever or a wheel. The quill's spring returns the bit and chuck (the attachment that holds the workpiece in place) to their original position when the drilling is done. Most drill presses have some means of adjusting the speed of the chuck, usually by a system of pulleys and belts. On some drill presses, the table can be set at different angles in relation to the drill bit. The same general rule applies as with all bits and cutters: The larger the bit diameter is, the slower the bit should turn; the smaller the diameter, the faster it should turn.

Tricks of the Trade

When drilling through a piece of wood, always support it below on a flat piece of plywood. Otherwise, the bit may tear out on the bottom of the wood as it breaks through the surface. Also, be sure to keep the bit over the hole in the center of the table so you don't harm the surface of the wood.

All sorts of jigs and fixtures are made for special drilling operations, but most people make their own fence for their drill press. Usually the fence is just a straight piece of wood clamped to the table. The fence allows you to drill holes a predetermined distance from the edge of a board and to do so identically on more than one board. Sometimes a stop is clamped to the fence so that multiple holes will be identical in two axes.

The advantage of the drill press is that it is capable of greater accuracy than the handheld power drill and can be set up for drilling identical holes in multiple parts both more accurately and faster than could be done by hand. You can also use larger diameter bits in the drill press than you can in a handheld drill.

The drill press is relatively safe, but you have to be extra careful of hair getting caught in the rotating mechanism. You also have to worry about the bit catching in the work and causing it to spin around. Always clamp work to the table when it's feasible.

The Stationary Belt and Disk Sander

Though sometimes found separately, the stationary belt sanders and disk sanders are usually ganged together and run off a single motor. They operate like their portable equivalents, but they have a stand and a built-in table to support the work. Generally, the table is used square to the sanding plane, but it can be angled if necessary. Belts and disks are available in different grits of sandpaper.

These machines, especially the disk sander, are generally used for shaping rather than surface finishing. They can be quite handy for shaping a curve. People who have not had the time to develop hand-shaping skills find them particularly useful.

When you use a sander, be careful to keep the work flat on the table, and don't let your fingers get caught between the abrasive belt or disk and the table or machine housing.

Dust Collectors

Dust collectors out there range from huge cyclone systems that collect the sawdust in a hopper you can drive a truck under to portable units that look like a vacuum and get hooked up to a machine when you need it, collecting the dust in a bag. The larger systems require a system of ductwork that runs along the ceiling, with drops to each machine; the portable ones use a hose that disconnects easily.

Dust collectors not only make the shop safer by removing unhealthy dust, they also improve the results you'll get from certain machines like the jointer, planer, and sanders. These machines produce so much sawdust that the sawdust will impair the ability of the machine to work if it is not cleared away. Dust collectors also keep your shop cleaner.

The Least You Need to Know

➤ Stationary woodworking machinery can improve the quality of your wood-working and allow you to do things faster.

➤ Stationary machines are inherently dangerous and require hands-on training.

➤ Stationary machines allow greater consistency when making multiple parts.

➤ Many stationary machines utilize a fence for consistency.

➤ You must understand a machine's cutting forces to use it safely.

➤ Dust collectors not only have health benefits, they also make some machines work better.

Chapter 8

Keeping Your Edge

In This Chapter

➤ Why you need to sharpen your own tools

➤ What makes a good edge

➤ How to use electric grinding wheels and whetstones

➤ Which sharpening aids you should use

➤ When you should use a professional sharpening service

To work cleanly and precisely, you have to use sharp tools. Period. Few things lower the quality of your work like dull tools. It takes more force to move a dull tool, and because dull tools don't want to slice through the wood, they tend to veer off unpredictably into things they're not supposed to cut—including hands and fingers. You are much more apt to cut yourself with a dull tool than with a sharp one. Sharp tools shear through the wood fibers cleanly, but dull tools crush fibers as they cut, leaving nasty marks that you may or may not be able to (laboriously) sand out later.

Handsaws, machine saw blades, and router bits can be sent out for sharpening by a grinding service, but you should sharpen your own chisels, plane blades, and utility knives. If you're hard at it on a project, you may well have to sharpen your chisels or plane blades two or three times in the course of a day, so it just doesn't make sense to send them out. This chapter shows you how to grind and stone your tools to hair-shaving sharpness, when to sharpen a tool, and when to use a sharpening service.

The Geometry of an Edge

Before we start grinding away, let's look at what we're aiming for. A cutting edge is the intersection of two planes. They may be curved, as in a carving gouge, or they may be straight, as in a chisel. The trick is to keep those planes true, sharp, and at the proper angle to each other. You'll learn what these terms mean later in the chapter. For clarity's sake, I'll leave curved tools out of it for now and concentrate on the basic chisel or hand plane blade.

Your Aim Is True

By true, I mean an edge that has absolutely flat planes and, when viewed from above, has a straight edge that is square to the chisel's sides. When you start using sharpening stones, it's hard to keep the tool at a consistent angle without rocking it this way or that. This motion leads to a rounded bevel or an edge with rolled off corners, cocked at some strange angle. It takes practice to hold a chisel steady, at a fixed angle, as it ice skates over a slippery sharpening stone, but with time, you'll get the hang of it. It's a bit like learning to ride a bicycle. If you hadn't seen someone do it, you wouldn't believe it was possible, but once you learn how, you can't believe you ever had a problem. The following illustrations show what you're aiming for and what you're trying to avoid.

The planes should be flat, not rounded.

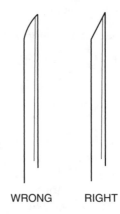

WRONG   RIGHT

The edge should be straight, not curved.

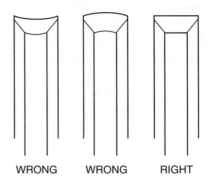

WRONG   WRONG   RIGHT

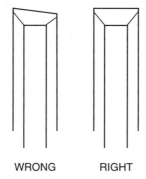

The edge should be square to the sides of the chisel.

WRONG   RIGHT

Look Sharp

Proper sharpness has two characteristics. First, the planes meet at a true edge, not a blunt, worn one. If you look at a good, freshly sharpened edge under mild magnification, you won't see the edge itself; you'll see the two flat planes intersecting. When you use the tool, infinitesimal bits of metal are removed from that delicate edge until it becomes rounded and blunt. As this happens, the edge starts to become visible; the more visible it becomes, the duller it is. If you can see the edge of a chisel under good light, chances are it's dull and could use a good sharpening. The trick to sharpening is to remove just enough metal to eliminate the radius between the two planes.

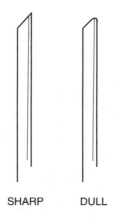

A sharp edge is the intersection of two planes. If you can see the edge, it's time to hit the sharpening stones.

SHARP   DULL

The second thing that affects sharpness is the grit of the final finishing stone used in the sharpening process. Sharpening stones, like sandpaper, come in different grits or degrees of coarseness. The coarser the stone is, the larger the abrasive particles and the faster it removes material; the finer the stone is, the finer the particles and the slower it removes material. These particles leave minute scratches in the edge.

The dotted line indicates how much material needs to be removed to sharpen a dull chisel.

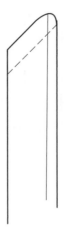

The finer you polish a tool, the smaller the scratches are, and the better the edge is. A coarsely sharpened edge may cut material very well at first (in fact for some applications, such as carving meat, a coarse or hairy edge may work better), but it won't hold up well. The microscopic points and irregularities formed by large scratches from a coarse stone snag as the tool cuts and wear away so that the blade dulls quickly. The time you spend polishing an edge with finer grit stones is well spent, because the edge will stay sharp longer and leave a smoother surface on the work.

The Sharpening Angle

The angle between the bevel and the back of a blade is always a compromise. A straight razor, with its ultra-low bevel angle, is dandy for shaving whiskers, but it wouldn't last long cutting wood. On the other hand, an ax may be fine for felling a tree, but I wouldn't try to shave with it. Basically, the sharper or more acute the angle, the more easily it will cut the wood, and the more fragile it is. The blunter or more obtuse the angle, the harder it is to cut the wood, but the more durable the edge is.

What this means is that over the years craftsmen have pretty much figured out the ideal sharpening angles for their tools. The standard angle for a western chisel or plane blade in hard wood is about 30 degrees. For a paring chisel that will be pushed, not struck with a mallet, and used for relatively delicate removal of stock, you can bring that angle down to about 25 degrees; it will be easier to push and will cut more cleanly at this angle. You can also drop the angle 2 or 3 degrees if you are working in soft wood, such as pine or spruce. If you're going to be doing some serious chopping, say timber-framing in oak, or if you're using an extremely hard wood, like bubinga or ebony, you might want to sharpen your chisels at 33 to 35 degrees to have more time between sharpenings.

The Stone Cold Truth About Abrasives

A sharpening stone or whetstone is just a solid block of abrasive grit with a flat surface to lap your blade on. A lubricant, either oil or water, is used to prevent the metal from clogging the stone. Like sandpaper, whetstones are rated numerically for coarseness, with 200 grit being a very coarse stone and 8,000 grit being about as fine as you'll see.

In the good old days, woodworkers used only natural stones like soft and hard Arkansas stones in this country or Belgian water stones in Europe. This century has seen manmade stones, which are abrasive grit baked into a matrix, rise from a cheap but inferior alternative into something even fussbudgets like myself use.

When I started woodworking, I learned to use man-made oilstones for rough sharpening and then move on to natural soft, then hard Arkansas stones for finishing. Sometime in the early 1980s, I was introduced to Japanese water stones, which were just appearing on the woodworking scene. At first, I was skeptical; now 95 percent of my sharpening is done on them. Water stones are inexpensive (the man-made ones anyway), are easier to keep flat, and cut the metal faster than an oil stone does. Also, you don't get oil all over your wood.

Water stones have swept the market so effectively that they are now being made in this country (Norton Abrasives makes a very good line). I still use my harder Western oil stones for sharpening carving gouges and small tools like $1/8$-inch chisels, which can dig into the softer water stones, but for general sharpening, the water stones rule. The description of the sharpening process that follows is for man-made water stones, but if you already have oil stones or just prefer them, simply substitute oil stones of a similar grit (you should always know the approximate numerical grit of the stone you are using).

Woodlore

In Japan, water stones were traditionally natural, and because of their association with the samurai sword, they are the subject of extreme connoisseurship. They have largely been mined out, and as with hard Arkansas stones in this country, the quality has dropped. Finer stones are highly sought after, with some examples selling for several thousand dollars.

You need a basic set of stones to get started; you can get more later if you want to fill in some gaps. For general sharpening, make sure the stones are at least ³/₄-inch thick, 2 inches wide, and 8 inches long; otherwise, they'll be awkward to use. I recommend getting these grits to start:

➤ **200 grit.** Used for very rough sharpening when the grinder won't do or is unavailable

➤ **700 to 800 grit.** The stone to use right off the grinder

➤ **1,200 grit.** A good intermediate stone

➤ **6,000 grit.** Finishing stone used to produce a mirror-like surface

Flatness is a virtue! If your stones aren't flat, your bevels won't be either. Keep stones flat by taping a piece of coarse sandpaper to a dead flat surface (a machine table or piece of plate glass works nicely) and lapping the stone back and forth. Check the stone with a straight edge across the length, width, and diagonally as you lap. It's best to use wet-dry sandpaper and water or oil as a lubricant, depending upon which type of stone you're using.

Sharpening the Easy Way

Lurking inside every woodworker there's a yenta who thinks he's Yoda. Woodworkers all have their own opinions as to how things ought to be done, and they're not shy about sharing them with you. I can think of no area of woodworking that sparks such fierce debates as how to sharpen a tool. Some people move the chisel in figure eights on the stone; others make circles, and both groups will argue until they're blue in the face about whose method is better. I've developed my own idiosyncrasies in how I sharpen this tool or that, but I won't burden you with them; it would just be confusing. What follows is a good, straightforward way to sharpen a chisel or plane blade that's relatively easy to learn. Later, you can embellish this method as you see fit. In the meantime, if some well-intentioned geezer tries to correct you, listen politely and go on about your business.

First, a Good Grinding

Every so often, when an edge needs a lot of metal removed (for example, if the bevel has gotten rounded or cocked at an angle from repeated novice sharpenings or if the edge is nicked from hard use), a grinder can save lots of time. If you don't have access to a grinder, though, you can start with the whetstones. I prefer an electric grinder with a coarse wheel on one side and a finer one on the other. When I did my apprenticeship, I used a hand grinder, which does the job and can be picked up cheap, but it's a bit of a feat of coordination at first to crank the wheel with one hand while you move the chisel back and forth with the other.

The first step is to set the tool rest to the right angle. The tool rest is an adjustable metal plate that supports the blade as it's ground; never use a grinder without one! Check the bevel angle of the tool you're sharpening. If it's too obtuse, adjust the tool rest, with the grinder turned off, so that the blade will contact the wheel toward the heel of the bevel. If it's too acute, adjust the tool rest so the wheel makes contact toward the edge on the bevel. If the angle is already good, see that the wheel hits the bevel dead center. Remember: The blade should always rest flat on the tool rest, and the wheel always makes contact with the bevel side, not the back of the chisel or plane blade.

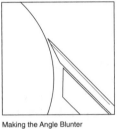

Making the Angle Blunter

Keeping the Same Angle

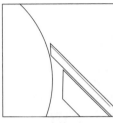

Making the Angle More Acute

Setting the angle of the tool rest.

Now you're ready to grind. First, with the blade on the tool rest, but not touching the wheel, turn on the grinder. Next, slowly slide the blade up the tool rest until it makes gentle contact with the grinding wheel. You'll know it has made contact because sparks will start to come off the blade and you will hear a grinding noise. As soon as this starts to happen, slide the chisel from side to side on the tool rest while keeping the blade in contact with the wheel. This sliding back and forth is a bit tricky at first, but with time you'll get the hang of it.

Very narrow or extra-wide chisels are the hardest, so practice on $1/2$- to 1-inch chisels at first. It's important to keep the blade facing the wheel straight as you slide it. If you angle it, that will translate into a skewed bevel and edge. It's also important that you don't apply too much pressure to the wheel or you'll overheat the blade and ruin the temper (see the following section, "Burning the Blade"). Remove the blade and check it frequently to see where exactly you're removing metal. Ideally, you should create a single straight, concave bevel that is square to the sides of the blade; in reality, you'll probably end up with a series of facets on the bevel at first, because you've been unable to hold the chisel consistently as you move it. Don't worry; this is normal. It takes practice to get the hang of the sharpening movement.

Tricks of the Trade

Keep a bevel gauge set to the desired angle at hand when grinding, so you can check the angle quickly as you go. If no measuring tools are available, you can guesstimate a 30-degree angle by making the bevel about twice as wide as the blade is thick.

"How do I know when to stop?" you ask. You grind just enough to remove the defects you're trying to correct. If you're trying to even out a rounded bevel, grind until the wheel just begins to touch the edge. To square a skewed blade, grind just until it's square. If you're getting rid of a nick in the blade, make sure you grind out the whole nick on a whetstone; it'll take some time to get the last bit.

Remember, the grinder is a power tool and should be treated with care. Don't even touch one until you review the safety checklist for power tools in Chapter 6, "Feel the Power: Portable Power Tools," and remember to keep the blade flat and firm on the tool rest. This not only maintains the proper angle, it also keeps the tool from bouncing around.

Burning the Blade

Grinding creates friction, which tends to heat up the blade. If you're not careful, a section of the blade can become red hot, which draws out the temper. If this happens, the part of the blade that has lost its temper will appear discolored; it usually will have a bluish color. The cure for this problem is to grind the blade past the part that has been discolored, which can be a time-consuming process. The edge of the blade itself, especially at the outside corners, is especially susceptible to burning because its thinner material doesn't dissipate heat as well as the thicker part of the blade.

To avoid overheating a blade, take the following precautions:

➤ Keep the pressure between the tool and the wheel light. More pressure means more friction. The tendency of beginners is to hold the tool in a death lock. Relax and develop a light touch.

➤ Keep a cup of cool water next to you as you grind, and dip the tool in the water as it starts to heat up.

➤ Keep the tool moving from side to side. Heat builds up faster in a stationary tool.

➤ If possible, use a slower grinder; slower grinders generate less friction.

➤ Use a coarser wheel; coarser wheels also generate less friction.

➤ Be extra careful when the wheel is near the very edge of the blade; a light touch pays off at this point.

I Woodn't Do That!

When you're putting the finishing touches on your chisel, don't forget about the danger of overheating. That's exactly when you're most likely to burn the blade, because by then, the wheel is grinding right at the edge, not in the middle of the bevel.

Using the Stones

After you're done grinding, it's time to hit the whetstones. The round grinding wheel leaves a hollow-ground blade, which means that the bevel is concave.

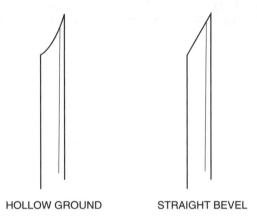

HOLLOW GROUND   STRAIGHT BEVEL

The grinder leaves a hollow-ground blade, which is easier to sharpen on a stone than a straight bevel, but the more hollow the bevel is, the more fragile it is. The more you lap the blade on a stone, the less of the hollow grind you leave, and the sturdier the edge is.

From the grinding wheel, I take the blade to an 800-grit water stone that I've placed on a stable surface just above waist level. It's important that the stone doesn't slide around. I keep mine on a thin piece of hard rubber, which keeps it from sliding and protects the work surface as well. Next, I touch the heel of the bevel at the back of the stone, rock the edge down until I feel it click as it contacts the stone, and hold the chisel at exactly that angle as I slide it forward toward the front of the stone. Then I pick up the blade and repeat the process—again—and again.

Now this process sounds easy, but until you've done it a few hundred times, it can be difficult to hold the chisel steady at the right angle. It wants to rock as you slide it over the stone, which rounds the bevel (something you don't want) and changes the angle you went to all that trouble to grind. Use the click as the edge hits the stone to find the right angle. Once the bevel gets rounded, you won't feel a click, and it will be difficult to know at what angle to hold the blade.

I Woodn't Do That!

Don't work just one area of the stone; use the whole surface. If you make a pass on one side, make the next pass on the other, and go the entire length of the stone. This helps keep the stone flat. I also rub the stones together when switching from one grit to another, which flattens the stones and creates a **slurry,** or abrasive paste, that speeds sharpening.

Holding the angle steady is easier if you go in only one direction. Figure eights, circles, and even merely sliding back and forth tend to rock the blade as you change direction, so save the fancy gyrations until you get the hang of things. Another thing that helps keep the angle is a proper grip: I hold the blade low and push with my right hand while using the fingers of my left hand to press down directly over the bevel to hold it steady. Angling the blade 45 degrees to the direction of the stroke also helps stabilize it.

Learn to feel the soft click as the edge contacts the stone; this means you're at the right angle. Keep downward pressure directly over the bevel to hold it as you glide the chisel over the stone.

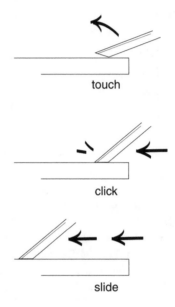

touch

click

slide

When is it time to go to the next stone? When the stone you're using has removed all the marks at the edge made by the previous step; in this case, the grinding marks left by the wheel. Each grit leaves a slightly different texture. When you have a consistent texture left by the current stone, it's time to move to the next. From 800-grit, you go to the 1,200-grit, and then move on to the 6,000-grit finishing stone.

The Finishing Touch

The finishing stone, a 6,000- or 8,000-grit water stone, is used a little differently than the ones preceding it. It *glazes* or clogs easily because it's so fine, and when it does, it stops sharpening. When the finishing stone starts to glaze, wet the stone and rub it face-to-face with the next coarsest stone, the 1,200-grit, for example. This rubbing cleans the surface of the stone and creates a slurry that helps the sharpening action (it also helps to keep the stones flat). The Japanese use a special small stone, called a *nagura,* to create a slurry and clean the stone's surface. You can purchase naguras, but they are not must-have items.

The coarser stones leave a burr or wire edge on the blade, which is like a minute flap of metal right at the edge. Resist the temptation to pluck it off with your fingers; rather, remove it by patiently lapping the bevel on the stone as discussed earlier in the chapter. When the burr is gone, flip the blade over, place the back of the chisel on the stone, and, with firm downward pressure, lap the blade back and forth on the stone 15 to 20 times; go back and make four or five passes on the bevel. Repeat this twice. This lapping of the back touches up the back surface of the blade, reestablishing that perfect plane you want.

When Do I Sharpen?

I suppose it is possible to sharpen too much, but I've never met anyone who does. Generally, we all procrastinate, and if you have an inkling that it's time to sharpen your chisel, then it probably is. If the blade is getting harder to push through the wood, if it's not leaving a clean surface as it cuts, or if you can see defects in the edge, then you should sharpen the chisel. Bear in mind that you don't have to grind the chisel every time you sharpen. Unless there's something wrong with the geometry of the blade, or there's a bad nick in the edge, just go to the 800-grit stone and progress from there. I learned as an apprentice that if you finish a task and have a little time to kill before lunch, coffee break, or at the end of the day, you should grab your chisels and plane blades and sharpen them. It's good psychologically to come back to work with all your tools sharp and your bench clean.

So You Have a New Chisel

I said earlier that an edge is the intersection of two planes. That means that the back of the chisel or plane blade has to be flat and honed as well as the bevel. You lap the back of the blade flat when you first buy a tool, but after that, unless something dreadful happens (like your brother-in-law uses your chisel to open a can of paint), you don't do much to it except a little lapping on the finish stone at the end of the sharpening process. Western blade makers have developed the irritating habit of buffing their blades heavily to make them shiny, and then lacquering them so they stay that way. The buffing rounds the edges and makes flattening the back a much longer process. Japanese blades, on the other hand, are generally well-finished and need just a bit of honing.

To flatten the back, place the first inch or so of the back of the blade on a flat, coarse stone (200-grit should work well) and, with plenty of downward pressure, lap it back and forth over the length of the stone. Flip the stone around every so often so you don't hollow out one side. At first, you'll notice that the stone leaves its minute scratches only on certain areas of the blade; other areas, the high spots, seem untouched. Do this until the entire section you're working on has a consistent pattern of scratches and the high spots are gone. With a heavily buffed or worn antique blade, this process could take a while. Once the blade is flat, use the same procedure on your 800-, 1,200-, and 6,000-grit stones until the blade back has a finishing-stone finish.

Sharpening Gadgets and Gizmos

Several companies make a variety of gadgets to help hold the blade at a steady angle during sharpening. Generally, these gadgets have a mechanism that holds the blade and a wheel or bearing that rolls on the work surface or on the stone itself. My feeling is that learning to sharpen tools freehand helps develop hand-eye skills that carry over into other areas of the craft, and that if you're into woodwork for the long run, it's worth practicing the sharpening process until you get the hang of it. But if you just want to sharpen your chisels for a project and can't take the frustration factor of freehand sharpening, then give one of these things a shot.

One sharpening tool that I don't own but came close to buying once or twice is a Japanese electric water stone. It resembles a record player (remember those?) where the record is a round water stone, onto which water drips slowly from a reservoir while the blade is held on a tool rest. You can swap different grit stones in and out. Electric water stones combine the grinding and the stoning process in one step. Their advantage is that they run cool so you don't risk burning your edge, and they don't put a hollow grind in the blade, which some people find objectionable.

Tricks of the Trade

Japanese electric water stones are great. The problem is that good ones are expensive, and they're not as versatile as grinders. I will probably never own one, but that's just because I'm set in my ways and cheap. If you're starting out and have the money, they are certainly worth looking into.

Sharpening Saws: Leave It to the Pros

Sharpening saws and other cutters like router bits or jointer/planer knives is best left to the professionals. I was taught to sharpen my own handsaws and even steel-toothed table saw blades as part of my training, but that's a holdover from the bad old days. It's too time-consuming to sharpen your own saws, and you can send them out cheaply. Save the energy for your projects. To find a professional sharpening service, look under grinding in your local yellow pages or check Appendix B, "Resources."

The Least You Need to Know

➤ To do good, clean work, you need to sharpen your own tools on a regular basis.

➤ A good edge is true, sharp, and the proper angle for the task at hand.

➤ Rapid grinding tunes up a blade before you sharpen it on whetstones.

➤ Progressively finer whetstones sharpen the edge and make it durable.

➤ Water stones are easier to use than oil stones.

➤ You need a range of sharpening stones from coarse to fine.

Part 3
The Word on Wood

Crafts are traditionally divided up according to materials: woodworking, stonemasonry, goldsmithing, and so on. This is because each material has its own character and properties. You don't cut stone with the same tools you would use for wood, and I can think of several pretty good reasons not to build your kitchen cabinets out of granite.

Ultimately, woodworking is about the wood. To be a great woodworker, you have to know the material and understand its structure, its strength, and its weaknesses and how it grows the way it does. You also need to know about the different varieties of wood and plywood, how and where to buy them, and how they should be stored.

The following chapters take you on a tour of the wide world of wood: from the forest where it grows, to the mill where it's cut up, to the lumberyard, and finally to your workshop. By the time we're done, you'll know how to buy and handle lumber with the swagger of an old-timer.

Chapter 9

Wood's Wild Ways

In This Chapter

➤ Wood as part of the natural world

➤ How a tree grows

➤ Rings and fibers: wood's natural structure

➤ Grain patterns and what they mean

➤ Moisture and wood movement

Wood is a natural material. We process it and manipulate it, but we don't manufacture it. Trees grow for their own reasons, not to make an ideal building block for our projects. We try to domesticate wood, but it always retains some of its wild origins, expanding and contracting, depending on the season, and warping, cupping, and bowing for its own mysterious reasons. If it weren't so beautiful, we could just make everything out of steel and plastic, but we can't seem to get away from its beautiful grain and reassuring warmth.

This chapter looks at how wood grows and how that affects the way woodworkers work with it. By learning wood's internal structure and idiosyncrasies, you come to understand what to expect from it and how to avoid some of the problems associated with it, such as splitting and warping.

The Call of the Wild

Wood is a natural material, not a man-made product. It hasn't been engineered solely with our convenience in mind, like some plastic. We do our best to keep it housebroken, but every so often, wood hears the call of the wild, like some Husky with too much wolf in it, and does something we don't like. You leave that table too close to the radiator, and a big crack opens up at one end, because the wood has dried out too quickly. You move that dresser from Los Angeles to New Orleans, and all of a sudden, the drawers won't open, because they've swelled up with moisture. Leave that dining table in front of the nice, sunny, bay window, and the top warps, and the finish darkens.

The other problem with wood is that trees are so unpredictable. One has a long trunk; another has a short one. This one has a trunk 14 inches wide; that one has a trunk 7 feet wide. Or maybe this oak tree grew fast, and the rings are $1/4$-inch wide. Another one grew slowly, and the rings are barely $1/32$-inch wide. Because trees aren't engineered in a laboratory, but grow according to their own genetics and climate, the boards you end up with are all different. You can't buy solid wood by the running yard the way you can fabric.

These problems all arise from wood's natural makeup. If you understand how wood wants to behave, you can head off disasters before they happen. To do that, you first have to understand how wood grows.

Tree Life 101

The tree is a system made up of roots, trunk, branches, and leaves. The roots draw water and nutrients from the soil; the trunk carries the nutrients to the branches, which carry them further to the leaves. The leaves draw carbon dioxide from the air and, with the aid of sunlight, carry out a process called *photosynthesis* that combines the nutrients to create sugars while releasing oxygen into the atmosphere. These sugars are carried by the tree's sap back down along the inside of the bark to generate new cells, allowing the tree to grow bigger.

The Trunk, the Whole Trunk, and Nothing but the Trunk

For most woodwork, we are interested only in the trunk of the tree up to the first branches. Branches bring knots to the trunk, and branches themselves are unusable because they grow fighting the pull of gravity and are so full of internal stresses that they twist and warp terribly when cut up. The trunk grows straight and relatively free of internal stresses (except when it grows on the side of a hill) and can most easily be sawn into lumber.

The trunk is basically a conduit and structural support for the leaf system. The more competition for sunlight that a tree has, as in a dense forest, the taller the trunk grows before it starts branching out. When there is less competition, as in the hedgerow trees that separate open fields, the less the trunk has to grow before it starts branching out. This is why the best wood is harvested from dense forests and jungles.

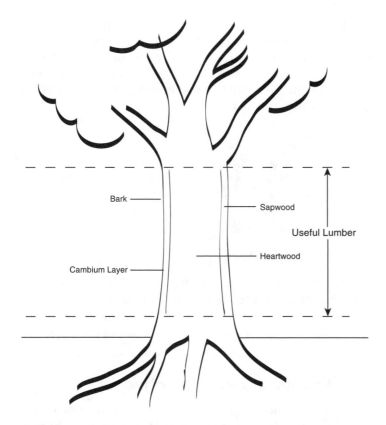

The tree is a system made up of roots, trunk, branches, and leaves.

Bark

Sapwood

Useful Lumber

Cambium Layer

Heartwood

Reading Rings and Following Fibers

Most of the trunk, the entire center or *heartwood* section, works to support the tree. The part that carries nutrients is the layer just under the bark, called the *cambium layer*. The nutrients travel through hollow fibers, which run up the length of the trunk. The tree is constantly creating new, active fibers at the outside of the cambium layer while older fibers at the inside of the cambium layer become inert heartwood.

This outward growth is fastest in the spring and summer and slowest in the fall and winter. If you slice through the trunk, the fast summer growth sections are more porous and wider, and the slow winter growth sections are denser, narrower, and darker. This difference gives the appearance of rings, one for each year of growth. Nearly everyone has seen growth rings and knows that you can determine a tree's age by counting them, but most people are not exactly sure why they form.

When growing conditions are favorable, when the climate is warm and wet with plenty of sunlight, for example, a tree's rings will be widely spaced. When climatic conditions are less perfect, the rings will be thinner and packed closer together. There are variations of ring thickness within the same tree due to yearly weather differences, and different trees vary widely from one to another because they grow in different locations under different conditions.

103

The thing to remember is that lumber from fast-growing trees with wide ring spacing is generally heavier, harder, and more difficult to work than slower-growing wood. It will also tend to have wilder grain patterns. This is especially true in certain species such as oak and ash. That's why it's a good idea to look at the ends of boards when selecting lumber. Unless you're making billy clubs or mallet heads, you probably want to look for slower-growing wood with tighter rings.

Woodlore

In the tropics, there is relatively little difference between the seasons. Consequently, the definition between rings is blurred. Rings are often quite wide, and the trees become huge because they grow so fast in the heat and humidity. All this makes tropical wood grain patterns very striking and exotic to people from the northern part of the world.

Wood Words

The core of the trunk is called **heartwood** and is generally the only part of the wood you will be interested in using. The first few rings inside the bark and cambium layer still contain vestiges of sap. This section of the trunk is called **sapwood** and is usually a different color and softer than the heartwood. A board with a section of sapwood is considered defective, though some woodworkers use sapwood decoratively, most notably the late George Nakashima.

Sapwood vs. Heartwood

In addition to the rings, a wood slice will reveal an area just under the cambium layer that is a different color from the rest of the *heartwood*. This area, generally lighter in color, still contains leftover nutrients (mostly sugars) and is called *sapwood*. Having a section of sapwood in a board is considered a defect because of its color variation, though in some cases it can be used as a decorative element. The one thing to bear in mind is that because sapwood is full of sugars, it is extremely attractive to boring insects (bugs who eat holes in wood, not ones that talk about their investment portfolios at parties), which is why you'll often see wormholes in the sapwood section of a board.

Fathoming Fibers

Because it's their business to support all those leaves, branches, squirrels, and whatever, the fibers that constitute the trunk have evolved into something of a structural miracle. Because they're hollow, they're relatively light; they're flexible and can bend without damage, and unlike most metals, they'll return to their original straightness. Fibers are what make wood strong, but it's important to re-member that wood's strength lies in the direction that the fibers run. So the strength is along a board's length, not across its width.

It's relatively easy to split the fibers apart. This is why firewood will split with a sin-gle, well-placed ax stroke, but chopping down a tree is hard work. It's also the reason why a karate chop always splits a board with the grain, not across it.

Wood also flexes more across its grain than it does with the grain. For this reason, shelves, table legs, and other load-bearing wooden parts must have the grain running in the direction that requires the most strength.

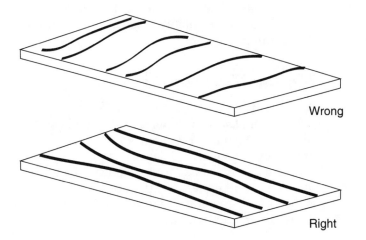

Wrong

Right

Wood's strength lies with the grain, so you must al-ways orient the grain in the direction where you need strength. A shelf, for example, that has its grain running the short way will sag or break.

Plywood is equally strong in both directions because half the layers run one way and half run the other. Consequently, it's a compromise for shelves and other parts that need most of their strength in one direction. Plywood shelves sag more than solid wood, and flakeboard, which has no grain direction at all, sags like crazy. When using plywood for shelves, it's a good idea to glue on a wide solid-wood edging for rigidity.

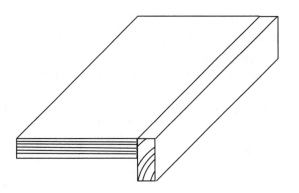

A wide, solid-wood edge helps keep a plywood or flakeboard shelf from sagging.

105

Grain's Beautiful Ways

Grain patterns give wood its beauty. If trees grew with perfectly straight fibers that didn't change density from season to season, wood would look very boring indeed. It's because the fibers change direction and density, undulate, and are generally unruly that wood has such beautiful surface patterns.

Rings do not grow in perfect, concentric cylinders. Like the human body, they narrow and widen unexpectedly, and the fibers may spiral clockwise for a few years only to reverse direction and twist counterclockwise for a decade. Consequently, grain never runs truly parallel to the planes of a board—when we speak of grain direction we are speaking *generally.* When a lumber mill cuts boards out of a log they align the saw in the *general* direction of the grain, but fibers are inevitably sheared off as they angle up toward and down away from the cut surface.

Wood Words

Plain-sawn or **flat-sawn** boards have been cut from the log so that the two primary surfaces are oriented tangent to the rings. **Quarter-sawn** boards are cut so that the surfaces are perpendicular to the rings. In **rift-sawn** boards the rings appear to run diagonally to the primary surfaces. Each type of board has its own characteristic grain pattern.

Name That Grain

Probably the most common grain pattern is that of *flat-sawn* or *plain-sawn* lumber. In this lumber, the main surface of the board is tangent to the rings. It leaves a preferably centered, undulating pattern, where the rings are nearly parallel to the plane of the surface. On the sections on either side, the rings curve at a sharp angle or are perpendicular to the surface, with a relatively linear grain pattern.

Flat-sawn boards are perfect for tabletops, because the undulating center looks striking, and the linear pattern at the edges hides glue lines and makes for a smoother visual transition from one board to another. They are also ideal for panels in frame and panel construction because they provide a balanced visual composition.

Another classic grain pattern is that of *quarter-sawn* boards. In this pattern, the primary surfaces of the board are perpendicular to the rings and give a consistent, linear grain that is understated, almost more of a texture than a pattern. This pattern is especially striking in oak and sycamore, where it reveals wood's *rays,* a secondary grain pattern caused by cells that travel radially in the trunk. Quarter-sawn oak is a hallmark of Arts and Crafts-style furniture.

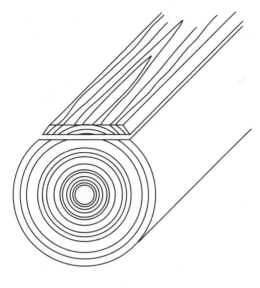

Flat-sawn boards have active grain in the center and linear grain on the outside.

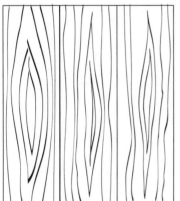

Flat-sawn boards work well visually for tabletops and for panels in traditional frame and panel construction.

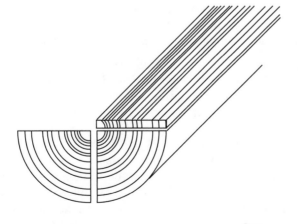

Quarter-sawn boards have a consistent linear grain pattern all the way across their surface.

Rift-sawn boards fall somewhere in between flat-sawn and quarter-sawn boards, with rings that are approximately 45 degrees to all the surfaces of the board. The outside sections of flat-sawn boards are generally rift-sawn. Rift-sawn boards have linear grain similar to quarter-sawn boards, but they don't have rays. Also, they have the advantage of a grain pattern that is similar on all four sides. This advantage makes them perfect for table legs and other corner elements where two or more contiguous sides are visible at the same time. It always looks wrong to me when two sides of a table leg have vastly different patterns; when the patterns are similar, it provides a sense of unity.

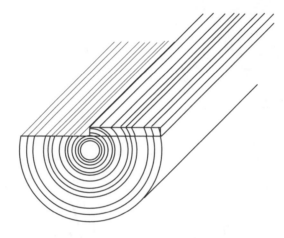

Rift-sawn boards have linear grain patterns on four sides, which make them ideal for legs and other corner elements.

I Woodn't Do That!

Don't build your first project out of figured wood; it may make you swear off woodworking. Get several projects under your belt before you start dabbling with the curly wood. It can be very frustrating because it requires so much more surface preparation before finishing. Make sure you've mastered the cabinet scraper before you tackle figured wood.

Curly, Bird's Eye, and Other Oddities

There is a category of grain patterns that are aberrations, freaks of nature that are sought after. In this category, secondary patterns combine with the normal grain patterns of the tree. When lumber has one of these oddball conditions, it is called *figured wood*. Certain woods are more prone to being figured than others, notably maple, mahogany, sycamore, oak, and anigre.

Probably the most common type of figure is *curly grain*, also called *tiger* or *fiddle back* grain, where the fibers grow in a tight wave pattern instead of straight, giving the impression of three-dimensional curls in the surface of the wood. Violin parts often use curly wood (thus the *fiddle back* moniker), and it can be quite beautiful, if a bit ostentatious. The problem with curly wood (and figured wood in general) is that it's a nightmare to work with. It tears out when planed and is better served by the cabinet scraper. One way or another, it requires beaucoup elbow grease and sanding.

Bird's eye maple is a very common figured wood. Interspersed in the normal grain pattern are small, swirled points, like miniature knots. Other woods are known to get bird's eyes, but it's relatively rare.

There are many rare and unusual figured woods that you may stumble upon: quilted maple or mahogany, plum pudding mahogany, and so forth. People either love figured woods or hate them; most woodworkers approach them with a touch of reluctance because these woods are so ornery. If you decide you like them, sharpen your cabinet scrapers, and happy hunting!

Water, Water, Everywhere

Wood is basically a fluid-delivery system; the fibers are just a bundle of straws. Consequently, wood wicks up moisture and disposes of it more easily than we might like. Wood also changes dimension as the moisture comes and goes, which can be problematic. When the fibers take on water, they plump up, and when they dry out, they slim down. They don't get longer and shorter, only fatter and thinner.

When lumber is freshly cut, it is holding a lot of moisture and must be dried before it can be used. When it dries, it shrinks dramatically in thickness and width, but not in length. If you were to build furniture out of wet lumber, this shrinkage could be disastrous, leading to cracks, open joints, and so forth. Lumber needs to be dried to about 6 to 12 percent moisture content to be ideal for most woodworking. You can learn about air- and kiln-drying in Chapter 11.

Wood and Weather

Despite initial drying, wood will continue to expand and contract due to moisture until somebody uses it for firewood. In summer, it will take on moisture and expand, and in winter, it will contract. Some finishes slow down the process, but nothing stops it. If you move to New Orleans, you may find that your drawers and doors stick, but don't worry; just move to Phoenix and they'll loosen right up.

Tricks of the Trade

Try to let your lumber get acclimated to your workshop before you cut it up. Leaving your boards stacked in your shop area with stickers (strips of wood used as spacers) between them so air can circulate will allow their moisture content to equalize with the ambient humidity. This acclimation will cut down on warping and cupping when you cut up the lumber. A couple of weeks will help, but the longer you can keep it in your workshop, the better.

Wood fibers take in and release moisture most easily at their cut ends, so the ends of boards tend to expand and contract faster then their centers. This is one reason why boards, tabletops, and other wide parts tend to crack at their ends first and why it doesn't hurt to make sure that the end-grain is thoroughly filled with finish. It's customary to paint the ends of rough lumber or baste them with paraffin to prevent them from cracking when they dry out and from shrinking faster than the center of the boards.

The Least You Need to Know

➤ Wood is a natural material and can behave in wild and unexpected ways.

➤ The wood that woodworkers use comes from the tree's trunk.

➤ Wood is made up of tiny fibers that hold moisture and are oriented in more or less the same direction.

➤ Fibers give wood its directional strength and grain patterns.

➤ Wood must be properly dried before it can be used for most woodworking.

➤ Moisture makes wood expand and contract over its width and thickness, but not its length.

➤ Seasonal and regional variations in humidity make wood expand and contract a significant amount.

Chapter 10

The Subtle Art of Buying Solid Wood

In This Chapter

➤ Knowing the different types of wood

➤ Making sense of the lumberyard

➤ Buying lumber: rough versus finished

➤ Choosing the right boards for your project

➤ Getting your lumber home

The lumberyard can be a daunting place, where you feel like a tourist who's walked into a bad neighborhood. First, there are boards the width you need in stock. Then crusty yardmen mutter some arcane nomenclature while measuring your crusty boards, only to tell you that you have *x* number of board/feet, whatever they are. Next, countermen ask you whether you want the boards left rough or if you want them surfaced for an additional 60¢ per linear foot. Finally, when everyone's done with you, you can't fit the boards in your car.

This chapter walks you through the process of buying wood and explains some of the lumberyard mysteries: the somewhat archaic and definitely complicated systems of measuring lumber, the different types of wood, how to pick the right boards, and how not to get taken to the cleaners.

Mother Nature's 37 Flavors

Like ice cream, wood comes in many different flavors, from plain vanilla to exotic tropical varieties. Novice woodworkers tend to be drawn to the exotic, and there's nothing wrong with that. Who wouldn't be titillated by bright orange padauk or the aptly named purple heart? However, most experienced woodworkers have simpler tastes. After the novelty of exotic wood wears off, woodworkers start looking for subtlety and substance. I remember the thrill the first time I saw padauk and thought, "I can make an orange cabinet," which I more or less did. Now when I see padauk, I think, "What a garish and difficult wood," but I do enjoy seeing my students get excited about it as I did 16 years ago.

The last 20 years or so has seen an explosion in the varieties of exotic wood on the market. This explosion is a direct result of the deforestation of tropical rainforests. As land is cleared in Africa, South America, and Southeast Asia, new varieties of trees are discovered all the time. Most of these trees grow in small batches in remote locations, and the wood is shipped north.

Woodlore

Twenty-five years ago, I could identify most of the hardwoods on the market in the Northeast. Today, hundreds of new types have appeared, and I don't even bother to learn their names, because I know that most will disappear and be replaced by new discoveries. Besides, most of these woods are mediocre; they're flashes in the pan. Some are beautiful, and some are not, but few have the workability, stability, and availability that, when combined with beauty, make a classic furniture wood.

I try to stick to North American hardwoods because they're time-tested, beautiful, available, and affordable. Some tropical woods (also called "exotics") have proved themselves over time to be great. Unfortunately, many of these woods have become extinct or are near extinction due to overharvesting in the last 200 years. Often, what you get now is a stunted shadow of past glory. The boards are short and narrow and have nasty sapwood, knots, and poor color. There are many types of wood out there, but your woodworking will go more easily, allowing you to improve more quickly, if you start with varieties that are workable and predictable.

The Domestic Woods

These are some of the classic woods:

➤ **Hard and soft maple.** The vanilla of woods, both hard and soft maple are light in color, relatively easy to work, and fairly stable (hard maple is more difficult to work). Maple is moderately inexpensive for a hardwood. Soft maple is often curly, but hard maple is rarely curly. Hard maple has greater visual depth to its grain, which makes it spectacular when it is curly.

➤ **Cherry.** This wood has a light but rich reddish color. Moderately hard and easy to work, cherry is very beautiful, especially when figured. This moderately priced and relatively stable wood is one of my favorites.

➤ **Walnut.** Rich, dark brown and very sought after, walnut has been overharvested, which has driven the price up and lowered the overall quality available. Boards frequently have defects and are narrow. When the quality is good, walnut is a joy to work, relatively stable, and expensive.

➤ **Poplar.** Cheap and soft for a hardwood, poplar is not very attractive, but it is used as a secondary wood for drawer sides, internal parts, and painted wood because it is workable and stable.

➤ **Birch.** A step above poplar, birch is used as a secondary wood and sometimes as a cheaper stand-in for maple, which it resembles.

➤ **Pine.** A softwood, pine is soft, cheap, and plentiful; it also works easily and can be quite beautiful.

➤ **Red and white oak.** Grain porous and dramatically grained, oak is moderately expensive, workable, and readily available. I prefer white oak for workability and appearance. Oak has a high rate of expansion and contraction.

➤ **Ash.** White oak and ash are often mistaken for each other. However, ash is lighter in color, less popular, and not as available. Ash is also moderately priced.

The Imports

Here is just a sampling of the world's vast number of tree types:

➤ **Honduran mahogany.** All South American mahogany is now sold as Honduran. It's a great furniture wood that grows in huge trees, which means that 30-inch-wide boards are often available. Although current crops of mahogany are much less fabulous than old stuff, great boards are still available. Honduran mahogany is super stable and workable. It's a bit expensive, though you save money on labor because it's so easy to work.

➤ **Luan mahogany.** Not a true mahogany, Luan mahogany is cheap and very stable. It has a reddish color similar to Honduran mahogany, but with pulpy grain and dark pores. Luan mahogany is used as a secondary wood because of its stability and price.

➤ **Brazilian rosewood.** One of the great furniture woods, Brazilian rosewood is effectively unavailable due to overharvesting.

➤ **Indian rosewood.** An expensive but somewhat available substitute for Brazilian rosewood, Indian rosewood is hard, beautiful, and dark.

➤ **Swiss pearwood.** With a beautiful rosy color, Swiss pearwood works easily and is moderately available. It is soft and quite expensive.

➤ **Padauk.** Bright orange when it's milled, padauk turns an ugly brown over time with exposure to light and air. It is hard, has unpleasant rowed grain, and is expensive.

➤ **Purple heart.** This wood has similar characteristics to padauk; the main difference is its color: It starts out purple before turning brown.

➤ **Wenge.** This wood is a beautiful chocolatey brown with strong grain. It is hard and difficult to work, gives toxic, festering splinters, and is expensive. What price beauty!

➤ **Gaboon ebony.** This wood is a beautiful black color when you have good boards, but it has become so rare that low-quality, white-flecked boards are now dyed black. Not stable and very hard, it is also fabulously expensive.

➤ **Zebra wood.** Light in color with dark stripes, this wood looks, well, like a zebra. It is hard and not easy to work, but it is very striking and expensive. When it's milled, it smells like I imagine zebra dung does.

Now it's on to the lumberyard!

The Lowdown on Lumberyards

Different types of lumber stores cater to different sections of the market. Within those divisions, lumber stores differ in the services they offer. Some stores are geared to the homeowner or handyman who just wants to fix a problem around the house and needs some bite-sized piece of wood; other, larger lumberyards sell construction lumber to carpenters and contractors. Serious woodworkers go to yards that specialize in fine hardwoods, such as cherry, maple, and mahogany

It's important to find the right type of lumberyard for the project at hand. You won't get good pricing on hardwoods at a handyman store that carries hardwood as a specialty item, and a hardwood yard generally won't have 2×4s at all. And within each category, it's important to find the best yard possible.

Ask professionals in your area whom they buy from and go look at the yards: Is the lumber stored flat and neatly on racks, or is it just dumped in piles on the ground (lumber should never be left on a concrete floor where it will suck up moisture)? Is the lumber kept dry and out of direct sunlight? Do the salespeople seem to know what they're talking about? Do they care about the lumber? After you've found a good yard, it helps to establish a relationship with the staff over time. You're much more apt to get special treatment, such as getting boards cut to size, free delivery, or even a call when something choice comes in.

Lumber-on-the-Side Stores

Some places that sell lumber are basically just hardware stores that sell a little lumber on the side. They generally sell a small selection of home-building supplies, such as 2×4s and cheap plywood, and they may have a rack of small, pre-milled pieces of hardwood at vastly inflated prices. The only reason to patronize a place like this is if you need a small piece of wood. And you need it now. Immediately.

I Woodn't Do That!

It generally doesn't pay to buy hardwoods at a construction lumberyard or hardware store. These stores treat hardwood as a specialty item and jack up the prices. Often it's all surfaced and dimensioned and in its own display case like brie at the gourmet store, and the price per pound may not be that different. A lumberyard whose business is selling hardwood to cabinetmakers will offer better deals, better service, and better selection.

The Builder's One-Stop Lumberyard

If you've been to one lumberyard in your life, chances are it caters to the construction trades. These lumberyards sell studs to build walls, fir plywood to sheath houses, nails, screws, and all the components used in home building. Fancy yards may sell some hardwood lumber and higher grades of plywood for finish carpentry, but they generally don't have the quality or selection that you want for fine woodwork.

If you need construction lumber for shop fixtures, rough shelving, or some house project, then you may want to go to a construction lumberyard. Or if you want to build something out of clear or knotty pine, then this is the place to go.

The Hardwood Yard

Yards that specialize in hardwoods are generally the best bet for the woodworker. They offer better selection, quality, and value for the fine woodworker and cabinetmaker, because we are their target customers. They will generally let you pick through their lumber, culling out the best boards for your project. They're more apt to have

Wood Words

Milling is the process of sawing or planing wood into boards. **Rough-milled** boards have rough-sawn faces as they come from the sawmill. **Surfaced** or **finish-milled** boards have been run through a planer so that at least one, and possibly four, sides have a smooth, clean surface that is ready for sanding. **S2S** or **S1S** written on boards or on signage mean **surfaced one side** and **surfaced two sides.**

I Woodn't Do That!

Don't assume that just because a board has been surfaced or milled that it will be straight, flat, and true. Most yards plane boards without jointing them flat, so the surface has been cleaned up, but not trued. Even if the wood was trued when it was milled, exposure to the moisture and heat can cause the wood to warp, bow, and cup. So check boards before you buy them for acceptable trueness and plan on remilling them.

higher quality wood and to have custom *milling* services. They will also tend to carry more unusual varieties, tropical and figured woods, for example, and a wider range of sizes. A good hardwood yard will have wider boards, which are ideal for tabletops and panels, and a wider range of thickness, so you don't have to pay for material that's just going to end up as shavings.

Hardwood lumberyards do not generally sell any construction lumber. Some, however, do stock premium hardwood and cabinet-grade plywood. This can eliminate a separate trip to the plywood yard, but I should point out that high-quality hardwood plywood is usually sold by a separate dealer. I discuss plywood in Chapter 12, "Plywood: The Engineered Natural Material."

Buying Hardwood: Surfaced vs. Rough-Milled

Most hardwood yards sell their wood *rough-milled,* that is, with the rough surface left by the sawmill and subsequent drying. This leaves the woodworker with the maximum amount of material to play with in the privacy of his or her own workshop. The problem is that the rough surface makes it hard to read the grain of the wood, see defects, and match color from one board to another because the color of the rough surface is different from that of the finished surface. Most dealers will allow you to bring a hand plane and clean up a patch on a board so that you know what you're getting yourself into.

Some yards also sell some of their wood *surfaced* or already planed, which leaves one or two wide faces of the board smooth and clean. You lose some of the thickness, but if you don't need it, pre-surfacing allows you to see exactly what you're getting. I used to think it was a badge of professionalism to buy only rough lumber, but now I prefer to buy surfaced boards, when possible, so I can match grain pattern and color more easily.

Other yards offer cutting and milling services, generally for a small fee. You choose the rough-milled board, and they will surface the sides and cut the boards to approximate length. Different yards offer different services. Some may cut boards to length and maybe rip them to width, but not plane the surfaces; others may offer surfacing, but not cutting. You may find it handy to have some preliminary milling done at the yard. Crosscutting will make transportation easier, and surfacing can mean less work and fewer wood chips for you to clean up later. If you don't have a jointer or a planer yet, finding a yard that does surfacing is key!

Buying by the Board/Foot

Remember how hard it was to learn cups, pints, quarts, gallons, and fluid ounces when you were in grade school? Most people find the *board/foot* system of measuring solid wood equally problematic.

Because wood is a natural material, and boards come in different sizes, a system was devised to measure the volume of any board, no matter what its dimensions are. The basic unit of the system is the board/foot, which in its idealized form is a piece of wood 1 foot square and 1 inch thick. Because board/foot is a volumetric measurement, the configuration of the dimensions doesn't matter as long as the volume is the same: A gallon of water is a gallon, whether it's poured into cups, filling a jug, or spilled on the floor. Thus, a piece of wood 2 inches thick by 6 inches wide by 1 foot long is a board/foot, as is a piece of wood ¹/₂ inch thick by 12 inches wide by 2 feet long.

> **Wood Words**
>
> The **board/foot** system is a volumetric measurement used to measure the quantity of wood in a board no matter what its dimensions are. It allows the dealer to value boards consistently that have inconsistent dimensions. Because construction lumber has been milled to consistent thickness and width it is sold in linear feet. Thus, an eight-foot 2×4 has eight linear feet.

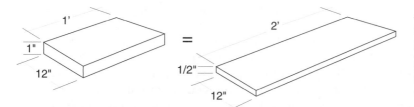

A piece of wood 1 inch thick by 12 inches wide by 1 foot long is the ideal board/foot; a piece ¹/₂ an inch thick by 12 inches wide by 2 feet long, also equals 1 board/foot.

To figure out how many board/feet are in a particular board, you multiply its thickness (T) in inches by its width (W) in inches by its length (L) in feet and divide the product by 12. Inches and feet are rounded off to the nearest whole number. The formula is as follows:

$$\frac{(T \times W \times L)}{12}$$

Tricks of the Trade

When measuring board/feet, you round off inch and foot measurements to the nearest whole number. Thus, 6³/₈ inches becomes 6 inches, and 5 feet, 5 inches is rounded down to 5 feet. Wood dealers almost inevitably round measurements up to the next higher whole number, when they should be rounding downward. Ask them how they're measuring your boards to make sure they aren't doing this.

Wood Words

Surfaced wood is measured in **nominal thickness,** which is its original thickness before surfacing. It's sort of a euphemism, a way of calling a ³/₄-inch or ⁷/₈-inch board a 1-inch board. It allows wood dealers to charge you for shavings that end up in the dust collector. When they figure how much lumber you have, they count the larger, original or nominal thickness instead of the smaller actual thickness.

For example, a board 3 inches thick by 4 inches wide by 12 feet long would be 10 board/feet ($3 \times 4 \times 10$ divided by 12). If that board were, say, cherry, priced at $4.50 per board/foot, that board would cost $45.

Why should you care about this obscure and confusing measurement system? Because many wood dealers are like used car salesmen, buyer beware is the rule. They frequently use the complexity of the system to bamboozle you and overcharge you for your lumber. It's like counting your change or checking your receipt; it's tedious, but you want to make sure you're not overcharged. I have had vendors (whom I deal with regularly, I might add) "miscalculate" my board/footage by as much as 50 percent; and in all the miscalculations I've experienced, not one was in my favor. Go figure.

Take a measuring tape, a calculator, and some scratch paper with you when you go to the lumberyard and be prepared to argue. If the wood dealers don't try to cheat outright, they will almost certainly round off dimensions in an upward direction when they should go downward. You want to count up your board/footage before you pay, not after you get your wood home.

More Measuring Madness

Sometimes it seems that the lumber industry wants to confuse you. I'm not sure it doesn't. Here's something else to bamboozle the uninitiated: The thickness of rough lumber is described not by the inch but by the quarter inch. Thus, 2-inch-thick lumber is called ⁸/₄; 1¹/₂-inch lumber is called ⁶/₄, 1-inch is ⁴/₄, and so on. It's a bit like counting your age in dog years. It's some archaic English system, and—this may seem paranoid—I believe dealers continue to use it because it makes their calculations that much harder to decipher for the person who walks in off the street.

To muddy the waters further, surfaced lumber is generally sold by its *nominal thickness* in inches. In other words, when lumber has been surfaced, it is usually, but not always, classified by its original thickness before milling. Thus, ⁸/₄ lumber is sold as 2-inch lumber after it has been milled down to a surfaced $1^3/_4$-inch thickness ($^3/_4$-inch × $3^3/_4$-inch) because this was its thickness as it was cut from the log before it was cleaned up. In case there's any doubt in your mind, you are charged for a full, presurfaced thickness when dealers calculate your board/footage. You pay for those missing wood shavings.

Getting Your Wood Home

One of the trickiest parts of a project for the amateur can be getting the lumber home. Lumberyards generally offer free delivery if you buy over a certain minimum amount. This amount is $200 to $500 in my neck of the woods, which isn't much for a cabinet shop, but a is bit steep for the hobbyist. It takes a surprising amount of rough lumber to build a dining table, hutch, or bookcase, more than will fit in your car, but often not quite enough to hit the minimum. With smaller projects, such as chairs or night tables, it may be possible to rough-cut the lumber into trunk-sized pieces. But if you're building a project with larger pieces, or don't want to start cutting boards until you get them home, the family car may not do the job. You can always rent a van, but that costs money. So the question arises: How do you talk the lumberyard into delivering your lumber for free?

First of all, it helps to be nice. I frequently see guys who think, "Hey, it's a lumberyard; I better act macho." Being nice works better; there's nothing blue-collar guys like less then a macho dentist—trust me, I know. Be cool: Don't overdo it, keep the piles neat as you go through them, keep what you're taking out of people's way, and treat the yard with respect. It may take a few trips before the yardmen notice you, but once you establish a rapport, they're apt to do you favors. Ask them when they're making a delivery to your neighborhood and see whether they'll throw your dinky order on for free.

Woodlore

I've found in the course of teaching that when I send students off to lumberyards, the women often get lots of helpful (read gratuitous) advice and free delivery. One young woman came back from a yard known for its grouchy yardmen to report, "I thought you said they were crusty. They were so friendly and helpful! And my lumber will be delivered free, tomorrow." The male students came back from the same yard looking browbeaten and broke and with their lumber in a taxi.

Skip the Middleman: Find a Mill

In some rural areas, you may be able to find small, local sawmills that will sell you lumber. They are usually limited in the services they offer, such as milling and delivery, but the prices are often better than other lumberyards. There's also something nice about buying local wood from the people that actually do the cutting and drying.

When buying from a sawmill, you can often get boards that have all been cut from the same tree, so the color and grain will match. You may also be able to buy lumber that has been air-dried instead of kiln-dried (more on this in Chapter 11, "The Sawmill: Where Trees Become Lumber"), which, although it is less dimensionally stable, often has more varied color.

The Least You Need to Know

➤ There are different categories of lumberyards.

➤ As a fine woodworker, you will use mostly hardwood and plywood yards.

➤ Hardwood is sold either rough–milled or surfaced.

➤ Hardwood lumber is measured in board/feet.

➤ Lumber dealers can be like used car salesmen, so you should know how to compute the cost of your lumber.

➤ In rural areas, you may be able to buy straight from the sawmill.

Chapter 11

The Sawmill: Where Trees Become Lumber

In This Chapter

➤ Cutting logs into lumber

➤ Plain-sawn and quarter-sawn: more than one way to slice a log

➤ Drying lumber

➤ The planing mill

➤ The veneer mill

After Mother Nature is done with the tree, it has to be processed into boards and dried to a workable moisture content before woodworkers can use it. Some woodworkers buy a portable chain saw mill, tow it out to the forest, and mill their own lumber. I am not one of them; I buy my lumber already processed, and you probably will, too, at least at first. So it's a good idea to have an overview of what happens between the forest and the lumberyard at the sawmill.

There is often confusion about the difference between sawmills and lumberyards. Basically, the sawmill (also called the lumbermill) is the manufacturer, and the lumberyard is the sales outlet. The wood goes from tree trunk to cut lumber at the sawmill and is sold to the consumer at the lumberyard. Like manufacturers, most sawmills do not sell lumber to the public directly, although some small ones will. These small mills are a great place for the discriminating woodworker to buy wood (more on this later in this chapter).

From Log to Board

The first thing that happens to the log is that it is placed in a *log carriage,* which is basically a cart that holds the log and rolls forward and backward on tracks. A saw blade is set to cut parallel with the tracks, just to one side of the log carriage. Some mills use a circular type saw, and some use a band saw. The log is positioned over the side, and as it slides forward, a slab is sliced off. The log carriage then slides back; the log is moved one board thickness over, and another pass is made, slicing off another slab.

The log is held in a log carriage and rolled on tracks into a saw blade, which cuts off a slab of wood.

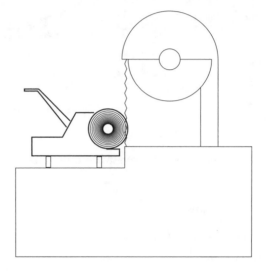

This process is repeated until the log has been sliced into a series of slabs or boards. These cuts may be consecutive, like bread, which is called *flitch-cutting* or *through-and-through cutting,* or the log may be rotated for greater yield or a particular grain pattern. The cuts are usually of varying thickness, some at ⁴/₄, some at ⁸/₄, and so forth.

Now come the edges. Some lumber is left untrimmed or *waney-edged* so that the edge still has sapwood, bark, and the whole outside surface of the tree left on. Small, old-school mills that flitch-cut logs often leave lumber waney-edged. It makes it easier to keep the boards in consecutive order, which makes board matching easier, because the bark surface indicates sequence. Large mills, however, don't cater to the purist and don't go to the trouble of keeping boards in order; plus it's easier to stack lumber with square edges, and the trimmings are ground up for flake board. So most lumber goes straight to the edger, which has two blades that cut the edges square and parallel.

The Cuts: Flat-Sawn, Quarter-Sawn, and Mixed-Sawn

In Chapter 9, "Wood's Wild Ways," I described flat-sawn, quarter-sawn, and rift-sawn grain patterns and how ring orientation causes them. Mixed-sawn or randomly sawn logs are cut for maximum yield (or bulk), with no regard for grain pattern. How the log is sliced at the mill determines ring orientation in the first place. In the good old days, logs were sliced specifically for pattern. Nowadays, getting maximum yield and avoiding defects are the primary concern of most mills.

 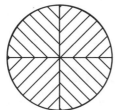 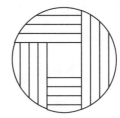

Flitch-sawn logs (left) offer a range of grain patterns. Quarter-sawn logs (center) provide lumber with characteristically uniform linear grain pattern. Sawing around the log (right) yields a hodgepodge of grain patterns.

Flitch-cutting, or sawing a log *through-and-through* yields flat-sawn, rift-sawn, and quarter-sawn boards, depending upon where in the log they're cut from, and fussbudgets like myself like nothing more than finding a complete flitch-cut log. Flitch-cut logs also make grain matching easier. Boards that have been sliced consecutively from a log will have grain patterns that are almost identical, because their surfaces were separated by a single saw kerf. Woodworkers use these boards to create a mirror image effect called *book-matching.* However, flitch-cutting can be wasteful, because it makes it hard to avoid defects that turn up as the log is cut, so most big mills don't like it.

Quarter-sawn logs provide lumber with characteristically uniform linear grain pattern. Quarter-sawing is usually reserved for oak, where it brings out oak's sought-after ray pattern. Some mills still quarter-saw logs, but they charge a premium, because quarter-sawing leaves a lot of waste. Sawing around the log yields narrower boards than flitch-sawing, but makes it easier to avoid defects.

Tricks of the Trade

You may be able to find a small local sawmill that will cater to your tastes. If you let sawmill workers know what kind of wood you like, they may call you when they get some. Small mills are more apt to flitch-cut logs, which would enable you to buy enough matched boards from the same tree to complete a large project and create a visual unity not possible with mismatched boards.

By edge-gluing boards with nearly identical grain patterns, woodworkers can create a mirror image effect, known as a book-match.

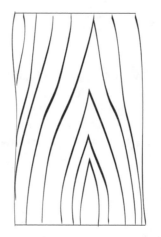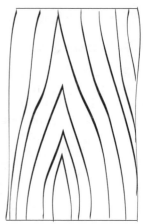

Wood Words

To bring down green (freshly cut) lumber's moisture content to the workable 6 to 12 percent range, lumber must be either air-dried or kiln-dried. **Air-dried** lumber dries over a period of years by controlled exposure to the atmosphere and is characterized by its rich color range. **Kiln-dried** lumber dries over a period of days in a heat- and humidity-controlled kiln. It is characterized by flatter color, but greater dimensional stability than air-dried lumber.

Drying Lumber

Because wood needs to be between 6 and 12 percent moisture content for most woodworking purposes, something must be done to green or wet lumber to dry it out before it can be used. Lumber is nearly always dried after it has been cut out of the log. Logs, half-logs, and even quarter-logs will *check* or crack as they dry because of internal stresses. These stresses dissipate more easily when lumber has been cut into boards (thicker boards still check in the drying process more easily than thinner ones). So after the sawing is over, the drying process begins. Wood is either *air-dried* or *kiln-dried*.

Air-Drying

In the old days, all wood was air-dried. In this process, the lumber is stacked out of direct sunlight and wind with *stickers*, or consistent spacers, between the boards so air can circulate on all sides evenly. Then the lumber is allowed to dry naturally over time. It is often weighted from the top to inhibit warping and twisting. The problem with air-drying is that it takes approximately one year per inch of thickness for the wood to dry; thus, a 3-inch-thick board needs to sit for about three years before it can be used. Extremely dense woods such as ebony, rosewood, and other tropical woods can take much longer. I recently cut up some ebony that I had sawn out of a log 15 years ago, only to discover it was still too wet!

It is possible to air-dry your own lumber if you have access to a mill that sells green lumber and have the space to store it. The trick is to set up an environment that won't foster fungus, but won't get too dry either; an outdoor shed that is open on one side is perfect. Keep piles well off the ground and stacked neatly with the same-size stickers throughout. Make sure the boards' ends have been coated with paint or the like so the moisture doesn't wick out too quickly. (For details on this process, check Appendix B, "Resources," for sources of information on the subject.)

Kiln-Drying

To avoid the delay of air-drying, most mills now kiln-dry their lumber, which means they dry it over a period of days or weeks in heated, moisture-controlled rooms with gently circulating air flow. Kiln-dried lumber is generally more stable than air-dried lumber, which means it's less prone to expansion and contraction. The problem with kiln-drying is that it tends to mute the wood's natural color variation, which is a major part of its beauty. For this reason, many purists prefer to work with air-dried lumber. Kiln-drying can also cause problems like case hardening and honeycombing (defects in the lumber due to the outside of the lumber drying more quickly than the inside) if it's not done properly. In case hardening cracks appear on the outside; in honeycombing they are concealed inside the board. Most of the hardwood lumber sold these days is kiln-dried, so unless you make a real effort, you're not likely to purchase air-dried wood.

I Woodn't Do That!

Do not start cutting a project out of a pile of freshly purchased air-dried lumber until you have checked it with a moisture meter. The potential for splitting, cracking, and project ruination is too great to risk taking some wood dealer's word about how long it's been seasoning. And, yes, if you're serious about woodworking, you need to buy a moisture meter.

Tricks of the Trade

When you get a batch of green lumber, write the date on it so you can keep track of the drying time. You think you'll remember when it came in, but I know I always forget if I don't mark it down.

Making the Grade

The last thing that happens to lumber at the sawmill is that it is graded. Grading is a way of classifying lumber by its objective qualities and its defects. I believe that lumber grading really concerns the commercial user, who wants to be able to order lumber of a particular quality, balanced against price, over the phone. As a small production woodworker, chances are you're going to pick out the lumber with an eye for how individual boards will work for particular parts. This process requires not just an eye, but subjective judgement, and grading isn't going to give you enough information. However, you should know the grading system because it can be helpful. If, for example, you call up a supplier and he tells you that he has only some inferior grade like No.2 Common, you know not to even bother going in unless you're building crates in which to ship your furniture.

The following is a list of the standard hardwood grades, as set forth by the National Hardwood Lumber Association (NHLA). I have not included the criteria for determining the grades, as it is very complicated and can vary from species to species. Suffice it to say that fine woodworkers usually use only Firsts and Seconds, abbreviated to *FAS* in the trade. A dealer might say, "I've got 1,000 board/feet of $^8/_4$ walnut, FAS."

The NHLA lumber grades are, in descending order ...

➤ Firsts.

➤ Seconds.

➤ Selects.

➤ No. 1 Common.

➤ No. 2 Common.

➤ No. 3A Common.

➤ No. 3B Common.

Wood Words

Wood sold as **rough lumber** has surfaces still fuzzy from the saw that cut it out of the log, and it's hard to see its grain patterns and potential defects. Many people prefer buying **dressed** or **surfaced** lumber, which is already planed on at least two sides, either because they don't have the equipment to do it themselves or because they like a clear picture of the grain pattern and color.

The Planing Mill

After the lumber is cut, dried, and graded, it either is sold as *rough lumber* or is sent to a planing mill. A planing mill *dresses* or *surfaces* it, running it through a planer to clean up the surfaces. A planing mill dresses at least the two primary surfaces (termed *surfaced two sides* and abbreviated to *S2S*) and often joints the two edges square and parallel (known as *surfaced four sides* or *S4S*). Some lumber, notably 2×4s, flooring, and other construction lumber, must also be milled to a consistent size.

The planing mill will also perform certain specialty operations to produce wood products. The mill may run wood through a *molder,* which uses special ground knives to cut profiles or shapes onto surfaces of the boards. It may cut tongue-and-groove profiles for flooring and wainscoting, or it may cut an elaborate profile for crown molding, baseboard, or some other purpose.

The Veneer Mill: Where the Best Logs Land

Unfortunately for those who prefer to work in solid wood, the best logs, ones that are exceptionally wide, figured, and so forth, generally go straight from the sawyer to the veneer mill. Veneer, the thin layer of wood laminated onto the surface of plywood and flake board, allows a much higher markup for the best-quality hardwood. You get so many square feet of veneer out of a log, compared to solid wood, that the veneer mill can afford to pay thousands of dollars for an exceptional log and spread out the cost. In a socialist sort of way, this is a good thing because it spreads the magic around: More people get to appreciate beautiful wood. But I can't help wishing that those extra-fine logs were available as solid lumber.

The veneer mill cuts the log into sheets of veneer, which are generally $1/10$ to $1/100$ of an inch thick, with $1/28$ and $1/40$ of an inch being the most common thickness. In the old days, veneer was sawn (some woodworkers still saw their own veneer on a band saw). But sawing creates waste, because the saw kerf turns a large portion of the wood into dust; it also requires that the veneer be cut thicker, which further cuts down on yield. Consequently, veneer is now almost exclusively sliced with a knife. To do this, the mill first boils the log until it becomes soft and wet so that the fibers will shear more easily. The log is then either sliced or rotary-cut.

Wood Lore

Old-fashioned sawn veneer was often as thick as $1/8$ of an inch. It had most of the advantages of thinner, sliced veneer, such as dimensional stability, less waste of precious wood, and better pattern matching potential, combined with some of the advantages of solid wood: It could be planed, and you didn't have to worry about sanding through it because it was so thick. It also lacked some of the flaws created by the slicing process, such as hairline cracks that show up dark in the finishing process. This is why some purists saw their own veneer.

Rotary-Cut Veneer

In the rotary-cut method, the log is held from either end in a device like a large lathe and spun. A long knife is then brought into the spinning circumference, and the veneer is sliced off in a continuous sheet, like tissue coming off a roll of toilet paper. This process is very efficient, but it creates a wild, undulating grain pattern that is not ideal for most furniture and fine cabinetmaking. Consequently, rotary-cut veneer is used mostly for construction grade and cheap architectural plywood.

Sliced Veneer

To slice veneer, the log is first sawn lengthwise into segments. Each segment is then held by an apparatus that brings it downward into a stationary knife, which slices off leaves one at a time. The leaves are kept in the same sequence in which they were cut, which facilitates future pattern matching, and dried. The complete stack of sequenced veneer is called a *flitch,* like a flitch of sawn lumber. Veneer dealers sell veneer in complete flitches, in smaller bundles of 32 or so sheets called *books,* or by the sheet.

Like sawn lumber, veneer is sliced for different grain patterns by angling the cuts at different orientations to the rings. You can buy flat-sliced, rift-sliced, and quarter-sliced veneer. Highly figured grain patterns that would be extremely rare in solid wood, like burls and crotch grain, are commonly available in veneer.

The Least You Need to Know

➤ Logs are cut in different ways for different grain patterns.

➤ Lumber must be either air-dried or kiln-dried to 6 to 12 percent moisture content.

➤ Lumber is graded for quality; woodworkers are generally interested only in Firsts and Seconds.

➤ Some lumber is sold in the rough and some is sold dressed or with planed surfaces.

➤ The best logs are usually sliced into veneer.

➤ Veneer is sliced in different ways for different grain patterns.

➤ High-quality veneer is sliced, not rotary-cut.

Chapter 12

Plywood: The Engineered Natural Material

In This Chapter

➤ Plywood versus solid wood

➤ Anatomy of a sheet of plywood

➤ The different types of plywood and other substrates

➤ Standard and semi-standard sizes

➤ Surface veneers and matching panels

By now you must be thinking, "This wood is ornery stuff. It cracks and twists, it expands and contracts when the weather changes, and it comes in unpredictable sizes and patterns. Forget natural materials; I think I'll become a plastic-worker instead of a woodworker. That plastic's good stuff." Fortunately, plywood is here to save the day.

Plywood is an engineered material. It's wood that has been housebroken, cured of most of its wildness and antisocial behavior. It doesn't expand and contract. It rarely cracks, and it comes in nice 4 × 8 sheets, in a variety of thicknesses. Sound ideal? Read on.

How Plywood Works

Plywood was probably first developed to deal with wood movement, which is wood's tendency to expand, contract, warp, and crack when the weather changes. *Veneer* was first used in ancient Egypt, but it was glued onto less desirable solid wood as a way to extend Egypt's limited stores of fine hardwoods. At some point, someone figured out that if you glued layers of veneer together with the grain direction running at 90 degrees to each layer, the resulting sandwich would be dimensionally stable.

By alternating grain direction, plywood negates wood's natural tendency to expand and contract across its width. Plywood panels are dimensionally stable and have equal strength in both directions.

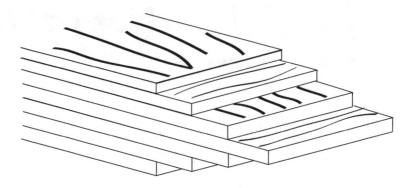

Wood Words

Veneers are the thin layers of wood that are glued together into plywood or glued onto the surface of a lesser-quality solid wood. Decorative surface veneers are called **face veneers** and are usually between $1/40$- and $1/28$-inch thick. The internal, structural veneers make up the **substrate,** or **core,** and are called the **core veneers;** they are usually about $1/16$-inch thick.

Because wood expands and contracts across the width of its grain, but not its length, each layer keeps the ones next to it from expanding or contracting across their width. The trick is that the panel must be balanced to be truly stable. A balanced panel has an odd number of layers: one center ply and symmetrical pairs on either side. A panel with an even number of layers with alternating grain directions would warp from unbalanced stresses when the outside layers changed moisture content.

Cores: It's What's Inside That Counts

Not all plywood has a veneer sandwich for its *core.* Although *veneer-core* plywood is the best known, other core materials have been developed to improve strength, lower cost, and minimize twisting and warping. Some you've probably heard of, such as flake board and fiberboard; you've been in contact with others, such as lumber-core, but you may not be aware of them.

Lasting Lumber-Core Plywood

When manufacturers sought to solve the sag problem that occurs when plywood is used for shelving and tabletops, they developed *lumber-core,* which has a core made up of narrow strips of wood, with the grain running in the same direction. The strips are laminated between two layers of veneer called *cross-banding,* whose grain runs opposite to theirs, and decorative face veneers are applied to the outside, with the grain direction reversed yet again.

The key to making the whole thing work is that the strips are not edge-glued together, they are held in place with minute gaps between them and the other layers of veneer. These gaps allow the strips to expand and contract ever so slightly as an autonomous unit, without causing the whole panel to move. Because most of wood's strength is in the direction of the grain, lumber-core is nearly as strong as solid wood in the direction the strips run in. I strongly recommend that you use lumber-core instead of veneer-core plywood whenever possible for bookshelves and any other weight-bearing cabinet part.

> **Wood Words**
>
> **Veneer–core plywood** has a core made from a sandwich of veneers. **Lumber–core plywood** has a core made from strips of wood bound together between layers of veneer. It may be solid flake or fiberboard, or it may be made up of a sandwich of either veneer, called **core-veneer,** or strips of wood and layers of veneer, called **lumber–core.** The core may require a layer of veneer below the face veneer to prevent surface cracks; this layer is called **cross-banding.**

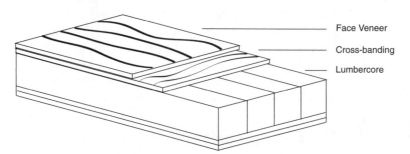

Face Veneer
Cross-banding
Lumbercore

By using strips of wood as its core, lumber-core has greater directional strength than core-veneer plywood, which makes it better suited to shelving and other applications that demand strength in one direction.

Flake Board and Fiberboard

Flake board (also called *particle board*) and *fiberboard* are composites made of wood chips or fibers that are reformed into panels. Flake board and its derivatives, such as *oriented strand board (OSB),* are made by combining wood fragments with an adhesive and forming the resulting mix into panels. Flake board has been around since the 1950s and has gotten rather sophisticated. Some flake boards have the fiber oriented for strength in a particular direction, or the fibers may be layered so that coarser particles are in the center and finer ones are near the surface for a smoother texture.

Fiberboard, or *hardboard,* is made by reducing the wood particles to individual fibers and making a slurry and then compressing the whole mess without adhesives, much like the way paper is made. Woodworkers mostly use medium-density fiberboard (called MDF) and sometimes use high-density hardboard. High-density hardboard is often called Masonite after the company that made the first hardboard in the 1920s. *Tempered masonite* has a resin surface treatment that makes it harder and water-resistant.

Fiberboard and particle board have a bad reputation because they are often misused. But they serve a valuable purpose. They save trees by using wood waste products. They are also affordable and make an extremely stable substrate for veneering. Their shortcomings are that they are heavy (especially fiberboard), have very little structural strength, generally dissolve in water, and create relatively toxic dust when machined. A new generation of fiberboards are being marketed that are waterproof and don't use toxic formaldehyde as an ingredient; ask your local plywood distributor whether he or she carries them.

I generally use flake board when I'm laying up veneer myself, because it makes a good substrate, and it's lighter than MDF and creates less irritating dust. I use MDF only when I'm planning a painted finish because it takes paint well, and you don't have to do anything to the edges before you paint them. Other types of plywood require *edge banding* (strips of solid wood or veneer) to cover the edges before painting.

Core-Veneer Variables

In addition to choosing among the different types of cores, you also have to think about which wood is being used in core-veneer and lumber-core plywood. Some use fir for the core material; others use poplar, aspen, or Luan mahogany (a "fake" mahogany grown in Southeast Asia). In my experience, the Luan mahogany, which has a reddish brown color, makes the best core because it's extremely stable, so the panels stay flat. It is also relatively free from *voids*, which are gaps left by missing knots and so forth. Fir core, which is yellowish, is the worst, with lots of voids and a disinclination to stay flat. Aspen (a light wood) and poplar (light greenish) are both fine. Check the edges when you receive the delivery; I've had dealers assure me they were sending poplar core, only to receive fir.

Playing with Platform Stock

Although much plywood used in cabinetmaking comes with a decorative veneer already applied to the surface, a category called *platform stock* is designed for woodworkers who want to do their own veneering. Platform stock may be made from flake board, MDF, Luan mahogany core-veneer, lumber-core, or some other stable core material. In addition, it usually has a number of particular features that make it suited to veneering.

Platform stock generally comes $1/16$-inch thinner than its nominal counterpart. For example, instead of being $3/4$ of an inch thick, it is $11/16$. This is because the veneer added to both sides will add about $1/16$ inches in thickness. Platform stock is also generally 1 inch larger in length and width than other types of plywood so that a full sheet can have its edges trimmed after veneering and end up at a finished size of four feet by eight feet.

If the plywood is core-veneer or lumber-core platform stock, then it will come with a choice of grain direction for the top veneers. This is because the layers must alternate direction, and the woodworker may need to run the decorative veneer either the long way or the short way, depending on the job.

Face Veneers: Book-Matching vs. Slip-Matching

Because most good decorative plywood uses sliced rather than rotary-cut veneer for its surface, there will be several leaves per face, with joints between each one. Each consecutive leaf should be placed in the order that it was cut out of the log, or flitch. Because the slices are so thin, the pattern on each surface is virtually identical to its predecessor's. This allows for two basic matching schemes: *book-matching* and *slip-matching*. When leaves of veneer are applied haphazardly with no consistent pattern, as happens on the secondary faces of some lower-grade plywood, it is called *random-matching*.

Wood Words

When a panel's veneer leaves are arranged so that the pattern on each is a mirror image of the ones adjacent, it is called **book-matching**. When they're arranged so that the pattern on each leaf is the same as the ones next to it, this arrangement is called **slip-matching**. **Random-matching** is the arrangement of leaves arbitrarily.

Book-Matching

The most common plywood veneer pattern is book-matching, where consecutive leaves are flipped with alternate faces pointing up. This gives the impression of a series of mirror images, which makes for smooth transitions over the joints and a feeling of symmetry.

If possible, center a glue line on a panel so that a balanced book-match is on each side. This arrangement gives the illusion of a custom veneer job. You may have to go through a pile of plywood to find sheets with veneer leaves that are the right width for your panel dimensions. (Here is where a sympathetic supplier who will let you pick your own material is important.)

Slip-Matching

Slip-matching is when veneers are laid out consecutively in the order they came from the flitch, with the same face up. This arrangement makes for a pattern that repeats across the panel, changing gradually as it goes. The slip-match is visually less static than the book-match because it is not symmetrical; it imparts a feeling of movement and, depending upon the grain, of direction.

Playing the Matching Panels Game

Whatever match you end up using, you may need to use more than one sheet for a project, and you may want the veneer pattern to match from one sheet to another. For this reason, sheets of plywood are kept together according to the veneer flitch used for the face and numbered sequentially in the order that the veneer leaves were cut from the log. If you look on the edge of each sheet, you will find two numbers printed: The first one is the flitch number and the second is the sheet's placement in the flitch. The second number allows you to keep track of the order if you want the pattern to match smoothly as panels progress around a room, as they do on kitchen cabinets.

Some flitches will have enough veneer for many sheets of plywood, and others will not; it depends upon the species and the individual tree. Some suppliers are not willing to let you pick through their stock because they don't want to break up the sequence of a batch of plywood.

Sizing Up Plywood

Unlike solid wood, plywood comes in standard dimensions. One of wood's most problematic aspects for manufacturers and woodworkers alike is the unpredictability of board sizes. So when plywood was developed as a product, standard sizing was a key selling point. The basic size for plywood width and length is four feet by eight feet. This size lends itself to house construction and architectural woodwork. It is the largest size that can be handled comfortably by a cross-section of workers, and it fits nicely in a light truck. It also rips nicely into floor-to-ceiling cabinets when you add a kick and crown molding.

The most common thickness of plywood is $3/4$ of an inch, which is the standard for cabinet boxes and doors as well as a host of construction applications from subflooring to sheathing. Other common thicknesses are $1/4$, $3/8$, and $1/2$ inch, which are commonly used for cabinet backs, drawer bottoms, and panels. Because these thinner panels are used for secondary purposes, they are not often available with the highest-quality surface veneers or may come with one good face and one not-so-good face. It's not necessary to use good veneer on both sides, because most people don't care what the underside of a drawer or the wall-side of a kitchen cabinet looks like. When a lower-quality veneer is used on the back of a sheet of plywood to balance the panel (not for decoration), it's called *backing veneer*.

Woodlore

Plywood is rarely the thickness it's supposed to be. There are two primary reasons for this: Either bean counters have figured out they can save a few percent by making the product $1/32$ inch thinner, or foreign plywood is made to metric measurements. Whatever the reason, plywood is usually thinner than its advertised thickness.

Plywood also comes in many semi-standard sizes. The sheets may be 4 feet by 10 feet, 5 feet by 8 feet, or 5 feet by 10 feet. Thicknesses of $5/8$, $7/8$, 1, and $1^1/4$ inches may be available. Ask your supplier what he or she stocks. Selection will be limited in oddball sizes. The key is to plan projects around what you know is available. Don't design something that requires 8 feet, 1 inch-thick lengths of cherry ply if it could easily be 7 feet, 11 inches, because you'll pay a premium for 10-foot sheets—if they're available in the first place. And don't plan on getting two 24-inch rips out of a 4-foot-wide piece. By the time you've cleaned up the factory edge and lost the saw kerf thickness when ripping the plywood, you'll be lucky to get $23^3/4$-inch pieces. Remember that every saw kerf turns about $1/8$ inch of material into dust.

Grading Plywood Grading

Like solid wood, plywood is graded for quality. Grading is based on color, pattern matching, and freedom from defects or patches. The premium grades are labeled with a letter on the primary face and a number on the secondary face; *A* and *1* are the top grades, with lesser grades denoted by progressive letters or numbers. Thus, an A-1 is the top-shelf grade. Plywood often comes with one premium face and one face with a lesser grade; this type of plywood is called A-2 or A-3. There is some confusion in the industry with different terms for different grades; some suppliers use terms like *cabinet-grade* or *furniture-grade* (for some reason, furniture-grade is lower than cabinet-grade).

The best way to buy plywood is to go and pick it out yourself. As a noncommercial user, you are probably interested only in the best grades. Look for pattern matching that lends itself to your project, good glue joints, good color, and wide, consecutive veneer leaves. The best plywood has wide leaves and therefore fewer joints per face.

Pointers on Buying Plywood

Many lumberyards sell low-quality plywood. When you need plywood for fine wood-working, however, you generally want something better than the run-of-the-mill, construction-grade stuff.

The best place to buy premium, hardwood-veneered, and cabinet-grade plywood is at a plywood specialist. Not only do specialists have a better selection, quality, and price, they also offer sequenced panels, where all the face veneers are cut sequentially out of the same log. This allows you to match color and grain patterns; the grain pattern will be virtually identical from one panel to the next. They also have plywood-support products, such as matching edge banding, which is used to cover unveneered plywood edges.

Make sure the plywood yard stores the wood in flat, horizontal piles and be suspicious of top and bottom sheets. These sheets tend to get banged up, and salesmen will try to pawn them off on the unsuspecting. Not all yards will let you pick out your own sheets; I won't use a yard that doesn't.

Plywood is sold by the sheet, but it is priced by the square foot. Some yards will sense that you're a noncommercial customer and give you per sheet prices, but if you want to sound like a pro, you can ask them the square foot price. I have had students say, "You said teak plywood was expensive, but it's only $4.10 per sheet!" To which I have to reply, "No, that price is per square foot; multiply that price by 32."

Wrestling with Edges

The big problem with plywood is what to do about the edges. Those funky lamina-tions just don't go with an elegant, book-matched, walnut face veneer. So most of the time, you just have to cover up edges with *edge banding*. You can use either solid edge banding or veneer edge banding.

Veneer edge banding comes in many forms. If you're using a relatively common sur-face veneer, your supplier should be able to supply rolls of veneer tape of various lengths. Veneer tape is just a strip of veneer made of spliced-together sections that should be $1/16$ to $1/8$ inch wider than your plywood edge. If veneer tape is not available for some exotic surface veneer you're using, you can make your own out of pieces of veneer.

Some veneer tape has a paper backing to help prevent splitting, and some comes with a hot-melt glue so it can be ironed on. I like the former, and I find that the latter leaves a thick, ugly glue line. If the veneer tape is not pre-glued, I recommend using yellow carpenter's glue and clamping the tape on with blocking strips or ironing it on; yellow glue is thermosetting. After the glue has set, the tape can be trimmed flush with the face of the panel, using a small router and flush trim bit, a sharp knife, or a chisel.

You have to make solid edging yourself by ripping strips of solid wood and clamping them on. It's more of a production to trim, but it makes for a much tougher edge on any part that is going to be exposed to traffic.

Some plywood is designed with decorative edges; the most common variety is called Baltic Birch, after its region of origin. The veneer laminations are very thin, less than $1/16$-inch thick, and they look good on modernist-style work. This plywood eliminates the need for edge banding, but the de-sign of the piece must be appropriate, or it will look dumb. You don't want to see a laminated edge of any sort on a Chippendale sideboard.

I Woodn't Do That!

Some people use contact ce-ment to apply edge tape, but I don't recommend it for any type of veneering. Contact cement breaks down with exposure to air, and because wood is porous, it's only a matter of time before the tape starts peeling.

The Least You Need to Know

➤ Plywood, because of its dimensional stability, alleviates a lot of the problems associated with wood.

➤ Plywood may have a core made of wood pulp, layers of veneer, or strips of wood sandwiched between veneer.

➤ Some plywood comes with a decorative surface veneer, some is ready to be veneered, and some is ready for paint.

➤ Decorative surface veneer may be book-matched or slip-matched.

➤ You can buy matching sheets of plywood with veneer cut sequentially from the same log.

➤ Plywood is graded for the quality of its surface veneers.

➤ Plywood comes in standard thicknesses, widths, and lengths, and it's good to design a project with the standard dimensions in mind.

➤ Plywood edges may be covered with strips of veneer or solid wood, painted, or used decoratively.

Chapter 13

Words to the Wise About Storing Wood

In This Chapter

➤ Storing solid wood when you get it home

➤ Dead stacking your lumber

➤ Precutting and premilling parts

➤ Building a lumber rack

➤ Storing plywood the right way

How you store your lumber has a great effect on how your work progresses. Nice, straight boards can become a pile of twisted, cupped lumber if left to their own devices. It's up to you to protect them from moisture, direct sunlight, and the other forces that conspire to ruin good wood, and allow them to adjust to the climate of your workshop.

Building a lumber rack and setting up plywood storage are the first steps. Precutting lumber to relieve internal stresses and speed-drying come next. This chapter shows you how to circumvent many of the problems that result from wood movement.

Why Store Solid Wood?

Inevitably, you have to store some lumber, if only the parts for the project you're working on at the moment, and for reasons that may or may not be obvious by now,

Tricks of the Trade

It's often a good strategy to develop projects around the lumber you have. If, for example, you have two $1^{1}/_{2}$-inch by 13-inch by 12-feet stunning cherry boards and some thicker stock all from the same log, then you can make a 49-inch by $5^{1}/_{2}$-foot dining table. Projects seem to have more grace when the materials suggest the form.

Wood Words

To **dead stack** lumber means to stack boards on top of each other without space between them, which slows down moisture exchange with the ambient air. **Stickering** boards means to stack them with strips of wood between them, called **stickers,** which facilitates air circulation and moisture exchange.

you can't just throw it in a heap on the ground. Plus, as the project progresses, you will find yourself with a growing pile of scraps that are too good to throw out and need to be kept somewhere until opportunity knocks.

If you're lucky enough to have room to store piles of lumber, then lumber storage takes on a new function. It allows you to buy exceptional lumber when it's available rather than mediocre lumber when you're desperate. Great deals on exotic wood always seem to present themselves when you're broke, have no room, and can't think of an appropriate project. A good storage area will solve the second of these problems and let you bide your time until the third one sorts itself out. (I leave the money issue up to you.)

Having ample lumber storage also allows you to dry your own lumber. Small sawmills frequently sell choice logs or half-logs milled, but still green. You can buy matching boards, perhaps cut to your own specifications, at a small sawmill for a fraction of what it would cost in a lumberyard. Don't forget that air-dried wood usually has better color than kiln-dried. The only catch is that you have to store it for a few years while it dries.

Store Smart

The goals with wood storage are to keep it flat, organized, and accessible and to gradually bring its moisture content to the same level as your workshop (which should itself be typical of your region). Once wood bows, twists, cups, or cracks, it's too late; you can't bring it back. Uneven moisture exchange is the primary danger, but wood will also move if it's forced by pressure or uneven support.

I like to store wood horizontally in piles. Because I live in a city, I keep mine on racks in my basement (not an ideal location because of a tendency toward dampness, but I have a dehumidifier down there). I've built racks made from arms cantilevered off the wall, so one side is open for easy access. The arms are close enough together that the boards won't sag from one to another and are lined up parallel and level.

If the lumber is already dry, I *dead stack* it, which means I lay boards directly on top of each other without *stickers* or other spacers that would allow air to circulate around them. By limiting air exposure, I slow down the warp-inducing effects of sudden changes in ambient moisture. To protect the top and bottom boards, I sandwich the pile between pieces of scrap construction-grade plywood.

If the lumber is green and needs drying, I *sticker* it. Stickers are strips of wood that hold the boards apart so that air can circulate over the two primary faces. It's important that the stickers are of consistent thickness, or the boards may not be supported evenly. I rip all my stickers at $^3/_4$ inch in both directions. That way, I don't have to worry about which side is which.

The stickers must be …

➤ Lined up vertically, or they'll cause the boards to bow.

➤ Long enough to support the entire width of the boards.

➤ Spaced close enough so that the boards don't sag under their own weight. Green lumber should not be kept in an overly dry environment, or it will crack.

I Woodn't Do That!

The worst thing you can do to a board is place it so one face is exposed to air and the other is not. This will cause the board to cup or warp for sure because the side getting air wicks moisture to correct any imbalance with the ambient humidity at a faster rate than the covered side. For this reason, you frequently see cupping in the top board on a pile.

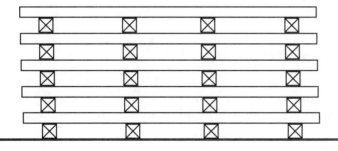

The pile on the top is dead stacked with scrap plywood top and bottom. The pile on the bottom is stickered properly so that the boards stay flat and air circulates.

Taking It Outside

If you have space to build a simple drying shed, outdoor storage is a good way to store larger amounts of wood, especially if you're drying green lumber. The shed should …

➤ Be open on two adjacent sides so that air circulates, but wind doesn't overdry the surface of the boards.

➤ Have an overhanging roof to protect the boards from direct sunlight.

In addition, the stacks should be raised a foot or two off the ground to protect the lumber from excessive moisture and insects.

Lumber can be stacked outside without a shed, but it should be next to a building that blocks the wind and covered with a sheet of corrugated metal or scrap plyood to screen it from the sun. Loosely covering the sides with plastic to keep out the rain is a good idea, too.

I Woodn't Do That!

Cement floors can wreak havoc on lumber. They tend to hold moisture, and when wood is stacked on top of cement, it will suck up the water like a sponge. This quality, along with its tendency to induce leg fatigue, makes cement a less-than-ideal surface for a shop floor.

Letting Your Lumber Adapt

Bring the lumber inside at least two weeks before you start cutting it up and stickering it to let it acclimatize to your workshop. Chances are it will dry out as it sits indoors. The longer it has to adjust, the less likely it will be to warp or crack when you start cutting it.

When boards are about to be cut, I often just lean them up against the wall rather then stack them. This allows air to circulate around the boards while letting me get a good look at them so I can think about how I'm going to cut out parts for the best grain patterns. The trick is to lean them vertically enough so that they don't sag, but angled enough so that they're stable. Many woodworkers keep all their lumber leaning against the wall, but I find it difficult to keep organized that way.

Make Sure with a Moisture Meter

Moisture meters read moisture content in wood by passing current between two sharpened electrodes that are jammed into the board in question. They display the reading, usually digitally, in percentage points. The ideal range for woodworking is within 6 to 12 percent.

Woodlore

I did some cabinetry once in a very fancy New York City townhouse renovation. (The budget was around $8 million.) When the wood flooring came in, the workers stacked it in the basement on a week-old cement pour, where it stayed for two months. The lumber, beautiful three-inch-wide ash boards, sat there in the humid basement on the still-wet cement, soaking up water like a sponge. When they laid the ash into an elaborate parquet pattern, it looked stunning. Then they turned the heat on. "And how the boards did shrink," to quote Coleridge. Within a month, $1/8$-inch gaps had opened up between each board, and most of the boards were cupped noticeably. The entire floor had to be redone, all for want of a moisture meter.

Moisture meters can be very useful for any woodworker and are essential for anyone drying his or her own lumber. There's no telling what's happened to lumber at a yard. Someone may have forklifted a pile of wood into a puddle or left it outside in the rain. I've seen some disasters that could have been averted by a moisture meter. Although some people claim that they can tell the moisture content by feel, I've never met anyone who was really accurate. I can tell if wood is green, for example, but I can't tell the difference between 15 percent and 8 percent moisture.

Storing Precut Lumber

If at all possible, I like to rough-cut solid wood parts slightly oversize and let them sit for a couple of weeks before I mill them. Cutting the wood helps release internal stresses in the wood and allows its moisture content to equalize with the shop's current ambient humidity level more quickly than whole boards would.

Often the moisture content of a board's surface is different than it is in the center of the board. The smaller the piece, the quicker it can respond to fluctuations in the humidity. If you slice a board into small pieces, and a dramatic difference exists in the moisture content at the center of the board, it may warp or bow. By cutting parts oversize and letting them season, you end up with less wood movement later, during the building process.

After cutting the parts, I like to stack them in the warmest, driest part of the shop (but not in front of a window or heater), either stickered or crisscrossed so that air can get to all sides, especially the freshly cut ones. Sometimes it's easiest to stack the parts out of the way on sawhorses.

Building a Lumber Rack

As I mentioned earlier, I like cantilevered supports for lumber storage. Several years ago, when I had a larger shop, I bought a heavy-duty, metal, cantilevered storage system. This sort of thing is great if you have the space and money for it, because you don't have to worry about overloading it. It's a bit much, however, for the average hobbyist.

You can make your own rack relatively easily out of construction lumber; you just have to be sure that it is strong enough. I recommend building it out of 4×4s with plywood gussets. You also have to be sure the wall it goes against can support the stress; a masonry wall is ideal. Don't make the arms too long (12 to 14 inches maximum), and don't overload it!

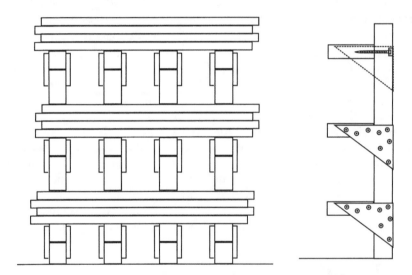

You can adjust the dimensions and number of shelves of the lumber rack to fit your space. The 4×4s should be lag-bolted together, and the plywood gussets should be glued and screwed on with #12 2-inch flat-head screws.

I store scrap wood on shelves. I don't like this method, but I've never found a satisfactory way to store scraps. I've tried bins and cubbies, but no matter what I do, my scrap wood is always a disorganized mess. If you come up with a good system for storing all the pieces that wind up on the cutting room floor, let me know. The best trick for organizing scraps is to know when to throw them out. Woodworkers tend to be a thrifty bunch and want to hang on to every hangnail they've ever clipped.

Sensible Plywood Storage

Like lumber, plywood needs to be kept flat. The task is easier, though, because plywood generally has consistent dimensions and thickness. Although plywood is dimensionally stable, it will warp if one side is exposed to air and the other is not. You also have to be more careful with plywood's surface than you do with solid lumber, because it has already been sanded and is covered with $1/40$-inch of veneer.

I like to store large pieces of plywood vertically in bays, with the faces perpendicular to the wall, like suits in a closet. This arrangement allows me to sort through and pull out a sheet in the middle more easily than if it were stacked vertically. It also makes for less lifting. I keep 4×8-foot sheets of cardboard on the outsides of the plywood to help reduce warping from moisture imbalance.

Half-sheets and rips can be kept in the full-sheet rack, but small scraps should be kept separately. As I do with solid scraps, I like to keep smaller plywood scraps on shelves, but vertically. Again, this arrangement makes sorting easier.

Tricks of the Trade

I like to write the species and dimensions of each piece of plywood on the visible edge, so I don't have to flip through the whole pile to figure out what stock I have.

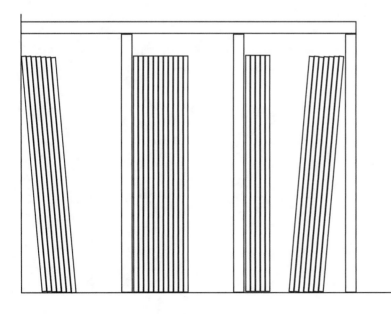

I like to store plywood vertically, in bays, for easy sorting.

The Least You Need to Know

➤ Proper wood storage helps keep lumber flat, organized, accessible, and dry.

➤ Having an ample storage area allows you to buy outstanding lumber when it's available and stockpile it until you're ready.

➤ A large storage area allows you to air-dry your own lumber.

➤ Stickering facilitates air circulation for drying.

➤ A moisture meter is a good investment.

➤ Wood should be kept away from sunlight and moisture.

Part 4

Putting It All Together: Means and Methods

When you think of fine woodworking you think of dovetails, mortise-and-tenon joints, and all the elaborate joinery of traditional furniture-making. Although there are many aspects to woodworking, the joinery is what has the greatest mystique and poses the most difficulty to the beginner. Once learned, however, joinery can provide tremendous satisfaction, because it is in the joinery that everything literally comes together.

Joinery is something of a science, with guiding principles, a bit of chemistry, and a healthy dose of seat-of-the-pants engineering. This section explains some of the mysteries, such as what joints to use in which situation, how adhesives work with woodworking joints, what the difference is between frame and carcass construction, and when and how to use screws and nails. Although these chapters may take some of the romance out of traditional joinery, they should also correct some of the myths and old wives' tales you may have picked up and, most important, help keep your projects together for future generations.

Chapter 14

All About Adhesives

In This Chapter

➤ Chemical bonds versus mechanical bonds

➤ The importance of long grain glue surfaces

➤ Different glues for different jobs

➤ Carpenter's glue, epoxies, plastic resin glues, hide glues, and some new additions

➤ The importance of clamping

The world of adhesives used to be small. You boiled down some horse hides and hooves or maybe some fish bones until you had a nice murky pudding, which you then smeared on your wood. Nowadays, however, there are lots of choices. Modern chemistry has greatly improved the adhesive arsenal.

Today's adhesives have lessened the need for elaborate joinery because they work so darn well. However, different adhesives have very different properties, and it's important to know which one to use in each application.

Bond: Chemical vs. Mechanical

One way to carve up the glue pie is to categorize glues by the way in which they bond: chemically or mechanically. Mechanically bonding adhesives work like cement or asphalt by keying into irregularities in the surfaces being bonded and binding them together as a third element. Chemically bonding adhesives require that the surfaces be clamped together without gaps, so the glue can cause the wood fibers to cross-link, creating a molecular attachment. You don't want surface irregularities with chemically bonding glue because they prevent the fibers from *cross-linking*.

When you edge-join boards, it's important to have plenty of clamping pressure. Space the clamps evenly, and then check the joint and add or move clamps where it's not coming together. Note: Alternating clamps over and under helps even out the pressure and prevents the work from bowing.

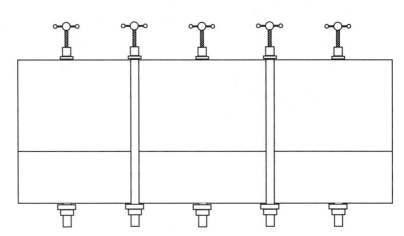

The advantage of *chemically bonding adhesives*, such as white and yellow carpenter's glue, is that they leave nearly invisible glue lines (when used properly). The problem with them is that they work best when surfaces being glued are perfectly smooth, joints are precisely machined, and lots of clamping pressure is applied. They have poor gap-filling properties. In other words, if the surfaces don't mate perfectly, chemical bonding adhesives don't fill in the boo-boos (a technical term). Obviously, they have some mechanical bonding characteristics, or they wouldn't be the most common glues sold in hardware stores to your average homeowner, who uses them for less-than-perfect joints. But they are much stronger when you can make a good chemical bond.

Mechanically bonding adhesives, such as epoxies, plastic resin glues, and mastics, work best with slightly rough surfaces, because they can grab hold of the irregularities. This quality can be a real advantage when you are gluing porous materials or if you can't machine the surfaces as perfectly as you might like. Mechanically bonding adhesives also tend to have much better gap-filling abilities, which can compensate for sloppily cut joints, poorly machined surfaces, and so forth. The problem with these adhesives is that they tend to leave more visible glue lines.

Wood Words

Mechanically bonding adhesives key into irregularities in the glue surfaces and lock the parts together like cement. **Chemically bonding adhesives** rely on smooth surfaces to cause the fibers themselves to interlock or **cross-link** with each other, forming a chemical bond.

Long Grain: Yes! End Grain: No!

One of the lesser-known facts about glue among the general population is that most adhesives don't work on *end grain*. On a normal board, the surfaces at the end, where all those fibers are sliced off perpendicular to the grain direction, are called end grain. The ends of the fibers act like straws, wicking glue away from the joint. Chemical bonding glues are particularly pathetic at gluing end grain. Some mechanically bonding glues, such as epoxy, work a little bit better with some coaxing. But end grain glue joints tend to have a short life expectancy.

Wood Words

A proper glue joint is made up of long grain–to–long grain glue surfaces. **Long grain** means any of the surfaces of the board that are more or less parallel to the direction of the grain and fibers. **End grain,** which does not generally glue well, is found on any surface that is perpendicular to the grain direction.

A *long grain-to-long grain* glue surface is what you want for a good joint. On this surface, the fibers bond along their length. Long grain-to-long grain glue surface is what allows the chemically bonding glues to do their molecular cross-link thing. One of the primary reasons that wood joints become complex is the struggle to get as much long grain-to-long grain glue surface as possible out of pieces that are butting into each other at right angles (such as finger joints, double mortise, and tenons).

Choosing the Glue for the Job

It's a good thing that there are so many different types of adhesive, because you run into so many different gluing situations in woodworking. You sometimes hear woodworkers say things like, "I only use X-type glue; those Y-type glues stink." This statement is foolish; modern science has bestowed upon us many types of glue with different characteristics; smart craftspeople figure out the differences and tailor the glue choice to the task.

When you're doing bent lamination, you want gap-filling properties, long *working time,* and good fiber saturation, so epoxy might be a good solution. Veneering requires a rigid glue film but low fiber saturation, or it'll wick through the veneer and mar the surface: Urea-formaldehyde glue might be the answer. When gluing together boards for a tabletop, or if toxicity is an issue, white or yellow carpenter's glue is a good choice. You get the idea. As they say in baseball: "You can't tell the players without a program," so what follows is a list of adhesives with a general description of their properties and applications.

White Glue

White glue, sometimes called white carpenter's glue, is a polyvinyl acetate emulsion (PVA). Developed in the 1920s, it is the classic wood glue we all grew up with and is

still a favorite because of its versatility, low toxicity, ease of cleanup, and effectiveness at bonding wood. It provides a chemical bond of long grain-to-long grain glue surfaces. It's water-soluble, and it's cheap. It is also thermosetting, which means you can speed its set time and likewise redissolve the glue by adding heat, which makes later repairs easier.

Its drawbacks are that it has a fairly short working time, so you have to get the work clamped up fast. Also, it is not water-resistant, so it should not be used on exterior work or anything else that may contact water. It also has a tendency to *creep* over time. Glue creep occurs when the glue line stays slightly elastic, and over time, the parts shift ever so slightly.

The PVA glues (white and yellow) are by far the most popular wood adhesives, and they are great for gluing joints. White glue is particularly well-suited to edge-joining boards, because of its ability to leave an almost invisible glue line. White glue is less well-suited to veneering, where its flexibility and tendency to creep can lead to surface checks.

Tricks of the Trade

The key to working with white and yellow carpenter's glue is a clean, flat glue surface and plenty of clamping pressure. Plastic resin glues are more forgiving of lower clamping pressure, although less pressure leads to thicker glue lines. Epoxies and hide glue work better with limited pressure; high pressure can starve the joint of glue.

Yellow Glue

Yellow glue, or yellow carpenter's glue, is a next-generation version of white glue, called a modified PVA. It is very similar to white glue, but it has less of a tendency to creep and a slightly faster set-up time. It is more heat-resistant, and some versions are quite water-resistant. Its applications are similar to white glue's, but it generally works slightly better in most applications, especially veneering.

Plastic Resin Glues

Plastic resin glues come in a variety of types. Some are urea-formaldehyde formulations, and others use a resorcinol-formaldehyde combination. These glues generally require mixing. Some come as a powder that must be mixed with water, and others are two-part adhesives, where you mix liquid resin and powder catalyst in a particular ratio. The latter type has the advantage that you can vary the working time (and set time as well) by adjusting the mix ratio within a range. Some manufacturers offer a color choice for matching either light or dark wood.

Plastic resin glues are water-resistant and extremely rigid when dry, which means they don't creep. Most also have good gap-filling properties, especially the two-part variety. Plastic resin glues are great for veneering, laminations (especially bent laminations, where their rigidity helps hold curves in place), and any outdoor joinery that will be exposed to water.

Their main drawbacks are their toxicity and difficulty to mix. You should always wear a good dust mask when mixing plastic resin glue and wear gloves during the entire time you're working with it. Plastic resin glues are also more expensive then PVA glues.

Epoxy Resins

Epoxies have become increasingly popular with woodworkers the past few years. They were first adopted by boat builders, who appreciated their resistance to water; unlike plastic resin, they can be formulated to penetrate deeply into laminations and create a fiber-resin composite that is extremely strong and waterproof.

Not all epoxies are created equal, though. Some are formulated to remain flexible; others set up stiff. Some have a long setup time, and some set up quickly. I don't recommend those little tubes of five-minute epoxy for use on anything important. Instead, look for one of the quality brands, such as Gougeon Brothers' West System, which includes an array of thickeners, protective gear, mixing aids, applicators, and different hardeners that allow you to control the set time over a wide time range. The Gougeon Brothers also publish several pamphlets that have epoxy how-to information and a hardbound book on boat building that has techniques you can apply to all types of woodworking.

Epoxy's drawbacks are that it is expensive, a pain to clean up (I recommend using the solvent acetone for cleanup), and quite toxic. You have to avoid skin contact with both the liquid glue and any sanding dust until it has cured thoroughly; the sanding dust is also toxic to inhale. You should use a respirator with an organic vapor

I Woodn't Do That!

Don't leave any glue on the surface of the wood. It will appear as a smear once the finish is put on, but it is often invisible up until that time. Try to clean up all glue before it dries, by using damp rags and chisels. Afterwards, check for any you may have missed by dampening the surface with water, which will penetrate and darken the bare wood, but not the leftover glue.

Tricks of the Trade

Some resinous tropical woods do not glue well. The resins on glue surfaces prevent the adhesives from bonding. To remedy this problem, wipe all joint surfaces with acetone immediately before gluing up parts to clean off the resins.

153

filter when working with it and follow all the manufacturer's warnings. Its super-penetrating characteristic can also be a pain in the neck, because epoxy spilled on a wood surface will go deep into the pores and stain it permanently.

I find epoxy unsurpassed for bent lamination and for gluing jobs that will be exposed to extreme weather conditions. It is also excellent for situations where you need gap-filling properties, but you may need to add thickeners so it doesn't all get sucked into the wood fibers.

Bent laminations are prone to gaps because it's hard to get even clamping pressure; they also tend to spring one way or another after they're released from the clamps. Epoxy and plastic resin glues fill gaps and set up hard, which minimizes spring back. They also have a long working time, which is easier on the nerves.

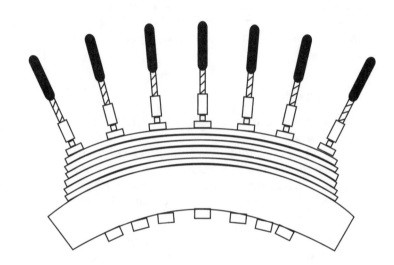

Hide Glue

Although it has a reputation as being old-fashioned, hide glue can still be very useful. It's made from the melted down hides and hooves of cattle (this stuff is not for vegans). It comes in the form of dried pellets, which must be remelted in a thermostatically controlled double boiler every time you use it. Sound complicated? It is, a little. It also smells terrible.

Still, it's great in situations where you can't use clamps, because you have to hold the parts together only for a few minutes while the glue cools to get a strong bond. I also use it occasionally for *hammer veneering,* a slightly archaic and complicated process for laying down veneer without a press that comes in handy sometimes.

Contact Cement

Contact cement has a somewhat cheesy reputation and deservedly so. It's okay for gluing down plastic laminate, but it should not be used for gluing down veneer or any other wood-to-wood application. It's broken down by contact with air, and because wood is porous, contact cement doesn't hold up well. It also tends to leave unsightly glue lines.

Other Glues

There are various other glues that are used in woodworking from time to time:

➤ **Construction adhesive** is a gooey, slow-drying mastic that can be useful when you are installing cabinets.

➤ **Cyanoacrylate ester adhesives**, such as Crazy Glue and Hot Stuff, can be useful for making jigs and for specialized situations where you can't use clamps.

➤ **Polyurethane glues** are a recent arrival in the woodworker's quiver. I've tried them only a couple of times and found them to be a foamy mess, but by all means, experiment with them; I know woodworkers who swear by them.

Woodlore

You have to be a bit careful with new products, especially finishes and adhesives. They don't have enough of a track record for us to know how well they hold up. Tage Frid, the octogenarian Danish master woodworker I studied with, used to tell a story of a Danish furniture company that started using a new, untried adhesive on all their wares during the 1930s. It seemed that after about five years the glue failed completely, leaving a pile of parts and peeled veneer. This simple mistake caused the company to go bankrupt. Tage used to say you shouldn't use an adhesive that hadn't been on the market less than 15 years.

Too Much of a Good Thing?

"How much glue do I use?" you ask. Probably less then you think. Generally, when I see beginners gluing up, it looks like a custard pie fight. I remember gluing up a table when I was first studying woodworking and a more senior student asking sarcastically, "Got enough glue there?" as it ran in puddles on the floor. You don't need much; the trick is to put it in the right place.

It's important to get a thin film on both mating surfaces that are to touch, but too much glue is hard to clean up and can affect the finish of a piece. Plus, when you're still a novice, you tend to be nervous at glue-up time, which doesn't lead to tidy glue application.

It can be hard for a pro to spread glue on all the surfaces on a complicated glue-up in the working time allotted on the back of a glue bottle. Wherever possible, glue up sections of the project separately, and then assemble the sections into the whole. There should be just an even line of small beads of glue along the joint, not dripping stalactites. The glue that is pressed out of the joint is called, appropriately, *squeeze-out*.

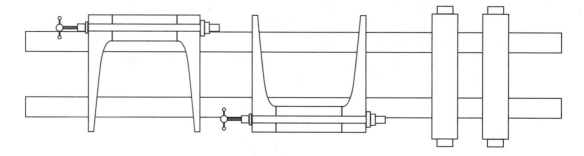

It can be less stressful and yield better results to glue up small sections first, and then glue these sections into the whole.

There are different theories about how to clean up glue. Some like to wait until it dries a bit to the point where it's leather hard. I like to clean it up immediately with a chisel that I keep dulled on whetstone so its edges won't dig into the wood, followed by a good rubbing with a slightly damp (not soaking wet) rag and a thorough drying. Under no conditions should you let the glue dry completely; going home without cleaning up squeeze-out is the mark of the boob. It is much more work to clean up dry glue, and dry glue nearly always damages the surface.

The Least You Need to Know

➤ Some glues rely on a chemical bond, causing wood fibers to cross-link on a molecular level.

➤ Other glues work primarily mechanically, keying into surface irregularities and cementing parts together.

➤ Different glues work best in different situations.

➤ Some glues are toxic, so read all safety precautions.

➤ Glues with gap-filling properties can save sloppy joinery and other boo-boos in a pinch.

➤ Clean up glue right after you are done gluing up.

Chapter 15

Frame Joints: The Skeleton as a Model

In This Chapter

➤ An overview of joinery

➤ The two categories: frame joinery and carcass joinery

➤ The classic frame joints

➤ A look at some classic frame structures

➤ A frame joint job description

If adhesives and finishing are the chemistry of woodworking, then joinery is the engineering side of woodworking. Joinery is what makes that table support your Thanksgiving spread and what keeps that frame-and-panel door swinging on its hundredth birthday. Joinery is how woodworkers hold the parts together so that they can withstand the myriad forces conspiring to break them apart while still accommodating wood movement and the need for long grain-to-long grain glue surfaces. The table has to do all this and look presentable.

Joinery is tricky, but fortunately we woodworkers have a few years of field-testing behind us to look back on. At this point, we've figured out what works and what doesn't. You have only to look through an antique shop and note the repairs to get some empirical knowledge about furniture engineering. This chapter examines the joints that are the staples of frame joinery and looks at some classic structures that use them.

Joinery: Who Needs It?

If life were simpler, you could just glue the ends of a table's *stretcher* to the side of its legs and then nail the top onto that. Unfortunately, wood is a finicky material, as you've learned by now, and a table constructed like that would self-destruct without ever being touched by human hands. First of all, the end grain of the stretchers doesn't work as glue surface; glue doesn't bond properly to it. During the first change of seasons, with a corresponding change of humidity, the wood will either expand or contract across its width; as the stretcher expands vertically and the leg doesn't (it's busy expanding horizontally), the joint will fail.

The tabletop, meanwhile, will also be expanding across its grain direction, and because white oak, for example, can change width by $3/16$ inch per foot from one season to the next, a 42-inch tabletop can move nearly $3/4$ inch! The force of wood movement is ineluctable, like weeds growing in asphalt; the nails will not hold the wood, and something will split.

Well-planned joinery avoids this sort of catastrophe. It works structurally in a dynamic way, allowing wood to move, as it inevitably will, without disasters. Later on in the chapter, we'll look at how a table should be constructed so as to ensure a long and fruitful life.

Wood Words

Frame joinery creates skeletal structure from frame parts, usually joined at right angles to each other, which may be filled in with **floating** (not glued in place) panels to create planes. The horizontal connecting members are called **stretchers** (in door construction, they're called **rails**). **Carcass joinery** starts with planes of wood that are used structurally and joined along common edges. It lends itself particularly to plywood construction.

Joinery: Frame vs. Carcass

Two different systems of joinery are used in woodworking: *frame joints* and *carcass joints*. Frame joinery works to create a skeleton-like structure or frame. It may contain flat, *floating* panels held within its frame members; these panels are not structural, but float inside the frame. Traditional chair construction uses frame joinery because it provides strength with lightness. The classic frame-and-panel door uses frame construction because the frame diminishes the overall wood movement that a door made of edge-glued boards would have. The filler panels are not glued into the frame, but float in a groove, which allows them to move autonomously with seasonal humidity changes.

Carcass joinery uses flat planes of either solid wood or plywood, which join at the edges to create boxes or carcasses. It is used primarily on cabinets, where the need for enclosure overshadows the need for strong structure. Carcass joinery does not try to limit wood movement; it just orients the planes so that they're moving in the same direction, and the parts don't break each other apart. I discuss carcass joinery in depth in Chapter 16, "Carcass Joinery: The Box as a Model."

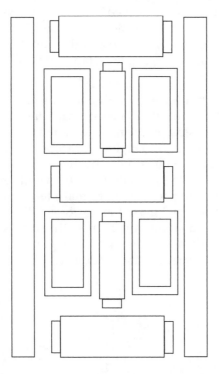

The frame of a classic frame-and-panel door provides structure while panels float unglued in a groove. A solid door would bind in summer and hang loose in winter, but the frame reduces overall dimensional change, making the door more stable.

Classic Frame Joints and Not–So–Classic Variations

The sections that follow describe a cross-section of popular frame joints. They have different applications based on their strength, ease of manufacture, and aesthetic considerations. Some, such as the mortise and tenon, have been in use for hundreds of years, yet none are obsolete. The mortise and tenon is still an ideal joint; it's just time-consuming to cut in production.

The attributes of a good joint are as follows:

➤ Plenty of long grain-to-long grain glue surface

➤ Enough wood for structural strength

➤ Some way of accommodating wood movement

➤ Decent appearance

The Mortise and Tenon

The mortise and tenon is the classic frame joint. It consists of a slot called a *mortise* that runs with the grain and a matching tongue, called a *tenon,* that is glued tightly inside. Although it has been largely replaced by the dowel and the biscuit joint (it's easier to make production versions of them), the mortise and tenon is still the reigning king of frame joints. It is strong, and its large glue surface holds far longer than dowels.

I use mortise and tenons for anything that's going to get a lot of stress: tables, standing cabinets, and definitely chairs. The tenon should be at least 1 inch long and no more than 3 inches wide to avoid expansion problems. The mortise should be about $1/16$ to $1/8$ inch deeper than the tenon is long so that glue and wood debris won't prevent it from closing when it goes together; you don't want the tenon to bottom out. The rule of thumb is that the tenon's thickness should be $1/3$ the width of the frame member it's cut from. I find, however, that people tend to make tenons too thick, in the superstitious belief that this thickness will make them stronger. I've rarely seen the tenon fail: It is nearly always the area around the mortise that cracks, because too much of its meat has been cut away for a big, beefy tenon. The *shoulders,* or surfaces surrounding the tenon, affect the joint's strength tremendously.

The classic mortise-and-tenon joint at the left, the lap joint at the center, and the bridal joint, right.

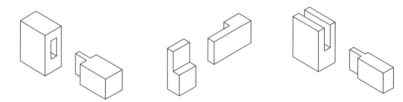

There are variations on the simple mortise-and-tenon joint. If the tenon completely pierces the wood it goes into, it's called a *through tenon.* Often, wedges of wood are then driven into the end of the tenon, in which case it is a *wedged-through tenon.* Double tenons are used to create more glue surface, but I think that with modern adhesives they are rarely necessary.

When wide boards are tenoned into frame members, the traditional joint of choice is the *haunched mortise and tenon,* which prevents cracking and other wood movement problems. This joint places a long tenon in the center and short stub-tenons, or *haunches,* on either side. The long tenon is glued in place and holds the joint together; the haunches are left unglued so that they can track back and forth in their correspondingly short mortise as the wood expands and contracts. The haunches provide more mechanical strength and keep the wide board from cupping. This is an example of a clever joinery solution to the problems of wood movement.

When cutting a mortise-and-tenon joint, you should always cut the mortise first, because it is easier to fit the tenon to the mortise than the other way around. The mortise is either chopped out with a chisel, a router, or a specialized mortising machine.

The tenon is marked out from the finished mortise, and then cut with a series of hand or power saw cuts.

The Bridal Joint

The bridal joint is like the mortise and tenon, but it works only in corners because it is not stopped at one end. It is not quite as strong in most situations, but it is much easier to cut. Because it's visible on both corner edges, it should be used in situations where a visible joint will not be distracting. Bridal joints are used most often in doors, where the visible parts of the joint are hidden most of the time by the doorjamb.

Lap Joints

Lap joints are weaker structurally than both mortise and tenons and bridal joints, but they are the easiest of the lot to cut and are simpler to fit. Lap joints can be used for frames that will be used in low-stress situations.

Spline Joints

Today, the spline joint is often used in place of the mortise and tenon because it's easier for some people to make, depending upon their equipment; nearly as strong; and still invisible from the outside. The spline joint is made by cutting two mortises in the opposing parts and then snugly fitting a piece of wood called a *spline* to bridge the gap. Because most mortise-and-tenon joints fail at their mortises, I prefer not to substitute the spline joint in situations that are going to get serious stress, like chairs.

The Dowel Debate

You probably are familiar with dowels, those round pegs of wood that serve as joinery in so much manufactured furniture and cabinetry. Mostly, you see them when their joints come apart, which seems to be fairly frequently. I must confess a prejudice against them that I picked up in my training. I know many woodworkers swear by them, but I am not a fan.

Here's why I think they don't work very well: Unless the grain of both pieces being joined is running the same way (in the same direction as the dowels), there will not be significant long grain-to-long grain glue surface, which is the only kind that counts. When the grain direction of the dowel is perpendicular to the grain direction of the wood it's going into, you get glue surface only at the points tangent to the dowel where the long grain passes over the hole; everywhere else the glue surface is effectively end grain. This problem is exacerbated by the fact that the seasonal humidity cycles change the round dowel hole into an oval as the wood around the hole expands and contracts in width only. The combination of poor glue surface and cycling wood movement breaks the bond between the dowel and the frame member, causing the joint to loosen.

161

Dowels are popular in industry because drilling round holes is so much easier (read: cheaper) than cutting mortises and tenons. Industry also can afford the machinery that makes *referencing* the dowel holes (locating them consistently in the correct position in the parts to be joined) easy. In the small workshop, referencing the holes can be a pain, which takes away their one big advantage: efficiency. Fortunately, in the past few years, biscuit joints have become available to resolve these dowel difficulties.

Wood Words

When cutting joints, you must locate the mortises and their corresponding tenons or slots precisely so that the surfaces of the parts end up in the proper alignment consistently and the joint faces fit tightly. To do this, you pick a common surface, usually a visible face, and use it as the reference surface. This process is called **referencing.**

Biscuit Joints

Since making its appearance in the late 1970s, the biscuit joint has become the new dowel. Biscuit joints are a great compromise between the dowel and the tenon, and they are perfectly suited to the small shop.

Originally developed in Switzerland, the biscuit joint is both a system and a product, which distinguishes it from traditional joinery. You need a special machine that cuts a specially shaped slot, into which a football-shaped spline, called a *biscuit,* is placed. These splines, which are sold in quantity, are stamped out of wood and compressed so that when they're inserted, the glue makes them puff up slightly, which helps bond them in place. The machines were very cleverly designed with an adjustable fence to make referencing easy in a variety of joining situations, from corner butt joints to miters. They also come with special glue bottles that inject glue into the slots.

The biscuit joint starts with slots cut by a special machine. Premade splines are then glued and inserted to join the parts.

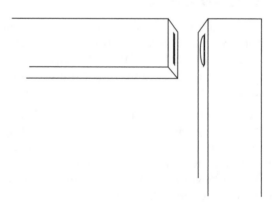

Biscuit jointers can be used for both frame joints and carcass joints. They are remarkably versatile and fast. I won't go so far as to say they're essential tools (certainly not if you want to concentrate on traditional joinery), but they can be very handy and efficient. My one caveat is that woodworkers tend to be seduced by their handiness and start using them where they ought to use a stronger joint. I don't think you should use them on traditional frame-style chairs; they aren't strong enough to replace a good tenon. I also have my doubts about using them on exterior doors, where moisture is going to conspire with high traffic to bust joints apart. But for cabinet carcasses, frames, and so forth, I think they're fine. It does make me a little sad, though, that nobody cuts tenons anymore.

Miter Management

Miters, like many other things in life, are beautiful and desirable, but difficult. A mitered joint is one that comes together with the faces cut at an angle, instead of butted together at a right angle. Whereas butt joints look utilitarian and structural, miters have a certain elegance.

The problem is that miters are harder to cut, measure, and fit and tend to open up due to wood movement. Miters can be held together with splines, tenons, dowels, or biscuits. The hard part is getting the miters cut at exactly the proper angle while keeping the parts at the proper length. This doesn't sound that difficult, but many professionals have a tough time getting it right.

The wood movement problem occurs regardless of whether the joints are cut properly. If the joints are weak because of some less-than-perfect craftsmanship, wood movement may worsen the problem, but wide miters tend to develop gaps one way or another, and they get worse as the seasons go on.

Miters are often used for cabinet doors, picture frames, borders around tabletops, and other situations where appearance is important. They tend to be weaker than other joints, in part because the faces of the miter are not true long grain glue surface.

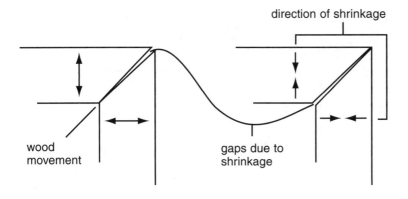

The miter on the left shows how a gap opens at the tip as the board expands in summer, because the angle effectively changes. The miter on the right shows how a gap opens on the inside as the board shrinks and the joints lock at the tip.

Frame Structures: Joints in Context

Because different structures have different stresses, joints have a variety of demands placed upon them. To understand joinery, you have to look at the joints in context and examine the nature of the stresses that they have to deal with. The following sections are brief examinations of the joinery in two wood structures. I've chosen traditional furniture structures as examples because they evolved over time through a process of trial and error, as in "Oops, the mortise broke. Let's try this instead."

Wood Words

In table construction, the accumulated band of stretchers supporting the tabletop is called the **apron.** It is important that the apron does not extend more than about $4^1/_2$ inches below the standard table height of 28 to 29 inches, or it will interfere with thigh clearance.

The Dining Table

A dining table does not have tremendous stress placed on its joints when it is stationary. Tables are, however, constantly being slid sideways, which, because of the long lever of the leg, exerts tremendous racking pressure on the joint. The *apron* can only be four or five inches wide, or it will clip the top of your thighs. Also, the mortise shouldn't be much more than three inches, so there is a limit to how much shoulder surface you have to prevent wracking. Each apron member resists wracking in one plane. A corner block screwed into adjacent apron members offers just a little more security.

Buttons are inserted into a groove on the inside of the apron and screwed into the top to hold it tight to the apron. The buttons can slide back and forth as the top expands and contracts with the seasons. Cracks would appear if the top were locked in a fixed position with screws around the perimeter.

The classic dining table has four legs, with an apron mortised in on four sides and a top held in such a way that it can expand and contract freely. In this case, it is held in place with buttons.

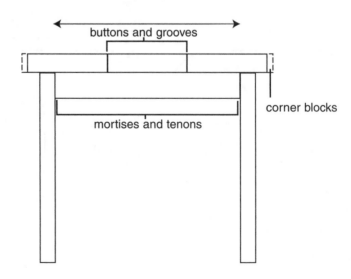

buttons and grooves

corner blocks

mortises and tenons

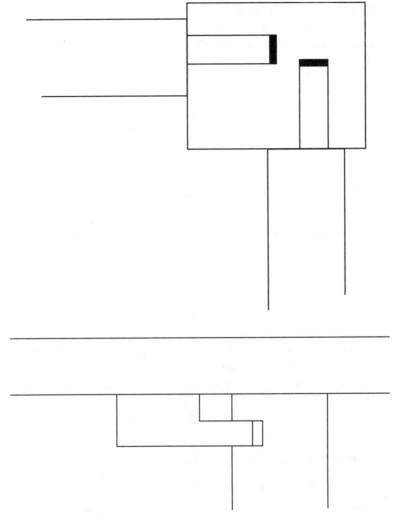

When laying out joints, it is a good idea to offset the tenons to the outside of the apron so that they can be longer without colliding in the middle of the leg. Some cabinetmakers angle the ends for a little added length.

The button pulls the table down to the apron, but it allows the top to slide back and forth with seasonal wood movement.

The Side Chair

Chairs have a tough time structurally. They have to support overweight, squirming people who drink too much wine at dinner and tip backwards, with no thought to the poor tenon gritting its teeth beneath them. They absorb stress from all angles, yet they have to appear light and graceful. The worst stress is certainly the tipping back business. Even with my professional experience, I do it myself, just ask my mother. It's irresistible, but it wreaks havoc on those tenons at the back of the side stretchers. This joint deserves to be a mortise and tenon. In the old days, it was often a double-mortise and tenon. The width of the stretcher needs to be at least 2½ inches, and it wouldn't hurt to have a second stretcher down below (the lower, the better). Corner blocks are almost a necessity as well. The rear stretcher is often offset down so that the side stretchers can use extra-long tenons without interference.

Chairs need all the structural help they can get. Secondary stretchers, at the bottom of the legs, greatly increase the strength. The joint that bears the brunt of the stress is the one where the side stretcher meets the back leg.

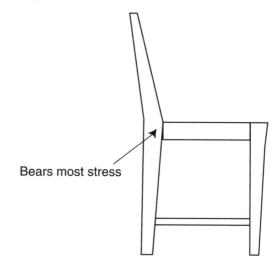

Bears most stress

The front legs have a relatively easy time of it, but they still need as much strength as they can get. The joints between the crest rail and the back legs receive very little abuse. They are often small in cross-section for appearance's sake, with a bridal joint for maximum glue surface.

The Least You Need to Know

➤ Joinery is the structural engineering of woodwork.

➤ Good joinery takes into account wood movement, glue surface, joint strength, and appearance.

➤ Joinery is divided into two categories: frame joinery and carcass joinery.

➤ Frame joinery offers strength and lightness; carcass joinery is ideal for cabinet boxes.

➤ Referencing is critical when cutting joints.

➤ Biscuit joinery has revolutionized small shop joinery.

➤ Miters are not easy and are probably best avoided for the first few projects.

Chapter 16

Carcass Joinery: The Box as a Model

In This Chapter

➤ Carcass construction in action

➤ Plywood versus solid wood carcasses

➤ A sampling of carcass joints

➤ Classic examples of carcass construction

As you may have read in the last chapter, traditionally, joinery has been divided up into two categories: frame joinery and carcass joinery. This chapter looks at the latter. In essence, carcass joinery is the science of attaching planes of either solid wood or plywood to form boxes. Kitchen cabinets, bookcases, and most other contemporary cabinetry sold in local shops use carcass joinery.

So much low- to medium-quality furniture is now put together with modern carcass joinery that people sometimes forget its august past. The finest eighteenth-century highboys and bombe chests were fastened with dovetails, which are the classic carcass joint and a benchmark for craftsmanship.

Old Carcasses and New

In the good old days, attaching flat planes of solid wood together was a challenge. Adhesives were primitive, wood was air-dried, and power tools had not yet been invented. So joints were developed that could be cut with hand tools and would not only offer lots of glue surface, but also would provide a mechanical locking action in case the glue failed.

In addition to regular dovetails, half-blind dovetails and full-blind dovetails were developed to conceal the joints, which were not considered decorative, but a necessary evil. Later, as adhesives improved and machine tools appeared, new joints were developed that could be cut with power saws and routers and that relied on glue surface in place of mechanical locking action. These carcass joints often relied on splines glued into slots to join the carcass members.

Carcass construction was revolutionized in the last half of the twentieth century by the growth of the plywood industry and the post–World War II development in Europe of standardized cabinet construction and hardware systems. Multiple dowels became the standard of industrial manufacturing, because doweling machines were easy to set up, and dowels work reasonably well in plywood and flake board, where grain direction and wood movement don't cause problems.

More recently, the biscuit jointer, mentioned in the last chapter, appeared. It was developed as an alternative to dowels for the small shop, and although it is flexible enough to work well on frame joints, its forte is carcass joinery. Although biscuits lack the mystique and romance of dovetails, they make plywood kitchen cabinet assembly a breeze.

I Woodn't Do That!

I'm not a big fan of dowels, for reasons I explained in the previous chapter. Although I think they're acceptable in flake board and plywood, I don't think they hold well in solid wood. I also think they are inefficient unless you're set up for production with a doweling machine.

Going with the Grain

When constructing cabinet boxes out of solid wood, you must consider grain direction. Although you would get great glue surface if you oriented the grain direction so that all edges met long grain to long grain, you would also end up with weak carcass members that would be prone to splitting. Even worse would be to have one side meet another with the grain running at right angles. The right way to build a solid wood carcass is to run the grain as though it were a continuous band around the perimeter of the box. This arrangement provides strength and allows the wood to move without causing problems.

The only rub is that you now have to plan your joints so that you get long grain-to-long grain glue surface. Finger joints and multiple splines (described later in the chapter) both offer a good solution, if you don't want to cut dovetails. Nails and screws can work as well, if you don't mind using metal fasteners.

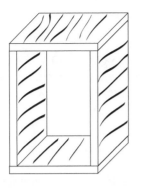 

If you were to run the grain parallel to the joint surfaces (left figure), you would end up with great glue surface, but weak cabinet members. By running the grain perpendicular to the joint faces (right figure), you get strength, but have to use joinery to gain glue surface.

The Practical Plywood Carcass

Plywood and its particle board cousins have largely replaced solid wood as the material of choice for cabinetry. They eliminate the need to mill boards and glue them together, and they're not subject to wood movement problems. Lack of wood movement problems definitely simplifies joinery. Plus, plywood brings down the material costs considerably.

Personally, I love to work in solid wood, and I still make solid wood carcasses for clients who are willing to spend the money for the feel that solid wood provides. But it is a lot more work. Let me put it this way: If I were making some utilitarian cabinetry around the house and just wanted it to look nice, I would probably use plywood. If, on the other hand, I were making a gift for my wife that might get passed down as an heirloom, I would use solid wood. It's just more personal.

One advantage of plywood is that it allows you to run the grain of the face veneer in whatever direction you want for visual effect. The convention is to run it as though the carcass were solid wood. I, however, sometimes run the grain the opposite way, if, say, I want the viewer to be pulled in visually to the box.

So Many Carcass Joints ...

The big challenge of carcass joints is to get as much glue surface as possible. Carcass joints do not generally have the same structural demands placed upon them that frame joints do, with the possible exception of drawer boxes. The structural demands are even less with cabinets that are to be fixed in place against a wall and/or floor, where the interior architecture helps prevent wracking.

Most of the joints described in the following sections will work whether the carcass corners are mitered or butted together. Some work better in plywood; others are solid wood joints. In each case, I list the joint's pros and cons.

The Single Spline

The *single spline* joint is easy to cut, which makes it a tempting choice. You simply cut slots in both frame surfaces being joined, and cut splines to glue in place. Where strength is important, the spline material should be solid wood, with the grain running the short way or across the joint line. If you run the grain of the spline parallel to the edge, it will tend to crack when stress is applied.

Wood Words

Single splines that don't run out the edges of the carcass members and thus are not visible are called **stopped splines.** Splines and dovetails that run out through the edge or surface of the members are called **through splines** or through dovetails.

To avoid problems with wood expansion when using solid wood splines in plywood carcasses, you should not use an unbroken spline all the way across, but rather use 2¹/₂- to 3-inch widths with slight gaps between them. This way, each spline can expand and contract independently. You can also make the spline out of thin plywood, and use one long spline, but such a spline is not as strong. Because a *stopped spline* doesn't run out past the edge, it makes the joint invisible, but it requires more work than a *through spline*.

The downside to this joint is that it is not all that strong when used with solid wood. With plywood, you get 50 percent long grain glue surface on any of the joint faces. But with solid wood, you get a lot of end grain glue surface plus short grain problems in the nonmitered version. I recommend using it only in situations that don't require a lot of strength, such as small boxes and cabinets that will be attached to a wall.

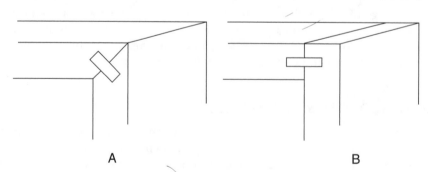

A   B

The mitered single spline joint (A) works in both solid wood and in plywood. It is mechanically resistant to pulling stress in two directions; the nonmitered version (B) is resistant in only one direction. The butted version works better in plywood where it gets better glue surface than in solid wood and is less prone to short grain breakage.

The Tongue-and-Groove Joint

The tongue-and-groove joint is a relative of the single spline butt joint. Instead of using a spline, you cut a tongue on one piece that fits into a slot or groove in the other. You should not use this joint in flake board or fiberboard, because the tongue will have no grain strength. It works best in plywood, but it can be used in solid wood if you are careful not to break the short grain on the outside of the slot. Like the single spline, the tongue-and-groove joint is an excellent joint for fixed shelves, where there is no short grain problem.

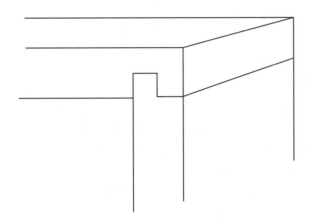

The tongue-and-groove joint is strong and easy to make.

The tongue-and-groove joint can be cut entirely on the table saw or else with a router and a table saw if you want to cut a stopped tongue. Like you would with a mortise-and-tenon joint, remember to cut the groove a little bit deeper than the tongue. You can always fill any gaps later.

The Biscuit Joint

The biscuit jointer, described in the last chapter, was developed primarily for carcass joinery. A handheld power tool, it cuts a football-shaped slot, which is like a section of the single spline joint. By cutting several of these slots in the joint surfaces and gluing in premade splines called biscuits, you can approximate the single spline joint. The biscuits come in several sizes, the most common of which are #0, #10, and #20. The biscuit jointer is generally faster, safer, and easier to use than the table saw for making joints (for the novice, anyway), and it has been a boon for small shops.

The biscuit joint can be used for miters or butt joints. It cuts blind joints that are not visible from the outside (unless you mess up) and are strong enough for most carcass construction applications. Biscuit joints work well in flake board, plywood, and even solid wood.

The biscuit joint has re-placed the single spline joint in most small shops. It is easier to cut in most small production situations and is plenty strong for most architectural cabinetry.

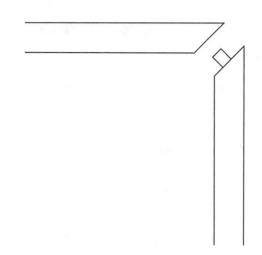

The trick to biscuit joints that come together neatly is to always reference off the out-side surface of the planes being joined, not the inside. That way, if the thickness of the material varies at all, the discrepancy will appear on the inside rather than on the more visible outside surface.

Tricks of the Trade

When you lay out the location of your biscuits, you have to mark both carcass members so the slots line up. Many people measure out the locations, which wastes time. If precise location is important, I just mark a refer-ence stick, and transfer the marks to the parts. If it's not, I just butt the parts being joined together and mark them by eye at the same time.

Because there are so many biscuit joiners on the mar-ket now, all of which work differently, I won't try to describe their operation. I will, however, warn you to be careful with yours; like the band saw, the biscuit jointer is considered nonthreatening by many people, who handle them more casually than they ought to. It is often the safe-seeming tools that people get hurt on, and I have seen some nasty accidents with the biscuit jointer. Always make sure that your work is clamped tightly, and don't ever hold a part in one hand while pushing the machine with the other hand. One of the largest, most elaborate bandages I've ever seen was worn by a man who won't do that again.

The Finger Joint

You don't see the finger joint so much any more now that glues have gotten so darn good. It still pops up, but it is relatively difficult to cut without fancy pro-duction cutters on a shaper or specialty machine. Smaller shops have gone to the biscuit jointer. The big advantage of the finger joint is that it offers a tremen-dous amount of glue surface on a narrow carcass edge.

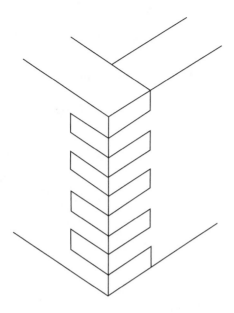

The finger joint is a machine-made approximation of the dovetail.

The finger joint is a solid wood joint. It is a bad joint in plywood and a terrible one in flake board, because it needs solid wood's grain direction for both strength and proper glue surface. It developed as a machine-made version of the dovetail, but it lacks the dovetail's mechanical locking action, so it is not very good for drawer boxes. Spline and biscuit joints, by comparison, can be oriented so that the spline has a mechanical resistance to the pulling stress that occurs when you open the drawer. Some people like the way finger joints look, but I find them neither elegant nor efficient. However, I do like to assign finger joints as a student project, because you can learn a lot about referencing and accuracy from them. If you don't get your setup right at the beginning, you'll find yourself suffering from accumulated inaccuracy. Any inaccuracy will be multiplied by the number of finger joints; by the end of the line, the fit will be terrible.

The Multiple Spline

Multiple spline joints are a rather large family. Some use slots that are cut with a router; others can be cut with a table saw. Splines are made by milling stock to fit the slots tightly, and then crosscutting them to length. Mock finger joints are a handy joint because they are easy to cut. You glue the miters together without joints, and then cut slots with a handsaw or table saw, which you then fit splines to.

I have a soft spot in my heart for the multiple spline joint, probably because the first real carcass piece I ever made I put together with half-blind multiple spline joints. They are strong and provide excellent glue surface. Their aesthetic appeal is a matter of opinion. I find them a bit mechanical looking and would use them on something

173

like a tool cabinet or some other utilitarian piece that requires extra strength. I would not use them on elegant dining room furniture, except in the full-blind version.

Multiple spline joints are ideal for solid wood, where they maximize glue surface, but they'll work in plywood and flake board as well. If you orient the grain of the splines parallel to the grain of the carcass members, multiple spline joints make a much better glue surface in solid wood than the single spline or tongue-and-groove joints.

The various multiple spline joints include the half-blind (visible from one side only) multiple spline joint.

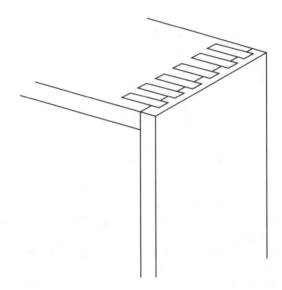

The Lovely Dovetail

If an aristocracy exists among joinery, then the dovetail certainly deserves a curtsey. It works well, can be elegant, and is a traditional badge of fine craftsmanship. Although adhesives have come a long way in the last 80 years, you still can't beat a dovetail for structural strength. The mechanical locking action makes them perfect for drawer boxes and other carcasses that are going to receive regular stress.

There are hand-cut dovetails and machine-cut dovetails. I'm sure that the latter work well enough, but when I talk about dovetails, I mean the hand-cut variety. Machine-cut dovetails always lack the charm of hand craftsmanship, which is a major reason woodworkers use dovetails, in my opinion. As woodworkers, we set our pieces apart from production work with little touches that humanize it. Hand-cut dovetails have an irregularity and feel you won't find in machine work.

It takes a lot of practice to become proficient at all the cutting and chopping that goes into dovetails, and you should definitely practice on scrap wood before you attempt them on a project. It's a good idea to use softer woods when you're learning, because they will compress to fit a little instead of splitting like harder woods. Practicing dovetails is a great way to practice your woodworking skills in general.

They require skill with a handsaw, chisels, and marking tools and help you develop a sense of process and accurate fitting. If you get good at making dovetails, you'll become better at woodworking in general.

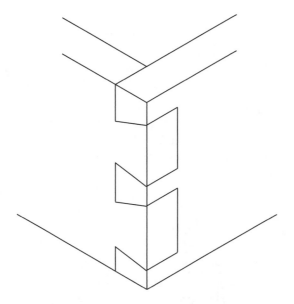

The classic, true dovetail has unsurpassed strength and is a symbol of fine craftsmanship.

There are three main types of carcass dovetails—through, half-blind, and full-blind. The through dovetail is the strongest, with pins and tails that go all the way through each other. The half-blind dovetail is often used on drawer fronts because the full-blind dovetail, which is not visible from the outside, is rather difficult to cut.

Woodlore

I cut my first set of dovetails in a class at the Rhode Island School of Design with the venerable Danish master cabinetmaker Tage Frid presiding. They came out pretty near perfect, and I was convinced that I was a complete natural. Unfortunately, it was about two years before I cut a decent set again. Far from a natural dovetailer, I was singularly mediocre. I worked diligently at making dovetails for my entire apprenticeship and eventually became pretty good. The moral is, class, that if I can do it, you can, too.

The Lowly Screw

Screws are much maligned in fine woodworking; they are frequently considered part of the carpenter's repertoire, not the fine woodworker's. They certainly require less skill to employ than cutting fancy joinery does.

However, screws can provide an excellent joint where strength and speed of construction outweigh aesthetic concerns. The reason you don't see many screws in antiques is not because they were undesirable, but because they were so expensive. When screws were made by hand, they took more time and skill to make than dovetails.

I frequently use screws for assembling plywood and flake board boxes where the screw heads will be covered by moldings, sit next to a wall, or be invisible for some other reason. Some people counter-bore screw heads below the cabinet surface, and plug the hole with round wood bungs. For carcass construction, I usually use #12 flat-head screws. I prefer Phillips head screws to slotted head screws, because they keep the driver centered.

Woodlore

Screws and nails were so desirable and expensive when they were made by hand that un-used buildings were frequently burned down to harvest nails and screws for new construction. The screw machine changed all that, and now screws are considered the cheesy woodworker's shortcut. The Great Dane, Tage Frid, told of his countrymen's prejudice against some of their neighbors to the north. As evidence of this, he cited their nickname for screws, which they called "Swedish dowels."

Sheet metal screws are more expensive then wood screws, but they are hardened so the heads don't strip out and leave them stuck. They are as strong as dowels or biscuits and are much faster. They also require no glue, which saves cleanup. Screws can be very handy for large built-in cabinets that are more conveniently assembled on site then awkwardly transported whole.

The trick to getting a good result with screws is to predrill a pilot hole, a free hole, and countersink and/or counter bore. For a fuller explanation of screw use, see Chapter 17, "Nails, Screws, and Bolts: When It's Okay to Use Fasteners."

Some Classic Carcass Types

To put these joints in context, the following sections look at some classic carcass structures and examine why you might prefer one joint over another. Because carcass construction is often used where great strength is not necessary, you can frequently choose joints for aesthetic reasons. Woodworkers also use different joints for different materials.

The Modern Kitchen Cabinet

Kitchen cabinets require relatively little of their joints. They are attached to the wall and generally to each other, so there's not a lot of wracking stress trying to work them apart, as there would be in a free-standing cabinet. In addition, the back of the cabinet can be screwed in, which further holds the joints together. Consequently, nearly any reasonable joint will be adequate. Doors are what get the worst abuse in kitchen cabinets.

Tricks of the Trade

To drill the pilot hole, free hole, and countersink at once, I use special countersinks, which attach to tapered drill bits. They are often called Fuller bits, after the company popularized them, even though they are now manufactured by many other companies. I just clamp the sides together and drill the holes, figuring screws as I go.

Considerations when choosing a joint come down to aesthetics and efficiency. I generally use biscuits, screws, single spline joints, or some combination thereof for kitchen cabinets. I don't like to use flake board or MDF (medium-density fiberboard) on any cabinet that may be exposed to water; thus, I would stick to plywood. If I had a production doweling machine, I might be inclined to use dowels because they work fairly well in plywood, but it would be a waste of time without one. The kitchen cabinet market is very competitive (even high-end stuff), and it's important to work fast.

Kitchen cabinets generally have adjustable shelves that sit on shelf-pins that fit in $1/4$-inch or 5 mm holes on $1^1/_2$-inch or 32-millimeter centers. The shelves should be about $^1/_{16}$ inch narrower than the cabinet opening so that they can be moved easily. It is critical to reference all the holes consistently so that the shelves don't rock.

Chest of Drawers

The classic chest of drawers has a carcass box with drawer dividers that carry drawer runners, a separate top that screws on from inside the cabinet to allow for wood movement, and separate feet that also screw on. The joinery was traditionally half-blind dovetails with the visible joints top and bottom so that they would not be visible. This arrangement also places the mechanical locking action so that it holds the sides on; gravity keeps the bottom in place, and the top carcass member doesn't get much stress.

Chests of drawers need strong joinery.

Tricks of the Trade

Wherever possible, I like to use a back that screws into place after the carcass goes together. It allows you to correct any out-of-squareness by tweaking the carcass with clamps and then screwing the back in when it's right. A floating back, or a back that glues into place when the carcass goes together, doesn't permit this.

Chests of drawers need strong joints because free-standing furniture gets pushed and slid about and is thus subject to wracking, especially at the bottom joints. Although dovetails are ideal, multiple spline joints would also work well. If you want to pass the chest on to future generations, you should stay away from single spline or biscuit butt joints, although mitered versions of both might be suitable because of their added mechanical advantage. Dowels would be the choice of many furniture manufacturers, but I don't recommend them. I do recommend screwing in the back of the chest to keep the carcass square, rather than having a back floating in a groove where it will do nothing structurally.

Now that dovetails are a badge of honor for many people, it would be tempting to cut through dovetails instead of half-blind ones and let them work as a visual as well as structural element. Of course, you can use dovetailing only if you're working in solid wood. In plywood, you would have to choose one of the other joints mentioned previously.

The Blanket Chest

Although the blanket chest is also pushed and slid around while loaded with stuff, its joints do not have the same stresses placed upon them. This is because the joint surfaces run vertically, so they naturally resist the wracking that occurs when the chest is pushed from above. The primary stress the joints have to contend with is that of the top opening and closing, which occurs right at the top of the joints at the back of the chest. For this reason, it would be good to orient any mechanical joint so that it holds the back carcass member tight to the sides. I would choose the same joints for the blanket chest as for the chest of drawers, although you could probably get away with tongue-and-groove joints and certainly biscuit joints.

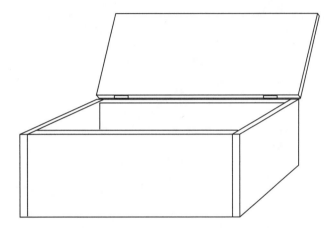

The blanket chest does not have the same wracking forces acting upon it as the chest because its joints run vertically.

The Least You Need to Know

➤ Carcass joinery is the joining together of flat planes of solid wood or plywood.

➤ The grain direction of solid wood should run continuously around the cabinet.

➤ Dowels don't work well in solid wood.

➤ Some joints offer mechanical locking action in addition to glue surface.

➤ Biscuit jointers have revolutionized carcass construction because they are fast and don't require a great deal of skill.

➤ Dovetails are the classic carcass joint, but they require time and skill.

➤ Some joints work well in solid wood, and some work well in plywood.

Chapter 17

Nails, Screws, and Bolts: When It's Okay to Use Fasteners

In This Chapter

➤ When fasteners do just fine

➤ Fastener types and sizing

➤ The ins and outs of pilot holes, free holes, and countersinks

➤ Pneumatic nail guns

➤ The right way to screw two pieces of wood together

Screws and nails have become second-class citizens in the world of fine woodworking. They have gone from expensive, handmade hardware in the eighteenth century to cheap, machine-made substitutes for good joinery in the twenty-first century. They do, however, play an important role in woodworking. Woodworkers use them to assemble jigs and fixtures and to work as part of the finished pieces.

Screws are used to join cabinet boxes (where they won't be seen) and to attach table-tops to bases, backs to cabinets, and hinges to doors. Woodworkers also use them for installation work to anchor cabinetry to walls and floors. Nails are used to locate parts while glue sets, to build jigs, and even to assemble cabinets that will be painted. Occasionally, bolts are used as well. This chapter makes sense of the array of fasteners that are used in woodworking and explains how to use them.

The Wonderful World of Wood Screws

The screws that woodworkers use are categorized according to a variety of characteristics: head shape, diameter, length, material, hardness, and drive type. Different situations demand different types of screws, and it's important to choose the right one. It's also important to be able to communicate your needs to your supplier. If you don't know the nomenclature, you won't be able to get what you want.

Woodlore

In grad school, I had a professor named Ken Hunnibel who oversaw the metal area. Ken was always urging students to communicate clearly. Students were always running into his office, with a project due in 10 minutes, pleading "Ken, have you got a bolt?" To which Ken would respond, with an almost imperceptible smile: "Yeah, what kind?" To which the unsuspecting student would answer, "Oh, you know, just a bolt." Ken would then pull out an Allen-head cap screw that he had bought specially for this sort of occasion that was about 3 inches in diameter and 18 inches long. "This what you were looking for?" he would ask innocently. He had a washer the size of a hula hoop, too.

Head Types (Screw Heads, That Is)

The flathead screw is the most common type of wood screw. It has a head that is flat on top and angled on the bottom, so that it wedges into the wood, locating it precisely. It is used to fix one piece of wood to another object without a washer. A *countersink* hole is drilled to accommodate its wedge-shaped head, the top of which then sits flush or slightly below the surface being screwed. A sure sign of the klutz is when you see a flathead screw used with a flat washer so that the head stands proud, ready to snag on something.

The roundhead screw and its fraternal twins, the button head and pan head screws, have a head that is flat on the bottom and hemispherical on top. These screws are used with a washer when a flush surface is not required and you want to skip the step of drilling a countersink. They are also used in situations where you need to allow for wood movement and don't want the firm locating effect of a flathead screw's wedged head. A roundhead screw will slide around on its washer, as long as it has an oversized free hole. This sliding could be a problem if you want positive location, but roundhead screws are commonly used to attach tabletops to their bases and in other situations where a wide piece of solid wood must be able to expand and contract with seasonal moisture changes while remaining attached to a frame or carcass.

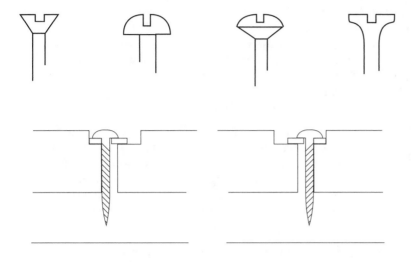

The screw head types most commonly used in woodworking are (left to right): the flathead, the roundhead, the oval head, and the bugle head.

This is a typical way to attach a tabletop to an apron. The roundhead screw's flat bearing surface will slide back and forth on its washer. In this case, the head is also counter-bored so that the head does not protrude and snag on things.

Oval head screws are just a decorative variation on the flathead. They have the flathead's angle, with a slightly domed top. They are most often used with hardware, so they are most commonly available in brass. I like the way oval heads look and use them whenever I can. They look great on hinges, but you have to be sure that they won't prevent the hinge from closing all the way.

Bugle heads appear on screws such as Sheetrock screws that are designed to be used on soft materials, without pilot holes or countersinks. Woodworkers use Sheetrock screws to attach softer materials like 2×4s and plywood to each other, where appearance is not important. The screw is designed to easily penetrate the wood without splitting. The heads are small in relation to the body, and the special bugle head does not displace as much wood as the flathead, so it sinks into the surface rather then jamming or breaking. Sheetrock screws don't work very well in hardwood, because they tend to break or bog down, and the heads don't sink into the harder surface.

Tricks of the Trade

Use screwdrivers that are sized for the screw you're driving. Slotted bits should just be contained within the slot. If they're too small, they'll mar the screw head, and if they're too big, they'll cut into the wood surrounding the head. Phillips screwdrivers must also be sized right. Phillips power drive bits are numbered p#1 to p#3: p#1 for screws up to #4, p#2 for #4 through #12, and p#3 for screws that are #12 or higher.

Drive Types

Most screws used in woodworking are either slotted or Phillips drive. Slotted screws have an old-fashioned feel that appeals to many woodworkers, but they are harder to use. Phillips head screws were developed to keep the screwdriver or power-drive bit centered, which is a big advantage when using screw guns. Drivers tend to wander in slotted heads and can damage the wood around the head or even the head itself, if you aren't careful. Phillips drive screws are much easier to install.

Tricks of the Trade

Apply some lubricant to the threads of a screw before you drive it in, especially if you're using a hand screwdriver. It makes for less work and prevents stripped drive slots. I like to use wax or soap, but I've seen Greek cabinetmakers use olive oil.

Square drive bits also keep the screwdriver centered, but it's harder to insert the driver in a square drive head than in a Phillips drive head. Square drive heads work well on very small-headed screws, such as trim head screws, and many people think they look more elegant or distinctive than the other types.

Allen and hex drive heads are used on bolts. Hex drive heads are more common and can be used with either wrenches or socket sets. Allen drive heads are used with counterbores and in other situations where there is limited clearance around the bolt head, and a conventional wrench or socket would not fit.

The most common drive types used on screws and bolts are (left to right): slotted, Phillips drive, square drive, Allen drive, and hex drive.

What's Your Screw Made Of?

Screws are made from a variety of different metals: steel pot metal, brass, stainless steel, and even silicone bronze. Some metals are weaker or stronger than others; some are corrosion-resistant; and others are decorative. The average zinc-plated wood screw is neither attractive nor particularly strong. They are, however, relatively cheap.

Where appearance is not an issue, I prefer to use sheet metal screws, which are hardened and stronger than wood screws. They also are threaded all the way to the head without the unthreaded shanks of wood screws. Because sheet metal screws are harder and stronger, they don't break as easily, and the heads aren't prone to getting stripped out by drivers. Sheet metal screws are more expensive, but it doesn't take many broken or stripped screws to convince you that they're worth it.

Brass, bronze, galvanized, and stainless steel screws were all developed for their resistance to corrosion. They're used in boat-building, for decks, in food service work, and wherever the elements would dissolve a conventional screw. However, many woodworkers use them decoratively. Brass screws are used with brass hardware, and stainless screws look better than zinc-plated ones.

Screw Sizes

The two standard dimensions used to size the standard screw are the diameter and the length. The diameter is indexed by a number, with a lower number being thinner and a higher number being fatter. The length is listed in inches. So a screw might be a #8 × 1^1/$_2$ inches or a #12 × 2 inches. Generally, only even number sizes are standard up to #18 or so, with odd and larger sizes available on special order. Odd numbers are, however, relatively available in the smaller sizes, where each increment makes more of a difference.

I Woodn't Do That!

Brass screws are very soft, and you can often break them or at least strip their slots, during installation. To prevent this, I drill pilot holes, and then thread in a steel screw identical to the brass ones I'll be using, remove it, and then install the brass one. This way, less torque is applied to the brass screw.

Screws come in boxes of a hundred. Rather than try to keep a supply of every screw size on hand, I keep a selection of the sizes I use the most and just keep track of my stock in those sizes (although I do have boxes of just about every size left over from one specialty job or another). To keep my screws organized, I keep them all in one area, with brass screws in one cabinet and steel screws in another. Each numerical size gets its own shelf, #4, #6, #8, and so on, with boxes arranged by group in order of length. This arrangement allows me to lay my hands on the ones I need quickly and to keep track of my stock.

Don't keep overflowing jars of mixed sizes. Your time is too valuable to waste sorting piles of screws. Anyway, you always end up two screws short and have to drive to the hardware store. It's important to be able to keep track of your supplies easily so you don't lose momentum by running out of things. Nothing leads to errors and slow-downs like having to stop a process in midstream.

Placing Your Order

Now that you know all the variables, you have the information to tell the clerk at the hardware store what you need. Instead of saying, "Uh, I need some, uh, screws," you can say, "Let me have a box of Phillips drive, flathead #12 × 2-inch sheet metal screws, my good man, and make it snappy."

Getting It Together

So now that you've got your screws, what do you do with them? Most people, including a lot of professional carpenters, don't know how to screw two pieces of wood together properly. The trick is to drill a *pilot hole* in the piece that takes the point and a *free hole* in the piece that holds the head.

Wood Words

A **pilot hole** is drilled for the screw to thread into. It should be slightly thinner than the **root diameter** (the distance between the threads) of the screw. The **free hole** drilled in the other piece should allow the threads of the screw to slide through. A **countersink** is a drilled hole that allows the flathead to locate below the wood's surface. A **counter bore** is a hole that allows the use of a bung, or plug.

The pilot hole should be big enough to ease the threading process and prevent the fibers from being overly distorted. In softer woods, the pilot hole should be 70 percent of the root diameter, and it should be 90 percent of the root diameter in harder wood. A screw joint is stronger with a pilot hole than if you just crank the screw in without one. The free hole should be big enough to slide the *shank* (the body of the screw) through by hand. Counter bores and countersinks are holes, and the tools that cut them, that allow the screw or bolt head to sit below the wood's surface. A countersink has an angled bottom and is used with a flathead screw. Counter bores cut a straight-sided hole and may be used with a plug.

The key to a strong screwed joint is that the head pulls the top piece of wood into the bottom piece that the tip is threading into: The screw should not thread into the top piece. If the screw threads into both pieces, it will prevent the pieces from pulling together as tightly as they should. For this reason, the free hole should be big enough to clear the threads so that the flathead screw, bearing against the *countersink*, pulls the parts together.

To screw two pieces of wood together properly, you need to drill a pilot hole and a free hole. Flathead and oval head screws require a countersink and sometimes a counter bore as well. Pan head screws are usually counter bored.

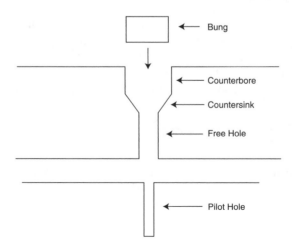

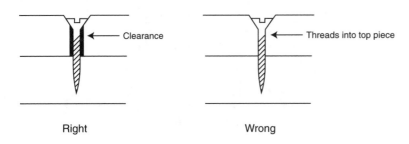

Right   Wrong

The head of the screw should pull the top piece into the bottom piece. The screw should not thread into both pieces if great pressure is important.

The Nuts and Bolts

Fine woodworkers certainly don't use bolts on a daily basis, but occasionally we do have call to tighten one, so it's good to know the basics. Bolts can be used to assemble utilitarian shop equipment, such as workbenches, shelving, router tables, and lumber racks. They also play a key role in holding your machines together, and sooner or later you're going to have to adjust, remove, and maybe even replace one.

Bolts have a length of threads that are designed to accept a similarly threaded nut. Real bolts do not have male threads designed to cut their own female threads in wood the way wood and sheet metal screws do. (What woodworkers call *lag bolts* are more properly called *lag screws*.) Machine bolts may have an unthreaded shank called the *grip length,* or they may be threaded all the way to the head. Hex bolts, named after their six-sided head, are the most common type and accept an open-ended wrench or socket wrenches. One rule: Do not use pliers on bolts! It ruins them.

Bolts are available in different grades or tensile strengths, measured in pounds per square inch. Marks on the head indicate the grade, with grade 8 being the strongest commonly available.

Bolts are sized by their diameter, their length, and the number of threads per inch. It's important that the threads of the bolt match those of the nut and that they are part of the same thread system. If they're not, they'll be ruined when you try to put them together. There are two main threading systems in use: national coarse and national fine, with national coarse being the ones you'll probably find at your local hardware store. Each system determines a specific number of threads per inch for any given bolt diameter.

Woodworkers often use lag bolts, or more properly, lag screws, because they thread into wood and don't need nuts; they are driven into pilot holes like screws. They're sized by diameter and length and are called bolts because of their hex heads.

I Woodn't Do That!

Unless it's an emergency, do not use pliers, channel locks, vise grips, or any other one-size-fits-all tool on nuts, bolts, or any other headed fastener. It will ruin the fastener, may or may not work, and is generally a finesse-less thing to do. Always use the correct size wrench or socket to drive a fastener. Even adjustable wrenches can mar a fastener.

A selection of bolts (left to right): Machine bolt with unthreaded shank, machine bolt threaded to the head, carriage bolt, and lag bolt.

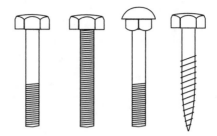

Carriage bolts have a driveless head, which is a round cap that prevents the bolt from being undone except on the nut side. They're used where security is an issue. The head has a square shoulder that locks it in place while the nut is tightened.

Welcome to Washers

Washers are used to distribute the pressure of the screw or bolt head over a larger surface area in order to prevent the head from burying itself. They also reduce friction, which can lock the head in place, allowing it instead to slide slightly, without marring the finished surface.

Washers are sized by their hole diameter: $3/16$-inch, $1/4$-inch, and so forth. Washers that have extra-large outside diameters are called *fender washers*. There are also many types of *lock washers,* which are designed to prevent the bolt or screw from rotating loose.

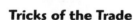

Tricks of the Trade

It's important to swing a hammer properly or the nail will deflect or bend. The trick is to hold the hammer as though you're shaking hands with it, down toward the end of the handle. Don't push it; swing it instead. Let the weight of the hammer do the work rather then your arm muscles. Move your wrist as the hammer swings so the hammer's face is parallel to the nail's head when it strikes.

Getting Nailed

Nails are sized by the penny system with a 2d (for some reason, *d* is the abbreviation of penny) being the smallest, and 60d being the largest. A 2d nail is 1 inch long, and each penny increment adds $1/4$ inch; thus, a 4d nail is $1^{1}/_{2}$ inches, a 10d is 3 inches, and so on. Nails over 20d are called *spikes*. Nails with flat heads are called common nails, and nails with very small heads are called finish nails. The heads of finish nails are set or buried beneath the wood surface with a punch called a *nail set*. Very small finish nails ($1/4$ inch or shorter) are called *brads*.

Fine woodworkers mostly use finish nails and brads. I use nails for installing trim on work that is to be painted (the heads are set and puttied-over) and for locating parts that won't be seen while glue sets. I also use nails for making jigs, fixtures, and crates.

Nailing Pneumatically

In the past 15 to 20 years, pneumatic nailers have become much more available to the population at large. Small compressors have made them portable to the job site, and it's gotten to the point where everyone's forgotten how to swing a hammer. I, too, have jumped on the bandwagon and would recommend them to anyone who can afford the setup. Buying a decent compressor, air hoses, fittings, and a gun or two can add up, but pneumatic nailers can speed your production tremendously. If you're going professional, they're almost a necessity.

Pneumatic nailers are not only faster, they're also more precise. The work doesn't move around as much as it does when you're hammering away. We've all been there, where you spend time lining up two pieces just right, only to have them shift just as the nail locks them together. Pneumatic nailers don't do that as much.

There are also *pin nailers,* which drive a headless nail too thin to drive with a hammer. They lock a piece in place and are so thin you often don't even have to fill the hole. Some woodworkers also use staples to attach thin backs and so forth, where a nail might pull through.

The Power Nailers

A new breed of cordless power nailer uses internal combustion to drive a nail. These nailers run off of butane cartridges, so they have no air hose. They're relatively expensive, but if you don't have a compressor, or if you're doing a lot of nailing outside the workshop, they might be worth it.

The Least You Need to Know

➤ Screws are categorized by head shape, diameter, length, material, hardness, and drive type.

➤ Understanding the varieties of screws enables you to specify the right screw for the job and order it without confusion.

➤ Keeping your fasteners organized in the workshop will prevent you from wasting time looking for the fasteners you need.

➤ Drilling the right pilot hole, free hole, and countersink for your screws ensures a strong screw joint.

➤ Washers are used to provide bearing surface and prevent surface marring.

➤ Nails are categorized by head type and penny weight.

➤ Pneumatic nailers can both speed your production and improve its quality.

Chapter 18

Doors and More Doors

In This Chapter

➤ Frame-and-panel doors

➤ Plywood cabinet doors

➤ Sliding doors

➤ A guide to hinges

➤ Pulls and knobs

➤ Stops, catches, and knobs

Door work is one of the hardest woodworking tasks to get right. A host of demands are placed on doors because they have to operate mechanically. A tabletop can have a hint of twist or be $1/8$ inch smaller than you'd planned, and no one will notice, but a door has to be absolutely flat and precisely the right size. Plus, there are hinges to be mortised in place, and knobs and locks to be set. And there are so many kinds of doors: sliding doors, inset doors, overlay doors, entry doors, cabinet doors, and on and on. This chapter clarifies door terminology and typeology so that you have a clear understanding of doorology.

Doorology 101

Some doors pivot on hinges, and some doors slide, but they all have more or less the same function: to seal an opening. Some have to keep out water or air; others have to protect homeowners from goblins. Glass doors have to keep dust off knick-knacks but permit the appreciative gaze; other doors provide a sense of calm by shutting life's clutter in cabinets and closets so that it can't be seen.

Basic components of the common entry door.

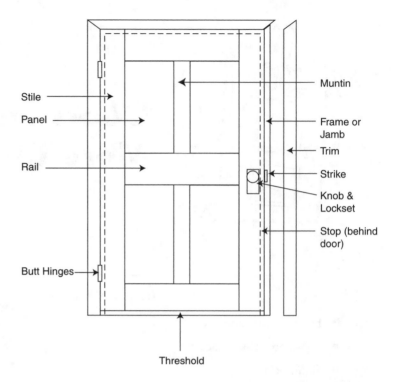

Muntin

Stile

Panel

Frame or Jamb

Trim

Rail

Strike

Knob & Lockset

Stop (behind door)

Butt Hinges

Threshold

A basic entry door is a good model to look at. It's hung from a doorframe with butt hinges. It has a lock set with knobs and a strike mortised into the frame. The door closes against a stop molding that runs around the door frame and locates the door when it is closed and seals against noise, drafts, and light. A threshold helps minimize drafts and noise while allowing the door's bottom to ride high enough to clear a carpet and any high spots in the floor. Trim molding bridges the gap between the frame and surrounding wall, simultaneously helping to lock the frame in place and cover up for any discrepancies in the plane of the wall. Double doors either overlap each other with matching rabbets, or have a strip of molding, called an *astragal,* that covers the gap where they meet. Exterior doors generally have weather stripping around their perimeters.

The tricky parts of getting the door to work properly are the following:

➤ Gluing up the door flat

➤ Installing the frame square, plumb, and flat

➤ Fitting and hanging the door so that the gap between it and the frame is tight and consistent all the way around

➤ Mortising the hinges and lock assemblies flush with the surface and lining them up properly

Those Swinging Doors!

When ordering hardware or talking over the phone with other tradesmen or designers, it's frequently necessary to specify how a door swings. Doors can swing into a house or out, and they can be hinged on the right side or the left. Locks, handles, hinges, and other hardware frequently work only one way. Doors themselves may have an inside or an outside, with decorative elements or weather proofing facing one way or another.

When entry doors open into a home, they are called *inswing* doors, and when they open out, they are called *outswing* doors. This is fairly straightforward. The hard part is determining whether a door is a left-hand or right-hand opening door. For some reason, everyone gets dyslexia when figuring out which way a door swings, which can have fairly catastrophic results. Here's how to remember: Stand in the doorway (or imagine you are) facing in the direction that the door opens. If the hinges are on your left, it's a *left-hand opening door;* if they're on your right, it's *right-hand opening door.*

Wood Words

It's important to be able to communicate to a hardware supplier which way a door is hung. Stand in the doorway (or imagine that you are), facing in the direction that the door opens. If the hinges are on your left, then it's a **left-hand opening door;** if they are on your right, then it's a **right-hand opening door.**

Choose Your Panel: Solid Wood, Plywood, or Glass

Solid wood panels give a traditional feel to a door. They are generally raised panels with a shaped edge or a rabbet where they meet the frame. Solid wood panels are not glued in place. Instead, they float in the frame, so they can expand and contract with humidity changes.

Nowadays, you often see flat, plywood panels. They can't be raised, or the laminations will be visible. Plywood, unlike solid wood, can be glued in place for added strength; this makes them useful for structural parts of the door.

Glass panels are common, especially for exterior doors, because they work like windows, letting in light and allowing you to see the great outdoors. The panes of glass themselves are known as *lights,* and they may be flat or beveled at the edges. Because lights must be replaced from time to time, they are never fixed in place permanently, much like their wood counterparts. Instead they are installed from one side and are held in place with removable moldings called *glass stops.* The permanent dividers that separate the lights, and to which the stops are nailed, are called *mullions.*

Because glass is breakable and therefore potentially dangerous to children and the clumsy, it's often a good idea to use tempered or laminated glass in doors, especially if the lights are large. Both are termed *safety glass.* Tempered glass is heated in an oven so that if it breaks, it will shatter into many tiny, squarish pieces. Laminated glass is a sandwich of two sheets of glass with a layer of plastic in the middle. In many cases, the building code requires that you use safety glass in doors, especially in commercial applications.

Acrylic plastic, often sold under the trade name Plexiglass, is also used for doors sometimes; and for high-security situations, there is polycarbonate, the generic term for the trade name Lexan), which is bulletproof in thicker dimensions. Remember, though, that plastic windows scratch easily and look dull after a while, and polycarbonate is pretty expensive.

Woodlore

Glass is heavy and fragile—a tricky combination. Several years ago, I made three doors for an architect that had a three-sided frame with a glass panel, with one edge exposed. The glass panels cost $1,300 each, were 5 × 9 feet, and made of a special acid-etched, low-lead glass that has a white (not green) edge and is more fragile than conventional glass. The doors were so big that they wouldn't fit into the elevator, so we had to carry them three flights up a switch-back stairway in a loft building. They weighed about 350 pounds each and had to be carried on end to fit, and flipped over the banisters. We made it, but it was a nerve-wracking day.

Cabinet Doors: Closing the Box

Traditional cabinet doors have many similarities to entry doors; they have butt hinges and frame-and-panel construction. As with entry doors, fitting them and getting them hung properly in the opening the first time is tricky. Unlike entry doors, however, there are many options to accommodate the multitude of cabinet variations.

Today, most cabinet doors are just cut out of hardwood-veneered plywood and edge-banded with veneer tape. Solid wood frame-and-panel doors can be more attractive and challenging. They are usually laid out like entry doors in miniature. The smaller doors, however, do not have the same stresses and do not place the same demands on their joinery. This has led to the cope-and-stick method of door construction.

Cope-and-stick cutters are matched sets of knives that are set up on a shaper or router table. They cut positive and negative mating surfaces on the edges of the stiles and ends of the rails. A groove runs the length of the stile, which accepts a short tongue called a *stub tenon* (which is usually ¹/₂ to ³/₄ inches long). Instead of square shoulders on the stub tenon, the cutters usually leave a profile to match a decorative molding on the edge side. This profile also provides a slightly better glue surface. You can choose the pattern of the molding.

Cope-and-stick setups are not for beginners. They require some experience setting up machines and can be confusing even for relatively experienced woodworkers. They can, though, be a great way for a small shop to make doors well and efficiently. They're something to think about down the line.

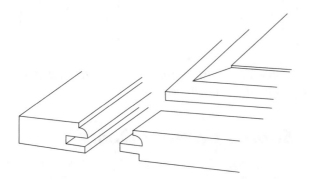

The cope-and-stick method of door construction is a production technique that has trickled down to the small shop. Matched sets of router bits are now available that cut the moldings and joints.

Full-Overlay, Half-Overlay, and Inset Doors

Typical kitchen-type cabinet boxes hang in a row, snug to each other, with doors that are either contained within the carcass or form a plane in front of the cabinet, covering both the opening and the front edge of the carcass as well. When a door is contained within the cabinet, leaving gaps between it and the carcass or frame members, it is said to be an *inset door*. When it sits in front, leaving gaps between it and its adjacent doors, it's called a *full-overlay door*. A subgroup of overlay doors called *half-overlay doors* are just overlay doors that are hinged from a common carcass member, so they overlap only half its thickness (minus a gap for clearance).

Inset doors require greater precision to fit because the gaps have to be calculated exactly. Overlay doors are more common because they are easier

Wood Words

There are three typical ways to hinge a door for a plywood cabinet. The door that can cover the entire edge of the carcass is called a **full-overlay door. Half-overlay doors** overlap half the vertical edges; they're used when doors are hinged or close on a common vertical member. **Inset doors** are contained within the box so that the edge is visible.

to fit. They have no gaps top and bottom, and with European-style hinges, you can just adjust the doors to even out the gaps. Overlay doors do not require a stop because they close against the carcass.

The inset door (left) leaves the cabinet edge visible; the full-overlay (center) and half-overlay (right) doors hang in front of the cabinet edge.

I Woodn't Do That!

When you're finishing a cabinet that has sliding doors, don't get finish in the grooves or on the tongues. It'll gum them up so they won't slide well. Instead, use wax on the grooves and tongues. A little wax will not only make the doors slide better, it will also darken the areas to match the finish on the rest of the piece.

Sliding Cabinet Doors

Sliding doors have a very different aesthetic from hinged doors. There is a simplicity to them. Long a tradition in Asia, they were adopted by modernists in the West and have become popular in the last 70 years.

They need to slide in a track, both top and bottom. You can buy a mechanical track (there are many on the market), but I prefer to make my own. Mechanical tracks are not necessarily easier to use, and they generally detract from the minimal feel that makes sliding doors attractive in the first place.

To make my own tracks, I cut a pair of parallel grooves called *dadoes* in both the top and bottom of the cabinet, just far enough apart to allow the doors to pass each other. I then cut matching tongues to fit into the grooves. The trick is to cut the top dado and the shoulder on its corresponding groove extra deep to allow the door to slide up and clear the bottom tongue for removal and installation. It takes some fitting to get the doors to slide easily but not rattle; a little beeswax or paraffin goes a long way.

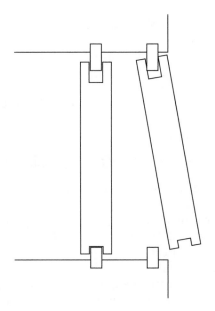

The cutaway view on the left shows two sliding doors in place, riding on lower tongues, with enough clearance to slide past each other. Note the extra depth of the top groove and shoulder. The view at right shows the front door as it is pushed upward and removed.

Hinges: The Usual (and Unusual) Suspects

Human ingenuity, spread out over a few centuries, has come up with more than one way to swing a door. Some, such as the butt hinge and strap hinge, have been around for hundreds or even thousands of years. Others are too young to go to college. Some are designed for strength or a special application; others are designed for fast production methods.

Traditional hinges may be made of steel, brass, cast iron, or various other metals. For fancy cabinets and doors, woodworkers usually use brass or sometimes cast iron for a rustic feel. The better brass hinges are cast, forged, or extruded; cheap ones are stamped out of sheet stock.

All hinges, but especially brass ones, are available in a wide range of surface finishes. Brass hinges are often available in polished, satin, or as-manufactured mill finish. Or they may come in nickel, silver, or chrome plate. The doors I once made for a certain conservative talk show host had gold-plated hinges costing over $1,500 per set. Brass hinges may come with different patinas: black oxide, antique brass, pickled, or various others.

Butt Hinges: The Old Standby

I like butt hinges. They have a traditional elegance, and they work well. It takes a little while to learn to install them neatly, but after you've done it a few times, it goes fast and is very satisfying in a meticulous sort of way.

The hard part is marking out the hinges, so take your time. If I'm just doing a single door or two, I'll mortise them in the cabinet or jamb first with a single screw holding them in place. I then line up the door with shims to hold the gaps I want top and bottom, and then mark where the hinges touch the door with a marking knife. This method is better then measuring because it gives you the real location of the hinges rather than the measured location.

Tricks of the Trade

When installing butt or other traditional hinges, I always use slotted screws made of the same material and with the same finish as the hinge. Slotted head screws are more traditional than Phillips head. I also make sure that I line up the slots so they all point in the same directions. As Mies Van Der Rohe said, "God is in the details."

European Cabinet Hinges

After World War II, German and Austrian manufacturers developed a systematic approach to plywood cabinet construction, with the goal of speeding production. Among other things, they came up with a new type of cabinet hinge that is easy to install because it doesn't need to be mortised flush. These hinges also can be adjusted for height, depth, and side-to-side location after they've been installed. They come in two parts: a *hinge cup* that screws onto the door after you drill a 35 mm hole to locate it and a *base plate* that screws onto the inside of the cabinet. These hinges are now the standard for kitchen and architectural cabinetry in this country, where they are known as European cabinet hinges, because they make door hanging so easy.

The European hinge has replaced traditional hinges because of its easy installation and adjustment.

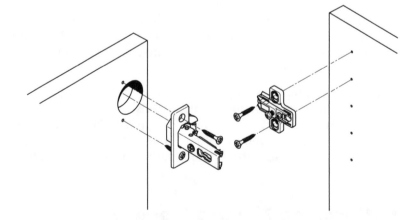

European-style hinges come with a bevy of variables. Some open 90 degrees, some open 135 degrees, some open 175, and so on. Generally, the wider the hinge opens, the bigger and clunkier it is, and also the more expensive it is. You can choose from hinges set up for inset doors, half-overlay doors, or full-overlay doors as well. And just in case you have the wrong hinges, you can buy different base plates to turn full-overlay hinges into either of the other two types and half-overlay into inset (unfortunately, it doesn't work the other way).

In the last few years, European hinges have been designed that snap onto their base plates rather than screwing together, so doors can be removed easily for installation and moving. They also come with or without an optional spring that makes them self-closing.

The downside of European-style hinges is that they're huge and ugly and look inelegant compared to high-quality, traditional brass hinges. They also tend to go out of adjustment over time, causing the gaps to become uneven or the doors to collide with their neighbors.

As a hobbyist, you can sacrifice efficiency for that old world craftsmanship and go for the brass butt hinges. If you intend to make a living from cabinetry, you might give European hinges a try. I used them on my own kitchen, despite the fact that I had originally wanted to use butt hinges. When push came to shove, I needed to save time wherever I could, because I was making my own cabinetry after normal work hours. As I often say, I can't afford to hire myself to do the kind of work I do for clients. There is always a compromise between quality and efficiency.

Other Hinge Options

When it comes to hinging a door, European-style and butt hinges are not the only tools in the shed. There's a host of alternative and special-purpose hinges at your disposal. Some, such as offset knife hinges, you might choose for their discrete good looks; others are available to get you out of a jam. Many oddball hinges are designed to solve an unusual clearance problem. There is, for example, a butt hinge with spiraling barrels so the door rises as it opens to clear high spots in the floor due to settling.

It's a good idea to familiarize yourself with the multitude of hinges out there (I recommend keeping a good cabinet hardware catalog near the toilet). See the following illustration of two most common hinges.

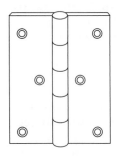

The two most common hinges: The butt hinge (left) and the knife hinge (right).

Knobs, Pulls, Catches, and Other Door Hardware

Various other bits of hardware grace entry and cabinet doors. Knobs and pulls come in handy when you want to open doors; locks and catches are handy when you want to keep them closed. Some hardware is recessed or mortised into the door; other items simply screw onto the exterior. The former is called *flush-mounted hardware;* the latter is known as *surface-mounted hardware.* As with hinges, there are many finish and material choices.

One rule for working with hardware: Don't start cutting wood until you have your hardware in hand. All sorts of things seem to go wrong when you make assumptions about hardware based on photos, drawings, or written measurements. Nothing is more frustrating than building furniture and finding out that your hardware won't quite work and nothing else is available. I was told this rule during my apprenticeship, and I would say that on 50 percent of the occasions that I have tried to get a jump on things by building before I had the hardware I've had a problem.

Also research standards before you start designing. Entry doors, for instance, come in standard thickness of $1^3/_8$ and $1^3/_4$ inches, so most hardware is designed for these sizes. If you choose nonstandard sizes, you may have trouble finding locks and hinges that will work. Most production cabinets are made with 1-inch plywood, so the majority of European-style hinges are made to work with this dimension. If you start to use $^7/_8$- or 1-inch thick doors or carcass sides, you've seriously limited the range of hinges that will work.

Pulls and Knobs

Door pulls are generally used on cabinets and do not operate a lock or mechanical latch. They just provide a knob for your hand to pull. Most common are knobs that are threaded for a machine screw that slips through a drilled hole in the door (or drawer). The head of the screw bears against the inside and holds the knob firmly in place. Some knobs simply have a wood screw thread protruding from their back. This type of knob is usually either cheap or antique because these knobs tend to strip out over time and do not have great longevity.

Entry doors have lock sets, which may consist of a pair of simple knobs and mortised latch or may involve elaborate box locks and handles. Generally, the lock part is mortised in with a router or a chisel, and a hole is drilled for the knob assembly.

Catches and Locks

Cabinet catches hold the door fully closed, but not locked, and come in many different styles and sizes. The most common have a magnet that mounts to the cabinet and engages a metal plate screwed to the door. They are simple, and they aren't pretty, but they work. *Ball catches* have two spring-loaded balls that catch a plate that is attached to the door. They are arguably better-looking than magnetic catches (they definitely have a more traditional feel), but they're harder to set. Another type of catch uses a positive mechanical trapping action that is accessible only from the inside, but I don't recommend this type. These catches look less cheesy than magnetic ones, but when they eventually jam shut and you can't get at them, that difference won't seem to matter much.

Many people like *touch latches,* which preclude the need for pulls. They have a spring-loaded plunger with a magnet on the end that engages a metal plate on the door. As you close the door, the magnet holds it, and the plunger is pressed in until it engages an internal latch. When you want to open the door, you push the door in a tiny bit, and it disengages the latch, allowing the spring to push out the plunger and open the door enough to grab. I have mixed feelings about touch latches. I like the option of not using door pulls, but touch latches do go out of adjustment very easily. I use them only when it's important aesthetically to have a pull-less face.

The classic mechanical cabinet door and drawer lock is mortised into the edge of the item being locked and uses an old-fashioned type key. It's a fair amount of work, but like mortising hinges, it can be satisfying for the persnickety.

I Woodn't Do That!

Don't set the depth location of a catch inside the cabinet; when the door is shut, you can't see where to put the catch. I take a cut-off from the door stock, attach the metal plate, and stick the catch to that. Then I just line up the cut-off where the door should end up and screw the catch in place. Then screw a plate onto the actual door.

The Least You Need to Know

➤ Doors must be glued-up and installed square, plumb, and flat.

➤ Doors must be fit to their respective openings.

➤ Doors are either right-hand opening or left-hand opening.

➤ Glass panels are called lights and are held in place by removable glass stops.

➤ Cabinet doors are either full-overlay, half-overlay, or inset.

➤ European-style cabinet hinges were developed to speed production.

➤ Traditional hinges, especially butt hinges, are still the standard for fine cabinetmaking.

Chapter 19

The Ins and Outs of Drawer-Making

In This Chapter

➤ Traditional drawer construction

➤ Modern drawer construction

➤ Mechanical drawer slides

➤ Fitting traditional drawers

➤ Applied drawer fronts

If any common woodworking job is thornier than door-making, it's traditional drawer work. Doors and drawers share many of the same challenges: You have to keep your joinery dead square, fit what is essentially a wooden mechanical apparatus so that it slides smoothly in winter and summer, and make it sturdy enough to hold up to lots of abuse. Drawers get overstuffed, yanked open, slammed shut, used as ladders by children, and generally taken for granted.

We tend to overlook what masterpieces of engineering drawers are because they are so ubiquitous. This kind of engineering became highly perfected through thousands of years of empirical, trial-and-error experimentation. Perhaps if Einstein had invented the drawer in a single stroke of genius, we might accord it more respect, though it probably would have a bug or two. By the end of this chapter, you should appreciate your drawers more than you do now, especially if you try to make one.

Crafting Traditional Drawers

I spent a lot of time during my apprenticeship and woodworking training building traditional dovetailed drawers out of solid wood. Now most of my drawers are made from plywood and hung on modern metal drawer slides, because I have to make a living in a big city. However, if I retired tomorrow and could build furniture purely for pleasure (which I would do), I would go back to traditional drawer-making techniques.

Making good, solid-wood drawers and fitting them like pistons is the mark of a real craftsman and very satisfying. It draws on all the classic woodworking skills: hand-sawing dovetails, deft chisel use, fitting with a hand plane, and generally keeping control of your material.

There is more than one way to make traditional drawers, but the classic way I learned consists of the drawer box with full dovetails at the back and half-blind dovetails up front. The bottom slides in a groove, or *dado,* at the bottom of the sides and front, screwing into the underside of the back piece. The drawer then slides on a *runner-kicker system* that is an integral part of the structure of the cabinet.

The traditional drawer is dovetailed together and has a solid wood bottom, which is screwed at the back, but floats in a groove unglued so it can expand and contract.

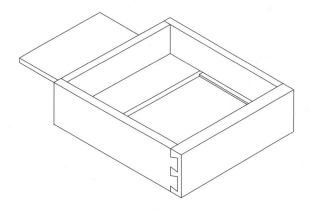

Wood Words

Traditional drawers are supported on the bottom by frame members called drawer **runners** and are kept level from above by drawer **kickers.** Strips of wood called **drawer guides** keep the drawer in place from side to side.

The cabinet is constructed so that each drawer opening has strips of wood that run front to back, above and below the drawer. The ones below are the *runners* and support the drawer as it slides in and out; the ones above are the *kickers* that prevent the drawer from tipping forward when it passes the balance point. If there is more than one drawer, the runners from the drawer above act as the kickers for the drawer below. If the sides of the cabinet do not come in contact with the drawers, it may be necessary to attach *drawer guides* to the runners to limit side-to-side movement. To operate smoothly, the runner-kicker system and the drawer itself must be perfectly square, parallel, and true. Each drawer must be custom-fit to its own opening.

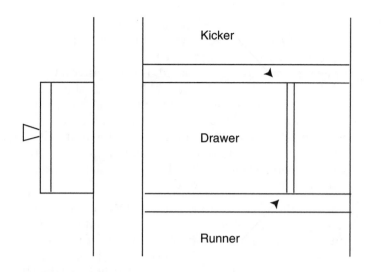

The runner-kicker system is fairly complicated looking. The drawer is supported below by the runner and kept from tipping downward by the kicker, above. Guides on either side prevent it from rattling left to right.

Sliding Dovetails

Another joint that is excellent for holding drawers together is the sliding dovetail. It is used with an integral, rather than applied, drawer front. It creates an excellent locking action and is a good intermediate choice. It is not as difficult as hand-cut dovetails, but it is a bit sturdier than simple tongue-and-groove.

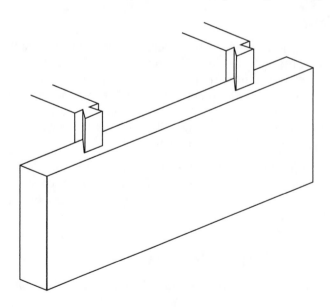

The drawer sides have male dovetails that slide into a matching female slot in the front. Generally, the drawer back is dovetailed into the sides.

I Woodn't Do That!

If you try to get a new joint, finish, or technique right the first time on an important project, you're asking for trouble. Make your mistakes on a test piece, and then you'll be able to sail through the real thing. I can't recommend doing samples or tests enough. It'll save time in the long run when you don't have to remake parts out of lumber you don't have.

The female dovetail slots are cut first with a router or router table with a special dovetail bit. Then the male dovetail is cut with passes on either side using the same bit. I strongly recommend using a router table because of its stability. It's critical to cut the slot first because getting the right fit becomes a nightmare otherwise. Make sure you have lots of scrap pieces for tests, including a test glue-up, because the joint will slip together fine without glue, only to lock up half together when the glue makes the wood expand. The glue-up is the tricky part of the process.

The first time I ever did a glue-up on this joint was during my apprenticeship, and I was working after hours on a commission I had gotten. As my boss at the time, Hank Gilpin, was leaving for the evening, he said, "You have to be careful those joints aren't too tight, or they'll lock up once the glue is on them. You did make a test, right?" "Oh no," I answered, "if anything, they're too loose." So, I spent the next night remaking parts. I'd just about destroyed them by trying to beat the joints together after they'd locked up halfway there.

The Dovetail Machine

During the last 80 years or so, various methods have been developed to cut traditional dovetails with machines, instead of by hand. Various jigs are available that allow you to cut "old-fashioned" dovetails with a router. I've never used them, because I think they miss the point. They end up being too regular in appearance and lack the fineness of good hand-cut dovetails. You don't cut dovetails because you need to nowadays, but rather because you're taking delight in a charming anachronism and taking pride in a symbolic act of craftsmanship.

This is just one man's view, and plenty of people take pride in machine-made dovetails. If you're interested, look at the various setups available and see which system you like best. Dovetail machines do make a strong joint. Then again, you could just practice cutting dovetails by hand.

Traditional Drawers: Fitting Words

Each drawer must be fit separately, and the process starts before you cut the joints:

1. Make sure the drawer opening is true. If it is not, do whatever you can to fix it.
2. Cut your drawer sides to length and rip them. Then plane them so they fit very tightly in each of their sides of the opening.

3. Fit your drawer front so that it just fits into the opening. I like to plane a slight angle (maybe a couple of degrees) on the edges all the way around so only the back fits in while the front is still a bit too tight. I then cut the drawer back to the same length as the front.

4. Lay out and cut the joints, assemble the drawers, and clean them up.

Woodlore

Some craftsman woodworkers who base their reputation on producing furniture of the best quality take things like drawer-fitting to a very high level. Hank Gilpin, the craftsman with whom I did the bulk of my apprenticeship, liked drawers to fit so perfectly that when you closed one quickly, the air pressure in the cabinet would pop out the other drawers slightly, proving that, though the drawers fit tightly, they slid smoothly. It's also possible to taper the runners slightly toward the back so that they snug up as they close and therefore won't slam. Another trick that works especially well with smaller drawers is to fit them to snug up as the back approaches the cabinet opening, so they won't fall out unexpectedly.

The drawers should now be a bit too tight to slide, so, starting at the back, I do the following steps:

1. Plane the drawers until they slide evenly all the way back.

2. Once a drawer slides smoothly, wax the runners, kickers, guides, and drawer sides to make the drawer slide that much better. If it's winter, I generally fit drawers a hair loosely, and if it's summer, I keep them just on the tight side, because the fit will change with the seasons, especially with deep drawers.

Traditional drawers often require a drawer stop that locates the drawer in a closed position so that the front lines up in the right place. One simple way to do this is to put a screw in the back of the cabinet;

Tricks of the Trade

For top-notch drawers, use quarter-sawn lumber for the sides and back. It expands and contracts less then flat-sawn stock, so it will fit more consistently from season to season. I used to make my best drawer sides and runner-kicker systems from quarter-sawn white oak, which was quite stable and quite hard, for long wear.

you can adjust it by screwing and unscrewing it until the front is where you want it. Other methods include attaching blocks to the drawer dividers or drawer backs.

Contemporary Drawer Construction

With the advent of modern adhesives and the quest for faster production, dovetails have become a quaint anachronism for commercial furniture-making. They are too time-consuming to make, and they don't work well in plywood, which has generally replaced solid wood for drawer box construction. Even small commercial shops have mostly given up on dovetails, leaving them in the hands of high-end craftsmen and hobbyists. Today, drawer boxes are generally made of plywood and put together with tongue-and-groove joints or biscuit joints. I prefer the tongue-and-groove joints, but I use both on occasion.

When the joints are oriented properly, the pulling stress applied to the drawer is resisted by the mechanical locking action of the joint. When the joints are oriented the wrong way, the stress is resisted only by the glue joint, which is more likely to fail over time.

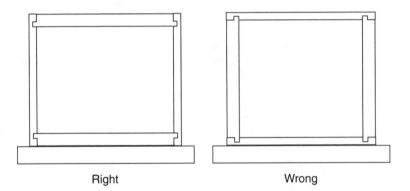

Right   Wrong

Usually, a box with an applied front is used, so that although the box is plywood, the drawer front can be solid wood. It's important to put the tongues on the drawer front and back and the grooves on the sides so that the pulling action is resisted by a mechanical locking action, not just the glue joint. When using biscuit joints, you should orient the biscuits like the tongues so that there is a mechanical resistance to pulling on the drawer front.

Surveying Drawer Slides

The innovation that has most affected modern drawer construction is the drawer slide. Primitive wooden versions were developed by industry at the end of the last century to avoid all the fitting necessary for runner-kicker drawer systems. The most common involved a groove milled in the side of the drawer, with a corresponding strip screwed to the inside of the cabinet. This system is still common among woodworkers looking for an easier alternative to the runner-kicker system that still has a rustic, crafty feel.

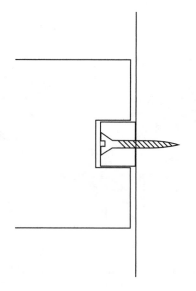

Many woodworkers hang drawers on strips of wood attached to the inside of the cabinet with a corresponding groove routed into the drawer side.

Most commercial woodworkers, however, now use metal drawer slides that they simply purchase and install. There are many different types on the market. Most are *side-mount,* screwing into the drawer and cabinet sides. Some, though, are *under-mount,* attaching to the underside of the drawer bottom and to drawer dividers below so that they are not visible when the drawer is opened.

There are many choices even within these categories. Some side-mount drawer slides screw onto the middle of the drawer side. Others wrap around the lower edge of the drawer side, which allows you to skip making the groove that the drawer bottom slides in and simply screw or nail the slide to the underside of the drawer box. This way, the slide conceals the edge of the plywood and supports the drawer bottom.

Wood Words

Drawer slides are divided into categories determined by whether they mount on the side of the drawer box or underneath; they are called **side-mount** or **under-mount,** respectively. They are also divided into **partial extension, full extension,** and **overextension** categories, depending on how far the drawer they are rated for will open.

There are many types of drawer slides on the market. Each type has its own advantages. All are designed to save you time over traditional drawer-hanging methods.

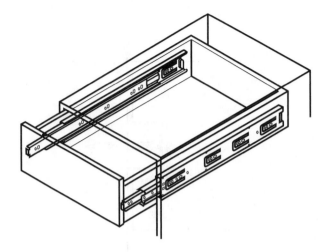

Various manufacturers are making a new type of under-mount drawer slide that is my new personal favorite. It is really a hybrid side-mount and under-mount. It screws to the side of the cabinet, but to the underside of the drawer bottom, so it does not require extra cabinet parts and is not visible when the drawer is open. The disadvantage to these new drawer slides is that they are quite pricey and a bit complicated to install.

Drawer slides come in different lengths, generally available in 1- or 2-inch increments, depending on the size and make. As I've said before about hardware in general: Don't start cutting parts until you have not only researched your slides, but have them in your hands. They may be a little different than the drawings and description indicated. This rule is especially true with drawer slides, where the industry works in the metric system and then rounds off the numbers to inches!

Drawer Slide Extensions

Drawer slides are available with different extensions. *Extension* refers to the distance a drawer will open. A *full extension* slide will open far enough so that the back of the drawer it's rated for will end up just past the front of the cabinet. *Partial,* or *three-quarter, extension* slides will leave the last quarter of the drawer still inside the cabinet. *Overextension slides* (which are rare) are designed to open beyond an overhang and still provide access to the back of the drawer.

Full extension slides are more desirable than partial extension ones, but they are nearly always much more expensive, often much larger, and unsightly. However, it's very frustrating not to be able to get to the back of a drawer, and partial extension slides are generally false economy. It's good to remember that traditional drawers were all "partial extension."

Drawer Slide Finishes

Many people feel that drawer slides, if not downright ugly, at least detract from the appearance of a piece of furniture. To minimize this problem, short of going with expensive nonvisible slides, you can choose drawer slides that come with a surface finish, usually a cheap-looking metallic one. Many slides, however, are available with durable epoxy paint, and some even offer a choice of color, generally white, almond, or black.

Applied Drawer Fronts

Separate drawer fronts that are attached to the drawer box after it has been assembled are another development to make drawer-hanging easier. After the slides are in and the box is hung in the cabinet, the front is attached to it from the inside with screws. This method is easier than trying to hang a drawer with the front already fixed. There are many variables when hanging a drawer, and it is complicated getting everything lined up properly. By keeping the front off, you can concentrate on setting the depth accurately, and then make up for any discrepancies in the height or left-to-right location later with the drawer front.

Many companies make a special device called a *drawer front adjuster* which holds the drawer front to the box while still allowing a $^1/8$ inch or so adjustment in any given direction. This can be very handy when setting all the gaps in a run of cabinetry with lots of drawers and doors. When the drawer gaps are right, you fix the front in place with regular screws.

Tricks of the Trade

I don't set my drawer pulls until I have the drawer exactly where I want it. Then I drill a hole for the machine screw through both the front and the drawer box to help hold them together. You don't want the constant stress of the drawer being pulled open to work the drawer front loose.

Drawer Bottoms, Then and Now

Solid wood drawer bottoms are not used too much anymore. I prefer them for fine work and use them if the client is willing to pay for the extra time involved or if I'm making a piece for a loved one. The grain on solid wood drawer bottoms should run side-to-side for strength so that as the wood expands and contracts, the movement can be absorbed at the front and back of the drawer. At the front, it can slide in and out of the slot that supports it, and at the back, it should be secured with pan-head screws with washers in oversize holes to allow movement. Solid wood drawer bottoms must never be glued in place, or they will break the drawer apart and/or crack.

Plywood drawer bottoms can be glued in place for added strength, though I don't glue them (unless I have an unusual situation) because I like the option of being able to disassemble the drawer. Although the grain of plywood's surface veneer could be oriented in either direction, it is customary to run it side-to-side, as though it were solid wood. I have, on occasion, run it the other way to cut down on waste, but it always looks wrong somehow.

The Least You Need to Know

➤ Traditional drawers are joined together with dovetails and run on wooden runners, kickers, and guides.

➤ Traditional drawers must be individually fit by hand to their respective openings.

➤ Modern drawer construction was developed to speed production.

➤ Modern drawers use metal drawer slides and do not have to be hand fit.

➤ Drawer slides come in different lengths and extensions and mount either on the drawer's side or bottom.

➤ Traditional drawers generally use integral drawer fronts; modern drawers generally use separate applied fronts.

Chapter 20

Edgings and Moldings: The Last Details

In This Chapter

➤ Where to use moldings

➤ Different types of moldings

➤ Buying premade moldings

➤ Making your own moldings

Although modernism, in its fascist "form follows function" enthusiasm, tried to do away with moldings in the early twentieth century, they just wouldn't die. They might have been easier to kill if they were merely decorative, but the fact that eluded the early modernists is that they serve a utilitarian function. They help make transitions, whether it's from one plane to another, one material to another, or one part to another. They bridge gaps, they hide uneven joints, they hold panels in place, and they make our woodworking lives easier in many ways.

They also look beautiful, which is a noble function. They can make a plain-Jane piece of furniture come alive. This chapter explains how to buy, make, and use moldings in your woodworking. It also explains the basic architectural moldings that are used in homes, as well as how moldings can be applied to furniture and cabinetry.

Whose Whim Were Moldings?

Moldings were originally developed as architectural elements; they were used on ancient Egyptian temples. The Greeks developed the form further, creating elaborate moldings that were used on their religious and secular buildings. The Greek moldings were based on abstract geometry, which had philosophical meaning for them. The curves in Greek moldings are all sections of an ellipse, but they were developed to be viewed from eye level, so their geometry was intentionally distorted to make them appear geometrically correct from that perspective. The Romans continued the Greek tradition, but changed it to express their worldview. Consequently, the curves in Roman moldings are all sections of a circle, which the Romans felt was an ideal shape, rather than an ellipse.

Today, most moldings are based on these Greek and Roman templates, and we still describe moldings based on the ellipse as "Greek," and those based on the circle as "Roman." The moldings you see at a lumberyard, however, have been watered down by time, popular tastes, and the need to make moldings easier to manufacture. The following figure shows a selection of common components of classical moldings and details.

A selection of classical molding details: A) Roman ogee B) Greek ogee C) Cove D) Bead E) Torus F) Cornice G) Ovolo.

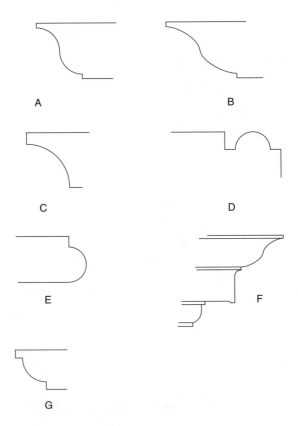

Interior Architectural Moldings

Interior moldings are taken for granted. They are another example of something ubiquitous that most people don't know much about. Maybe they know what a crown molding is or a baseboard, but a chair rail? Or picture molding? Let's look at the moldings found in a traditional home.

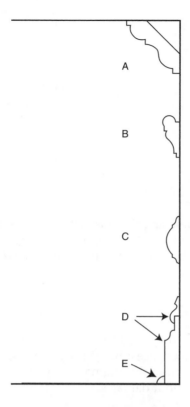

The moldings found in a traditional home are: A) Crown molding B) Picture molding C) Chair rail D) Baseboard with cap molding E) Shoe mold. The geometric details are arranged to be seen in foreshortened perspective from eye level, so the crown molding has the finer details toward the bottom, the baseboard has them on the top, and the chair rail and picture moldings are more centered.

The Majestic Crown Molding

The *crown molding* is the grandest molding; it bridges the planes of the ceiling and the walls. When it has a line of applied rectangular "teeth," it is called *dental molding*. Traditionally, these large moldings were made of plaster, but ornamental plasterers have become rare as hen's teeth, so it's become the woodworker's responsibility to fill the gap. The problem with making them out of wood is that wood expands and contracts, which can lead to gaps at the edges of these wide expanses. For this reason, it's a good idea to limit the size of wood crown moldings, or else build them up out of smaller moldings; that way, each piece will expand and contract separately, leaving you with several small gaps rather then one or two big ones.

Wood Words

Some **crown moldings** are not just profiles, but also have separate, rectangular pieces of wood glued on in a repeating order. These moldings are called **dental moldings,** because the repeating rectangles resemble teeth.

Two of many styles of crown molding available.

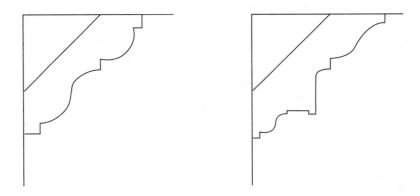

Crown moldings should be nailed to blocking that has been attached to the wall and ceiling first. The edges may have to be planed to accommodate irregularities in the walls and ceiling. After the molding is in place, any open joints along the edge can be filled with caulk.

Picture Moldings

Picture moldings are less common than they used to be. They sit a foot or two below the crown molding and are designed to engage a hanger used to suspend pictures. They are handy, because they keep you from putting nails in your beautiful walls. Paintings can be moved or changed without damage.

Picture molding must have a lip on top to engage a bracket from which the picture is hung.

Chair Rail

Chair rail is a generally symmetrical molding that protects the wall from chair backs, which were usually pushed back against it when not in use. Like the picture molding, it has waned in popularity, but it is often used with wainscoting as a cap molding. It is nearly symmetrical because it is so close to eye level that you can see both the top and the bottom.

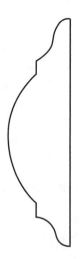

Chair rail generally has a blunt half-round or similar shape in the center that can survive repeated impact with chair backs.

Basic Baseboard

Baseboard is the most common molding out there. It exists even in most modernist homes because you have to bridge the gap between the floor and the wall somehow. It is often a single molding consisting of a flat expanse with a detail molded into the top edge. At its most elaborate, it has two separate cap moldings attached to a flat section, which may itself have a rabbet or two, as well as a shoe mold where it meets the floor. The top cap will be mitered at every door opening and continue around the door casing. The shoe mold holds tight to the floor to avoid gaps between the floor and the baseboard. In modern homes, baseboards (and crown moldings, too, to an extent) are often hollow in back and used to run communications wiring. Some have special removable cap sections for access to jacks.

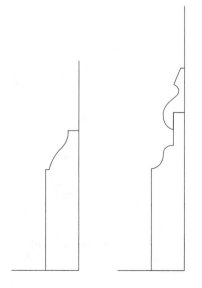

Baseboards can range from a simple, single piece of wood to a base with two molded caps (the elaborate one on the right is from my Victorian home).

Coping with Corners

When installing molding, woodworkers commonly miter all corners, inside and outside. Outside corners must be mitered to get a clean joint, but inside corners are better off being *coped*. As I pointed out in Chapter 15, "Frame Joints: The Skeleton as a Model," miters have a tendency to separate due to seasonal wood movement. You have no choice but to use miters on the outside corners, but on the inside, you do, so cope them.

Tricks of the Trade

Mitering crown molding can be tricky because it must be cut at a compound angle relative to the back of the molding. If there's enough clearance under your blade, hold the crown molding against a support at the same angle at which it will ultimately hang. If this is not possible, you'll have to consult a table, and then cut the crown at a compound angle, which is a pain in the neck.

A coped joint is a fancy butt joint. The profile is traced on the end of the molding and cut with a coping or fret saw so that when you're done, the end of one piece will mate perfectly with the face of the other. A coped joint will not separate as much as a miter, and whatever separation does occur will be less visible. One way to cope a joint is to use a compass to transfer the pattern (see the following illustration). It's important to hold the compass flat for an accurate profile. This process is called *scribing*. Then, cut the molding with a coping saw and do some final fitting with a rasp. It helps to angle the saw blade back from the line so that only the front edge of the molding makes contact with the face of the other piece; this is called *back-cutting*.

Another way to find the right profile to cut on the end of the molding is to miter it as though it were going into an inside miter, and then follow the line where the face of the miter meets the front face of the molding. This will give you the right profile. Try it!

Use a compass to trace the pattern; it may help to bend the leg out so it can reach the nooks and crannies.

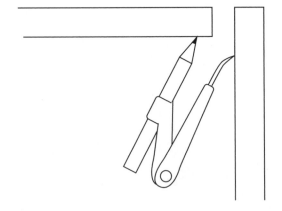

When joining sections of molding in the middle of a long, straight run, you should not just butt them together, because this will be visible later. Using a scarf joint will blend the pieces more smoothly. To make a scarf joint, just cut both pieces in a matching 45-degree joint and glue and nail them together as you install them. Sand the joint after the glue has dried and fill any irregularities with caulk or putty.

Furniture and Cabinet Moldings

Moldings are used in many disparate ways on cabinets and furniture. Large separate molded pieces are used for crowns and cornices on armoires and other architectonic cabinets to make them more closely resemble buildings. Smaller strips of molding are used to frame raised panels and glass lights on doors and cabinet faces. The use of molding often goes beyond mere decoration, serving to hold the panels in place when it's desirable to install them after the frame has been assembled.

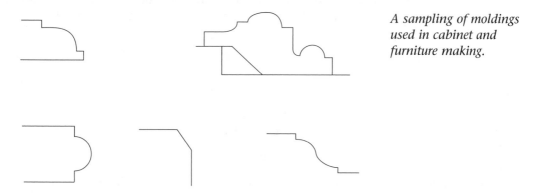

A sampling of moldings used in cabinet and furniture making.

Integral molded edges are often cut on the edges of tables and furniture tops. These may be as simple as a bevel or a bull nose or as elaborate as the Victorian imagination could contrive. The edges of doors and drawers often have bevels, beaded moldings, or cock beads that are not only decorative, they also conceal minor misalignments that would be visible otherwise between the door or drawer front and surrounding cabinet front. Because misalignments are inevitable with wear and tear over time, these edge details are a considerate insurance policy. In the cope-and-stick joint system discussed in Chapter 18, "Doors and More Doors," the moldings on the joint surfaces provide better glue surface and also make a transition between the frame and panel.

Often, eighteenth- and nineteenth-century furniture included moldings and other architectural elements, such as pilasters, capitals, and plinths, that reflected the interiors in which they were placed. You may notice that often casework from this golden age of cabinetmaking resembles individual buildings set in the interior. Moldings go a long way toward creating this illusion.

Large moldings that curve gradually may be veneered, although this is tricky to do. Often, clamping pressure is applied with sandbags that will conform to the profile. Vacuum systems work in some instances. In the good old days, cabinetmakers would hammer-veneer the moldings using hide glue; this is a particularly appropriate application for hammer-veneering.

Buying Basic Molding

Any good lumberyard will sell basic architectural moldings in pine or poplar and may have some in oak or mahogany. The lumberyard will probably also have a catalog of available moldings. A good hardwood yard may even stock a selection of hardwood moldings. Molding usually comes in lengths from 6 to 14 feet. It is sold by the linear foot, with smaller, less intricate moldings selling for less than larger, more complicated ones.

Some mills will cut custom moldings to match something existing or just to suit your fancy. Custom moldings are, however, much more expensive. Generally, you pay to have a custom knife ground, a setup fee (the cost of having a person install the knives in the molding machine), and then you pay a linear foot charge. If you're having a lot of molding of the same profile run, the knife grinding cost and setup fee are spread out over many feet, and it's not so bad, but if you just need a few feet, it's not cost-effective.

Woodlore

Before power tools, all wooden moldings had to be cut by hand with special molding planes, which was no mean feat. A typical cabinetmaker had perhaps hundreds of wooden planes, each with the sole and blade shaped to a particular profile. Some would be simple beads or chamfers; others were quite elaborate with adjustable fences. In the early 1950s, before I was born, my mother came across an eighteenth-century cabinetmaker's tool chest with a vast quantity of exquisite molding planes. She gave it to a friend who had taught her to refinish furniture (and gone on to become a restorer at Colonial Williamsburg). He refused to work on a piece with any tools made after the piece itself. I've never entirely forgiven her for giving these planes away.

Rolling Your Own

You can make simple moldings in a small shop. This skill can be handy if you're working with an unusual wood that is unavailable in stock moldings. It also allows you to customize a molding for a particular project. Or it may be easier to run a few feet of a simple molding (if you have the router bit) than it would be to drive down to the lumberyard.

Lumber mills cut moldings on a special machine called, not surprisingly, a molder. If you have a shaper (which is not really a beginner's tool), you can have knives ground and moldings cut quite efficiently. But most small shops cut smaller, simple moldings on a router table.

The selection of available router bits is getting larger and larger, and it is now possible to cut relatively sophisticated moldings, maybe not big crown moldings, but other, smaller ones. Often, the molding has to be cut in sections, using more than one bit and making multiple passes. You might, for instance, cut an ogee, then a cove, and then a rabbet, all with different bits. Small moldings, like a bead for glass stops or a bull nose for the edge of a tabletop, could be cut with a single bit, though you might have to make several progressive passes.

If you have a shaper, you can get special cutter heads that hold matched sets of knives that have profiles ground into them. The knives have various systems that hold them. Some have corrugations in the back that key into matching corrugations in the cutter head; others have a series of notches in the edge that lock into a screw, which allows you to adjust them in and out.

I cannot, however, emphasize enough how dangerous these shaper cutter heads are in the hands of the untrained. You must get proper training and have qualified supervision with them, because they are about as dangerous as anything you are likely to come across in the world of woodworking. This past year, I gave expert testimony in a case that involved a man running a shaper, who was killed when the knives came loose and one went through him after passing through a guard and bouncing off a power feeder. Give woodworking a few years before you think about using these cutters.

The Least You Need to Know

➤ Moldings are used to ease transitions between planes, materials, or parts.

➤ Moldings can be used to conceal misalignments, gaps, and other idiosyncrasies.

➤ Most moldings have their origins in Greek and Roman architecture.

➤ Many moldings have details that are designed to be viewed from a particular perspective and may look strange from another.

➤ You can buy many basic moldings in common woods at lumberyards.

➤ You can make smaller moldings yourself with a router table to match the wood in a particular project.

Part 5

From Principles to Practice

So you understand the tools, the machines, the materials, and the general theory of joinery and construction. Now it's time to start building something. This means you have to think about the various processes that woodworking entails and put them together into the larger process of getting something built. This part of the book looks at how to break a project down into its component processes and how to organize and order these processes to get the job done efficiently and successfully.

This part of the book starts with drawings and planning, proceeds through the milling process, cutting joints, and assembling the parts. It then provides two examples, making a tabletop and building a door, that offer lessons that will help you tackle nearly any project.

Chapter 21

Plan It on Paper: Drawings, Cut-Lists, and Procedure Lists

In This Chapter

➤ Drawings as a means of communication

➤ Drawings as a way to work out details and preclude problems

➤ Seat-of-your-pants drafting

➤ How and why to do a cut-list

➤ Procedure lists to keep the ball rolling smoothly

Woodworking is a technical process. It requires precision, and you have to get things right on the first cut if you don't want to waste a lot of time (and money) redoing previous steps. It also requires that steps be taken in an order that makes sense. Consequently, careful planning is the key to successful projects.

Drawing out your project is the first step to clarifying the details. Making a detailed cut-list with the dimensions of all your parts is the next step, followed by creating a step-by-step procedure list that walks you through the project from start to finish. Getting organized will do more to get the piece finished than anything else. This chapter shows you the ins and outs of drawings, cut-lists, and procedure lists so that you can avoid frustration in your woodworking life.

What Drawings Will Do for You

Mechanical drawings serve several functions. They force you to work out the details, the transitions where parts meet, the joinery, and the relationships between parts. They serve as a reference that you can go back to as you work. You may sort out everything in your head at the beginning of the job, but will you remember the tricky stuff weeks later? I don't think so. Cut-lists can also be a means of communication between you and your clients, your shop assistants, and your suppliers.

Nail Down the Details

Making drawings of your project is an important step in the design process. Sketching out details and doing mechanical drawings that show the dimensions of parts, reveals, and joints, forces you to clarify your vision. Can the tenon be long enough, given the size of the leg? How large a reveal is possible between it and the stretcher? How deep can the drawers be? Will there be enough thigh room under the table apron? These are examples of questions that can't be answered unless you do a drawing.

We all have an ability to visualize spatial relationships. It is highly developed in some people and less so in others. Most of us can improve this ability like an athlete develops a sports skill, through practice. Drawing and sculpting are the best ways I know to improve your visualization skills, and in the meantime, they help you to visualize the work at hand.

Very often, you have an idea for a project in your mind, and it seems like all the details are worked out. Then, when you sit down and start drawing, you find that there are all sorts of problems and conflicts. There isn't enough room in the leg for two tenons long enough to support the table; the drawer will be only one inch deep; the curve of the leg would require a board five inches thick, that sort of thing. Or perhaps aesthetic problems suddenly become obvious when you draw your project. The drawing becomes a preview of the building process, allowing you to solve problems before you ruin good lumber.

When Memory Fails

There are so many details to keep track of in a project. Some are obvious, but if you're like me, you can't keep track of everything without something to jog your memory. That's where drawings come in. I keep a copy of the project drawing pinned to a board that I can carry around the shop wherever I'm working. (I'm so forgetful that I can check a detail and forget my findings by the time I cross the shop.)

Drawings are particularly helpful for the hobbyist who may put a project aside from weekend to weekend or longer. Working sporadically makes it even harder to keep track of the details. It becomes critical to have a reference you can check.

A Drawing Is Worth a Thousand Words

It's nearly impossible to successfully explain three-dimensional objects to another person. You both think you're on the same page while you're imagining completely different things. Usually, it's something simple that seemed so self-evident you didn't describe it properly, so you and the other person are imagining the same chair, with the same ornament, only yours has four legs and theirs has three. When this happens with a client, the results can be disastrous: You can end up inadvertently making yourself a new piece of furniture.

Architects and designers do *sketches* to help themselves think, and make drawings to communicate. They do *presentation drawings* for clients to clarify their design and make sure it's what the client had in mind. They do *working drawings* for their fabricators. Working drawings are what you build from; they have the construction details and the dimensions of all the parts. Generally, the builder and the designer discuss the working drawings, with the builder making suggestions about construction details.

As a designer/builder, you make your own working drawings. The advantage of making drawings for yourself is that they don't have to be pretty. I know I always become self-conscious when I do drawings that someone else will see and spend far longer on them than I would otherwise. Drawings for myself end up smudged and stained with coffee, and nobody complains.

Working drawings also become part of the contract between the designer and the builder. Generally, when the deal is worked out, the deposit paid, and the details agreed upon, the various parties all sign the drawings and everyone receives a copy as a record. That way, if there is a disagreement or a design flaw, the drawings are the final arbiter.

Wood Words

Presentation drawings are a type of rendering shown to clients to give them an idea of the aesthetic aspect of the design. They emphasize what the piece will look like, not the technical aspects. **Working drawings** provide technical information. Designers use **sketches** to develop the design and as a means of thinking on paper.

I Have a Pencil, Now What?

There are plenty of courses and books on drafting, and it's not within the scope of this book to teach you how to do a good mechanical drawing. I will, however, explain what I think should be included in a working drawing that you are going to use as a guide to building a project yourself.

Your drawing should have a *front elevation,* a *side elevation,* and a *plan view.* If a view is not going to have any pertinent information because it will be a view of a blank surface, such as a plan view of a rectangular table, then substitute a *section* or *cutaway view.* For example, instead of a proper plan view of a tabletop, I would draw the

perimeter of the top, but then draw a top view of the base with all the details. Or instead of a simple side elevation of a boring kitchen cabinet, I would draw a side section showing the drawers, shelves, shelf pin locations, and any other important details.

Section views are usually necessary in addition to the three primary views, because they reveal technical information such as joinery and part dimensions. Often, however, you can get away with just doing a detail drawing. For example, rather than draw the entire apron of a table with four identical quadrants, I would just draw a section of one leg with its surrounding area, showing the joinery and the apron dimensions. It may help to draw in phantom lines of details behind the plane of the drawing, such as rabbets, grooves, and so forth, so you don't have to do multiple section views.

I like to draw details such as joinery, where precision is critical, in life size. With a life-size drawing, I can take measurements right off the drawing; I can even lay parts against the drawing and check things visually. Life-size drawings also help give you an intuitive sense of whether the joinery is going to be adequate for the job; sometimes what seems right in a small scale looks all wrong in life size.

Wood Words

An **elevation** is the frontal view of the vertical face of a project with no perspective. So a **front elevation** of a house is how a child would draw it: roof, windows, door, and walls. A **side elevation** is what your next-door neighbor sees. A **plan view** is what a bird flying directly overhead sees. A **section view** is like seeing a slice of the project's interior.

The basic three views are the plan, front elevation, and side elevation. By aligning them on the page, you can speed your layout by carrying lines from one view to another. In addition to speeding the layout, the alignment helps check for errors.

PLAN

FRONT ELEVATION

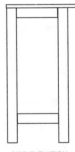

SIDE ELEVATION

JOINERY DETAIL

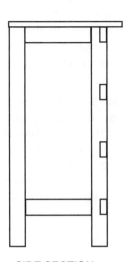

SIDE SECTION

Here are examples of a section view and a detail drawing. These types of drawings are often what hold the most technical information for the maker.

In proper drawings, the details are noted on the main drawing and then cross-referenced from one drawing to another. I don't bother with this protocol if I'm just drawing for myself; I just draw the detail. You can take liberties with personal drawings, ignoring conventions and including practical information for yourself. It's like taking notes in class: Drawings have to make sense to you only. But be sure the drawing has enough information for it to be comprehensible a few days down the line when your memory has faded a bit.

Perspective drawings and any drawing that depicts the object in three dimensions are very helpful when you're trying to visualize the piece. They can orient you in a way that flat elevations and plans cannot. They help you see the relationship between parts and shaped details more clearly.

Tricks of the Trade

There are some great drafting programs for the computer on the market; some do three-dimensional modeling and rendering as well. These programs are generically called CADD (computer-aided drafting and design) programs. They can save a lot of time, but good ones are expensive. It's also important to know how to draft on paper before you go to computer.

Will a Sketch Do?

Sometimes a sketch is all you need. If a project is very simple, or something I've done a million times, I won't bother with the drafting table. I'll just sit down with a pad of paper and sketch my plan, elevations, details, and a perspective view freehand. Freehand drawing is faster than drafting and is perfectly fine for a project that does not have a lot of minute details. I find sketching much faster for perspective views, but that may be because of my own limitations as a draftsman.

Sometimes I use a cross between sketching and drafting, which is a trick I picked up in a rendering class in art school. I draw freehand, but I use a straightedge and triangle for straight lines. This way, I get the speed of sketching, with neater lines for greater clarity. This method is often helpful for people who don't have much experience drawing and complain of "not being able to draw a straight line." The straightedge gives them the confidence they need to get started. This technique can also be used to improve the quality of presentation drawings when you're giving a client a preview of the finished project.

Good Old Graph Paper

Graph paper is an excellent tool, especially for the inexperienced draftsperson. It helps you to establish the proper proportions for a drawing. All too often people start sketching a project with no thought to the dimensions that the thing will have to be. I see this happen with students all the time. Chairs can't have a seat 48 inches off the ground, a bookcase may have to fit into an opening that's 6 × 8 feet, and so forth. People get carried away sketching freehand and come up with something that looks great, but bears no proportional relationship to reality. Then, when they change the proportions so it will fit where it has to go, it doesn't look so good anymore.

With graph paper, you decide on a unit that each box represents (six inches, three inches, or whatever), and you draw the thing in proportion. The graph paper does leave you with a stiff, orthographic view, but you can always sketch freehand on separate blank paper and just use the graph paper drawing as a template to check back to. Sketch paper can work well as a template under *trace*, which brings us to the next section.

Trace It and Save Time

Tracing paper, called simply *trace* in design circles, can be a big help when you're still developing a design. It allows you to generate sketches quickly so you can try out different details or configurations without having to redraw the whole piece from scratch every time. I'll draw the project on a piece of paper, taking time to make the proportions correct and put all the elements where they are supposed to be. Then I'll overlay a roll of tracing paper and quickly trace the overall structure, but with different details drawn in that I want to try out. Using this method, I can quickly produce many different versions until I develop a design I like.

For amateurs who see a drawing or picture of something they like and want to personalize, tracing can be a great way of developing their own version of an existing design. Or you may want to do your original template on graph paper and overlay trace on top of it.

The Cut-List: Hallmark of a Pro

Your next organizational tool is the *cut-list,* which is an itemized list of every part in the project with the quantity of each, its thickness, width, and length, and notes describing any special characteristics, such as rabbets, chamfers, or joints to be cut. To be efficient and for consistent sizing, you should mill and cut all your parts at once (there are certain exceptions, but this is the general rule). Beginners often rough out, mill, and cut all their legs, say, and then go back and do all the short stretchers, and then all the long stretchers. This is not the way to do it. You should set up and do everything at once: Do all your roughing, then all your jointing, and then all your planing. To do this effectively, you need to stay organized and clear-headed, and a cut-list is crucial to organization.

I like to give each part a number, which I write along with the name of the part on the piece in crayon or soft pencil as I cut it out. This system helps me keep track of my pile of parts as the project progresses. You may know what all the parts in a stack are right after you cut them out, but will you remember what that blank piece of wood is a week or two later? If you're working with someone else on a project or working in a large shop with several people, everyone must know what all the parts are, which is impossible if they are not labeled. The name lets you know what it is immediately, and the number helps you find it on the cut-list quickly. I also include a spot to mark a check once the piece is done so I can keep track of where I am in the process.

Cut List

Part#	Done	Description	Quantity	Material	T	W	L	Notes
		Legs	4		2 1/4"	2 1/4"	28 1/2"	Each leg gets 1/2 x 3 x 1 1/4" mortise
		Stretchers	2		1"	3 1/2"	41"	Each stretcher gets 1/2 x 3 x 1 1/8" tenon and 1/4 x 5/16" groove for cleats
		Stretchers	2		1"	3 1/2"	23"	Each stretcher gets 1/2 x 3 x 1 1/8" tenon and 1/4 x 5/16" groove for cleats
		Top	1		1"	34"	52"	Top to be glued-up from boards of whatever width is available
		Cleats	10		15/32"	2"	2 1/2"	

This sample cut-list has all the information you need organized clearly. If you keep blank cut-lists printed and ready to go, you can speed up the process considerably.

Make your cut-list directly from your drawing so that you can check and double-check all the information. I have a standard cut-list form that I use, so when I need to write one up, all the formatting is already done, and I just have to fill in the blanks. I then stick it on a clipboard and carry it to whatever machine I'm using for speedy reference. I worked in a Swiss-run shop for a while, and they used an elaborate system of abbreviations that I've adopted. They also installed eye-level cut-list hangers at every machine to make the process that much more efficient (it's true what they say about the Swiss).

Cut-lists can also be very helpful when you go to buy lumber. I like to pull out boards, mark the pieces as I intend to cut them out right on the rough lumber in crayon, and check them off the cut-list as I go. This process helps me ensure that I'm buying the right amount of lumber. It also speeds up the rough-cutting process when I get back to the shop, because I choose certain boards of a particular width for specific parts. I don't want to cut parts out of the wrong board and end up with a lot of waste later.

The Procedure List: The Project's Rudder

The last piece of paper in your organizational trinity is the procedure list. It's your project's itinerary, an optimum order of procedures to complete the job as efficiently as possible. The primary function of the procedure list is to prevent a misstep that would make an operation more difficult. For example, it's easier to sand frame parts before they're assembled, so you're not sanding into corners; you may have to touch them up in the end, but the bulk of the work is done while they're easy to handle. Another example would be cutting joints on oddly shaped parts: It may be necessary, or at least preferable, to cut the joints before you shape the parts, because once they're shaped, you won't have flat surfaces to lay against the machine table for referencing.

The trick to doing a procedure list is to walk through the building process in your head, imagine yourself performing each task, and try to visualize any problems ahead of time. Clearly, it's easier to do this after you've had some building experience. Do what you can, and if you know someone more experienced, have that person look over your list to see whether he or she can locate glitches. It may help to break things down into categories, such as milling, joinery, shaping, sanding, and finishing, and approach each one separately.

The other thing that a procedure list does is prevent the kind of procrastinating that occurs around tricky procedures. I see colleagues, students, and myself do this all the time. You're nervous about a difficult or unfamiliar technique, something that, if you mess up, will ruin several prize pieces of wood that you've already invested a great deal of time in. So you sand the underside of drawer bottoms, clean behind the drill press, reorganize your sock drawer, and do just about anything but the job at hand. Woodworkers do twice as much work as they have to by avoiding a risky procedure. The procedure list puts the thing you should be doing on your plate, in your face, and right in front of you.

Procedure List:

1) Pick lumber

2) Lay out parts on rough lumber

3) Cut out parts from rough lumber slightly oversize

4) Sticker and let sit

5) Rough mill slightly oversize

6) Sticker and let sit

7) Final mill parts to size

8) Lay out and cut mortises

9) Cut tenons

10) Run groove for panel

11) Raise panel and fit to groove

12) . . . . .

The procedure list does not have to be elaborate; in fact, simpler is better.

The Least You Need to Know

➤ Project drawings are used to communicate with clients and builders.

➤ Doing mechanical or working drawings helps you work out the details in a project.

➤ Working drawings are a reference all through the building of a project and should be readily accessible.

➤ Plan view, front and side elevations, section views, and detail drawings are different views of a project that help clarify it.

➤ Working drawings do not need to be meticulously drafted if you are the only one who will be reading them.

➤ Cut-lists allow you to work efficiently and prevent errors.

➤ Procedure lists help you work productively and prevent procrastination.

Chapter 22

Milling: How to Make Parts That Fit

In This Chapter

➤ Rough milling

➤ Jointing and thickness planing

➤ Squaring the edges

➤ Ripping to width

➤ Crosscutting to length

The milling process is where the shop work begins. You've planned your project, you've purchased the lumber, and now you have to cut those rough boards into parts. You rough-cut the parts, use the jointer and planer to clean and square the surfaces, and then cut the parts down to size on the table saw. This chapter shows you how to mill your parts square, true, and sized correctly. It also outlines the order of tasks to follow to complete your work efficiently and safely.

Cut It Out!

The first thing you do with your pile of boards is cut out your parts. As I said in the last chapter, I like to mark my boards as to their intended use as I pull them out at the lumberyard, but you can do it in the shop if you prefer. When I start to cut out my parts, I take my cut-list, decide how much oversize to cut them, and mark them with a long straightedge and a medium-soft pencil; I don't use crayon, because it leaves a sloppy line. Remember: Longer parts need to be cut more oversized then smaller parts, and woods that move a lot when cut need to be more oversized than ones that don't move much.

I do my crosscutting first either on sawhorses with a circular saw or on a radial arm saw. Then I do my ripping on the band saw. Why don't I use the table saw? Two reasons: First, rough lumber is not flat, so if you try to rip it on the table saw, it will twist and rock on the bed, which leads to pinching the blade and kickback. This is dangerous and nerve-wracking, and I don't like it. The band saw doesn't pinch nearly as much because the blade is so narrow, and if it does, it won't throw the board back at you. The second reason I prefer the band saw is that it allows me to angle the orientation of the part in the board to alter the angle of the grain pattern. This affects the graphic quality of the grain in the finished piece. With the table saw, I'm stuck cutting parallel to the existing edges.

The band saw allows me to angle my parts in the board to improve the graphic effect of the grain. Here I am aligning the grain direction with the direction of some stretchers.

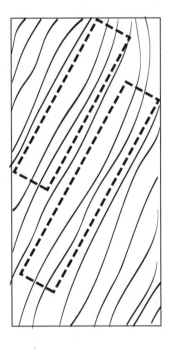

As I cut out the parts, I write on them which part they are so that I'll be able to keep track later. If it's a large, complicated project with many parts, I'll write its part number on it as well to make it easier to find on the cut-list later. As you go through the milling process, you'll have to transfer the markings from surface to surface as you remove material from one or another of them.

Avoid Warping: Premill

As wood is ripped or planed, its internal balance is changed. It has grown with varying amounts of internal stresses; some fibers pull this way, and some pull the other, creating a balance. When you separate the fibers, they can each go their own way, causing the respective boards to warp. If you're cutting those two boards to their final dimension, you're going to be disappointed. They'll be the right dimension, but they'll be bowed and twisted.

I frequently see beginners and poorly trained professionals alike make this mistake, thinking they're saving time by jointing and planing a wide board to final thickness, and then trying to rip it into four or five strips for stretchers or something, only to end up with banana-like boards. The problem escalates when you try to cut joints on the boards, and they won't lay flat. The rocking leads to miscut joints that won't fit. Later, these people will say "That batch of wood was no good." No wood is perfect; it's up to you to finesse it.

Certain species of wood, like maple, are particularly bad for having internal tension; others, like mahogany, are usually stable and don't move much when cut, although any given tree can be problematic. Rough milling or premilling is a preliminary step that helps nip destructive wood movement in the bud. Rather then fight it, you cut the wood a little oversize, stack it, and let it move as it will for a couple of days. Then you flatten it on the jointer, joint an edge square, plane it, and rip it to a little bit thicker and wider than the final specifications. Then let the wood sit on stickers for a few more days. This sitting time allows the tensions to release, and the moisture content to equalize; the longer the wood sits, the better. Finally, after waiting as long as you can stand it, rejoint the wood flat and straight and go through the whole final milling process.

Woodlore

My old boss, Hank Gilpin, works to an extremely high level of craftsmanship. To ensure absolute flatness and precision, he lets boards season for at least two weeks after rough milling. Then he does it again, milling them even closer to final size and letting them sit for another week or more before final milling to size. People wonder how he gets such glass-like flatness to his tabletops and general trueness. This is one of the tricks that help. Nowadays, people aren't as patient as they used to be. Premilling is like letting wine breathe; you just have to wait.

Let me point out that not everyone premills lumber. In fact, not many woodworkers ever do it. But I guarantee it will prevent a huge percentage of your wood movement problems.

Flat's Where It's At!

After premilling, the final milling process begins at the jointer. The initial goal is to flatten one of the primary surfaces. By primary surface, I mean a wide face, not an edge. If all four surfaces are to be more or less equal, as in a square leg, then just choose a side. You want to start with a wide face so you have maximum bearing surface on the fence later, when you're squaring an adjacent surface.

Some woodworkers like to joint a face and immediately square an edge. I don't. I joint all my primary faces flat, run them through the planer, and then come back to the jointer to square an edge. This process adds a trip and slows things down a bit, but it means you can choose which surface to run against the fence, the jointed or the planed face, when squaring the edge. This allows you to get the grain direction right and avoid tearout. I don't know about you, but I'd rather add a trip back and forth to the jointer than sand tearout.

I Woodn't Do That!

Don't let your hands flutter around when you're working on the jointer or other power tools. Establish a routine way of doing things that involves regular movements. It's not only faster, it's safer, too. If you design your routine to keep your hands away from spinning blades, your hands will continue to work safely even when your mind wanders.

To set up the jointer so I can work quickly with the least amount of wasted steps, I keep either a pair of sawhorses or a rolling cart at either end. (A rolling cart has the advantage of easy adjustability.) I pile the parts on them close to the in-feed table, and I position the second pair or cart within an arm's length of the out-feed table. I keep my jointer and planer side by side, feed direction reversed, so I can usually position the second pile so that it sets me up at the in-feed of the planer.

Before I make the first pass on the jointer, I decide which way the grain should run on each part for minimum tearout. I make sure I keep the parts oriented the same way as they come off the jointer, jointed side down, so I don't have to look at each one again when I get to the planer. I just pass the parts through the planer in the same way. If you have a lot of parts, this saves plenty of time.

Pick Your Thickness

The planer is your next step. Now that the parts are flat on one side, it's time to mill them to final thickness. Starting with the parts that are to be thickest, run them through the machine. For the first pass, set the planer about $1/6$ inch thinner than the thickest piece and keep milling until you're through the thickest ones. Set them aside and proceed through the pile until the thinnest are done.

As with the jointer, I keep sawhorses or rolling carts at either end of the planer oriented for the least amount of steps and so the parts at the outfeed are reachable when I go back to the jointer. It is sometimes easier to keep sets of horses on the left and right sides of the planer instead, so you can go back and forth when making progressive passes. It helps you keep track of which parts have been through the planer and which ones haven't.

Another Jaunt to the Jointer

After the boards are at their proper thickness, it's back to the jointer for edge jointing. The idea is to make the edge square to the two parallel faces. To do this, you first have to square up the jointer fence, which I do with a six-inch engineer's square.

Tricks of the Trade

I keep a six-inch rule graduated in $1/32$-and $1/64$-inch increments with me when I'm working on both the jointer and planer, and I check boards frequently. It helps you avoid removing too much stock on the jointer, and it improves accuracy on the planer. Most planers have a thickness gauge built in, but a rule is more accurate.

Again, I orient all the boards the same way as they come off the out-feed table and onto a rolling cart or sawhorses. This way, when I bring them to the table saw for ripping, I have the jointed edge on the entire pile already aimed in the direction of the saw fence. This just simplifies my hand movements and helps keep my hand motions regular and consistent for safety and speed.

It's a good idea to mark the edges as you joint them to keep track. Woodworkers have used a traditional squiggle for at least 200 years (I've worked on eighteenth-century antiques that have the same marks we use today), so I figure, why not keep the tradition going and use the same marks? The mark indicates not only that the edge has been jointed square, but which primary face was used as the reference; this mark can help trace problems later should they turn up.

Let 'Er Rip!

After the pile has been edge-jointed, it's time for the table saw. Keeping the rip blade so it just clears the top of each part, the splitter and guard in place, and your push stick firmly in hand, it's time to start ripping. You can arrange your sawhorses or cart for easy access. I usually pile the parts to the outside of the fence on the side table after they're cut. Do not leave parts on the saw table as you are cutting! You have to keep the cutting area clear.

I Wooldn't Do That!

I've said this elsewhere in the book, but it's worth repeating: Never, ever, put your hand behind the saw blade when the saw is cutting. The wood wants to go toward the front of the saw when it kicks back, and it will take your hand with it. It's tempting to put your hand back there when you're ripping and the part comes away from the fence. Don't do it!

I start ripping the widest parts first, and then proceed through the pile to the narrowest ones; this order helps cut down on mistakes, such as cutting a wide piece too narrow. Make sure your fence is set accurately by tapping it lightly to fine-tune it. I generally set the fence to cut parts $1/32$-inch wide, and then go back to the jointer, set it for a $1/32$-inch cut, and clean up any saw marks.

Parts that are close to square in section, like legs, I'll rip $1/16$ inch over width, and I'll clean up with a $1/16$-inch pass on the planer. Safety note: Always push the piece all the way through, past the back of the blade and the guard when you are ripping, so the piece won't kick back.

If I have several identical, short, wide parts, I'll try to keep them together in the board end to end. I'll rip them to width while they're still together for safety's sake, because a longer board is safer to rip, and then crosscut the parts apart later.

Crosscutting Cautiously

Crosscutting requires that the ends wind up square and the length is correct. Although crosscutting can be done on a radial arm saw or even a chop saw, it is usually done on a table saw. You should never try to crosscut parts by running one end against the fence. This is about the best way I know to seriously hurt yourself. The cutting action of the blade twists the part, pinching it against the fence and either throwing it at you or pulling your hands into the blade.

To crosscut properly, the table saw needs a fixture to hold the board and move it square to the cutting axis of the blade. Although some table saws have a built-in crosscutting fixture called a *sliding table,* most do not. Nearly all table saws, however, do come with a miter gauge. The *miter gauge* is just a fence with a protractor adjustment attached to a square bar that slides in one of two slots on the saw table. It's useful for cutting small pieces and for cutting odd angles, but it is not stable enough for crosscutting large pieces of wood. Neither are miter gauges particularly accurate, because they slide on only one track, and that one track is usually a sloppy fit.

Smooth Sledding

To crosscut a range of wood sizes, you need to make a table saw sled. A sled might just be the single most important shop fixture you can make. I know that when I've set up the various shops I've had, it's always been the first thing I've made. The table saw sled consists of a flat plywood bed that fits on the saw table. It has two strips of solid wood attached to its underside that slide in the two slots intended for the miter gauge. The plywood table is held together by two fences, one at the out-feed side and one at the in-feed side. The out-feed side fence is just there to hold the two halves of the table together; the in-feed side fence is set dead square to the cutting axis of the blade.

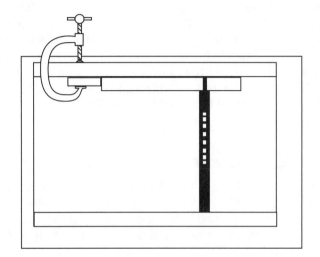

The table saw fence is used for crosscutting. By clamping a stop in place, you can make a series of parts exactly the same length without wasting time measuring each one.

One of the greatest things about table saw sleds is that they enable you to achieve a much higher degree of consistency. By placing parts on the sled table, holding them tight to the fence, and sliding the sled into the blade, you can get a nice, square cut. By clamping a stop to the fence, you can cut multiple parts exactly the same size without having to measure each one separately. Multiple long parts may require that a long strip be clamped to the fence to extend it, with a stop in turn clamped to that.

The sled should be hung out of harm's way when it's not in use. Dropping a sled will knock it out of square. Most shops end up with several sleds: small ones, big ones, ones for cutting miters that hold the work at 45 degrees, ones for use with the blade angled, ones for dado cuts, and so forth.

Milling (Continued)

You've finished ripping your wood, and you've cleaned up your ripped edges on the jointer or planer. I like to set up the sawhorses or cart again within arm's reach on either side of me in front of the saw. I stack the uncut pieces to my left. On goes the sled, and I set up a stop to the right side of the fence. I adjust the stop to cut the longest pieces first, because it prevents the mistake of accidentally cutting long parts too short. I keep the cut-list handy, and as I cut each group of parts, I check it off the list, reset the stop to the next longest part, and resume cutting.

Before I cut each part to length, I must first square one end. It's a good idea to check the rough length of each batch of parts and see how much extra you have, so you don't cut too much off with the first squaring cut. I check each part to see if there are defects on either end, such as end checks or waney edges, that I want to remove. If so, I may make my first cut as heavy as I can to get rid of the defects. The second cut just squares the good end.

As I cut, I take the piece from the pile on the left, put it on the left side of the fence to cut the first end, slide it to my right to square the other end, and then place the piece on the cart or sawhorses to my right. This smooth series of actions from left to right is just one more routine to help prevent accidents and mistakes by being consistent. When I'm done, I dead stack the parts so that air cannot get to them, putting a piece of plywood on top, until I'm ready to start secondary milling operations, such as rabbeting and grooving. Your parts should be stored this way between milling operations to keep them flat and straight.

Rabbets, Grooves, and Chamfers

Secondary milling operations may be performed before or after the joints are cut, depending on the situation. Generally, I like to cut the joints first, so I can adjust grooves for panels to the joinery layout. It's also better sometimes to have as much bearing surface as possible when cutting joints, so you don't want to cut rabbets or chamfers until later.

Rabbets, chamfers, and grooves may be cut on the router table or on the table saw (it is possible to cut chamfers and rabbets on the jointer, but I don't recommend it for safety reasons). For beginners, the router table is safer for most operations. Later, you can explore the table saw when you want greater speed. The router table has a wide range of bits and bearings for these operations; for the small shop and for beginners, it takes the place of the shaper. It, too, can be used with stops clamped onto its fence when cuts don't run all the way through. The router table can also be used to cut the bevel and tongue for raised panels, cutting the bevel and fitting the tongues to the grooves simultaneously, with bits specially made for this task.

Side view of a setup to cut a groove for a panel. You can adjust the depth of the groove by moving the fence in and out. Safety note: Always move the piece against the cutting action of the blade, not with it, or it will throw the piece.

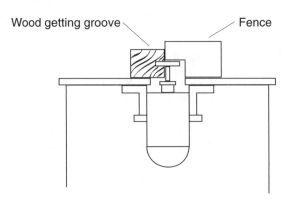

Wood getting groove — Fence

A Shapely Form

After the parts are milled, the joints cut, and the secondary milling operations completed, you're ready to do some shaping (if the project has shaped parts). Shaping begins with laying out lines on the parts, proceeds to the band saw, and moves on to the workbench, where rasps and planes and sandpaper finish the job. Some shaping may occur with templates and routers or the shaper. Profiles, such as bull noses, ogees, and beads, can be cut on edges with the router table. Moldings can be made out of strips that have been milled, but not yet cut to length.

Milling Plywood

Milling plywood starts with the table saw. You don't ever run plywood over the jointer or through the planer; it wrecks the knives. I like to do all my ripping first (when cutting plywood, ripping means cutting parallel to the grain direction). It's generally necessary to cut your first rip a $1/4$ inch or so wide, and then flip the piece to rip off the factory edge, which gets damaged in transit. Then I just go through ripping parts and marking where and what they are in the rips with chalk or crayon.

When I have a pile of eight-foot rips, I start crosscutting. Some parts will have to be reripped narrower, because they may have been part of a wider initial rip. I organize piles on rolling carts or sawhorses, just as I would with solid wood. You have to be extra careful handling plywood because the thin surface veneer can be damaged easily. It is sometimes easier to lean long rips up vertically against a wall, but you shouldn't let them bow for long, or they'll lose their flatness. Plywood should be stored overnight like solid wood: flat, with a protective sheet of scrap plywood on top to protect it from ambient humidity.

The Least You Need to Know

➤ Parts should be marked on the lumber and cut out on the band saw, with an eye for the graphics of the grain.

➤ Premilling prevents most of the warping that occurs during the milling process.

➤ Parts should be marked individually for identification, and the markings need to be rewritten as the surfaces are machined.

➤ Set up each process for efficiency, organization, and safety by using sawhorses or rolling carts.

➤ Crosscutting is done with a fixture, usually a sled, on the table saw.

➤ Secondary milling operations and shaping are usually performed after the joints are cut.

Chapter 23

How the Parts Become a Carcass

In This Chapter

➤ Preparing for a glue-up

➤ Doing a dry glue-up

➤ Marking parts to avoid mistakes

➤ Making sure things end up flat and square

➤ Mastering miters

A final glue-up is the moment of truth. You've milled and prepared your parts, cut your joints, and finished all your shaping and sanding. Now all the parts have to go together. The final touch-up and finishing still has to be done, but for most woodworkers, the glue-up is when they feel as though they've accomplished something. The project looks like a piece of furniture for the first time.

The glue-up can also be a time for catastrophes. Many projects are permanently damaged, if not ruined, during the glue-up. The fight against the clock as the glue is setting combined with poor planning, unexpected problems, or joints that need too much pressure to close can lead to panic and trouble. The result can be frames out of square or not flat, joints locked partway open, parts with hammer or clamp dents, or parts glued in upside down. This chapter aims to help you prevent these catastrophes by showing you how to plan, prepare, and choreograph a glue-up.

On Your Marks

Marking your parts to orient them is a process that begins before you cut your joints and is crucial for assembly. Over the years, a system of arrows has developed that indicates the front and the back of the project. The arrows marked on the parts indicate the part's location and orientation so that when joints and rabbets are cut or parts are assembled, the part isn't reversed, flipped upside down, or generally confused.

The best way to explain how to mark parts with arrows is with sample illustrations of different types of structures. The rule is that the arrows always point up or back and are drawn only on one side of any plane; left and right sort themselves out, as you'll see. Many parts have arrows pointing up and arrows pointing back for clear orientation.

This illustration shows how a door is marked for joinery and assembly. The arrows always point up and back. The centerline of the arrow is always the middle of the door.

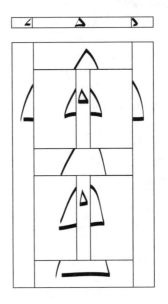

This illustration shows how a drawer would be marked: The arrows on drawers are usually marked on the underside, so they don't need to be sanded off. A plywood cabinet would be marked the same way, but with the arrows pointing up.

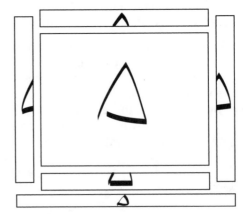

Students often ask me, "Why not just write words, like 'up' and 'down' or 'right' and 'left' instead of using arrows?" The reason becomes clear when you're in the middle of a complicated glue-up. You can read the arrows immediately, but it takes a while to process the words written on the various parts; if a part is out of place and the arrow is upside down, your eye catches it instantly. When the glue is drying, speed and clarity count. You want mistakes to jump out at you; you don't want to go looking for them when your mind is busy with half a dozen other things.

Time to Clean Up!

One of the major mistakes that beginners make is to assemble the project before thorough sanding and cleanup. You can't sand a project properly after it's glued together. Frame and carcass members should be sanded on the workbench so that you're not sanding into corners. You'll have to go over the project later to touch it up, but any internal surfaces and corners should be thoroughly sanded through the entire spectrum of sanding grits while the project is apart. I generally scrape and sand any outside surfaces to 120-grit before the glue-up as well, so all I have to do is sand the piece with the higher grits after it is together. I don't sand the surfaces further before assembly because they get handled so much and may get dinged by clamps.

While I'm sanding, I also check over each piece and look for problems, especially where the joints are concerned. I check to see that the shoulders on tenons are flat and square. If they're not, I pare them with a very sharp chisel. I also look for debris that may cause the joints to bind; there is often waste at the bottom of mortises or in the slots for biscuit joints and in grooves for panels.

It is sometimes a good idea to *prefinish* parts before glue-ups. A box that has a built-in bottom or a carcass with a glued-in back, for instance, is nearly impossible to spray: You don't want to spray into a closed box. So if you're doing a sprayed lacquer finish, you would want to prefinish the inside of the parts before you assembled them.

It's also a good idea to prefinish solid wood panels before they go into their frames because they generally shrink over time. If the tongue does not get finish on it before it's placed into the groove and is then finished after assembly, an unfinished strip will appear when the panel shrinks and pulls a bit of the tongue out. It's probably smart to finish any visible area that will be hard to get to after assembly. Be sure to keep finish off glue surfaces and joints, though, because glue doesn't stick to most finishes. Covering glue surfaces with masking tape usually works.

Wood Words

It's sometimes a good idea to apply finish to parts or sections of parts before the project is assembled and before the general finishing takes place. Woodworkers do this because it would be hard, or even impossible, to apply finish to these areas after assembly, despite the fact that they will be visible. This process is called **prefinishing**.

Gluing Up in Sections

It's often too much to expect to glue up a whole project in one shot. It may be safer to glue it up in sections, and then glue the sections together. For instance, if I'm working on a big tabletop consisting of four or five boards, I'll glue up two pairs of boards separately, let them dry overnight, and then glue the pairs together. If you were to try to glue all of the boards together at the same time, they would slide around, and you would end up with uneven joints you had to plane-flush. I would rather spend my time waiting for glue to dry than spend it flushing and sanding tabletop boards.

Another example would be a frame-and-panel chest of drawers. It would be way too ambitious to try to glue up an elaborate chest of drawers in one shot. I would glue each side together separately, let them dry overnight, and then glue the two sides together. It's hard enough to put a single frame-and-panel unit together square and flat; to do four at the same time with any precision is next to impossible. Break down your projects and figure out how to glue up sections rather then tackling the whole thing at once.

I Woodn't Do That!

When you're gluing up boards for a tabletop, don't tighten all the clamps at once, because this makes it hard to get the boards to end up flush. Proceed one clamp at a time from the center out, tightening the clamps part way, working the boards flush with your hands, and then tightening the clamps all the way.

Setting Up the Glue-Up

You need all the time you can get for a glue-up. Most glue-ups are done with white or yellow glue, which means that the whole thing should take about 10 minutes. You don't have time to be running for clamps or mallets or things you've forgotten or klutzing around because your setup is sloppy. Everything you need has to be there. If something goes wrong (and it often does), you'll need all the time you can get. Bumbling for things breaks your confidence, which leads to panic.

A Solid Foundation

To glue up a project, you need a clean area and a flat surface. I like to do my glue-ups on two or three identical wood battens placed on top of my workbench or else on sawhorses. By raising the parts up, I can arrange clamps underneath, which is sometimes necessary, and the project doesn't rock if something is uneven. I also find that the surfaces of the parts don't get damaged as much or as smeared with glue if they're raised up.

It's important that the sawhorses or battens are parallel and create a flat plane so the work doesn't end up with a twist. With the battens, flatness is easy to check; if the workbench surface is flat, as it should be, and the battens are the same thickness, then you're fine. With the sawhorses, you should sight from one to another to see whether they're parallel. They may require some shimming, because floors are rarely flat.

Hey, Back Off!

Make sure you have plenty of clamps. Plan it out and figure how many you're going to need: Don't just guess! Also, make sure they're deep enough and long enough for your purposes. Place them within arm's reach so that you can get to them quickly.

Also make sure that the clamps are *backed off*. This just means that the tightening screws have been opened all the way. When the glue is drying, as you're tightening, you won't have time to run out of threads, remove the clamp, back it off, readjust it, and start over. I see people, panicked-looking people, do this all the time.

You should also have plenty of pads to protect the wood from the clamp faces. I like to use small squares of $1/2$-inch Homosote. It's rigid enough so that the clamps stay square, but it's soft enough not to damage the wood. It helps save time to attach the Homosote to the clamp faces in advance with masking tape.

Other Accoutrements

You'll need various items in the course of your glue-up, and you should get them ready beforehand. Here's a list:

➤ Glue spreaders. Some people use their fingers; others like small strips of wood.

➤ A tape measure, a square, and a straightedge to check for trueness as you go.

➤ Dull chisels and a damp cloth to clean up glue.

➤ A mallet and block to coax parts together while protecting the wood's surface.

The Dry Run

If you have a tricky glue-up or if you're a beginner and every glue-up is tricky, consider doing a *dry glue-up*. The dry glue-up mimics the real thing in every respect but one: You don't apply any glue. You assemble everything and clamp it together just as you would if it were the real thing, but if you encounter an unforeseen problem, it isn't a catastrophe. When you're done, you carefully tap everything apart and do the real one. Doing a dry glue-up speeds up the real glue-up, because you've already rehearsed it, and it reveals any slowdowns or problems, allowing you to deal with them panic-free.

To do a dry glue-up, you have to take it seriously and prepare as though you mean it. Set all your clamps out ahead of time, get your pads ready, have your measuring devices to check for squareness and flatness after the piece is in the clamps. Remember, the real glue-up will be harder because you'll have to spend time spreading glue, and the glue may expand the joints, which makes them harder to pull together. You'll also be nervous.

Show Time!

You have all your clamps and tools together, the parts are marked, you've done a dry run, and now it's time for the main event. It helps to have a friend to hold the other side of a long clamp, to help spread glue, and to give you a shoulder to cry on when things go wrong. If you have a big glue-up with long parts and lots of long clamps, it's worth postponing it until you can get someone to help. Otherwise, here we go!

Tricks of the Trade

If you can't find anyone to help with a glue-up, and you have to use long clamps that are hard to position alone, you can make blocks to hold them the right height from the work. Set them in place and measure how far up they need to go to get the screw centerlines in line with the joint centerlines and then cut blocks that will hold the clamps at the right height.

First, start spreading the glue. Be sparing; most novices lay it on too thick and end up cleaning it off the floor. If you get it exactly right, you should end up with tiny beads of glue in a row along the joint line; they can be deftly removed with a chisel. Experience will guide you in the future; in the meantime, give it your best guess.

Put a thin film of glue on both mating surfaces. With mortise-and-tenon joints, I like to put a line of glue on the rim of the mortise and on the leading edge of the tenon. When the joint slides together, it spreads the glue across the mating surfaces for you. This way, the glue doesn't dry out as quickly as it does when you smear it over each face; gluing also takes less time this way. I do something similar with dovetails, finger joints, and tongue-and-groove joints, applying glue to the leading edges only. When edge-joining boards for a tabletop or the like, I run a bead along both edges out of the glue bottle, and then smear it across the entire edge, either with my finger or with a flat strip of wood.

When you glue together large, flat surfaces, such as when you're laminating sheets of plywood or gluing wide boards face-to-face, you have to cover a lot of surface area fast. I like to use either a paint roller with a short nap or a flat, serrated glue spreader. These tools work well when spreading glue for veneer, too, but remember that you spread the glue only on the substrate, never on the veneer, which will curl.

I like to start assembling the joints by hand as I spread the glue. The glue will stay wet longer if it's not exposed to air. One caveat, though: Tight tenons and dovetails may lock up if you get them partially together and then stop. In these cases, you should tap them all the way together immediately, before you apply clamping pressure.

The Pressure's On

As I said in the preceding section, I like to pull the joints together by hand rather than with the clamps. It often helps to tap them together with a hammer, holding a block of softer wood against the part you're tapping. If you use Homosote, or something really soft, it will deaden the shock of the hammer blow, which you don't want.

After I get the parts at least partially together, I bring the clamps into action. It's important to position them properly, and most beginners have trouble with this task. The clamps' faces should be square to the planes of the wood they're engaging, and the centerline of the screws should be aligned with the centerline of the joint. If you get it wrong, the parts will want to slide, or the plane of the parts will bow away from or toward the clamp. You may find you have to adjust the clamp to correct some problem created by uneven clamping pressure. When frames are glued up out of square, the problem is often angled clamps.

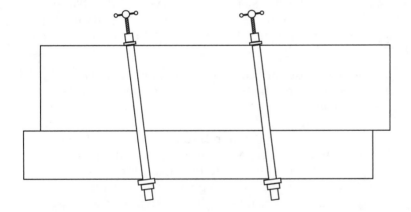

If the clamp is angled, it will slide the parts to try to correct the mistake, pulling parts out of alignment.

When you position the clamps where you want them, start tightening them. It's a good idea to tighten all the clamps lightly, and then gradually tighten them all a little bit at a time. This process ensures even clamping pressure.

251

If the axis of the clamping pressure is not centered on the joint, it will bow the plane of the parts. At left, the clamps are too far back; in the center, they are too far forward; at the right, they are centered.

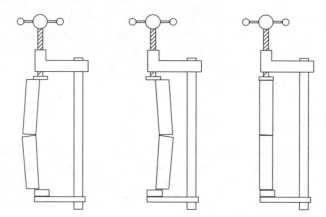

Be Square, Be Flat

After you have pulled the joints together and clamped them, it's time to check for flatness and squareness. Checking for flatness is easy; all you need is a long straight-edge. Place it across the surface, and you will immediately see whether a bow exists. If it does, you need to move the clamps. Move the clamps in and out to change the centerline or flip them around to the other side.

Cabinet frames and carcasses have to be checked for squareness as well as flatness. You can't always do it with a square because clamping pressure bows parts slightly. Instead, you check for squareness by measuring the diagonals with a measuring tape or folding rule.

Tricks of the Trade

Because bar clamps and pipe clamps bow themselves as they are tightened, they naturally tend to bow the work away from them, even when the centerlines seem correct. For this reason, it's a good idea to alternate clamps from side to side to balance the tendency to bow.

First, you measure the distance between diagonal pairs of corners where frame members meet. If the two diagonals measure the same, then the frame is square; if not, they need some adjustment. To correct the problem, the best solution is to loosen and angle your clamps as though you're trying to pull together the two corners that are farther apart. If this doesn't work, then you can resort to plan B, which is running a clamp diagonally to pull the two more distant points together. You have to be careful when you do this because it's easy to overdo it. Often, you'll tighten the clamps more, and nothing will happen. Then, as you give them one more twist, the joints suddenly free up, shift, and throw the frame out of square the other way. Then you have to start over from the opposite direction.

The Colossal Cleanup

You breathe a sigh of relief; your joints went together, and you managed to get everything square and flat. Your problems are over. Well, almost. You still have to clean up the glue.

There are many theories on glue cleanup, all of which try to minimize the amount of work you have to do. Some people wait until the glue is "leather hard," which I think is more trouble than it's worth. Others splash water all over the place, which is really a bad idea, and the truly misguided wait until the glue is hard and then chisel and sand it off. My method requires some industry just when you want to relax and celebrate, but it's designed to minimize disturbing the wood surfaces, which saves time correcting damage later.

I like to remove the glue as soon as I can. First, I take one of the chisels that I dull specially on my sharpening stones so they won't gouge the wood, and I scrape all the glue off that I can while it's still wet. Always move the chisel with the grain, to avoid cross-grain scratches.

As soon as I've scraped one area, I take a lightly dampened cloth and feverishly rub where the glue has been removed. Let me stress that you do not want a wet cloth that sends drips cascading down the woodwork. You just want to soften the residual glue film. It may help to go back over it with the chisel, and then hit it again with the damp cloth. After the glue has been totally removed, get rid of any dampness with a dry, absorbent cloth.

It may be necessary to flip the assembly over to clean up the other side. If so, be careful not to move any clamps. When I had a big shop I used to keep an auto mechanic's creeper to get underneath tabletops and the like to remove glue when I was assembling on sawhorses.

The Morning After

After the glue-up has set completely (I know what the label says, but I like to let it sit overnight), you can remove the clamps and clean up the damage. First, make sure that there are no glue blobs that hid under clamps and require scraping and sanding. Then check the areas where glue was cleaned up. The damp cloth will have raised the grain; with luck the chisel has not scratched the wood. Smooth any raised grain with extremely fine sandpaper (220-grit to 320-grit); scratches may require a lower grit.

If you think there might be residual glue on anything, you need to find out now before the finish goes on. To find out, go over the area with a damp cloth again. The parts with glue on them will stay light; the clean areas will soak up water and darken (this same thing will happen with finish). If there is glue, you'll have to sand and possibly scrape it off. Be as gentle as you can to keep the surfaces flat.

Royal Flush

Surfaces that are supposed to be flush, whether adjacent boards in a tabletop or frame members, invariably need some trimming after the glue-up. Here is where your plane and cabinet scraper skills come in. Use a straightedge to check that you are flattening surfaces and not creating hollows. The way to avoid making hollows is to work a broad area, not just a small section. After planing and scraping, run through the spectrum of sandpapers by using a cork block.

Miter Matters

As I've said elsewhere, miters are a challenge. (I've heard them called less-flattering epithets around the shop from time to time.) They are particularly difficult to glue up, but there are techniques that help the process, or at least correct problems.

The biggest problem is clamping. If you run clamps in both directions, the joints inevitably slide unevenly, and it becomes a festival of dismay as you try to make the thing square. The Lamello company has developed a system of miter clamps that use four corners combined with a special strap clamp; they're great for carcass miters. They aren't cheap, but I recommend them wholeheartedly.

Another trick I use is to tape miters together. That's right: I tape them. First, I take one length of fresh masking tape, and I hang it from something. Then I "laminate" a second length on top of it so I have a double thickness for strength. Next, I rip the tape into three four-inch segments, one end of which I tack onto my bench or elsewhere for safekeeping. I glue my parts and assemble them as tightly as I can by hand. Then, I burnish one end of the tape down near the edge of the miter and stretch it over the corner, then burnish it down onto the other side.

Woodlore

Fresh masking tape stretches and pulls the joint together; old tape loses its stretch, so don't use it. I describe this miter-taping process to other woodworkers, and they look at me like I'm an idiot. But done properly it works brilliantly. I learned it from a friend and business partner who had been the lead cabinetmaker at a shop renowned for their high-end veneered cabinets. Everything seemed to have impossible curved miters; it gave me the shivers just to look at work like that.

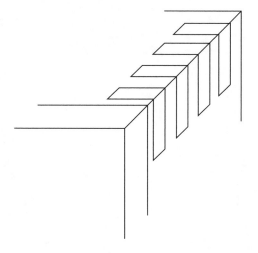

Taping miters sounds silly, but it works great if you get the feel of it. Make sure you burnish the tape down and then stretch it and burnish it again so it holds. I should warn you, though, that it works only if the joints have been cut accurately in the first place.

If your miters still don't quite pull together at the ends, it's time for the miter hammer. While the glue is still wet, you lightly tap the edges where the miters meet just a few degrees off flat to close the open miter. Make sure you do both sides. Don't overdo it and dent the surface, just do lots of light taps. Later, you can sand the area gingerly.

The Least You Need to Know

➤ Arrows indicating part orientation prevent mistakes and save time.

➤ You should sand parts thoroughly before assembly.

➤ Projects are often glued up in sections rather than all at once.

➤ Dry glue-ups prevent disasters and are a rehearsal for the real thing.

➤ Everything you're going to need for a glue-up should be set out, organized, prepared, and within arm's reach beforehand.

➤ Proper clamp position is subtle and critical.

➤ It's important to check for flatness and squareness when gluing up.

➤ You should clean up glue immediately.

Chapter 24

Woodworking Art: Tabletops and Other Flat Surfaces

In This Chapter

➤ Matching boards for a balanced grain pattern

➤ Orienting the growth rings

➤ Gluing up

➤ Final surfacing

➤ Detailing edges for style and function

➤ Attaching the top to allow for wood movement

The last chapter examined the general processes that go into gluing up a typical project. This chapter focuses on a particular task that you will encounter on a regular basis: making a solid wood tabletop. The lessons learned here resonate to other projects: cabinet tops, floating panels, and any situation where you have solid wood boards glued up to make a panel.

This chapter delves into aesthetics and how technical issues work in the service of beauty. I'm talking about grain patterns and how to work with them. In the course of walking you through the making of a tabletop, I will introduce another key technique: using cleats to attach a solid wood top to a frame.

Not Just Another Pretty Tabletop

When you look at a tabletop, what do you see? I'm not talking about a photograph of a tabletop in some interiors magazine or a furniture company brochure's dog's-eye-view; I mean, what do you see as you stand in a room with a tabletop? The average dining table is 29 to 31 inches tall (lower than you thought, right?). Consequently, what you see of the table is the top, and not much else. You may see a little leg and foot as well.

Because of this, the tabletop is the most important thing on a table. Architects, who are in the habit of drawing everything in elevation, usually put elaborate details down around the apron and at the top of the leg, where they're never seen. A good furniture designer puts the most effort into the top, into its shape and its grain pattern. The top's graphic effect is even more important on a coffee table, because it's lower, and on a small table, because it's read better as a shape than a larger one.

This is why a tabletop is like a picture. It reads as a graphic image, which means that you have to work extra hard when choosing, matching, and arranging the boards you use. The sign of a cheap production table or of a table made by a less-than-sensitive woodworker is a top with randomly matched boards, where the grain and color of one board has nothing to do with the one next to it. Certain species with dramatic grain, such as oak and mahogany, can look particularly disagreeable if you don't take care to match the boards.

Tricks of the Trade

The trick to a good book-match is to remove as little material as possible from the visible matched faces. The more you remove, the less they look alike. You have to be very careful when jointing them not to get carried away. I always joint the book-matched faces with shallow passes, and then run the back side through the planer.

Matchmaker, Matchmaker

What makes a good match between boards? As usual, beauty is in the eye of the beholder. Some things are simple, such as color. Nearly everyone agrees that boards in a tabletop or panel should have a similar color; commercial furniture is nearly always stained to even out the color. Most people also prefer a sense of balance and symmetry to a disjointed, unbalanced look.

The most symmetrical and balanced match is the book-match, and it is the classic choice for panels and tabletops. Book-matching, as I've explained in Chapter 11, "The Sawmill: Where Trees Become Lumber," gives an almost mirror image by joining consecutive boards and exposing faces that have been separated by a common saw cut. The less material that is removed between the two faces, the more similar they will be. This is why veneer gives a closer match than solid wood; it's sliced, so you don't lose material to the saw kerf and subsequent planing. I should point out that book-matching is much more common in veneer work than in solid wood, because sequenced boards are hard to come by.

Not only are they hard to come by, book-matched boards sometimes seem a little formal. Sometimes boards that have a generally balanced feel seem more natural, less artificial. For a quietly balanced match, I look for boards with a centered grain pattern, which is the classic flat-sawn board with active grain in the center and quiet linear grain that hides glue lines on the edges. Look for boards that have ellipses or gentle cathedral grain in the center.

The two boards at the left have centered grain patterns; the two on the right have generally less desirable, unbalanced grain patterns.

I've seen beautiful tabletops that are made with neither centered grain boards, nor book-matches. My own dining table, made by my old mentor Hank Gilpin, is made from exquisite flame-grain cherry; the boards are not particularly centered, and they have plenty of sapwood, which is generally considered a defect. But Hank, who is known for his eye with wood, has somehow chosen and arranged them so that they have an active grain pattern that waterfalls from one to another, achieving an unexpected balance and symmetry. Of course, masters can break the rules and achieve success in ways that ordinary craftspeople cannot. That's what makes them masters.

The message is: Don't be afraid to take chances and trust your instincts. There are no hard and fast rules. I just lay boards next to each other and flip them this way and that until something makes sense. The sense of movement in one board may be balanced by the movement of another. If there is an art to woodworking, it includes grain-matching.

Picking the Winners

When you shop for lumber for tabletop stock, you're going to have to spend a little extra time at the lumberyard. You need to find boards that have similar color and grain patterns that relate to each other in some way.

If possible, for tabletops I like to buy lumber that has already been surfaced or planed on the two primary faces (S2S in lumber industry parlance). Surfaced boards are just easier to read than rough-milled boards, which are dark and fuzzy. You also get a more accurate reading of their color. The disadvantages of surfaced lumber are that it is a little bit more expensive than rough lumber and is significantly thinner than equivalent rough lumber, yet not necessarily flatter. So-called 2-inch S2S lumber is usually 1³/₄ inches thick, and ⁸/₄ lumber is usually a bit over 2 inches. If you're going for a nice thick top, you may have to use rough lumber, because you'd mill it more carefully than some Joe in a planing mill would.

Wood Words

The **scrub plane** is a specialized tool that used to be quite common. It looks like a thin bench plane, but it has a slightly curved edge ground on its blade and a large throat opening. This shape is so you can remove a lot of stock quickly. Before electric planers, when milling was done by hand, scrub planes were used for preliminary flattening of rough boards.

On-the-Job Planing

If I have to buy rough lumber, then I make sure to take along a *scrub plane* and a block plane, so I can quickly remove a section of the fuzzy, dark surface. I use the block plane to smooth the surface a little after the scrub plane does its work. Most reputable lumberyards will let you do this, but you should ask first and make sure you clean up any mess.

You can usually eliminate most boards without planing them. Just look at the surfaces, and you should be able to get a general idea of the grain pattern; most will be an easy cut. If a board seems to have promise, then pull out the planes. You'll find that the color changes dramatically as you delve beneath the surface, so don't think that boards that seem to have similar color in the rough will look the same after milling. Color variation will eliminate more boards, especially after you've already chosen a board or two and have to find ones with similar color.

Cleaving to a Tree

The best way to match boards is to buy ones that have been flitch-cut from the same tree. Boards from the same tree will have identical color, texture, and general grain patterns. When a tree is flitch-cut (sawn in a series of consecutive slabs, like slices of bread), the grain tends to be centered nicely, which makes for a balanced feel. Flitch cutting also makes it possible to book-match boards, which many consider the ultimate way to match them. (See Chapter 11 for more on flitch cutting.)

The problem is that buying consecutive, flitch-cut boards isn't easy. You have to be prepared to hunt, which is why professional woodworkers don't bother. As a hobbyist, you may be more willing to spend some extra time searching for this ultimate solution to the matching problem. The best places to look are at small lumbermills and at specialty lumberyards that cater to fine woodworkers.

Small lumbermills will require more of your time spent hunting and negotiating. But there is a certain satisfaction in the hunt, and I can think of worse places to spend my time than in the country going from mill to mill. Besides, if you go to a fancy lumber dealer, you'll pay more, usually much more, because the dealer has done the hunting for you, and dealers do it for the money, not the sport. Many lumber dealers are very fair, though, and you may well prefer to spend your time working with wood than hunting for it.

Milling About

You have your carefully selected matching boards back at the shop, so now it's time to mill. The first problem you may encounter is the width of your jointer. Tabletop boards are generally chosen in part for their width. Woodworkers are always looking for 12-inch, 14-inch, or as-wide-as-they-can-find boards. Inevitably, they end up with boards that are wider than they can fit on their jointer.

Tricks of the Trade

Over time, flat-sawn boards tend to cup slightly away from the center of the tree, as though the annular rings were straightening out. Woodworkers often argue about whether it's better to alternate the ring direction and get a ripple effect or to face them the same way and pull one big curve flat. I think both methods are ridiculous because they ignore aesthetics. Just flip the boards the way that looks best.

Woodlore

During my apprenticeship, I had to joint boards by hand. I wasn't being paid, so it didn't matter if I spent a few sweaty days flattening 30-inch mahogany boards with hand planes. You just have to keep planing and checking and planing and checking. You start with your old friend the scrub plane, and then move on to a medium–length bench plane. Then you finish up with a smoothing plane, checking the board all the time with winding sticks and a straightedge. To plane the other side parallel, you mark the edge with the desired thickness from the jointed side using a marking gauge and connect the lines, using the same tools you used to joint the first side.

You have several options for jointing wide boards. The most basic option is to joint them by hand. If you really like handwork or are remarkably patient, then maybe hand-jointing is an option for you. A speedier method is to run the board on your jointer (the jointer must be over half the width of the board) and keep flipping it around. You joint half the board and spin it so you can joint the other half of the same face. You'll get tearout because one direction will be against the grain, and there will be ridges, which you will have to remove with a hand plane, but it will expedite the process.

A third method, if you are plugged in to the local woodworking network, is to find someone with a wide jointer and rent some time on it. You have to spend time lugging the boards around, but you get a good job when you're done. I had a 34-inch wide by 16-feet long mahogany board that I had to take on a three-hour truck ride to get planed a few years ago. Because mahogany is so stable and stays so flat, I didn't have to joint it. I was able to just run it through a planer on both sides, but finding a 36-inch planer isn't easy.

Long, wide boards are hard to joint evenly, so crosscut them to a couple of inches longer than you need, and be careful. It's easy to take too much off one end due to uneven pressure. If you can, get a helper to support the end of the board overhanging the jointer bed. You can also buy adjustable roller stands to do the same thing.

Gone Clamping

To prepare my boards for clamping, I mark them with an arrow that orients them. As soon as I determine the match, I lay them out and mark them this way before I mill them, and I keep transferring the marks from side to side as I mill each one. But I always re-evaluate the boards after I'm done planing them to thickness. The grain pattern changes during milling, and sometimes defects appear, or patterns change, or sometimes my taste changes.

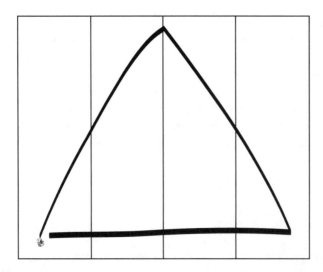

Once again, the arrow indicates the order and orientation of the boards to be glued up.

As I said in the last chapter, I like to clamp boards in pairs, let them dry thoroughly, and then clamp the pairs together. I glue them up on sawhorses that have been shimmed parallel. It's a good idea to clamp boards together without glue first to check the joint line and to make sure the joint faces are square and will yield a flat tabletop. It's good practice to rejoint the edges to be glued after you've glued up the pairs, but before you glue the whole thing together. Clamping has a way of wrecking edges.

You need good clamping pressure, and you need to make sure that the clamps are positioned correctly so the top goes together flat. Tighten one clamp at a time, working the boards flush at that point.

The Final Surface

I Woodn't Do That!

Many people feel that it's necessary to put a spline joint, biscuits, or dowels between edge-joined boards to get a good joint. In this case, a good glue joint is better than a mechanical joint, and the preceding joints can all cause problems of one sort or another. It's better to improve your gluing skills than resort to unnecessary joinery.

After the glue is dry and the clamps are off, it's time to flatten the surface. This can be a grueling process (remember what I said about jointing boards by hand), but it has to be done. Always do the underside first, because the side you do first tends to get scratched from being face-down with so much activity going on above it when you do the other side. The bottom isn't seen, so it doesn't need as thorough a job.

The following instructions are for the top surface. I recommend starting with a #4 smoothing plane and a straightedge. Invariably, one edge on each glue joint will be proud and the other shy, and they may switch back and forth. Start working on the high one with the plane. Take broad strokes and feather out the high spots gradually. It's best to work the boards with diagonal strokes going one way and then the other, so you make an X-pattern over the glue joint. You will almost inevitably get tearout. This can be removed later with a cabinet scraper and sandpaper.

After you flatten the surface, you can switch to a #3 smoothing plane and try to minimize the tearout. Take light passes, with the blade sticking out just far enough to get a shaving. Make sure the blade is extra sharp and keep the chip-breaker about $1/32$ inch from the edge of the blade. You can take passes with the grain, too. It helps to angle the plane to the direction of the pass for a better shearing action. When you seem to have stopped improving the surface with the smaller smoother, it's time for the cabinet scraper.

I sharpen three or four scrapers at a time because they're inexpensive and they get dull quickly. It takes a long time to get the hang of the cabinet scraper, but it's worth it. I give an explanation of how to use it later on in Chapter 28, "Surface Prep: Groundwork for a Great Finish," but it just takes practice. The scraper will remove all of the

●

263

tearout and minimize your sanding. As with the plane, it helps to work the scraper in an X-pattern and hold it at an angle. The scraper is particularly handy when you're working on curly or figured woods that tear out hideously with a hand plane.

When you're done getting rid of the tearout, you can move on to the sandpaper. I recommend starting with 100-grit, moving on through 120-, 180-, 220-, and possibly further, depending on the finish and the hardness of the wood. The harder the wood is, the finer the final grit should be.

Getting an Edge

When the top is flat, you can detail the edge. There are many options for a molded edge. You have to be careful to choose a profile that doesn't leave sharp corners (you don't want the children of the house walking around with pirates' eye patches unless they're playing dress-up). Blunter moldings are damaged less and so look better longer.

A sampling of edge moldings.

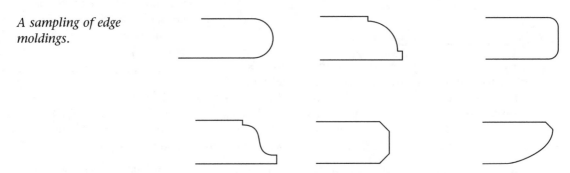

Most profile choices come down to issues of style, and that is your business. I will point out, though, that if the profile is visible from above, it will read thicker and give a sense of three-dimensional form. Moldings that undercut the edge from below make it read sharper visually, so a shaped top will pop out graphically.

Profiles that are visible from above read thicker and give a sense of three-dimensional form. Moldings that undercut the edge from below emphasize the graphic shape of the top.

Attachment Anxiety

You probably know by now that you can't just screw a wide solid wood tabletop to a base, because it will crack when the humidity changes. Some method of attachment has to be used that will hold the tabletop flat and fast, but let it expand and contract when the weather changes.

One option, if the top is not too wide, is to screw it down from below using pan-head screws and washers in oversized holes. This allows the screw to slide on the washer sideways, absorbing the movement. The problem is that this is only good for about $1/8$ inch in either direction, at most. It also requires long screws for wide aprons. This method is best left for small tabletops with narrow aprons.

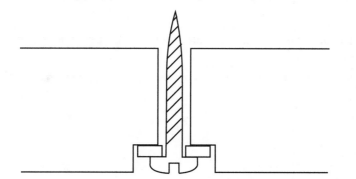

A pan-head screw with a washer in an oversize hole will accommodate a small amount of expansion and contraction.

The classic way to attach a tabletop is to make small cleats, often called buttons, that screw to the top with a tongue that slides back and forth in a groove in the apron. Because the buttons can slide either side to side or in and out, you can run a groove all the way around the apron for them. Make sure there's enough depth in the groove for the cleat to move in and out enough to accommodate the expansion differential of the tabletop. To play it safe, allow $1/8$ inch per foot. It's best to lock the top in the middle with a screw at either end so that seach side expands and contracts evenly.

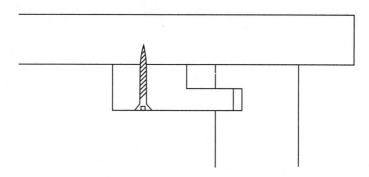

The cleat, or button, can slide either side to side or in and out of a groove in the apron. This allows it to be used around the entire perimeter of the base.

The Least You Need to Know

➤ Tabletop boards must be chosen for their graphic effect.

➤ Tabletop boards must be matched for grain pattern and color.

➤ You must see the board at least partially planed to evaluate it.

➤ Consecutive boards from the same tree are ideal.

➤ After boards are glued together, they must be carefully flattened with hand planes and cabinet scrapers.

➤ Edge details can make a shape read graphically or provide a sense of thickness and form.

➤ Tops may be held to the base with cleats, called buttons, that permit expansion and contraction.

Chapter 25

HOW'S IT HANGIN'?

PRETTY GOOD.

The Well-Hung Frame-and-Panel Door

In This Chapter

➤ Milling door parts

➤ Marking door parts

➤ Cutting joints

➤ Raising the panels

➤ Gluing it up

➤ Hanging the door in the opening

Our next step-by-step project is a four-panel, frame-and-panel cabinet door. Like the tabletop of the last chapter, this project raises issues that carry over into all sorts woodworking projects, such as fitting, raising panels, cutting joints, and working with hardware. A frame-and-panel door is a close cousin to the side of a frame-and-panel cabinet, so many of the techniques will carry over to cabinet construction. The door also involves aesthetic issues and grain-matching.

Choosing the Best Boards

The door raises some new issues about wood choice. Like the table, it has panels that require expanses of grain, though not as wide. But the door panels are in a frame.

One of my pet peeves is when frame parts have wildly incongruous grain patterns. This problem is particularly common with production red oak cabinetry, where the strong grain texture accentuates the randomness of random-matched parts. Many people think they don't like oak, when in fact they just don't like cheap oak cabinetry. The stronger a wood's grain, the more important it is to match it carefully.

I choose all my frame parts from rift- or quarter-sawn boards so that they have a subtle linear grain pattern that accentuates the rectilinear lines of the frame. The pattern harmonizes with and underscores the form and sense of structure. Quarter- and rift-sawn frame stock is also more stable and will expand and contract less in the opening. For the panels, I generally use flat-sawn boards with centered grain patterns. The undulating flat-sawn grain gives the panel a softer graphic quality, and centered grain gives a feeling of symmetry. On a door that has over and under panels, I like to cut the top panels off the same boards I use for the ones below, so the grain continues through. This unifies all the panels.

My other favorite trick is to book-match the panels as well, which is relatively easy in this case. Because the panels are thin, I don't need to buy consecutive boards from a specialty wood dealer; I just buy a thick board and resaw it in half on the band saw into two thinner book-matched boards. An $^8/_4$ board should yield two $^3/_4$-inch boards if you're careful, which is enough thickness to make a cabinet door panel. The combination of the book-match and the continuous grain from top to bottom makes a unified and balanced door.

Using rift- or quarter-sawn lumber for frame parts and flat-sawn lumber for panels gives a nice contrast, accentuating the structure of the frame with linear grain and softening the panels with the flat-sawn grain. In this case, the grain on the panels is book-matched and continuous from top to bottom.

If you can't get rift- or quarter-sawn boards in the wood you are looking for, then you can buy flat-sawn lumber, rip the sides off (which will have rift-sawn grain), and use those. You'll have to do something else with the centers, which have nonlinear grain. If they're wide enough, you can use them for narrow panels.

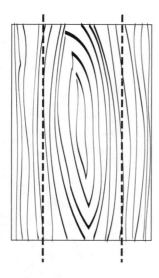

The sides of a flat-sawn board have rift-sawn grain because the rings cross the face at an angle. By ripping them off, you can get perfect linear grain for frame stock; you just have to figure out something to do with the middle.

It's Milling Time!

The milling sequence is the same as described previously in Chapter 22, "Milling: How to Make Parts That Fit." It's particularly important to mark the parts correctly and to maintain the marks as you go through the process. Doors need to be completely flat, and this means you have to be extra-scrupulous about making the parts and ensuring that they stay true. Be sure to premill the stock, because nothing helps maintain stability as much as premilling does.

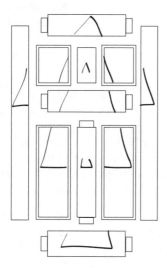

All the parts should be marked with arrows indicating their positions. This system is especially helpful when you're book-matching panels and trying to maintain continuous grain.

As I noted previously, I like to resaw panel stock on the band saw. To do this, you joint one face, and then joint an edge square. Using your marking gauge, make a line down the center of the board along the unjointed edge; if it's too rough to mark legibly, then rip it clean on the table saw before you mark it. Next, set the jointed edge on the band saw table and rip it in half, thickness-wise. If the board is thin and tall, it may be precarious and dangerous, so you should set up a resaw jig, which is an L-shaped piece of plywood clamped to the table to hold the board vertical, the desired distance from the blade. Do not use a flat fence for resawing, because the wood will bind. You should use a wide blade, at least $3/4$ inch or 1 inch, with relatively few teeth, 2 or 3 to the inch. Make sure the table is dead square and the guides are adjusted properly.

When you are milling the boards, treat them like any rough-sawn lumber. As with any book-matched boards, you should gingerly joint the matched faces first and run the back faces through the planer. Make sure you let the boards sit for a few days after resawing before you mill them to let any residual stresses equalize.

One note: I like to make my doors $1/4$ inch oversize in both height and width so that I can cut down the doors to size after they are glued up. One reason is that this allows me to clamp them together without having to use protective blocks to protect the edges. I just cut the dented edges away when I fit the door. It also gives me some leeway if there's an unexpected problem, like out-of-squareness. I make them up wider by adding $1/8$ inch to the width of the stiles and outside rails when I'm milling.

The Joints Are Jumping

You could put doors like these together with a variety of joints. You could use a cope-and-stick router bit set, stub tenons, dowels (yuck!), or even lamellos, which are not that strong. (Small doors do not get a great deal of stress, so you don't necessarily need the strongest joint.) I don't recommend using lap joints because they're a bit cheesy.

Bridal joints might be a good choice because they're strong and easy, and they have a workman-like integrity that lends itself to doors. Also, you see the joint only when the door is open, so it doesn't detract from the exterior look of the cabinets. Bridal joints can be cut entirely on the table saw, which makes them nice and low-tech if your shop machinery is limited. You can align the grooves for the panel with the female part of the bridal joints by cutting them on the same dado setup and merely lowering the blade to make a shallower pass; just make sure to reference the same face against the fence.

Raised Panel Picks

You have a lot of profile choices for your raised panels. They can be simple, or they can be elaborate. You can cut a square or angled rabbet that will work fine on the table saw. Or you can shell out some money and buy router bits or shaper cutters that will cut almost any profile you can imagine. If you have a hankering to experience a little bit of the good old days, you can even plane the angle with a hand plane.

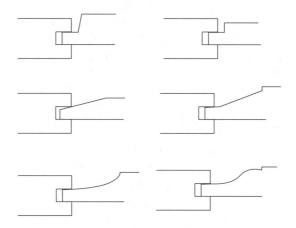

These section views show a variety of panel profiles: The top and middle left views are rabbets cut on the table saw (the middle one can be planed by hand if you're industrious), and the rest must be cut by router bits in a router table or on the shaper.

The panels should always be raised after the grooves are cut, because the tongues must be fit to the groove, rather than the other way around. Always make several test pieces out of scraps to trial-fit the joint.

Flat Is Where It's At

When gluing up a frame-and-panel door, you have to keep track of several things. First of all, it's crucial that it goes together flat and square. A door that is not flat will always have a corner that sticks out from the opening, which looks terrible. If it's not square, you may end up with crooked reveals between panels and frame or even between the door and the opening, unless you've made the door oversize enough to compensate.

To keep a small door flat, I glue it up on battens on my workbench. I make sure the battens are straight and identical. I like them to be square in section,

Tricks of the Trade

To keep the face of the panel flush with the face of the frame, or in some other specific relationship, you can adjust the fit of the tongue in the back with a shallow rabbet. Or if the back is flat and the panel is tight, you can fit the panel with a plane in the back. You can fit panels raised on both sides by adjusting from the back.

so if they roll over accidentally, and I don't notice, it won't affect the glue-up. I make sure that the door's stiles rest firmly on the battens, which ensures that the door will not be twisted. One tip: Don't use clamps that are any longer than they have to be; the weight of long clamps cantilevered off the door twists it off the batten. If necessary, to keep the door flat, clamp it to the battens and the bench.

If the door has more than one panel, then you have to worry about the spacing of the *muntins* (internal vertical frame members) and internal rails. If the parts are not lined up, panels, reveals, or even frame members may look crooked. One handy solution is to cut spacers that either fit between the frame parts and the raised section of the panels or between the frame members themselves, which will hold them the right distance apart during the glue-up. Small spacers between the frame and the panels work best if the fielded sections of the panels have square shoulders.

Make sure all your arrows are facing up and in the right direction when you start your glue-up. I recommend that you lay out the parts exactly as they are going to go together and assemble the parts by hand as you apply glue; when you start, it should look like an exploded view lying on your bench. Laying out the parts keeps things organized and prevents you from reversing parts in the heat of the moment.

I like to put a dab of glue in the center of the tongues on the top and bottom of each panel. This prevents the panel from shifting in the frame, which can lead to uneven reveals, while allowing the sides to expand and contract evenly.

But I'm Not Finished Yet!

Before you glue up, all the inside faces of the frame should be completely sanded; it's too difficult to sand these areas once the parts are together. But whatever you do, don't sand the joint faces! Beginners often make this mistake. In the course of sanding the inside edges of the frame, they sand the joint faces that meet the shoulders of the tenons, which causes gaps and undoes all the care you took to cut accurate joints. Mark the location of the end-of-the-joint surfaces on the face of the frame members. When you sand the edges, just make sure to stay within these marks.

If possible, panels should be finished before glue-up, so unfinished sections of the tongues don't appear when the panels shrink. Some woodworkers just finish the tongue area and leave the fielded part of the panel to be finished with the rest of the door.

I think it depends on whether you're wiping, brushing, or spraying the finish; you can decide this issue yourself. If the panels have square shoulders at the tongue with tight reveals, you may want to finish the frame edges as well before the glue-up, because getting finish down in there with a brush or spray gun may be a mess of a job.

Getting a Snug Fit

After the glue has set, you can clean up the door and cut it to size. First, flush up the faces of the frame with a hand plane, scraper, and sandpaper. Do the inside first and then the outside. Sand the entire frame with a series of sandpapers up to 120-grit, and then stop while you complete the cutting and fitting process, because you'll probably scuff it up a little.

Now you have to fit the frame to the opening. First, you have to figure out your door gaps. If you're using butt hinges or knife hinges, you can keep them tight, in the $1/32$- to $1/16$-inch range; if you're using European-style cabinet hinges, you'll have to make the gaps closer to 3 millimeters (about $1/8$ inch), or they may bind (check the manufacturer's recommendations). To figure out your door size, measure the opening and subtract your door gaps.

Before you do any cutting, check that the opening is square. If it's out-of-square, you'll have to cut the door oversize and adjust it accordingly by hand-planing one corner or another to fit. This is a fussy process. You'll have to hold the door in the opening with shims to check it for square as you go, bringing it back to the workbench for a few swipes of the plane, and then checking it again, and then taking it back to the bench, and so on.

To cut a door to size, you should first joint the opening edge with a light pass to straighten it out. Next, on the table saw, cut half the amount you have to remove from the hinge side, joint that side lightly, check the width, and rip the remaining amount off the opening side. To cut the height, first square an edge, removing half the total you have to; then measure again and remove the remaining excess from the other side. Check the door in the opening with shims, and if it's good, sand the edges.

When the gaps are tight, you must relieve the inside edge of the opening side of the door, or it will bind.

If I'm doing really fine work and trying to keep the gaps tight, I'll rely on the hand plane for final fitting of the width, so I can bevel the opening edge to clear the cabinet. In this case, I'll cut the door a tad full to allow for a few plane strokes.

Fit for Hanging

How you hang the door depends upon the type of hinges you're using. If you are using European-style hinges, it's a piece of cake. Using the manufacturer's recommendations, you determine the locations to drill the holes for the hinge cups in the doorframe, and screw on the hinges. Then you just measure back, screw the base plates in the appropriate places, attach the two together, and play with the adjusting screws until the gaps are even.

Butt and pivot hinges require more precision. I like to mortise the hinges in the cabinet, install them with one screw, and then shim the door in place so the gaps are where you want them. Then, using an Exacto knife, or reasonable facsimile, transfer the hinge location to the door, mortise the hinges in the door, and again use one screw to screw on the door. I give the door a swing and see how it looks. I do any necessary adjustments with the hand plane and reinstall the door.

Once I have it where I want it, I set my stops, catches, pulls, and any other hardware. When it's right, I disassemble everything, sand it, and finish the whole cabinet. Only on the final assembly do I install all the screws in the hinges, just in case I have to move a hinge slightly.

A Touch of Glass

When using glass lights instead of wood panels, you'll have to hold them in with glass stops. The glass stops will be nailed in with brads from the back. The wood parts all need to be finished before the glass goes in. To do this, I like to fit and cut all my glass stops, sand and finish them, and then nail them in to the doors as the last thing. It helps to put a drop of silicone in the corners to keep the glass from rattling.

Mission Control: We Have a Problem

Every so often problems arise. The most common involve mortising the hinges wrong. If you get them too deep, you can put rectangles of paper or masking tape in the mortise to shim them out a little. If you need to move them up or down or in or out, you should plug the screw hole and start with another hole.

If a door is twisted, you may have to kick a hinged corner in or out to split the difference with the diagonally opposite corner. One note: Check your pull location twice or three times before you drill the hole; people always screw that up because it's so easy, and they've just been doing all that tricky fitting.

The Least You Need to Know

➤ Frame members must have coherent grain patterns for a unified look; rift-sawn wood gives a good linear look and reduces movement.

➤ You need to take extra care when milling door stock to ensure that it stays flat, or the door will not operate properly.

➤ You also need to take extra care to keep the door flat when cutting joints and gluing up.

➤ Solid panels need to be prefinished at the tongues to prevent a dry edge when they contract.

➤ A tight-fitting door requires a planed fit and a beveled edge to prevent binding.

Part 6

The Finishing Touch

Most woodworkers concentrate their time and interest on the building of projects rather than on finishing them. Perhaps this is because they are drawn to woodworking because they like to tinker. Whatever the reason, the result is that they craft beautifully made projects and then slather on some second-rate finish in a half-hearted attempt to get the job done. The problem is that the average person cares most about the finish and doesn't notice all that old-world craftsmanship.

I frequently see people cooing over some slapped-together flake-board monstrosity with a fancy stained finish (nothing irks woodworkers more, I might add). We may not like it, but the surface is what turns people on. Besides, a well-crafted piece deserves a well-crafted finish.

This part of the book explores the slightly separate world of finishing. It looks at the history of finishes, exploring the traditional favorites, such as shellac and oil-based varnish, and offers a look at the modern finishes, which have changed dramatically in recent years, with synthetic varnishes and now water-based finishes appearing on the scene.

Chapter 26

A Fill-In on Finishing

In This Chapter

➤ Why we use finishing

➤ Oils

➤ Shellac and French polishing

➤ Asian lacquers versus nitrocellulose lacquers

➤ Modern synthetic finishes

➤ Water-based finishes

Finishing has developed in the past century as a result of extraordinary innovations in the field of chemistry. Most of today's finishes are essentially plastic dissolved in solvent or water-based mediums that bear no relation to the finishes of the past. Yet they are still called *lacquers* and *varnishes* because people are familiar with these old-fashioned names. For this reason, I think it's important to follow the development of finishes from traditional to modern, in order to try to make some sense out of the crowd of products on the market.

Finishing: A Woodworker's Story

I'm a woodworker. What do I know about finishing? I was lucky enough to have been thrust into the world of finishing despite myself. My parents owned an antique shop when I was very young, and they were always refinishing pieces. When I was 13, I decided I wanted to be a cabinetmaker and took a job with a well-known furniture

Wood Words

Many people think, incorrectly, that **French polishing** involves a separate specific finish. It is just a technique for applying **shellac.** Shellac, made from the secretions of the lac beetle that are dissolved in alcohol, is normally applied with a brush or a spray gun. In French polishing, shellac is padded on with a **tampon,** or small pad, in a fairly complex process.

restorer who happened to have a shop nearby. I worked for him after school and summers for two years. I did stripping, sanding, and eventually some finishing. He worked on what I call serious furniture: museum-quality seventeenth-, eighteenth-, and early nineteenth-century stuff. He never let me do much woodworking, but I managed to learn a lot about *French polishing* and other *shellac* finishes that are used on good antiques.

Later, when I graduated from college and was trying to figure out what to do next, I met this kind of gorgeous older woman at a party. She was all of 28 and had a finishing business doing furniture and architectural woodwork. When she offered me a job, finishing suddenly seemed like a good idea, so I took it. I worked for her for about a year before getting back to building furniture, and in that time, I learned more about traditional finishes and branched out into colored finishes and varnishes.

Since then I've learned how to use modern finishes, spray lacquer, water-based finishes, and catalyzed varnish. I also developed an appreciation for oil finishes along the way. I'm not a professional finisher, but I have a pretty good understanding of the field, and perhaps most important, I know when to ask for help.

What's Finish for, Anyway?

The main reason people finish wood is to make it more beautiful. All the common finishes are formulated to accentuate wood's natural beauty by bringing out the grain and making the color deeper and richer. Anyone who has worked with wood has experienced the thrill of applying the first coat of finish and seeing the wood come alive. In addition to making the color more vibrant, finishes can fill the wood's pores and create a shiny, smooth surface that many find appealing.

Finishes protect the wood's surface against the dirt and grime that life hands out. If it weren't for finish, wood's porous surface would absorb all the fingerprints, dirt, and grease that came its way. Some finishes, though not all, protect from water stains that occur when, say, a wet glass is put on a tabletop.

Finishes also slow down the effects of airborne humidity on wood movement. As you know by now, changes in ambient moisture levels cause wood to expand and contract when the air's moisture enters the wood through its surface. Finishes form a barrier, slowing down (but not stopping) this moisture exchange. The degree to which the moisture exchange is slowed differs vastly from finish to finish. Some *penetrating finishes,* such as oil, offer negligible protection from ambient moisture; on the other hand, *film finishes,* such as lacquers and varnishes, can slow down moisture exchange substantially.

Why is this a good thing, you ask? Because when a board absorbs or sheds moisture quickly, the change is greatest at the ends and near the surface. The center is slower to exchange moisture content, and this differential between the center and the perimeter can lead to cracks and surface checking. It's like when you pour boiling water into a thick glass, and the inside expands faster than the outside, causing it to crack. By slowing down moisture exchange, a finish can prevent cracking. As a rule, the finishes that offer the greatest moisture resistance are thick, built-up ones rather than thin, "natural"-looking ones like oil and wax.

You hear a lot about finishes "allowing the wood to breathe" or "nourishing" or "feeding the wood." This is a lot of malarkey dreamed up by marketing people and propagated by well-meaning romantics. Once a tree has died, it no longer breathes or eats. Now that you know why woodworkers use finish, it's time to look at the various players in the field, starting with the old-timers.

Wood Words

Finishes that are absorbed by the wood and do not build up thickness on the wood's surface, like the oils, are called **penetrating finishes.** Finishes that do build up on the surface, filling the pores and hardening into a coating, are called **film finishes.** Penetrating finishes offer little protection from moisture and wear compared to film finishes.

Essential Oils

Oils and waxes are probably the oldest finishes known. In ancient times, it was discovered that oils would protect wood from fingerprints, dirt, and the like while bringing out the grain and beauty of the wood. Originally, any available oil was used: olive oil in the Mediterranean, animal fats in the north, and so on. Eventually, people got tired of using oils that would go rancid and figured out that certain oils would *cure* or harden as they oxidized. The most popular oils for finishing became linseed oil in the West and tung oil (or China wood oil) in the East. Eventually, it was found that chemicals called *dryers* could be added to the oils to speed the curing process.

As other finishes, notably shellac and varnishes, made their appearances, oil became a second-class citizen, but it remained commonplace, if not popular, because it was cheap and readily available. Today, people have a romantic notion about oil as a sign of "old world craftsmanship," but historically, oil was not held in particularly high esteem. It was traditionally used on country furniture and lower-quality stuff while the top-shelf furniture got a shellac finish such as French polishing.

Today, oil finishes are popular with craftspeople because they are easy to apply and relatively idiot-proof. Oil finishes became especially popular with consumers in the 1950s and 1960s with the rise of Danish Modern furniture because it had a "natural look." This look was the result of its nonbuilding quality: Oil doesn't fill the pores and build into a thick film; it penetrates and dries. The downside of this characteristic is that it offers little protection.

Shellac: Beetlemania

Somehow or another, somebody in the Far East a few hundred years ago figured out that the secretions of the lac beetle made a great furniture finish. (I don't even want to think about how they figured this one out.) The good news is that they were right, and shellac has turned out to be one of the most enduring finishes in both life expectancy and popularity.

How many products can you think of that are still in use, largely unchanged, for several hundred years? (Well, there is beer.) A shellac finish, if left alone, will last indefinitely, unlike varnish, which crazes (cracks), darkens, and gets an alligator texture. Some eighteenth-century furniture still looks great with its original finish over 200 years later. (I'm guessing the owners didn't have kids.)

> **I Woodn't Do That!**
>
> I don't recommend using shellac on tabletops or any horizontal surface that is going to get a drink placed on it. On the other hand, you can finish the supporting structure with shellac, and apply varnish to the top. Applying varnish to intricate structures can be tricky anyway, whereas shellac is relatively easy to apply if you thin it down.

French Polishing (Ooo La La!)

At some point in the eighteenth century, the technique of French polishing was developed to apply shellac. The process involves mixing the shellac with oil and pumice and applying it with a pad (or *tampon*). French polishing fills the pores and imperfections of the surface and yields a built-up, glass-like finish that is quite beautiful if it's done properly. It is, however, quite a production and is very time-consuming compared with other finishes.

The big plus that French polishing had in the good old days is that it went on so smooth and shiny that you didn't have to do anything to level or polish it, and this was a huge plus in the days before sandpaper, steel wool, and polishing compounds. Now that we have these abrasives and can spray and polish a finish, French polishing does not seem like such a miracle and is hardly worth the trouble unless you're restoring a period antique.

Shellac 2000

Today, shellac is still remarkably popular and is used clear on woodwork and as the base for some paints. Although it's not used much as a commercial furniture finish anymore, it is favored by the home handyperson because it's easy and by the professional for specific applications. For example, I like it as a finish for the inside of drawers. In deference to the modern consumer, it comes in liquid form packaged in cans. It is still brushed on, and with modern technology, it is sprayed as well. Some restorers and die-hard traditionalists even apply the old French polishing technique from time to time.

Traditional Varnishes: Finishing's Best Friends

Varnish is the product of finishing oils combined with resins and *dryers,* which are then heated and thinned with solvents. Adding resins to oil made a finish that hardened when it was *cured* and could be built up into a thick film. It revolutionized finishing because it was strong, water-resistant, heat-resistant, and cheap. Although fine furniture was still finished with shellac, varnish was the workhorse used wherever something tougher was called for, such as in boats, exterior work, tabletops, and instruments.

Early varnishes used tough pine resins, generally in fossilized form, because these were the best available. In the twentieth century, with the development of early plastics like phenolic resin (bakolite) and alkyd resin, *synthetic resins* replaced *natural resins* in varnish. Today, natural resin varnishes are quite rare and are used only by specialized finishers like instrument makers and antique restorers. Shortly before World War II, polyurethane became a resin of choice; mixed with alkyd resin, it is now probably the most common form of varnish because it is extremely tough.

The major drawback of early varnishes was that they were hard to apply and took forever to cure. Modern varnishes cure much faster, but they're a little tricky to apply. They've been profoundly affected by the Environmental Protection Agency (EPA), and though it is a good thing to reduce the solvents released into the environment, the EPA hasn't made the wood finisher's life any easier. Many of the things that made varnishes work well have been removed by government mandate.

Wood Words

Resins are the part of film finishes that harden and build up on the surface of the wood. There are **natural** and **synthetic resins.** The process of hardening, after the solvents have evaporated, is called **curing.** Some modern synthetic resins require a catalyst to enact a chemical curing process. Older varnishes relied on chemical **dryers** to speed the curing.

The Lacquers of the East

In Asia, mankind's quest for finishing materials found a new finish in a plant resin. Called Urashi in Japan, it's the resin from a plant in the poison oak family. Popular throughout Asia, this extremely labor-intensive finish became much sought-after throughout the world after China began to export objects finished with it. In the West, it became known as Chinese lacquer (in the misconception that it had something to do with the lac beetle).

I don't know as much as I should about the process of Chinese lacquer, but it can be practiced only by people who are not susceptible to the rash-inducing properties of this poison oak-type plant. Apparently, if you're a normal person, you'll look like something out of a horror movie if you handle the stuff. Just imagine finishing furniture with poison oak or poison ivy! I know that Chinese lacquer requires many layers to build up—thousands, I've heard, but that may be an exaggeration. There is more mystique about it out there than real information.

Spray Lacquer for Speed

Modern spray lacquer was developed about 1920, just after World War I, as a by-product of gunpowder manufacturing. I'm a little vague on the chemistry, but someone figured out that he could turn gun cotton into a finish called nitrocellulose lacquer that was perfectly suited to the new spray technology that had been developed. It protected like a varnish, but it dried in minutes, rather than hours, like shellac. Although this new finish bore no connection to Chinese lacquer, the name was appropriated for marketing reasons; it sounded more attractive if people thought they were getting a version of that exotic and expensive finish.

Woodlore

Chinese lacquering is not practiced much in this country. I've met only one person who did real Urashi work, and he didn't speak English, so I was unable to learn much about it. It's primarily of interest because its name was appropriated in the twentieth century with the invention of nitrocellulose lacquer, which bears no relation to Chinese lacquer.

Up until that time, finishes were brushed or padded on. Even cars were painted with a brush. If you ever see pictures of early Ford manufacturing plants, there was a bit of a bottleneck where they brushed on black paint. By spraying lacquer, they not only sped the application process, they also reduced drying time. Consequently, the fledgling automobile industry embraced this winning combination and invested heavily in developing the finish and the application process.

Since then, modern lacquer has become the preeminent furniture finish for commercial furniture. Small shops embraced it, too, because once you learned to spray, it was fast, easy, and it looked great. It became a highly engineered finish, by which I mean that many varieties of lacquer and thinners were developed for various different applications and weather conditions. Lacquer comes clear or in colors and in different degrees of hardness and flexibility.

Today, modern lacquers are still extremely popular. Unfortunately, they are toxic and pose a threat to the environment. Some states, notably California, have taken steps to ban solvent-based lacquer entirely.

Tricks of the Trade

The early lacquers were all nitro-cellulose-based. Later, other resins were developed, and today acrylic lacquers are used heavily in the after-market automotive industry. Acrylic lacquers are quite hard, but they are ill-suited for wood because they are not flexible and tend to craze, or develop small cracks, as wood expands and contracts.

The Complex Conversion Finishes

Conversion finishes are creations of the furniture manufacturing industry and are intended for factory conditions. They are complex chemical configurations that use plastic resins in combination with chemical catalysts, so they don't dry through evaporation, but rather harden through a chemical process. There are epoxy finishes, various polyurethanes, polyesters, catalyzed lacquers, and conversion varnishes. Because they cure through a chemical process rather than evaporation, they can generally be sprayed on quite thick for fast film build.

They all have different characteristics: Epoxies are tough and waterproof, but sensitive to ultraviolet light and expensive; polyesters are less expensive and can be built up quite thick very quickly; catalyzed lacquers are much more durable than conventional lacquer; conversion varnish cures more slowly, but is more durable than catalyzed lacquers. Conversion varnish and catalyzed lacquers are the ones that are used most often in small shops because they are the most manageable to spray. Although they require fewer solvents than noncatalyzed finishes, conversion finishes still pose a threat to the environment and to the user's health. Some, like epoxies and polyester resins, are extremely toxic and should not be used by the amateur.

Generally, conversion finishes are two-part finishes, which means that you have to mix two chemicals, the resin and the catalyst, to begin the chemical reaction. Some finishes are precatalyzed for ease of use. This means that they have the catalyst already mixed in, but they also have special solvents added that prevent the catalyst from kicking in. When the finish is sprayed, and the solvents evaporate, the chemical reaction is free to take place.

Water–Based Finishes: Wave of the Future

Because all these other finishes are so bad for the environment, something had to be done to create a new type of finish that did away with the conventional solvents. Since, the EPA has been limiting the use of some solvents, which has diminished the quality of varnishes, lacquers, conversion finishes, and paints dramatically in the past couple of decades finishes have been developed that use water as a primary medium.

At first, these water-based finishes were awful. They were soft, cloudy or milky, and very expensive. They have gradually improved and are now acceptable alternatives to the old favorites. I'm sure that they will continue to improve, and the day will come when they are just as good. I use them because of their reduced toxicity as well as their environmental advantages.

The Name Game

The names of finishes can be confusing. Chinese lacquers have nothing in common chemically with nitrocellulose lacquers, which have little in common with catalyzed lacquers, and absolutely nothing in common with water-based lacquers. Besides, the word lacquer comes from the lac beetle, which is the basis of shellac, not Chinese lacquer. What we have here is a foreign finish named by another culture and based upon a misconception. It's name, lacquer, was later appropriated for a modern finish in the West, Chinese lacquer. Since then, it has again been extended to new chemical formulations to make them seem familiar to finishers so that they'll be comfortable with them.

The current crop of conversion finishes and water-based finishes are all complex chemical formulations that have virtually nothing to do with the original varnishes and lacquers. Generally, the way it works is that finishes that are formulated to cure harder are called *varnishes,* and the ones formulated with the priority on speed of curing are sold as *lacquers.*

The Least You Need to Know

➤ Oils penetrate into the wood and do not build up a film; they offer little protection from wear and humidity.

➤ Shellac offers good protection from humidity in the air but not from water or heat.

➤ Varnishes provide a tough surface but are harder to apply.

➤ Lacquer is best sprayed, but it can be applied quickly, is relatively durable, and looks great.

➤ Conversion finishes are great, but they are for the advanced finisher.

➤ Water-based finishes are the wave of the future because of their environment-friendly nature.

Chapter 27

Choosing Finishes: Knowing Fact from Fiction

In This Chapter

➤ Facts and myths about finishes

➤ What's easy and what's hard

➤ Spraying finish

➤ The pluses and minuses of individual finishes

➤ Stains and pigments

There are more and more finishes out there on the market, and they all have different characteristics. Some have remained unchanged for hundreds of years; others came out of a lab within the last decade. Some finishes are tricky to apply, and others are a breeze. The problem is that few aspects of woodworking are clouded by as much confusion or misinformation as finishing. This chapter picks up where the last one left off in attempting to clarify the finishing maze. It examines the good and bad points of various finishes and helps you navigate through the selections to an appropriate choice.

Finishing Mythology

Part of the problem in selecting a finish is that the field is so rife with misinformation. Old wives' tales propagated by your Great-aunt Sadie circulate among the civilians. Manufacturers appropriate misleading names for new finishes (which I discussed in the last chapter). And many finishers impart half-knowledge instead of the whole picture.

Consumers are often suspicious of this finish or that because they had some bad experience with it. You hear things like, "Shellac is so cheap-looking, so orange and shiny." Well, if you use white instead of orange shellac and rub it out with steel wool, it is neither orange nor shiny. Or you hear, "You should rub oil into the wood once a year to nourish the wood." Your wood couldn't care less about what's for dinner; a little oil may buff up the surface of an old oil finish, but it does nothing for your wood's health. Many old-timers had problems 30 years ago with polyurethane varnishes yellowing; they should try them now—modern science is a wonderful thing. My point is, don't believe everything you hear.

Even finishers are not to be trusted. I don't mean to impugn the trade, but an awful lot of them, even good ones, have a less-than-scientific understanding of their craft. Most have learned to finish, not in school, but in the field, where a good end product is more important than a complete understanding of how you got there. Good finishers are more like artists than scientists, and when some of the better finishers I know start explaining something to me, I have to bite my tongue because, even with my scant knowledge of chemistry, I know that they don't know what they're talking about. But they can make this particularly tricky process work, and I can't. Maybe the solvents cloud their minds.

Tricks of the Trade

When you call manufacturers for technical advice about finishing or whatever the subject, don't be satisfied with whomever answers the phone. Usually, it's some well-meaning flack at the other end of that customer service line. Instead, ask to speak to a product engineer or the product engineering department. You may have to wait for a call back, but you'll get better information.

I should point out that woodworkers are worse than finishers at explaining this cloudy realm. Most woodworkers are afraid of finishing, and many who aren't should be. I see perfectly good woodworkers ruin pieces by slathering drippy, shiny messes all over them. Tage Frid, ever the diplomat, used to say (imagine thick Danish accent here), "My God, it looks like dat came out your nose."

For good information, read books, go to seminars, and call manufacturers. There are books on finishing listed in Appendix B, "Resources," seminars now abound on all aspects of woodworking, most manufacturers have 800 numbers, and finishing companies as a group are particularly good about giving advice.

You Think It's Easy?

Many woodworkers opt for finishes that seem easy. Oil, for instance, has a reputation for being easy. Nothing could be further from the truth. Finishing with oil is simple, but it isn't easy. A good oil finish requires blood, sweat, and tears. If you learn how to spray nitrocellulose lacquer, it requires less hard work to finish a large project than it would with oil, but it also requires an initial investment of time to learn the more complicated spraying process. Because oil is a penetrating finish, any gloss is dependent on a polished wood surface, which needs more surface preparation. With lacquer, the surface requires less attention because the film buildup provides the shine, and if you have to, it's easier to rub out finish than it is to polish a lot of wooden real estate.

There's a lot to learn in woodworking, but don't let your curiosity stop when you get to finishing. There's a difference between low tech and low effort. The trick to learning finishing is to practice (a lot!) on samples. Many people retreat to low-tech solutions after they have a disaster trying out a new finish on a piece of furniture, and have to strip it. Get the hang of a finish on scraps over a period of time before you attempt it on the real thing.

To Spray or Not To Spray

Spraying finish is not for everyone, and teaching you how to do it is not within the scope of this book. There are many reasons not to spray finish. Spraying finish is more toxic than brushing on a finish, and you should have a spray booth to do it. It takes an investment of time before you get the hang of it. It also requires an investment of money to set up the equipment. On the positive side, it opens up the possibility of using a whole new range of finishes that cannot be brushed on effectively. It is much faster for jobs with a lot of surface area, where the setup time is outweighed by the time spent brushing. The advent of water-based finishes and *high volume/low pressure* turbine spraying systems makes spraying more of a reality for small shops because they lower the toxicity levels.

Learning to spray can be daunting. First of all, it can be hard to find a knowledgeable teacher. I had several woodworkers try to give me lessons in my youth, where I could tell they didn't really know what they were talking about. I finally took a training seminar offered by the Binks spray equipment company that gave me the information I had been looking for, rather than the "Well, you kind of do this, and if that doesn't work …" stuff I had been getting. From there, I read and experimented until I got that combination of correct technical information and real-world experience that's so important. I also made sure I had the direct line of the man who taught the training seminar, and I hounded him for years. I still call him with a question from time to time, and I hope he doesn't take early retirement.

Wood Words

Traditional spray systems are high pressure/low volume, and although they have good atomization (ability to break up fluids), they have a poor transfer ratio. That means that a lot of the finish ends up in the air, which is bad for the environment and toxic. Newer **high volume/low pressure** systems have better fluid transfer ratios and are now mandated in some states.

But Will It Last?

When you evaluate a finish, perhaps the main issue is whether it is up to the task at hand: Will it be strong enough for its chosen task? Certain applications, such as table-tops and bar tops, require a tough surface. The last thing you want is a call from a client in a few months complaining about some finish problem.

The first time I ever used a water-based finish was on the dining table of the older sister of my best friend. I gave her a price on the table that was about a quarter of what I normally charged, so I figured I could take some liberties and try one of these new-fangled water-based finishes I'd been hearing about. I chose the wrong one, especially given the fact that she had a maid who liked to clean the table with a scouring sponge. I refinished the table with another water-based finish, which didn't work either. Finally, about 40 hours later, I put a good, old-fashioned hand-rubbed varnish finish on it, which I should have used in the first place.

The following sections survey the various common finishes, listing their advantages and disadvantages. This information should help you choose which finish will work best for your project.

You've Struck Oil

Oil finishes are the hands-down favorite of woodworkers everywhere. Perhaps their folksy appeal strikes a chord or maybe it's the "ease of application" they boast about on the labels or the ease with which you can touch up an oil finish that's been damaged. Finishes sold as oil finishes cover a wide range of products, and many have been engineered by modern chemistry to the point where they have more in common with a modern varnish than a traditional linseed oil finish. Many are, in fact, varnishes that have been thinned way down so that they can be wiped on.

There are two types of oil sold in pure form that I recommend for finishing: boiled linseed oil and tung oil. They are among the few oils that truly *cure,* or change to a solid state, when exposed to air. Mineral oil can be used on salad bowls and cutting boards because it's nontoxic, but it always remains in a liquid state.

The problem with even the best oil finishes is that they offer little protection against humidity or water. This means that they don't slow down moisture exchange, and they offer no protection against wet glasses or water spills. Water will stain an oil-finished tabletop within seconds.

The Linseed Oil Legend

Boiled linseed oil enjoys a venerable reputation because it was used in the "good old days," but people in the good old days used it because it was available, not because it was such a great finish. It does little to protect the wood from moisture or abrasion; you have to build up several coats to get any kind of shine; and it darkens wood dramatically, yellowing over time. I use boiled linseed oil on dark woods if I want a darker, natural finish and don't mind doing a lot of rubbing.

The Buzz on Tung

Tung oil, or China wood oil as it is sometimes called, is similar to linseed oil, but it offers slightly better protection against moisture. It is, however, far more expensive and requires more coats and more elbow grease to achieve a good finish. My feeling is that if you're looking for moisture resistance, you don't use an oil finish, so it's not worth the added expense and trouble. Various stores that cater to the fussy woodworker have been touting it in recent years because it's uncommon compared to linseed oil, but, obviously I think there's a reason it's less common.

Several companies have been marketing polymerized oils in the last few years. They seem to dry harder and resist moisture better than standard oils, but they are extremely expensive, and I find them harder to work with because they dry so fast.

I Woodn't Do That!

Ironically, boiled linseed oil is not really boiled; it's just raw linseed oil with dryers in it so it will cure overnight, instead of over weeks. When my parents had their antique shop, my mother, not knowing this, decided to boil her own linseed oil. It's almost as flammable as gasoline, and she nearly burned the house down. Like they say at KISS concerts: "Don't try this at home, kids."

Is Danish Oil Really Oil?

A variety of finishes on the market are sold with names like "Danish oil" or "furniture oil" that are just a synthetic varnish mixed with oil, dryers, and thinners. The synthetic resins in these oils are what cause them to protect the wood better than straight oils. When I'm doing an oil finish, these are generally what I use because they cure faster, offer slightly better resistance to moisture, and don't darken the wood as much as linseed oil. Then why don't I just thin a good varnish down with oil and spirits until it becomes wipeable? It's probably just force of habit: After years of using this stuff, I know how it behaves, so why switch?

Caution: Flammable!

You can't be too careful with oils. They are extremely flammable and should not be near open flames. Perhaps the most dangerous thing about them is that if you leave oily rags piled around, they'll spontaneously combust. I've seen this happen several times, usually when someone throws them in the garbage pail without thinking. The finisher I worked for had a terrible fire in her shop and nearly burned the building down because some rags with linseed oil on them caught on fire in a garbage pail. Again, used rags must be laid out flat to dry or soaked in water.

A Word on Waxes

Waxes may be used as finishes in their own right, although they're usually used over another finish to give it a final polish. Used alone, wax offers even less protection than oil. Some "purists" like it because it darkens the wood less than other finishes. Frankly, I think many people choose it as a lifestyle thing. Finishing furniture with beeswax is just so natural, like driving a VW micro bus or wearing patchouli oil.

Wax is handy for touching up finishes that have become lightly scratched or dull, and it will help protect other finishes from wear. Among the waxes, carnuba wax is about the toughest, but it should be used mixed with another wax so you can buff it out without killing yourself. There are many good furniture paste waxes on the market.

Oil's Pluses and Minuses

Oil's pluses are its …

➤ Simple application method.

➤ Rich, natural look.

Oil's minuses are that it …

➤ Has poor resistance to much of anything.

➤ Requires extra-fine surface preparation.

➤ Is highly flammable, and dirty rags can spontaneously combust.

Getting a Shellacking

As you may have read in Chapter 26, "A Fill-In on Finishing," shellac is made from the secretions of the lac beetle (pretty picture, huh?). It is a resin that is refined into flakes, which can then be dissolved in alcohol. In liquid form, it can be either sprayed or brushed onto wood, or it can be applied with a pad called a *tampon* in the process called *French polishing*.

I have a soft spot in my heart for shellac, perhaps because it was the preferred finish of the restorer I worked for when I was a kid. The smell of it brings back fond memories. It's a finish with pronounced strengths and weaknesses. Many people have had mishaps with it in the past, and my parents' generation associates it with cheap furniture. But used in the appropriate application, it's a sterling performer, is easy to apply, and looks beautiful. Unfortunately, it's a bit of a princess among finishes, being just a little bit fragile in certain circumstances.

Shellac's weaknesses are that it is dissolved by water and alcohol and melted by heat, so it makes a lousy finish for tabletops. (Coasters were invented with shellac and oil finishes in mind.) It also has a shelf life. It starts to age as soon as shellac flakes are dissolved in alcohol, and as it ages, it loses its resistance to water and gets to a point where it won't dry hard, but just remains tacky. It will last longer if you keep it in a cool place. Several years ago, without thinking, I finished a cabinet with old shellac—boy, have I learned my lesson! Now I date my shellac and throw it out after six months. You can always do a test on a piece of wood, but I figure it's not worth taking any chances.

You can buy shellac in flake or liquid form. Liquid form is easier, but you're stuck with its shelf life, which should be listed on the can. Flakes will last longer, and you can mix them as you need shellac.

Tricks of the Trade

The viscosity or thickness of shellac is determined by the ratio between the weight of the flakes and the volume of the alcohol and is called the **cut.** A pound of flakes per gallon of alcohol is a one-pound cut, two pounds per gallon is a two-pound cut, and so on.

Shellac comes in either orange or white, sometimes called clear. White shellac has been bleached. I often mix the two colors to get different tones. The orange is a bit dark most of the time, so the white is better on lighter woods. By mixing them, you can get a moderate, warm tone. White shellac has a much shorter shelf life in liquid form and has a shelf life in flake form as well.

Shellac's pluses are that it …

➤ Seals against stains well.

➤ Is easy to apply when thinned out.

➤ Is easy to rub out.

➤ Is easy to touch up.

➤ Has low toxicity.

➤ Is extremely resistant to ambient humidity exchange.

➤ Can have its tone adjusted through a mixture of orange and white varieties.

➤ Has longevity if not tampered with.

Shellac's minuses are its …

➤ Poor resistance to water and solvents.

➤ Susceptibility to heat.

➤ Lack of toughness.

➤ Short shelf life.

The Varnish Vista

Varnishes are tough. They provide tough surfaces that resist the elements, and they're tough to put on. Varnishes, which are resins cooked with oil, offer considerable protection for high traffic and exterior surfaces.

The good news is that varnishes aren't as difficult to apply as they used to be. Modern synthetic varnishes need far less drying time than their predecessors. They do, however, still require some work and patience. Varnishes generally brush on better than they spray. This is not true of so called conversion varnishes, but conversion varnishes are not really varnishes in my book; they're some modern chemical creation.

The original, natural varnishes that used pine resins as a base are not used anymore except in highly specialized applications. Synthetic resins are commonly available, and each kind has different characteristics. Here are the three resins commonly found in varnish, and their attributes:

➤ **Phenolic resin.** The first one available, phenolic resin is quite tough, but it yellows over time. Phenolic varnishes are often sold as *spar varnish* or *tabletop varnish.* Spar varnish is a so-called *long oil varnish,* which means it has a high percentage of oil, making it flexible and suited for outdoor work. Tabletop varnish is a *short oil varnish,* which means it has a low percentage of oil, making it harder for abrasion resistance.

➤ **Alkyd varnish.** The second type to come along, alkyd varnish is not as tough as phenolic, but it doesn't yellow as much, either. It's cheaper, too. If your varnish doesn't list a resin on the label, it's probably alkyd.

➤ **Polyurethane varnish.** This varnish combines polyurethane resin with alkyd and is the most resistant to abrasion, but it does not have the depth of the others, leaving a plastic look. It also breaks down in ultraviolet light and so should not be used in exterior situations. It's tricky to apply properly, as well, because you have to time the coats carefully. I personally am not a huge fan of this varnish, but many swear by it.

Varnish's pluses are that it ...

➤ Builds thickness quickly.

➤ Is extremely resistant to water.

➤ Is extremely resistant to humidity exchange.

➤ Is extremely resistant to solvents and most chemicals.

➤ Resists wear and heat.

Varnish's minuses are that it …

➤ Yellows after a while.

➤ Dries slowly, which makes it difficult to apply.

➤ Is so tough that the finish is hard to rub out.

➤ Eventually darkens and forms alligator-skin texture over a long period of time.

Nitrocellulose Lacquer

Nitrocellulose lacquer's main advantage is that it sprays on so well. If you are not interested in spraying finish, then it's not for you. It is flexible in formulation and can be mixed for different weather conditions and applications. It comes in any color you can imagine, and some you can't. It is also a great-looking finish, whether it's clear or colored. It's moderately tough; it's water-, humidity- and solvent-resistant.

The downside is that it is toxic and bad for the environment. Spraying it on requires extra time for setup and cleanup. Lacquer thinner is not only toxic, it is also extremely flammable.

Lacquer's pluses are its …

➤ Great depth and clarity.

➤ Extremely quick cure time.

➤ Variety of formulations, which offers great flexibility.

➤ Beautiful results when sprayed.

Lacquer's minuses are that it …

➤ Is highly toxic.

➤ Must be sprayed.

➤ Is not as tough as varnish.

I Woodn't Do That!

I wouldn't use lacquer for a dining tabletop or something that is going to get a lot of wear and tear; I'd defer to varnish. But I like lacquer for most light-to-moderate duty applications.

Water-Based Finishes

Like it or not, water-based finishes are the look of things to come. Water-based finishes come in both brush-on and spray formulations. There are so many different types that it's hard to generalize too much. Each type has very different characteristics; some types are great, and some are el stinko. The primary advantage water-based finishes have is that they're environmentally friendly. They are supposed to have low toxicity, but I'm waiting until they've been on the market longer before I accept that claim. You know how it goes; after a few years, the new product turns out to be just as bad as the old one, but in a new way.

Water-based finishes' pluses are ...

➤ Low solvent content, which is good for the environment.

➤ Low toxicity (the jury's still out).

Water-based finishes' minuses vary from product to product but may include ...

➤ Cloudy, milky appearance.

➤ Thick viscosity, which makes spraying difficult.

➤ Rubbery surface and poor sandability (many sand fine).

It's Raining Stains

We stain wood for many reasons: to darken it, to even out color variation from one board to another, or because we want a particular color not found in nature, to name a few. There are many different types of stain with very different qualities. Stains are formulated to work with different finishes, or to work on refinished wood versus old wood, or to be sprayed on versus wiped, or to work under any number of distinct conditions. Let's look at the different categories that separate one stain from another.

Where Colors Come From

Stains get their color from two different types of coloring agents: dyes and pigments. Dyes dissolve in a solvent and penetrate into the wood's fibers, saturating them and changing their color, which is the same way you dye your hair or clothes. Pigments, on the other hand, do not dissolve; they are finely ground particles of colored material that are suspended in a liquid binder. They color wood by settling into the wood's pores and drying there. Paint uses pigment for color; wine is a stain.

I generally recommend a dye stain for most applications. It is easier to control the degree of color change: You can go much darker with dye as a rule; it colors the wood more deeply, because it penetrates. Perhaps most important, it gives a clear color because it does not sit on top of the wood surface.

Binders and Solvents

Pigments and dyes need liquid to make them work. Pigments use a *binder* that adheres the particles to the wood. The binder can be any of the finishes previously mentioned: oil, shellac, varnish, lacquer, or water-based finish. Dyes need a *solvent* to dissolve them. Different types of aniline dyes are formulated for different solvents, and you should not use powdered dye intended for one solvent with another; likewise, you should not mix different types of premixed stains without checking with the manufacturer. The solvents used for dye stains are water, alcohol, lacquer thinner, mineral spirits (oil-based stain), and glycol ether. You have to decide which stain is best for your needs.

Following is a brief description of the various types of stain to help you make your choices. The thing to remember is that the compatibility of stains and finishes is the opposite of what most people automatically think: You don't want to use a water-based stain with a water-based finish, or an alcohol-based stain with shellac, or an oil-based stain with oil or varnish. The reason is simple: The finish redissolves the stain. You want to use a stain that won't be dissolved by the finish you're using.

Tricks of the Trade

In the old days, dye stains were all made from natural sources: berries, roots, and so on. Later, the textile industry developed synthetic aniline dyes that are better in so many ways that they have come to dominate the industry. You can buy powdered dyes that you then mix yourself, or you can buy already mixed dyes.

Wonderful Water-Based Stain

Water-based stain is a great choice on new wood with any finish except brushed-on water-based finish or lacquer, both of which dissolve it. It penetrates well and has good clarity. It also fades the least of any aniline stain from exposure to light. The only problems are that it is prone to streaking if it is brushed on, and it *raises the grain* of the wood. It works best when sprayed, which is beyond the range of most beginners, but feel free to give brushing a try.

As for raising the grain, you must go back and sand the wood lightly with very fine sandpaper to take the *hair* off, and then reapply more stain. The stain can also redissolve with lacquer finish. If you spray the lacquer or water-based finish, compatibility should not be a problem, because the dye will just dry again. Only the brushing or wiping action disturbs the redissolved finish.

NGR: Non-Grain-Raising Stains

In the past 15 or 20 years, NGR, or non-grain-raising stains have appeared. They use aniline dyes suspended in glycol ether, which is the secret ingredient in most water-based finishes. In theory, the big advantage of these stains is that they don't raise the grain of the wood much, and so don't require sanding and recoating the way water-based stains do. I don't particularly like these stains, but I haven't used them in years, and now that I think about it, I can't remember why I abandoned them. I know some people like them, so see what you think. They will be redissolved by water-based finishes.

Effortless Oil-Based Stain

Oil-based stains that combine both pigment and dye generally give the best results for the beginner. They are easy to use, and they can be wiped on and fiddled with for a while before they dry. They do require the longest time to cure before the finish coating, generally overnight. They work well over stripped wood when refinishing, but many oil-based stains have pigment only, and I find that these stains tend to just sit on the surface without penetrating for a really deep stain. The problem with oil-based stains is that they are redissolved by oil and varnish finishes. They may also have to cure longer than overnight when used with water-based finishes. Before you do the work, check with the manufacturers of both the stain and the finish.

Wood Words

After wood has been sanded, water and some other solvents cause the grain that has been burnished down by the sandpaper to raise up and feel **hairy.** This process is called **raising the grain.** To cure the problem, you have to resand the wood lightly with a fine sandpaper to cut the **hair.** Sometimes, it's a good idea to raise the grain and resand it in preparation for a subsequent grain-raising finish.

Alcohol-Based Aniline Dye Stains

Alcohol-based aniline dye stains work very much like water-based stains, with good clarity and penetration, but they're not as light and fast as water-based dye stains (I don't know why). I use alcohol-based stain when I use brush-on water-based finish and don't want to disturb a water-based stain or NGR (non-grain-raising) stain.

Enter the Gel Stains

Gel stains are a recent addition to the stain roster. I don't have that much experience with them; mostly, I've helped some of my students use them. They have a thicker, jelly-like viscosity, so they don't penetrate as deeply. Their claim to fame is that, because they don't penetrate so deeply, they give a more even finish on woods that tend to look splotchy when stained, notably pine and birch and woods with figured grain. The downside of this is that I've found it hard to get good color saturation.

The Least You Need to Know

➤ The science of finishing is clouded by lots of misinformation.

➤ Some finishing techniques, like spraying, are hard to learn but make for easy work.

➤ Some low-tech finishes, such as oil, are simple to learn, but require a lot of elbow grease.

➤ Some finishes, such as lacquer, are best sprayed; others, such as varnish, are best brushed.

➤ You choose a finish because it is easy to use, low-tech, low toxicity, durable, attractive, or some combination thereof.

➤ Many finishes are toxic and/or flammable.

➤ Stains must be compatible with your finish.

Chapter 28

AHHHHHH....

Surface Prep:
Groundwork for
a Great Finish

In This Chapter

➤ The different needs of different finishes

➤ Abrasives: sandpaper, steel wool, and friends

➤ How to sand

➤ The cabinet scraper

➤ Sanding figured woods

Many bad finishes were doomed from the start. The surfaces they covered were not ready for them. The wood was either undersanded or oversanded, or else it was just sanded wrong. The finish begins with the surface preparation. This chapter examines the various components of surface preparation. It also discusses the requirements of different finishes.

Different Facts for Different Finishes

All finishes are not created equal. Some require a nearly polished surface beneath them; others need only to be moderately sanded. The difference lies in whether they are penetrating finishes or built-up film finishes. Penetrating finishes, specifically oil, do not build up on the surface; they sink below it. Consequently, if the surface of the wood is rough, the finished surface will be rough; if it is finely polished, the final surface will be polished. With built-up film finishes, a rough but clean surface can be covered with a separate surface that is itself smooth and polished.

This difference is what made French polishing so popular in the late eighteenth and nineteenth centuries. You couldn't just buy sandpaper to finish the wood surface, which made surface preparation for an oil finish just that much more grueling. French polishing yielded a built-up finish that did not require rubbing out. It would cover a surface beautifully that had been scraped with a cabinet scraper, but not sanded.

Woodlore

The antique restorer I worked for when I was 14 and 15 finished most of his work with a French polish. He would not allow sandpaper to touch any flat surfaces that were to be French-polished because he insisted that the sandpaper dulled the surface and ruined the depth of the finish by clogging the pores with dust. Instead, he would scrape the surface and do French polishing directly over it. The scraping allows you to see down into the pores through the finish, giving the appearance of great depth.

The Japanese do unsanded, hand-planed finishes for the same reason. I recently saw a Japanese tea house in a museum that had a planed and waxed finish with great depth, despite the fact that it was only wax on the surface. However, these techniques are for aficionados only.

Varnishes, lacquers, and shellac may need to have a wood surface sanded to only 220-grit or so, because the finish itself will be rubbed out later. Oil, on the other hand, needs a surface that has been polished much farther. Some people apply a heavy coat of oil to seal the grain a bit, and then *wet-sand,* using more finish as a lubricant, with a very fine grit, say 400-grit or 600-grit, which is just polishing the wood. They then wipe off the wood and apply more thin coats of oil.

When you start your surface preparation, think about what kind of finish you're using and proceed accordingly. Later in this chapter, I go through the steps of surface preparation for both penetrating and built-up film finishes.

The Gritty World of Abrasives

As woodworkers, we are very fortunate to live in a world populated by such an array of abrasives and sanding machines. The main weapon in the abrasive arsenal is sandpaper. Everybody knows what sandpaper is, but most people are not aware of all the different types available. There are sandpapers that have been engineered for metal, and others made especially for wood; there are those for sanding finish between coats without clogging, and others that are just designed to be cheap. Sandpaper also comes in different *grits,* or degrees of coarseness. Let's start this sandpaper survey by looking at what sandpaper is made of.

Is There Sand in Your Sandpaper?

When you choose sandpaper, be aware of the variety of abrasive materials available. The stuff you get at the local hardware store is probably the infamous *flint* paper. Stay away from it! The best thing that can be said for it is that it's cheap, but this is false economy. It's good for about two strokes before you need a new sheet.

The best sandpapers for use on wood are *garnet* and *aluminum oxide.* Garnet is a natural crystal material, and though soft, it fractures in use, revealing new sharp edges.

Aluminum oxide is a synthetic material and is much harder than garnet. Another option is *silicon carbide,* which is the hardest material of all and is excellent for metal. Some finishers prefer silicon carbide for sanding finishes, and it may well be better, but to keep my life simple, I just buy aluminum oxide and use it for everything but metal and wet sanding, in which case I use a wet/dry silicon carbide.

Tricks of the Trade

Order your sandpaper from an industrial supplier in boxes of 50 or 100 sheets. You'll be able to get much better quality paper at a significantly lower price. Generally, the paper at a local hardware store is low-quality and overpriced. Look in your local Yellow Pages under "abrasives" to find a supplier.

The size of the grit is the most important aspect of sandpaper, which is often sold as coarse, medium, fine, and extra fine. Serious sanders specify an exact grit size. The lower the number is, the coarser the grit, and the higher the number is, the finer the grit, with the range commonly used by woodworkers being from about 60-grit to about 600-grit. A series of standard grits runs as follows: 60, 80, 100, 120, 150, 180, 220, 240, 280, 320, 360, 400, 500, 600.

Sandpaper's Mysteries Solved

Within each type of sandpaper, there are different grades or qualities. Often, they'll have the same trade name, but there will be mysterious numbers on the back. These numbers indicate the grade, and the numbers change from time to time, so be careful. I used to wonder why one batch of sandpaper would last four times as long as another even though they shared the same name. Eventually, I talked to a product engineer at Norton Abrasives who explained it to me. Now, instead of just ordering Norton Adalox, I order Adalox A273, which he tells me lasts as much as seven times longer than Adalox 212 in tests. Find an industrial abrasives dealer and ask for his or her advice (you'll find suppliers in Appendix B, "Resources").

Another variable with sandpaper is the thickness of the paper. The weight of the paper is designated by a letter, with *A* being the lightest and *C* or *D* being the heaviest commonly available. Thinner papers conform to intricate shapes, and thicker papers hold up better.

Sandpaper also comes in *open-coat* and *closed-coat* configurations. Closed-coat papers have abrasive grit over 100 percent of the paper; open-coat paper has grit over about 50 to 60 percent of the paper, which makes it faster-cutting, resistant to *loading* or clogging with particles, and more flexible. Use open-coat paper for woodworking.

Yet another choice is between stearated and unstearated papers. Stearate is a lubricant that helps keep the sandpaper from clogging. It is particularly useful for sanding finishes, which can cause severe loading or clogging.

Papers are available for dry sanding or for wet/dry applications. Wet sanding uses water or a solvent to lubricate the sandpaper as it cuts, which dramatically reduces clogging when you're sanding finishes.

Other Abrasive Characters

Besides sandpaper, other abrasive tools are used to smooth wood and finishes.

Steel Wool: A Staple

Steel wool is a staple of the woodworking field. Coarse steel wool is used for stripping furniture that is being refinished, while extra fine steel wool is used for rubbing out finishes. The degree of coarseness is designated by numbers, with higher numbers like 3 or 4 being coarse, and finer versions down past 0 to 00, 000, and 0000 or 4 × 0. I use 0000 for rubbing out finishes such as shellac and varnish to a satin sheen and for polishing wood that is getting an oil finish after sanding. I use the coarser grades when stripping off old finish.

Variations on the Steel Wool Theme

Bronze wool is a nonrusting alternative to steel wool that is used with water-based finishes. Little fragments of any metal wool will snag on wood fibers and lodge in the rubbed surface. Those fragments will rust if you use steel wool on a surface that will subsequently get a coat of water-based finish or be exposed to water and will stain the wood under the finish. To avoid this staining, you can use bronze wool or Scotch-Brite pads. You can use steel wool on the final rub out if you are absolutely sure that you will not need to apply another coat of finish.

Scotch-Brite, made by 3M, is an abrasive plastic wool that was originally developed for getting rust off metal. Since then, it's been adapted to many other uses. That scouring sponge with the green scratchy face? That's Scotch-Brite. And those white abrasive complexion pads? They are Scotch-Brite as well. In the extra-fine grades, it's a perfect replacement for steel wool if you're rubbing out water-based finishes. I keep a selection of the stuff around the shop for a variety of applications (you never know when you're going to need to do a little exfoliating).

The traditional way to rub out finishes was to use an abrasive powder like pumice or *rotten stone* with a lubricant such as linseed oil or paraffin oil and a felt pad. I've used this method, but frankly, we have much better abrasives today. The automotive industry has all sorts of abrasive compounds if you want to explore them.

Sanding Made Simple

The hardest part of sanding is the first step, getting all the marks and defects out of the surface before you run through the grits. When you start, there will be tiny ripples left by jointer and planer knives, maybe saw or router marks, some tearout, and maybe a ding or two where a tool slipped or the part was dropped. You have to remove all these marks completely with your coarsest paper before you move to the next grit. Most beginners sand *almost* as far as they should with a particular grit and switch to the next finer paper, which just adds to the heartache. Do your time with the coarse stuff, and then breeze through the finer grits.

The Basic Moves

I do my flat sanding with a cork sanding block to speed the cutting action and to prevent dust from clogging the paper. Cork sanding blocks are available from any good woodworking catalog, or you can make your own by gluing some $1/4$-inch-thick cork to a piece of wood and beveling the corners on top. It must be absolutely flat. Mine is $1^1/_2$ inches thick by $3^1/_2$ inches wide by $4^1/_2$ inches long. I rip the sandpaper in quarters and wrap it around the block. As I sand I rotate the paper frequently on the block to reduce clogging and expose fresh sanding surface; as I rotate it, I tap it to loosen any clogs. I also brush off the surface frequently to further reduce clogging. The reason clogging, or *loading,* is so bad is that it not only ruins the sandpaper, it will also burnish streaks in the wood surface, which can show up later.

For shaped parts, I retire the cork block and just fold one of the quarter-sheets in thirds. I know this sounds like nitpicking, but how you fold it is important. Fold it in thirds, which ensures that the paper side is always touching an abrasive face. This method of folding keeps the paper from slipping, which is not only annoying, it also leaves swirls in the wood that will magically appear when the finish is on and it's too late to fix. If you fold the sandpaper in half or quarters, you'll get paper-to-paper contact, and it'll slip. As each of the faces gets dull, I refold it to expose a new one.

Change your sandpaper when it gets dull. Don't try to milk the last drops out of it; it's false economy. Your time is worth something, and you'll waste less of it if you use fresh paper. With sanding, the name of the game is efficiency.

I like to tear a sheet into quarters and either wrap it around a cork sanding block or fold it in thirds for shaped work. Folding it in thirds prevents slipping.

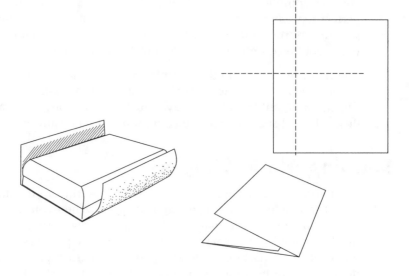

Make sure you sand in long, straight strokes with the grain. Never sand across the grain or even diagonally, because you'll end up with scratches that are very hard to get out. Run the block halfway off the edge, but be sure you don't roll the edge over. Cover the entire surface evenly and move sideways gradually by overlapping the strokes. It's easy to get swirls when you switch from a forward movement to a backward one; be sure that you make it a straight transition.

Smoothing Things Out, Grit by Grit

The first thing you want to do is remove all the milling marks, which are all the little ripples left by the jointer and planer. I start at about 100-grit, and I sand until all the marks and any dings or tearout are gone. Then I sand with 120-grit and sand until all the scratches left by the 100-grit are gone. I then go to 150-grit, through 180, 220, and so on until I've taken it as far as I need to go. Ultimately, you save time by not skipping grits. And don't sand beyond the time it takes to get rid of the previous paper's scratches.

As a final touch, you may want to go over the piece with a damp cloth to raise the grain, let it dry thoroughly, then hit it again with the final grit, ever so lightly. This is a must if you're using a water-based finish.

Breaking Edges

When you're done with two adjacent surfaces, you can *break the edge* between them. This is just a way of softening the edge slightly with sandpaper. It adds longevity to the edge; a sharp edge will snag on something or get dented. Also, it makes the edge more comfortable to touch. How much you should break the edge depends on you. This subject is the center of many heated debates among woodworkers. I don't break edges much because I like to keep a nice, crisp appearance, but it's for looks, not practical reasons, so you can break yours as much as you want.

Power Up!

I used to think that power sanders were too rough, but that was when I was a perfectionist working for a perfectionist. Now I do most of my sanding with a German-made Fein random orbit sander. It is so fast and does such a great job that I have to pinch myself from time to time. It's also very expensive, but my feeling is that anything that saves you time sanding is worth its weight in gold.

As I've said elsewhere, I don't like those little pad sanders. I think they're slow and leave swirls. Belt sanders are okay for fairly rough work, but these days, I use planes and scrapers to level things, and then go to the random orbit sander. Make sure you keep the sander moving, or it will create a hollow.

One trick I have, though, is that after I'm done with the final grit of the random orbit sander, I step back a grit with the cork block and hand-sand all the swirl marks out. I don't care what anyone says: Random orbit sanders leave swirls; the swirls are not as bad as those left by orbital sanders, but they're noticeable when finish hits the wood. I should point out that stain brings out swirl and cross-grain marks that you might not see otherwise, so be extra careful when you're staining.

Getting Out of a Scrape

The hand scraper is one of the unsung heroes of the toolbox. It doesn't have rosewood handles or brass ferrules, but a cabinetmaker wouldn't trade his or her cabinet scrapers for all the overpriced tools in a fancy woodworking catalog. It will save you untold time sanding and yield a better result in the end.

Before you can work with a hand scraper effectively, you'll need some one-on-one instruction and a surprising amount of practice to learn how to use one, and you'll need even more practice to learn how to sharpen one. Once you've learned both skills, it seems incredibly easy, but it takes a lot of frustration to get the hang of it. Like surfing or skiing, it's a very simple process with a lot of feel to it.

The scraper uses a minute hook burnished into its edge (exaggerated here for clarity) to carve shavings from the wood surface.

The scraper is just a flat piece of steel that has a hook burnished onto its edges. By drawing this hook over the surface of the wood you can pull up a shaving in a way that is a little different from that of the hand plane. Unlike the hand plane, it will not tear out the wood, so it's perfect for removing tearout where grain reverses. Prior to sanding, you can use it to remove tearout left by the jointer or the thickness planer; I use it to remove the jointer and planer marks. It is useful in many situations as a prelude to sanding.

It is also very useful, once you become extremely proficient with it, for leveling finishes. You can use the scraper to remove sags, drips, and brush marks from shellac, varnish, and lacquer surfaces. It doesn't clog like sandpaper and can save a lot of time.

To sharpen a scraper, you must file the edge square, remove the file marks on a whetstone, and burnish a hook about 5 degrees off square with a piece of harder steel (an old push rod out of an engine does nicely, but so does a chisel).

You burnish the hook with a hardened piece of steel, like an automobile push rod or a chisel.

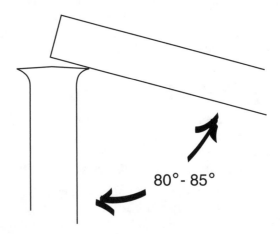

80° - 85°

I don't see any point in wasting space with a step-by-step photo essay on how to use and sharpen a scraper. Plenty of other books have them. Of course, I've never met anyone who learned to do it properly out of a book; you really need someone to show you. It's one of those things where seeing is believing.

The Goods: Figured Woods

Figured woods such as curly maple offer a special challenge when it comes to surface preparation. They are so prone to tearout that you are guaranteed a little quality time with the scraper or sander. I find the scraper invaluable when it comes to figured woods.

There are, however, some tricks to minimize tearout. My favorite is to dampen the surface being planed right before I run it through the planer. Wet fibers cut better than dry fibers (why do you think they wet your hair before they cut it?), and wetting reduces tearout. Just make sure you dry off the wood when you're done.

When you sand curly wood, even a cork block will tend to sand the curls inconsistently because they have different densities, and this difference leads to ripples. If this happens, I switch to a hardwood block. It will clog more, but it will keep the surface flat because it doesn't conform to the surface as cork does. This also works on grain-porous woods that have very different fast- and slow-growth densities.

So You Want to Be a Stripper

Refinishing generally involves stripping off the old finish. I don't like to do this anymore because I don't like using chemical strippers. The good strippers, the ones with methylene chloride, cause cancer and heart, liver, and kidney disease and are bad for your central nervous system. When I was young and very, very foolish, I used to spend hours and days elbow deep in stripper without a mask. Do not make the same mistake. Wear lots of protection. I often say, "I know what I'm going to die of; it's just a question of when."

If you want to strip wood, I recommend that you do it right: Use a powerful stripper, but take all the precautions recommended by the manufacturer. Strip outdoors or in a spray booth with the fan on and wear a respirator with fresh cartridges intended for organic vapors. Also, cover your body and wear heavy gloves that are designed for toxic chemicals.

I believe the best strippers to be ones that use methylene chloride and methanol as the active ingredients. Alkali-fortified methylene chloride strippers are stronger, but unless you're stripping polyester resin, epoxy, or some other two-part conversion finish, I would avoid them. I had some doors stripped with it recently, and it ruined the surface of the wood.

I Woodn't Do That!

Never work with strippers without great ventilation. They're even more toxic than the various solvents used in finishing. You should do stripping outdoors if possible or else with a commercial-grade exhaust fan nearby. A respirator that's set up for organic vapors and heavy gloves are also musts.

I find that thicker, gel-type strippers work best because you can leave them on and let them work, and they'll neither drip nor evaporate as fast as liquids. A new trick that I picked up recently when I was stripping some marble mantles in my house is to cover the stripper with plastic to prevent evaporation and let it work overnight. If you can let the stripper work for you, you should.

After the stripper has done its thing, scrape off the mess with a putty knife and deposit the sludge into a container that you don't mind parting with; a cardboard box will do nicely. I then go over the surface, especially curved ones, with coarse steel wool. You may have to apply stripper several times to remove all the old finish. After this is done, you should neutralize the finish with lacquer thinner or paint thinner. Keep in mind that these are general instructions; you should read the instructions on the stripper you've chosen and do what they tell you.

The Least You Need to Know

➤ Different finishes require different surface preparation.

➤ Good quality sandpaper is worth the investment.

➤ You should use a sanding block on flat surfaces.

➤ Always sand with the grain.

➤ Scrapers are hard to get the hang of, but they are worth the effort.

➤ Stripping is the ultimate toxic woodworking activity.

Chapter 29

Let's Get It On!: Applying Finish Step by Step

In This Chapter

➤ Brushing finish

➤ Special demands of water–based finishes

➤ Staining wood

➤ Filling the pores

➤ Problems that arise and how to avoid them

Applying your finish is the last thing you'll do to your woodworking project, so you want to get it right. You want your finish to be like glass, with no brush marks, drips, or air bubbles. This requires some knowledge and some patience. There are basic rules to finishing, but each finish is a little bit different and requires its own approach. Often, beginners will master one finish only to experience disaster when they try an unfamiliar one. This chapter looks at both the general and the specific rules and methods of finishing to help you avoid that sort of debacle, because nothing is so disheartening as messing up your piece at the eleventh hour.

I've chosen not to get into spraying finish, because I don't think it's for the beginner. This may seem unfair after I've told you how great a sprayed lacquer finish is, but I believe you'd do better to master the brushed finish before you start spraying. Appendix B, "Resources," lists books that go over the details of spraying, and I suggest that you also find a good seminar or course to get hands-on training with a spray system.

Finally! The Finish Line

If you've been patient and thorough with your surface preparation, then the hard part's over. You still have to be patient, and you need to know what you're doing, but I can assure you that what happens from here on in sure beats sanding.

Dissing the Dust

Probably the most important thing in applying finish is to work in a dust-free environment. Often, dust is the cause of bubbles that show up in the finish, because surface tension forms a bubble around each dust particle. Finding a dust-free environment is a problem, because woodworkers and finishers inevitably produce lots of dust. Dust is probably everywhere in your workshop; just try knocking a ceiling fixture and see what rains down. If you can, do your finishing in a different place from where you do your woodworking and sanding. Outside can be a good choice because it solves ventilation problems; just make sure you set up something to block the wind.

Wood Words

A **spray booth** is the ideal place to do your finishing. It's a special room with a sheet metal shroud holding filters placed in front of ductwork, with a powerful fan that draws air though the filters. If you place your work within the shroud, any particles of dust or finish and solvent fumes will be whisked away. Some shops rent time in their spray booths, so ask around.

If you can't work out a dust-free environment, you can take action to minimize the problem. First of all, vacuum the area and the piece the night before you plan on getting started. Be thorough, and make sure you get any surfaces that are above the finishing area.

Right before you start finishing, fill a spray bottle with water and spritz the floor so that you won't kick up dust as you move around. Also, wipe down the piece with a tack cloth immediately before you start. Blowing off the piece with compressed air is a great way to remove dust from the pores, but it deposits the dust particles in the air. Do this only if you're working in a *spray booth* or can do it in your shop and then move the piece to another area for finishing.

A Little Atmosphere

The environment and weather conditions can wreak havoc with your finish. Humidity is the most dangerous culprit. It slows down the cure time of most finishes, which allows more time for dust to collect. It also causes lacquers to *blush* (form hazy spots).

Extreme heat and cold will also speed or slow (respectively) the cure time and hot, dry weather can cause tiny bubbles to form, which ruins a finish. What happens is that the surface of the finish dries too quickly and skins over, and as solvents evaporate below, they can't escape, forming bubbles that are trapped against the skin. This happens when the finish is applied too thick, so always apply film finishes extra-thin in hot weather. They should also be applied thin in cold weather, because the cure time will be extended and thick coats will take forever to dry.

When the weather is inclement, put off your finishing if you can. It may save you time in the long run by preventing problems.

The Brush-Off

The first thing you need to do is buy finishing brushes. You will need different brushes for different finishes. You'll need a good natural bristle brush for solvent-based finishes and a synthetic (polyester or nylon) brush for water-based finishes. Natural bristle brushes have a better feel in solvent-based finishes, but they get too soft in water-based ones, and the water-based finishes tend to dry them out. The better natural bristle brushes are made from Chinese boar bristles. I recommend a brush in the two- to three-inch range. Look for brushes that have a chisel end rather than a flat end, and tapers from the metal ferrule to the end. You also want individual bristles that taper from the ferrule down to a flagged tip; that's one that has split ends that hold more paint and give a finer finish.

Also, keep some lower quality brushes around for rough work. Disposable foam brushes are handy and cheap, but they dissolve in alcohol and some other solvents. However, foam brushes are good for water-based finishes.

Make sure you clean and store your brushes properly. Clean them in the solvent that dissolves the finish you're using. It helps to use a brush comb when cleaning them to remove finish and straighten the bristles. Brush combs are available at any decent paint store.

After you're done, you can store your brushes in one of two ways: If you use a brush for only one finish, you can leave it suspended with the tip in some of the solvent appropriate to that finish: alcohol for shellac, mineral spirits for varnish. To do this, you just drill a hole above the ferrule and put a dowel through, which rests on the rim of a jar with solvent in it. Make sure the bristles do not touch the bottom of the jar, or they will bend. My old boss maintained that this method keeps the bristles soft. Because I don't finish every day or even every week, I find it simpler to fold the brush in the little jacket that good brushes come in or in brown paper to protect the bristles.

Woodlore

My friend Sean Webster's father, Jack Webster, was a master finisher in England and used to set up schools for finishing around the world. Sean does finishing and painting to support his sculpture in this country. During one of Sean's visits home a few years ago, the old man, in a rare tender moment, took Sean up to the attic saying he had something for him. He pulled out his old roll of sable brushes, a complete set for regular and decorative painting, the kind of quality that existed 50 years ago in Britain. He made a little speech and opened the roll, only to discover that moths had eaten all the bristles. Sean said it's one of the few times he's ever seen his father speechless.

Different Strokes

If you follow some basic rules, you'll be able to lay on a smooth finish with the best of them. First, decant some finish into a can big enough to fit your brush. Holding it low, dip your brush into the material about a third of the way up the bristles. Remove any drippy excess by tapping the metal ferrule against the edge of the container. Do not wipe the bristles against the lip, because this is messy, gets finish in the upper section of the bristles, and can create drips on the outside of the can.

Start your stroke a couple of inches from the edge and, brushing with the grain, run your stroke off the edge; then, overlapping the stroke, come back the long way so you have one long stripe of finish. Repeat this process, overlapping the strokes slightly. Keep your brush fairly wet, and when you reload your brush, start your first stroke a few inches from the last one and work back to it, so you don't have a strip that is extra-thick. I like to start at the far side of a surface, so long as I can reach across it comfortably, and work toward myself, so I don't drip on already finished surfaces as I reach over.

Don't move your brush too fast, or the material will not flow properly; you can go faster with thin finishes because they flow faster. With finishes that are slow-drying, like oil-based paints and varnish, it is sometimes better to lay the paint on and then go back over the whole surface carefully with your brush. I sometimes apply paint with a roller for speed and then brush it out to smooth it.

Applying an Oil Finish

Now it's time to discuss the finishes individually. I'll start with the oil finish because it's the low-tech favorite. I've worked for people who apply oil finishes in a number of different ways. Each method has advantages and disadvantages.

Some put it on heavy at first to saturate the wood; they let it dry, and then wet-sand it with more oil as a lubricant, and wipe off the residue. They then lay on several lighter coats, one day apart, making sure to wipe off the finish before it gets tacky. The problem with this method is that after wet-sanding with oil, wood tends to sweat oil from its pores for several hours. If you don't wipe it off right away, beads of oil will dry on the surface, at which point you have to rub them off with steel wool.

The way I do it now is that I sand the wood to a very fine grit, say 320- or 400-grit; I then go over the wood with a damp cloth to raise the grain and resand with 400-grit paper. Then I go over it with 4 × 0 steel wool before applying oil. I apply the oil very lightly, polishing it hard as I go with a wool cloth to generate heat, which lowers the viscosity. I wipe off the excess after a few minutes (forget about that "wait 25 min-

utes" business on the label; if you do, you'll have a sticky mess). I go on to apply several coats in this manner, allowing each of them to cure overnight. When the coats cease to improve the appearance of the piece, I stop. I think that polishing as you rub in the oil does as much for the surface as the additional coats after a certain point. You have to revive the finish every so often by coating it with more oil when it gets dull and dry-looking.

Although oil finishes are simple, they are not easy. They require a lot of elbow grease. Because true oils don't build up significantly, any shine comes from polishing the surface before and during the application. Basically, this means more surface preparation. The so-called Danish oil formulations build up a bit, because they have some varnish in them, and I prefer that.

Tricks of the Trade

Use good rags. Don't use rags made with polyester or other synthetics; they don't absorb material, and they don't polish well. I use only rags made from cotton or wool. Wool gives the best polishing action with oil-based finishes.

Step On It with Shellac

Shellac is an easy finish to apply. The one thing that is tricky about it is that the solvent, alcohol, dries quickly, so you can't go over an area after you've laid finish down. You have to keep moving to overlap your strokes, or you'll start tugging it up and leave brush marks.

When applying shellac, a one-pound cut is good as an initial sealer coat. You may recall from Chapter 27, "Choosing Finishes: Knowing Fact from Fiction," that a one-pound cut means one pound of shellac flakes per gallon of alcohol. Let it dry for three to four hours and then sand the hair off with 320-grit sandpaper: Don't overdo it! After that, I use a two- to three-pound cut (two to three pounds of shellac per gallon). The thicker it is, the harder it is to brush, so you may want to keep it on the thin side. Apply a coat and wait three to four hours again.

I like to sand between each coat to level the finish out. If you don't sand between each coat, especially on grain-porous woods, you'll get a built-up finish with hollows wherever there are pores; this is called a *hungry* finish, because the pores have sucked up the shellac. To me, a hungry finish looks cheap. If you sand the finish flat between coats, you not only get rid of the brush marks, you also end up filling the pores with shellac for a glass-flat finish. Keep applying coats until you get the film thickness you're after. After your last coat has dried, you can rub it out to a matte sheen with 0000 steel wool; again, don't overdo it.

Shellac forms clots of finish on your sandpaper as you work. Tap them out if you can and change paper if you can't, because they will streak the surface. It helps to use stearated paper. Shellac is also prone to skinning over and forming bubbles if it goes on too thick, so if you see bubbles, just sand them out and thin down your material.

Wood Words

A **tack cloth** is a piece of cloth treated with a small amount of sticky varnish so that dust sticks to it when you wipe a surface with it. You can buy commercially made ones that seem to use a special varnish that never hardens, or you can make your own. Cheesecloth is the common choice because it doesn't shed fibers. I keep my tack cloths in a sealed plastic container.

Varnish: Hurry Up and Wait

Varnish brushes on easier than shellac. It flows out, and you can rework areas for a few minutes after you've laid it down, as with paint. The big problem with varnish is that, because it takes a long time to cure, it tends to pick up dust. For this reason, you have to work extra hard to control dust. Use a *tack cloth* after you sand between coats. Varnish is also very sensitive to temperature. It can take forever to cure if the temperature is below about 60 degrees, which just makes the dust problem more of an issue. In hot weather, varnish can be prone to skinning over and getting trapped bubbles and may not flow out well, leaving brush marks.

I don't use a sanding sealer with varnish; I just thin out the first coat with mineral spirits. It won't sand quite as well, but I use varnish when I want real toughness, and the sanding seal works against toughness. Besides, this way I only have to buy one product. You must stir varnish before you use it, but do so gently. Never shake varnish, or you'll put bubbles into it that can mar the finish, especially if the viscosity is thick.

Apply the first coat quite thin (about 50 percent thinner than normal) and let it cure for 24 hours; because you're really going to sand it, you want to let it get good and hard. Sand it with 320-grit, preferably outdoors or at least away from where you're finishing, and remove all the dust thoroughly. After that, you can apply another coat. I like to thin out varnish with about 20 percent thinner, because I find that if I don't, I get brush marks, and it goes on too thick and ends up with bubbles. I just prefer the way varnish feels thinned out, and I think it's much easier to work with for beginners. Expert finishers probably like to lay it on thicker for speed's sake, but if you don't finish furniture all the time, you're better off thinning it out as I do.

I like to alternate coats with and across the grain, making sure that the last coat goes with the grain. Let it cure for 24 hours and sand out any blemishes and brush marks with 320-grit sandpaper. Repeat this process until you have a sufficient film, usually four or five coats after the sealer coat (if you're thinning it out 20 percent).

You may want to try wet sanding, because the paper will clog quickly otherwise. Use wet/dry 400-grit paper with mineral spirits as a lubricant. Some people like to use mild liquid soap and water, but I prefer thinner, for no very good reason than that it seems wrong to me to put soap and water on wood, even if it's protected.

Once the varnish has enough buildup, I like to wet-sand it and rub it out with 0000 steel wool to a matte finish. You can buy gloss finish and rub it out, or you can buy a semigloss or satin varnish. I use gloss, because I always rub out the finish anyway for flatness, and I've heard that gloss is stronger because it doesn't have flattening agents. Regardless of whether this is true, the flattening agents don't improve the clarity or depth of the finish.

Water-Based Finishes: Stirred, Not Shaken

Water-based finishes vary tremendously from one to another, so you should read the directions for each type and do what the manufacturer says, not what I tell you. Still, there are certain characteristics that are common to most of them. For instance, they all need to be stirred thoroughly, but they must not be shaken, or they will foam. It's a good idea to strain water-based finishes, because they tend to get floating chunks of dry finish that can mar your surface.

Before you use water-based finish, you should definitely raise the grain and resand, because water-based finish raises the grain badly. I find that the first coat always raises the grain again, so I always use sanding sealer and give it a good sanding with 320-grit sandpaper. You shouldn't use a tack cloth with a water-based finish, because it can affect adhesion. The good news is that you can use a plain damp cloth instead.

I just keep applying coats of water-based finish, sanding only if blemishes exist or if the pores on a grain-porous wood are looking hungry. At the end, I rub it out with steel wool or Scotch-Brite, but don't use steel wool until you're sure you won't be applying more coats.

Water-based finish tends to look terrible until it has cured overnight, because it flows out for a long time. This is particularly true when you're spraying. The first few times I used water-based finish I left the shop in the evening thinking I had a disaster on my hands only to come in the next morning to a perfectly fine-looking finish.

The Many Ways to Stain

Stains can be wiped, sprayed, or brushed on. You should read the directions on the product you're using and see what the manufacturer recommends. I usually brush thin stains such as water-based stains, NGR, and alcohol stains and wipe oil-based stains. However, stains go on more evenly if you spray them.

Wood Words

Different parts on the same project made from different boards of the same type of wood often have differences in color and texture and take stain differently. It's hard to even out the color simply by applying stain to bare wood. In this situation, you can use **toning,** which is adding stain to the finishing material, to create a unified color.

Stains that overpenetrate are one of my pet peeves because they produce a blotchy surface on woods that have lots of open fibers, such as pine, cherry, and birch. This occurs when sections with lots of open pores suck up more stain than areas with fewer pores. My solution is to apply a very thin wash coat of shellac or some other finish and sand it before I stain. The finish seals the pores so they don't end up darker. To me, this step gives a much more professional-looking result. The only wrinkle is that this limits the effectiveness of the stain; it won't get as dark, which may or may not be a problem.

If you need the piece to be darker, you can always add some stain to the final finishing material. This is called *toning,* and you have to use a dye or pigment appropriate to the finish you're using. Call the manufacturer and ask which stains are compatible with its finish. The only problem is that adding color to the finish will hurt its clarity. This is especially true if you use pigment stains.

Filling the Pores

If you want an ultra-flat finish with no porosity, then you need to fill the wood's pores. Certain woods are very porous and tend to look hungry if you don't do something to fill them. You can fill pores with the finish by applying the material and sanding it back so that eventually the pores fill with finish and rise to the same level as the surrounding area. This method works very well with shellac, lacquer, varnish, and water-based finishes, but not with oils, which won't fill the pores.

As an alternative, you can use a paste wood filler. It is different from putty; paste wood filler just fills pores. Although there is more waiting time with a paste wood filler, this method may take less work, and it allows you to tint the color to match the color in the pores to that of the rest of the surface or to color them to contrast with the rest of the finish.

Paste wood filler can be hard to use at first. The first time I tried it was a nightmare. I had seen my boss do it previously, and when I was in grad school, I decided to try it myself, thinking the instructions on the can would be enough. I was wrong. I ended up with a walnut tabletop that had horrible streaks burnished into it, and I had to sand it out all over again right before the graduate student show.

Here's the method I use now for oil-based paste wood filler: Thin it out with mineral spirits until it's the consistency of heavy cream. Don't use naptha, as is often advised; mineral spirits give you more working time. Stir it well and brush a heavy coat on the surface. Don't do too large an area, because you have to wipe it off before it dries too much. Work it into the pores with a plastic squeegee, sold at paint stores for applying putties and filler. Work it in with the squeegee diagonally to the grain. Let it dry to the point where the surface gets dull, but don't wait too long, or you'll kill yourself wiping it off.

At this point, start wiping across the grain with clean burlap rags. I know you're not supposed to do anything across the grain, but this motion cleans the filler off the wood surface while keeping it in the pores. Wipe until nothing more comes off onto your rag. Do the rest of the surface in manageable sections.

When you're done, let the surface sit for several days. Wait a week if you have the time so that it's good and dry. For particularly porous woods, you'll probably have to apply a second coat and go through the whole process again. After the pores are filled and the filler has cured thoroughly, go back and sand very lightly with the grain using 320-grit paper. This is the point where people generally have problems. (I know I do!) There are usually cross-grain streaks, and you have to sand them out. The problem is that you have to try to not sand through the stain. I find I generally have to reapply stain when I'm done sanding, because I create thin spots. You can now apply finish.

As you can see, oil-based paste wood fillers are quite a production. To be honest, I rarely use them. I don't use them with water-based finish because there are special water-based fillers that cure quickly and don't hurt the adhesion of the finish. I don't use wood fillers with lacquer, because lacquer thinner disturbs the filler, and it's so much easier to fill the pores of most wood with sanding sealer when applying lacquer. The same goes for shellac. The only time I use paste wood filler is if I'm applying varnish, where filling the grain with finish by sanding back coats would take longer than doing it with filler. I would also use it if I wanted to tint the pores a contrasting color, but I never do finishes like that.

The Least You Need to Know

➤ Dust is the enemy: Finish in a dust-free location.

➤ Temperature and humidity affect your finish application.

➤ Use a synthetic brush for water-based finishes, and use natural bristles for solvent-based finishes.

➤ Apply finish in thin coats to avoid problems, especially in hot weather.

➤ To get an even stain, you must either seal the pores first and/or tone the finish material.

➤ To get a glass-flat finish, you must fill the pores either with finish or with paste-wood filler.

Glossary of Woodworking Terms

across the grain   Perpendicular to the grain direction.

against the grain   If, when cutting into the surface of the wood, you do so such that the blade lifts up fibers rather than shearing them off. This leads to tearout.

air-dried   Wood that has been dried to at least 12 percent moisture content by exposure to air over a period of time, generally one year per inch of thickness. Contrast to kiln-dried.

applied drawer front   Separate front that is attached to an assembled drawer box.

arbor   A rotating machine part that holds blades, cutting heads, or chucks in place.

astragal   A strip of molding that prevents drafts and light leaks between French doors.

backing veneer   The veneer face on the secondary or back of a panel.

balanced panel   A veneer core panel with an odd number of layers so that the stresses will be balanced as moisture comes and goes.

base plate   Mounting bracket for a European-style hinge.

baseboard molding   Molding that makes a transition between floor and walls.

bearing   A friction-reducing device that holds spindles and moving parts while they rotate or slide.

bench dogs   Metal or wood fixtures that fit in slots in the workbench and vise to hold parts.

blemish   A defect in the wood's appearance.

board/foot   The volumetric unit used to buy and sell wood. It is equivalent to 1 inch in thickness by 12 inches in width by 1 foot in length. For example, a piece of wood 3 inches in thickness by 8 inches in width by 6 inches in length is a board foot. To calculate how many board feet are in a board, you multiply the thickness in inches, by the width in inches, by the length in feet, and divide by 12.

bole   The useable section of the trunk of a tree that may be cut into lumber.

book-match   To match consecutive boards or veneer leaves so that there appears to be a mirror image, because the grain of the two faces separated by a saw kerf or knife slice are nearly identical.

boring insect   Common small insect that ruins wood by boring into it. They tend to concentrate on *sapwood* because it holds sugars.

bowing   A type of warping where the board is bent along its length.

burl   A growth at the bottom of the trunk of a tree that has wildly figured grain and is often used for turning or cut into veneer. It has no grain strength, so it is not used in solid wood form.

butt chisel   Flat-bladed cutting tool with a wooden handle. Its short blade is used for mortising butt hinges and other work where control is important.

button head screw   A screw with a flat-bottomed head. Also called a roundhead screw.

cambium layer   The living layer at the outside of the trunk's wood where it meets the bark. New cells are created in the cambium layer, and it is where the outward growth of the trunk occurs.

carcass joinery   Joinery designed around the joining of flat planes of wood.

case hardening   A defect caused by poor kiln-drying, where the outside of the board is hardened by compression and the inside is in tension, often leading to interior checks known as honeycombing.

chair rail or **molding**   Strip of molding that runs around walls to protect them from chair backs.

chamfering   Beveled edge on a workpiece.

checks   Splits or cracks in the grain that occur because of stresses due to uneven shrinkage and expansion. Usually they occur at the ends of boards and on the surface.

chemical bond   Glue bond formed by chemical cross-linking of fibers between the two faces being joined.

chisel   Flat-bladed cutting tool with wooden handle.

clear   In reference to wood, free from blemishes or defects.

clearance angle   The angle between the back of a cutter like a plane blade or a jointer knife and the wood left by the cut.

closed set-up time   Amount of time an adhesive will remain viable after it has been applied to parts, and they have been assembled but not clamped.

comb grain   *See* rift-sawn.

conversion finish   A modern finish that cures by chemical reaction rather than by evaporation of solvents. Conversion finishes usually require the mixing of two components to get the chemical reaction started.

core   The center material or layers of a sheet of plywood.

counterbore   A cylindrical hole above a screw head that can accept a plug.

countersink   An angle hole designed to accept the head of a flathead screw so that it can be recessed below the surface of a part. Also, the tool that cuts such a hole.

crack   A radial check due to shrinkage. Note: This is the technical definition; the term is used more broadly in normal usage.

creep   Tendency for a glue to allow parts to slide slightly along a glue line after the glue has cured.

crook   A type of warping along the length of a board where the part that is not straight is along the edge of the board.

cross-banding   The layer of veneer in plywood that is just below the face veneer and whose grain direction is perpendicular to the face veneer.

crosscut   To cut a board or part perpendicular to the grain direction, or to cut plywood perpendicular to the grain direction of the face veneer.

cross-grain   Perpendicular to the grain direction.

crotch-grain   Figure produced by slicing through the crotch, or junction, of the tree trunk where each branch begins its separation from the trunk. The grain of the branches is visible on either side of the trunk's centerline.

crown molding   Often elaborate moldings that join walls to the ceiling.

cup   Type of warping where a hollow occurs across the width of the board.

curing   The set-time of adhesive or finish due to chemical reaction after drying.

curly grain   Type of figure caused by fibers that grow wavy rather than straight. It's very desirable in some instances and a defect in others.

cut-list   List showing all the parts of a project with dimensions and details necessary for their fabrication.

cutting angle   Relation between the angle of the face of a blade and the surface of the wood.

dado   A groove.

dado set   A set of saw blades that can be put together in different order and shimmed to cut grooves or dadoes of different widths.

dead stacking   To stack lumber face to face without stickers so that air cannot circulate around its faces.

decay   Wood rot due to fungi.

deciduous trees   Trees that drop their leaves every winter; contrast to evergreens.

defects   Wood abnormalities or damage that reduces its quality or value.

delamination   When the layers of plywood or laminated solid wood separate due to adhesive failure.

density   The weight of wood per unit volume. This measurement is often connected to its hardness.

dental moldings   Crown moldings with applied rectangular pieces that resemble teeth.

drawer guides   Strips of wood that position drawers side to side.

drawer kicker   Frame member above the drawer that prevents it from tipping downward in front.

drawer runner   Bottom supports that drawers run on.

drawer slides   Commercial sliding mechanisms that allow quick drawer installation.

dressed lumber   Boards that have had their surfaces cleaned up on the jointer and planer. Often wood is sold D2S, which means dressed two sides.

dry rot   Term for wood that has rotted due to fungi but is now dry and crumbly. Dry rot is a misnomer; no wood rots while dry, because fungi need moisture to grow.

dryers   Chemicals added to varnishes and other finishes to speed curing.

earlywood   The wood that grows quickly, in spring, and is more porous and less dense than that which grows the rest of the year.

edge banding   The veneer or solid wood strips that are glued onto the edges of plywood and other sheet goods.

Elevations (front and side)   Orthogonal view of a project from front or side.

end grain   A surface that intersects the grain's fibers at any angle blunter than 45 degrees, but especially at 90 degrees, so that it is all pores. End grain is a poor glue surface.

epoxy   A modern two-part adhesive that is great for bent lamination but is expensive and toxic.

face veneer   The exterior veneer surfaces on plywood or other veneered panels.

FAS grade   Top grade of lumber. It is an abbreviation for Firsts and Seconds.

fiddle back grain   *See* curly grain.

figure   Unusual grain pattern in any given wood due to atypical fiber growth. For example, curly maple is a type of figured wood.

film finish   A finish that builds in thickness on top of the wood's surface, offering greater protection than penetrating finishes.

flake board   Sheet material, like plywood, whose core is made up of ground particles of wood that have been mixed with glue and formed under pressure and heat. It may or may not have face veneers.

flathead screw   Screw with a head that is wedge shaped on the bottom and flat on the top. It's used for positioning parts positively.

flat-sawn   Refers to wood that has been sawn so that the primary two faces are tangent to the growth rings and the majority of the rings intersect the face at an angle more oblique than 45 degrees.

flitch   Series of consecutive boards or slices of veneer where all the pieces have been cut parallel to each other, as though with an egg slicer.

flitch-cut log   Log that has been sawn so that the boards are cut consecutively, starting on one side and continuing through to the opposite side.

floating panel   A panel that is not glued in place but floats in a frame.

frame joinery   Joinery that builds a skeleton-like structure that may or may not be filled in with panels.

French polishing   Technique for applying shellac with a tampon or pad.

full-overlay doors   Doors that completely cover the carcass sides of a cabinet.

grade   Level of quality according to an official organization applied to lumber, veneer, plywood, or similar product on the market.

grain direction   Direction of the fibers or long cells in a board.

green   Term applied to wood meaning that it has not been dried or to certain adhesives, such as epoxy, meaning uncured.

growth ring   The layers of wood that grow consecutively every year around the perimeter of the tree, below the bark. They are characterized by early and late growth, which have low and high density, respectively.

half-overlay door   Door that sits halfway over the carcass sides of a cabinet so that other doors may share the sides.

hardwood   Trees in the group called angiosperms, which basically means they have broad leaves instead of needles. Surprisingly, it does not mean that the wood is necessarily hard.

heartwood   Wood from the center of the log, generally characterized by darker color than sapwood on the outside. All heartwood starts out as sapwood, but it becomes heartwood when it stops carrying sap.

hide glue   Glue made from boiled animal hides, hooves, and bones.

honeycombing   Interior checks that appear due to poor drying conditions, especially bad kiln-drying. They are often not visible until you cut into the board. Usually appearing in thick boards, certain species are particularly prone to them, such as white oak and maple.

H.V.L.P. spray equipment   High-volume, low-pressure equipment that is designed to lessen overspray and solvent emissions that are toxic and bad for the environment.

inset door   Door that is set within a carcass.

interlocked grain   Grain that occurs when the fibers spiral one way and then another around the trunk. This results in boards whose faces have grain that runs in at angles in both directions, which leads to tearout. Also called roed grain.

kiln   A room or building used for drying wood with humidity-controlled heat and air circulation.

kiln-dried   Wood that has been dried in a kiln as opposed to air-dried.

knot   An early section of a branch that the trunk of the tree has subsequently grown over and that is then encapsulated in the board. Some knots are loose, and others are held.

lacquer   Refers to both Chinese lacquer, which is an ancient finish, and nitrocellulose lacquer, which is an 80-year-old finish that bears no connection to Chinese lacquer. Nitrocellulose lacquer is probably the most common commercial finish in use today.

latewood   The wood that grows slowly, after spring growth, and is less porous and more dense than that which grows in the early part of the year.

lights   Glass panels in a door or window.

linear foot   Wood measurement alternative to the board/foot where the board or molding is measured by length only, in feet, as opposed to board/foot, which is a volumetric measurement.

log carriage   Rolling apparatus that holds a log for cutting into lumber.

lumbercore   A sheet material like plywood, but with strips of solid wood as the center core for greater directional strength. This strength makes it ideal for shelves.

MDF (medium-density fiberboard)   Sheet material, like plywood, whose core is made up of individual wood fibers that have been mixed with glue and formed under pressure and heat. It may or may not have face veneers.

mechanical bond   A glue bond where the adhesive keys into irregularities in the surfaces being joined.

medullary ray   Cells that grow from the pith radially to the perimeter.

milling   The process of flattening, cleaning up, and cutting lumber to dimension.

moisture content   The amount of moisture in a volume of wood, expressed as a percentage by weight of the wood were it dried completely in an oven.

moisture meter   Device used to measure the moisture content of wood by testing its electrical conductivity.

mortise   Slot into which a tenon is placed to form a mortise-and-tenon joint.

mortise chisel   Flat-bladed cutting tool with a wooden handle where the sides of the blade are high and square for chopping mortises, as in mortise-and-tenon joints.

mullions   Divisions between lights (glass panes) in windows.

muntin   A central, vertical frame member on a door that separates wood panels.

nitrocellulose lacquer   Spray finish that is fast-drying, flexible, inexpensive, and attractive.

nominal dimension   The dimension of parts or lumber before machining.

oil stones   Sharpening stones that use oil or kerosene as a lubricant to prevent clogging.

open time   Amount of time an adhesive can remain exposed to air and still be viable after it has been applied to parts.

oval head screw   Decorative version of a flathead screw that has a domed top for appearance.

pan-head screw   *See* button head screw.

paring chisel   Long, thin chisel used by resting the back of the chisel on the work and shearing an object like a bung or dowel off the surface.

particle board   *See* flake board.

peeled veneer   *See* rotary-cut veneer.

penetrating finish   Finish that penetrates into the wood, rather than building up a film on its surface. Oil is a penetrating finish.

picture molding   Thin strip of molding below the crown molding from which pictures are hung.

pitch   Resinous material that collects in pockets and runs through resin canals of softwood. It gums up power tool cutters and stains through finish and paint if not cured in a kiln or sealed in by shellac or some other sealer.

pitch pocket   An elongated pocket that appears in some softwoods containing soft resin.

pith   Pulpy center of trunks and branches.

plain-sawn   *See* flat-sawn.

planing mill   A sawmill that planes and molds lumber for sale in lumberyards.

plan view   Technical drawing showing the view from above the project.

platform stock   Sheet material designed to have a face veneer glued on by the purchaser.

plywood   Sheet material made from layers of veneer laminated together with the grain at right angles.

pore   The open mouth of a wood fiber that has been sliced open.

pot life   The length of time that an adhesive that cures by chemical reaction, rather than evaporation, has before it becomes unworkable after it is mixed. Conversion finishes have a pot life, too.

powder post beetles   Common small insect that ruins wood by boring into it. They tend to concentrate on sapwood because it holds sugars.

prefinishing   Finishing parts before assembly that would be difficult or impossible to finish after assembly.

premill   *See* rough-mill.

presentation drawings   Drawings of finished project to indicate to a client what it will look like.

procedure list   List of processes necessary to complete a project in step-by-step order.

push stick   Shaped stick that serves as an extension of your hand when you are using machinery. Push sticks prevent injury by keeping your hand away from the cutter.

quarter-sawn   Lumber in which the rings run perpendicular to the primary two faces. It takes its name from the fact that it comes from logs that are generally cut in quarters first.

quick-release coupling   Snap-together coupling for pneumatic hoses and tools.

rabbet   A recess at an edge designed to accept a back or other panel.

rail   A horizontal frame member on a door.

raised grain   Grain that has gotten furry after sanding by coming in contact with water or some other liquids. Raised grain must be resanded to be made smooth.

raised panel   A panel that sits in a frame with a tongue that raises up to a field or flat surface with a molded transition.

rays   *See* medullary rays.

reaction wood   Wood that has tremendous internal tension because it has grown fighting gravity, such as wood grown on the side of a mountain or wood from branches.

reference surface   The one surface on a part that all measurements or cuts are made from for consistency.

resawing   To cut a board into two or more slabs that have the same width and length but fractional thickness.

resin   Class of solid or semisolid organic substances. Natural resins and synthetic resins are used in adhesives and finishes.

rift-sawn   Boards that have been cut so that the rings cross the two primary faces at approximately 45 degrees.

ring-porous wood   Certain woods that have a pronounced difference in density between earlywood and latewood, such as oak, ash, and chestnut.

rip   To cut solid wood parallel to the grain direction and plywood parallel to the grain direction of the face veneers.

roed grain   Grain that occurs when the fibers spiral one way and then another around the trunk. This results in boards whose faces have grain that runs in at angles in both directions, which leads to tearout. Also called *interlocked grain*.

rotary-cut veneer   Veneer that is cut off a spinning log from the perimeter so that it comes off like toilet paper.

rough lumber   Lumber that is sold unplaned as it comes cut off the log, with rough, wooly surfaces and saw marks.

rough-mill   A preliminary step to get the parts cut out and milled slightly oversized so that internal tensions may relax before final milling.

sap   Water with dissolved nutrients that keeps the tree alive.

sapwood   Wood near the cambium layer at the outside of the trunk that still conducts sap. After it is cut into lumber, it is usually lighter than heartwood and is prone to rot and insects because it contains sugars. It is considered a defect in lumber.

sawmill   A manufacturing facility that saws logs into boards or lumber. Most do not sell lumber directly to the public, but small ones may.

seasoning   The process of drying lumber by air-drying.

section view   Technical drawing showing a slice through a project.

shelf life   The amount of time a chemical mix, such as an adhesive or finish product, will remain viable if left unused.

shellac   Ancient finish still in use that is made from the secretions of the lac beetle.

short grain   Situation where the grain either runs in the wrong direction in relation to the structural axis of a part or fibers are simply too short to hold together and will break apart.

shrinkage   Change in the width of a board due to moisture loss.

sled   A sliding fixture that allows you to crosscut parts and boards.

sliced veneer   Veneer that has been sliced off the log into leaves with a knife, as opposed to sawn off.

slip-matched   Consecutive flitch-cut boards or slices of veneer matched so that seemingly identical patterns face in the same direction, in contrast to a book-match that appears to be a mirror image.

soft wood   Wood from coniferous trees of the family gymnosperms. The term paradoxically does not mean woods that are softer than so-called hardwoods.

spalted wood   A defect that is sought after by some for its decorative value and is caused by controlled decay that leaves light patches and dark lines. Spalted wood loses much of its strength, and its dust can cause potentially serious lung problems in rare individuals who are sensitive to it.

splitter   A thin piece of metal that sits behind a saw blade as a kind of a guard.

spray booth   A ducted enclosure that circulates and filters air so you can spray finish without ending up in a cloud of solvents.

stable   As applied to wood, it means wood that stays flat and does not expand and contract much with moisture change.

stearated sandpaper   Sandpaper that has been impregnated with a special lubricant to reduce clogging. It is especially useful when sanding finish.

stickers   Wood strips used to separate boards in a stack so that air may circulate around them for moisture equalization.

stile   A vertical frame member on a door.

stretcher   A horizontal frame member.

substrate   The central core of a sheet material upon which face veneers are applied.

summer wood   *See* latewood.

surface checks   Generally small checks that appear on wood's surface and do not (with luck) penetrate deeply. They are often caused by wind while the board was air-drying or by short exposure to sun or heat at the surface.

surfaced lumber   Boards that have been planed on at least two sides.

swelling   Wood expansion due to added moisture.

swirls   Scratch patterns found under finish that are created by nonlinear sanding.

tack cloth   A sticky, varnish-impregnated rag that picks up dust more efficiently than a plain rag.

tampon   Pad used in French polishing and for padding lacquers.

through cutting   Sawing a log into a flitch of consecutive slabs.

tiger grain   Old-fashioned term for curly grain, as in tiger maple for curly maple.

timber   The wood in trees before they are cut down.

toning   The technique of adding color to the final finish so that you can adjust color after the staining process.

trunk   The main structural support between the roots and the first branches.

two-part adhesives   Adhesives that require that a resin and a catalyst be combined to bring about a chemical process that makes the glue cure.

varnish   Finish made by cooking oils and resins (either natural or synthetic) and adding dryers. Resins used include phenolic, polyurethane, and alkyd resins.

veneer   Sheets of wood cut from a log by slicing, peeling, or sawing and applied to the surface of parts and panels or laminated together into the same.

waney edge   Edge of a board showing the bark or uneven outer surface of a trunk; edge untrimmed when milled out of log.

warp   Twisting, bowing, cupping, or any other distortion of a board due to internal stress, external pressure, or uneven humidity balance.

water stones   Sharpening stones that use water as a lubricant instead of oil to prevent clogging. They generally cut faster than oil stones.

wet-sand   To sand with a liquid introduced, generally soapy water or a solvent, to reduce sandpaper clogging. Special wet/dry sandpaper must be used.

white glue   Polyvinyl acetate (PVA) glue.

with the grain   As in a cutting operation, shearing the fibers so that they are not torn and damaged.

wood movement   The tendency for wood to expand and contract or warp due to changes in its moisture level.

working drawings   Technical drawings that communicate the detailing and construction information necessary to construct a piece.

working time   *See* pot life.

yellow glue   Modified polyvinyl acetate (PVA) glue.

Resources

Suppliers

Here is a list of woodworking resources—suppliers of tools, materials, videos; a list of books; and some Web sites. They should help you set up shop and continue your "studies" now that you've gotten this far.

The following is a list of suppliers that I would recommend. The list favors the Northeast, because that is where I have always done business, but they all have mail-order service. They cover a wide range of products that you will need in the course of your woodworking. You will have to find suppliers, especially suppliers of lumber, near you, but this should help get you started, especially if you live in an area where it is difficult to buy high-quality tools.

A & M Wood Specialty Inc.
358 Eagle Street North
P.O. Box 3204
Cambridge, Ontario N3H 456
519-653-9322

I don't know of a better place to order wood over the phone; they are the only wood dealers that I would buy wood from sight unseen. They are honest and very knowledgeable. Shipping anywhere is not a problem.

Binks Inc.
1 Chapin Road
P.O. Box 696
Pinebrook, NJ 07058-0696
973-575-6660

This manufacturer of professional-quality spray equipment sometimes runs finishing seminars.

Certainly Wood
13000 Strykerville Road
East Aurora, NY 14052
716-655-0206
Fax: 716-655-3446

This is a supplier of top-quality veneer. Mail orders are a specialty.

Charrette, Inc.
To order a catalog:
1-800-367-3729
www.charrette.com

This is the major supplier of drafting tools and supplies, with stores in most major cities.

Albert Constantine & Son
2050 Eastchester Road
Bronx, NY 10461
718-792-1600
1-800-223-8087

This supplier of veneer, veneering supplies, veneering kits, and exotic woods has a catalog available.

Charles G. G. Schmidt & Co. Inc
301 West Grand Avenue
Montvale, NJ 07645
1-800-544-2447

This supplier of table saw, jointer, planer, and shaper knives also has an excellent sharpening service by mail.

Do-All Eastern
36-06 48th Avenue
Long Island City, NY 11101
1-800-765-4595

Through its catalog and stores, this industrial supply company is a great source for band saw blades, abrasives, and machinist's tools.

Forrest Manufacturing Co.
461 River Road
Clifton, NJ 07014
1-800-733-7111

This maker of top-grade table saw blades also has a top-notch sharpening service by mail.

Frog Tool Co. Ltd.
700 W. Jackson Boulevard
Chicago, IL 60606
312-648-1270
1-800-648-1270

Through its catalog and store, this company is a good source of woodworking tools and books.

W. L. Fuller Inc.
7 Cypress Street
Warwick, RI 02888
401-467-2900

This great old-school company makes and supplies drill bits and countersinks.

Garrett-Wade
161 Avenue of the Americas
New York, NY 10013
212-807-1155
1-800-221-2942

Through its catalog and store, this company is a source of high-end tools, books, and other woodworking supplies.

Gougeon Bros.
P.O. Box X908
Bay City, MI 48707
517-684-7286

This company manufactures and supplies West System Epoxy and support products, including literature about working with epoxies.

Hafele America Co.
3901 Cheyenne Drive
P.O. Box 4000
Archdale, NC 27263
1-800-423-3531

The largest supplier of European style hardware I know of, this company has a great catalog with more hardware than you can shake a chisel at, everything from drawer pulls to Murphy bed hardware. Most of the products are made in Europe. Although the catalog is aimed at production furniture manufacturers, it has something for everyone.

The Japan Woodworker
1731 Clement Avenue
Alameda, CA 94501

This company provides a great selection of high-quality Japanese tools.

Lee Valley & Veritas
1090 Morrison Drive
Ottawa, Ontario K2H 1C2

or

12 East River Street
Ogdensburg, NY 13669
1-800-871-8158
Fax: 1-800-513-7885

Originally a Canadian company, it now has a division in the United States. It carries an excellent selection of woodworking tools, books, videos, and related products, and has a great catalog.

Madsen & Howell, Inc.
500 Market Street
Perth Amboy, NJ 08862
908-826-7651

This supplier of top-quality Norton brand sandpaper also has a line of industrial equipment.

Mohawk Finishing Products, Inc.
Rt. 30 North
Amsterdam, NY 12010
518-843-1380
1-800-545-0047

This company is a manufacturer and supplier of high-quality finishing supplies.

MSC Industrial Supply
151 Sunnyside Boulevard
Plainview, NY 11803-1592
1-800-645-7270

This supplier of fasteners and industrial supplies has a great catalog.

Nanz Hardware
20 Vandam Street
New York, NY 10013
212-367-7000

This company manufactures and supplies very high-quality reproduction architectural hardware. Have your wallet stuffed and ready.

The Sanding Catalog
P.O. Box 3737
Hickory, NC 28603
1-800-228-0000

This company offers sanding supplies, including papers and sanding machines.

Select Machinery
64-30 Ellwell Crescent
Rego Park, NY 11374
718-897-3937

This company supplies Lamello products and others.

Star Chemical Co. Inc.
360 Shore Drive
Hinsdale, IL 60521
708-654-8650
1-800-323-5390

This company is a manufacturer and supplier of high-quality finishing supplies.

Vacuum Pressing Systems
553 River Road
Brunswick, ME 04011
207-725-0935

This company is a manufacturer and supplier of vacuum veneer presses and veneering supplies.

Whitechapel Ltd.
P.O. Box 136
Wilson, Wyoming 83014
1-800-468-5534
Fax: 307-739-9458

Founded by an English harpsichord maker, this company puts out a catalog that is an excellent source for traditional hardware. It sells my beloved scalpel/marking knives.

Woodcraft Supply
210 Wood County Industrial Park
P.O. Box 1686
Parkersburg, WV 26102
1-800-535-4482

Source of high-end tools, books, and other woodworking supplies. I bought my first set of carving tools from it when I was 11 in 1970. In addition to its catalog, it also has stores scattered around.

The Woodshed
1807 Elmwood Avenue
Buffalo, NY 14207
716-876-4719

This company sells veneer and veneer products.

The Woodworker's Store
21801 Industrial Boulevard
Rogers, MN 55374
612-428-2199

This store sells a wide variety of tools, books, and other woodworking supplies.

Woodworker's Supply of New Mexico
5604 Alameda Place
Albuquerque, NM 87113
505-821-0500
1-800-645-9292

This store sells a wide variety of tools, books, and other woodworking supplies.

Books and Videos

Now that you've gotten your feet wet, you might as well jump in. The following is a list of books I recommend to keep the ball rolling. They cover a range of topics. Some are general in focus, and some concentrate on one aspect of woodworking. A few are on the old-fashioned side; some are books that I used when I was starting out. Others are new publications.

The best resource I know for books, videos, and the like is Taunton Press in Newtown, Connecticut. They also publish *Fine Woodworking* magazine, which has become something of a bible for the woodworking field.

Charron, Andy. *Spray Finishing*. Newtown, CT: Taunton Press, 1996.

Conover, Ernie. *The Router Table Book*. Newtown, CT: Taunton Press, 1994.

Flexner, Bob. *Understanding Wood Finishing*. Emmaus, PA: Rodale Press, 1994.

Frid, Tage. *Tage Frid Teaches Woodworking Books 1 & 2 & 3*. Newtown, CT: Taunton Press, 1979, 1981, 1985.

Hoadley, R. Bruce. *Understanding Wood*. Newtown, CT: Taunton Press, 1980.

Joyce, Earnest (revised by Alan Peters). *Encyclopedia of Furniture Making*. New York: Sterling Publishing Co., Inc., 1987.

Krenov, James. *A Cabinetmaker's Notebook*. New York: Prentice Hall Press, 1975.

——. *The Fine Art of Cabinetmaking*. New York: Prentice Hall Press, 1976.

———. *The Impractical Cabinetmaker*. New York: Prentice Hall Press, 1979.

Landis, Scott. *The Toolbox Book*. Newtown, CT: Taunton Press, 1998.

———. *The Workbench Book*. Newtown, CT: Taunton Press, 1998.

———. *The Workshop Book*. Newtown, CT: Taunton Press, 1998.

Lee, Leonard. *The Complete Guide to Sharpening*. Newtown, CT: Taunton Press, 1995.

Lincoln, W.A. *The Complete Manual of Wood Veneering*. New York: Charles Scribner's Sons, 1996.

Odate, Toshio. *Japanese Woodworking Tools: Their Tradition, Spirit and Use*. Newtown, CT.: Taunton Press, 1998.

Tools and Their Uses. New York: U.S. Navy publication published by Dover Press, 1978.

If you're interested in videos, Taunton Press has the most comprehensive selection on all aspects of woodworking. Contact Taunton Press at 1-800-447-8727 or on the Web at www.taunton.com.

Web Sites

Of the many woodworking Web sites, I think these three are the best starting point.

www.taunton.com

www.woodworking.com

www.woodzone.com

Organizing Your Project

The hardest thing for beginners, and often for experienced woodworkers as well, is to maintain a clear overview of their project. It's critical in woodworking to perform tasks in the right order and perform all the operations necessary. This is particularly hard for the hobbyist who doesn't have a master there barking instructions and who often goes for days at a time without working on a project, which tends to glaze the memory a bit.

For this reason, it is critical that you work from drawings, make a cut-list, and sleep with a procedure list beneath your pillow (or keep one pinned to the bulletin board anyway). This appendix has an example of each of these critical items: drawings, cut-list, and procedure list. I discuss these items in depth in Chapter 21, "Plan It on Paper: Drawings, Cut-Lists, and Procedure Lists." Here I focus on a single sample project, a small dining table, so you can chart the relationship between the three. Use these lists as a guide or build the rather undistinguished table if you care to. I chose it because it's not too hard and not too easy.

Cut-list.

Cut-List

Part#	Done	Description	Quantity	Material	T	W	L	Notes
		Legs	4		2 1/4"	2 1/4"	28 1/2"	Each leg gets 1/2 x 3 x 1 1/4" mortise
		Stretchers	2		1"	3 1/2"	41"	Each stretcher gets 1/2 x 3 x 1 1/8" tenon and 1/4 x 5/16" groove for cleats
		Stretchers	2		1"	3 1/2"	23"	Each stretcher gets 1/2 x 3 x 1 1/8" tenon and 1/4 x 5/16" groove for cleats
		Top	1		1"	34"	52"	Top to be glued-up from boards of whatever width is available
		Cleats	10		15/32"	2"	2 1/2"	

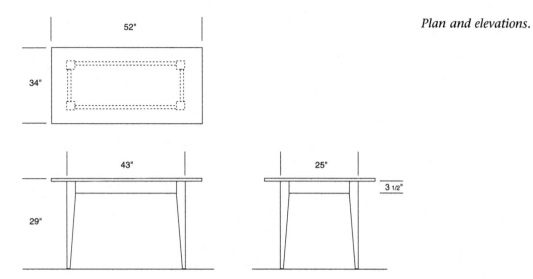

Plan and elevations.

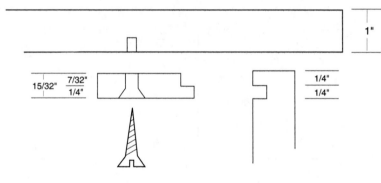

Detail showing buttons used to attach top to apron.

*Section through leg
showing joinery.*

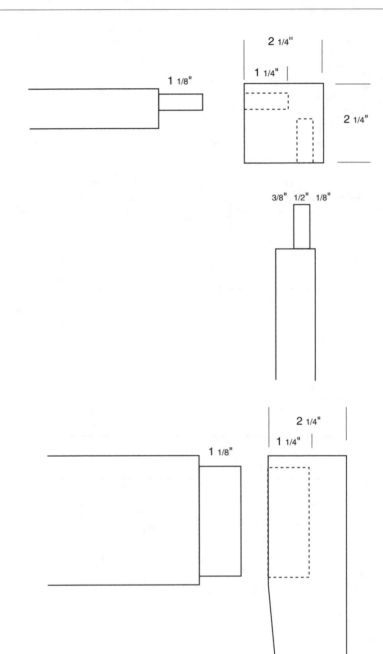

Side view of joinery.

Procedure List for Small Dining Table

To begin your project, take the cut-list that you generated from your drawings to the lumberyard along with a marking crayon, tape measure, scrub or block plane, and pencils. Pick out and purchase your lumber. Once the wood is in your shop, follow these steps:

1. Lay out parts on rough lumber in pencil.

2. Cut out parts from rough lumber, slightly oversized.

3. Rough-mill parts $3/16$-inch oversize in thickness and width. Note: It is not necessary to crosscut parts when you rough-mill. Follow these steps:

   a) Joint a face.

   b) Plane the opposite face.

   c) Joint the edge.

   d) Rip the boards to width.

4. Stack and sticker the wood and allow to sit for a few days (the longer the better, to relieve internal stresses and allow the moisture level to equalize) before proceeding to step 5.

5. Mill the pieces to their final size by following these steps:

   a) Joint a face.

   b) Plane the opposite face for thickness.

   c) Joint the edge.

   d) Rip the pieces to width.

   e) Joint the ripped edge.

   f) Crosscut ends square to final length.

6. Cut taper on table leg.

7. Cut mortises in legs.

8. Cut tenons.

9. Cut a groove in stretchers with dado blade in table saw or with router.

10. Sand the parts.

11. Glue up base.

12. Make cleats to hold top by following these steps:

   a) Mill stock to thickness and width, but long enough to get all the cleats by crosscutting.

   b) Crosscut cleats.

   c) Cut tongues to fit groove in stretchers.

   d) Drill and counter-sink a free hole for #12 flathead screw.

13. Glue up the top out of the boards.

14. Flatten the top with hand plane, scraper, belt sander, or whatever method is available to you.

15. Cut the top to its final width and length.

16. Mark and drill pilot holes in the top for attachment screws.

17. Final sand the top and base in preparation for finishing.

18. Apply finish.

19. Assemble the base and top with cleats.

20. Stand back and admire what a great job you've done.

Index

Symbols

3M Scotch-Brite pads, 306

A

aberrations, 108-109
abrasives, 306-309
    bronze wool, 306-307
    sandpaper, 304-306
    sharpening stones, 91-92
    steel wool, 306
accessories, tooling, 29
acrylic
    lacquers, 285
    plastic windows, 193-194
adhesives, 155-156, 167-168
    chemical bonds, 149-150
    construction, 155
    contact cement, 154
    cyanoacrylate ester, 155
    end grain, 151
    epoxy resin glues, 153-154
    hide glues, 154
    long grain, 151
    mechanical adhesives,
      149-150
    plastic resin glues, 152-153
    selecting, 151-155
    white glues, 152
    yellow glues, 152
adjustable wrenches, 55-56
aiming, cutting edges, 88
air-dried wood, 124-125
alcohol-based aniline dye
  stains, 300
alkyd resins, 296-297
Allen drive heads, 184
Allen keys, 55
aluminum oxide sandpaper,
  305
American tools, 9

angles, cutting edges, 90
apartments
    woodworking, 12-14
    workspace, 12-14
aprons, 164
Arkansas stones, 91-92
ash wood, 113
aspen wood, 132-133
astragal, 192
auctions, tools, 10

B

back saws, 40-41
back-cutting, 218-219
backing veneers, 134-135
balancing, chisels, 39
ball catches, 200-201
Baltic Birch, 137
band saws, 15, 81, 122
banding, edges, 132, 137
base plates, 198-199
baseboards, 217
basements
    woodworking, 15
        machines, 15
        open space, 16
        storage, 15-16
    workspace, 15-16
        machines, 15
        storage, 15-16
beams, 26
beds, 74
beeswax, 294
beetles, shellacs, 282, 294-295
belt sanders, 9, 65-66
benches
    dogs, 23-25
    planes, 42-43
    slaves, 24-25
beveling
    files, 39
    gauges, 8, 49, 93
    paring chisels, 38

binders, stains, 299
Binks spray equipment, 291
birch wood, 113
biscuit joints, 9, 68-69,
    162-172, 208
    butted, 171-172
    mitered, 171-172
bits
    drills, 62
    Fuller, 177
    spade, 9
blades
    chisels, 39
    circular saws, 63-64
    grinders, 94
    jigsaws, 64
    saws, 122
    table saws, 80
    tooling accessories, 29
blind joints, 171-172
block planes, 8, 42-43
blocks
    cork sanding, 307-308
    corner, 164-166
    sanding, 8
board/foot system, 117-118
boards
    flat-sawn, 123
    quarter-sawn, 123
    rift-sawn, 123
boiled linseed oils, 292-293
bolts, 187-188
    carriage, 187-188
    grade, 187-188
    hex, 187-188
    lag, 187-188
    machine, 187-188
    washers, 188
bonds
    chemical, 149-150
    mechanical, 149-150
book-matching, 123, 133-134

books
Cabinetmaker's Notebook, A, 340
Complete Guide to Sharpening, The, 341
Complete Manual of Wood Veneering, The, 341
Encyclopedia of Furniture Making, 340
Fine Art of Cabinetmaking, The, 340
Impractical Cabinetmaker, The, 341
Japanese Woodworking Tools: Their Tradition, Spirit and Use, 341
Router Table Book, The, 340
Spray Finishing, 340
Tage Frid Teaches Woodworking Books 1 & 2 & 3, 340
Toolbox Box, The, 341
Tools and Their Uses, 341
Understanding Wood, 340
Understanding Wood Finishing, 340
veneers, 128
woodworking, 340-341
Workbench Book, The, 341
Workshop, The, 341
bottoms, drawers, 211-212
bow saws, 40-41
brads, 188
brakes, circular saws, 63-64
branches, 102
brass
hinges, 197
screws, 184-185
Brazilian rosewood, 114
bridal joints, 161
bronze
screws, 184-185
wool, 306-307
Buck Bros. chisels, 39
budgeting, woodworking, 5-6
bugle head screws, 182-183
bullnose planes, 9
bungs, 186
bushings, tooling accessories, 29
butt chisels, 8, 36-37

butt hinges, 194-198
butt joints, 170
butted biscuit joints, 171-172
butted single spline joints, 170
button head screws, 182-183
buttons, 164
buying plywood, 136

C

cabinet doors, 194-195
cabinet scrapers, 8
Cabinetmaker's Notebook, A, 340
cabinets, 167-168
carcass joints, 169-170
European hinges, 198-199
grain patterns, 168
kitchen, 177
moldings, 219
particle board, 169
plywood, 169
tools, 27-28, 57
calipers, dial, 9
cambium layers, trees, 103-104
carcass joints, 158, 167-168
biscuit joints, 171-172
dovetails, 174-175
finger joints, 172-173
glues, 169
grain patterns, 168
multiple spline joints, 173-174
particle boards, 169
plywood, 169
screws, 176-177
single spline joints, 170
tongue-and groove joints, 171
carcass structures, 177
blanket chests, 179
chest of drawers, 177-178
kitchen cabinets, 177
carnuba wax, 294
carpenter's glue, 149-152
carriage bolts, 187-188
carts, rolling, 28
carving gauges, 9
cast iron, hinges, 197

casters
lockable, 28
swiveling, 27
catalogs, 10-12
catalyzed lacquers, 285-286
catches, 200-201
caulk, 216-219
cement
contact, 154
floors, 142
chair rails, 216
chairs, 165-166
chalk, 52
chalk lines, 8
chamfering, paring chisels, 38
channel locks, 187
chemical strippers, 13, 311-312
chemically bonding adhesives, 149-150
cherry wood, 113
chests, 179
Chinese lacquers, 283-284
chip-breakers, 42-43
chisels, 6-9, 36
butt, 8, 36-37
choosing, 39
cutting edges, 88
aiming, 88
angles, 90
sharpness, 89-90
mortise, 36
paring, 8, 36-38
beveling, 38
chamfering, 38
cranked-neck, 36-38
sharpening, 92-97
chop saws, 82
chopping, butt chisels, 36-37
chucks
drills, 61-62
keys, 61-62
circular saws, 9, 63-64, 122
classic frame joints, 159-161
claw hammers, 53
closed-coat sandpaper, 305-306
closets, woodworking, 13-14
clubs, woodworking, 17
coarseness, sandpaper, 304-306

coarseness, steel wool, 306
collecting tools, 9-10
collectors, dust, 85
collets, 67
combination squares, 7, 48
commercial shops
  woodworking, 17
    electrical service, 17-18
    setting up, 18-19
  workspace, 17
    electrical service, 17-18
    setting up, 18-19
common nails, 188
compass planes, 9
Complete Guide to Sharpening,
  The, 341
Complete Manual of Wood
  Veneering, The, 341
compound miter saws, 9
compressors, 9, 69-70
construction adhesives, 155
contact cement, 154
conversion varnishes, 285-286
cope-and-stick cutters,
  194-195
coped corners, moldings,
  218-219
cordless screw guns, 9
core veneers, 130-133
cork sanding blocks, 307-308
corners
  blocks, 164-166
  coping, 218-219
counter bores, 186
countersink holes, 9, 176-177,
  182-183, 186
couplings, quick-release, 69-70
cranked-neck paring chisels,
  36-38
cross-banding, 131
crosscut saws, 40-41
crosscutting, table saws, 79
crown moldings, 215-216
curing
  oils, 292
  varnishes, 283
curly grain, 108-109
cut-lists, project planning,
  343-348

cutters
  cope-and-stick, 194-195
  tooling accessories, 29
cutting
  edges, 88
    aiming, 88
    angles, 90
    sharpness, 89-90
  logs
    flitch-cutting, 122-123
    through-and-through,
    122-123
cyanoacrylate ester adhesives,
  155

D

dadoes, 196, 204
Danish oils, 15, 293
dead blow mallets, 9
dead stacking, 140-141
decorative plywood, 133
  book-matching, 134
  flitches, 134
  slip-matching, 134
dehumidifiers, 16
dental moldings, 215-216
dial calipers, 9
dimensions
  plywood, 134-135
  screws, 185
dining tables, 164
disk sanders, 65, 84-85
domestic woods, 113
doors, 191-196
  cabinets, 194-196
  catches, 200-201
  entry, 191-192
  frame-and-panel, 194-195
  full-overlay, 195-196
  glass, 194
  half-overlay, 195-196
  hardware, 200
  hinges, 197, 199
    butt, 197-198
    European cabinet,
    198-199
  inset, 195-196
  inswing, 193

knobs, 200
locks, 200-201
outswing, 193
panels, 193-194
pulls, 200
sliding, 196
swinging, 193
dovetails, 167-170, 174-175
  drawers, 204
  full-blind, 174-175
  half-blind, 174-175
  machines, 206
  sliding, 205-206
  through, 174-175
dowels, 161-163, 167-168
drawer guides, 204
drawers, 177-178, 204
  bottoms, 211-212
  constructing, 208
  fitting, 206-208
  fronts, 211
  pulls, 211
  slides, 208-210
    extensions, 210
    finishes, 211
  sliding dovetails, 205-206
drawings, project planning,
  343-348
dressed lumber, 126
drills, 8, 61
  bits, 62
  chucks, 61-62
  free holes, 186
  pilot holes, 186
  presses, 15, 84
  speed, 62
drive head screws, 184
dry-sanding, 305-306
dryers
  oils, 281-282
  varnishes, 283
drying
  sheds, 142
  wood, 140-142
dust collectors, 85
dust masks, 64, 75
dyes, stains, 298-299

E

ear protection, 64, 75
edge-band, 194-195
edges
    banding, 132, 137
    cutting, 88
        aiming, 88
        angles, 90
        sharpness, 89-90
    plywood, 137
    sanding, 309
    waney-edges, 122-123
electrical service, three-phase
    power, 17-18
*Encyclopedia of Furniture
    Making*, 340
end grain, adhesives, 151
engineer's squares, six-inch, 8,
    49
entry doors, 191-192
environment, 6-7
Environmental Protection
    Agency. *See* EPA
EPA (Environmental
    Protection Agency), 283-286
epoxies, 149-152
    finishes, 285-286
    resin glues, 153-154
Eskiltuna chisels, 39
European cabinet hinges,
    198-199
evaluating, woodworking, 4
exotic wood, 112
extensions
    full, 210
    overextensions, 210
    partial, 210
eye protection, 64, 75

F

face veneers, 130-133, 169
    book-matching, 134
    flitches, 134
    slip-matching, 134

fasteners, 187
    nails, 188
        pneumatic nailers, 189
        power nailers, 189
    nuts and bolts, 187-188
    screws, 182
        contents, 184-185
        drive types, 184
        head types, 182-183
        joinery, 186
        ordering, 185
        sizes, 185
    washers, 188
fences, 63-64, 74-77
fender washers, 188
fiberboards, 130-132
fibers
    grain patterns, 106
        aberrations, 108-109
        flat-sawn, 106-108
        plain-sawn, 106-108
        quarter-sawn, 106-108
        rift-sawn, 10608
    trees, 103-105
fiddle back grain, 108-109
figured wood, 108-109, 311
files, 8, 39-40
    beveling, 39
    flushing, 39
film finishes, 280-281,
    303-304
    lacquers, 283-285
    shellacs, 282-283
    varnishes, 283
Fine Art of Cabinetmaking, The,
    340
Fine Woodworking magazine,
    39, 340
finesse, woodworking, 5
finger joints, 168, 172-173
finish hammers, 7
finish nails, 188
finish-milled boards, 116
finishes, 155, 279-281, 286,
    303-304
    conversion, 285-286
    drawer slides, 211
    epoxies, 285-286

film, 280-281, 303-304
    lacquers, 283-285
    shellacs, 282-283
    varnishes, 283
French polishing, 282
lacquers, 283-285, 297
lasting, 292
mythology, 289-290
oils, 281-282, 290-292
    Danish, 293
    flammable, 293
    linseed, 292-293
    pros and cons, 294
    tung, 293
penetrating, 280-281,
    303-304
    oils, 281-282
    waxes, 281-282
problems, 289-290
shellacs, 282-283, 294-295
spray, 291
stains, 298
    alcohol-based aniline
        dyes, 300
    binders and solvents,
        299
    gels, 300
    NGR, 300
    oil-based, 300
    water-based, 299
varnishes, 283, 296-297
water-based, 286, 292,
    297-298
waxes, 281-282, 294
finishing stones, 96-97
fir wood, 132-133
firsts, lumber, 126
fixed based routers, 67-68
fixtures, 22
    beams, 26
    jigs, 30
    push sticks, 29
    rolling carts, 28
    sawhorses, 25-26
    storage shelves, 30-31
    tool cabinets, 27-28
    tooling accessories, 29
    workbenches, 22-25

flake boards, 105, 130-133
   carcass joints, 171-172
   multiple spline joints,
     173-174
flammable oils, 293
flat-sawn boards, 123
flat-sawn grain patterns,
  106-108
flathead screws, 182-183, 186
flattening planes, 42-43
flea markets, tools, 10
flint papers, 305
flitch-cutting, 122-123
flitches, 128, 133-134
floating panels, 158
flush-mounted hardware, 200
flushing, files, 39
flutes, 62
folding rules, Lufking Red
  End, 50
formulas, board/foot systems,
  117
Forstner bits, 62
fractional, wrenches, 55
frame
   joints, 158-161
   structures, 164
     chairs, 165-166
     dining tables, 164
frame-and-panel doors,
  194-195
framing squares, 8, 49
free holes, 176-177, 186
French polishing, 279-282,
  294-295, 303-304
Frid, Tage, 155, 175-176
Frog Tool Co. Ltd., 337
fronts, drawers, 211
full extensions, 209-210
full-blind dovetails, 174-175
full-overlay doors, 195-196
Fuller bits, 177
furniture
   conversion finishes, 285-286
   moldings, 219
   stripping, 13

G

gaboon ebony, 114
galvanized screws, 184-185
garages
   woodworking, 15
     machines, 15
     open space, 16
     storage, 15-16
   workspace, 15-16
     machines, 15
     storage, 15-16
garnet sandpapers, 305
gauges
   bevel, 8, 49, 93
   marking, 8, 51-52
gel stains, 300
Gilpin, Hank, 207
glass, 194
   panels, 193-194
   stops, 193-194
glasses, safety, 8
glaze, 96-97
glues, 22-25, 155-156, 167-168
   bonds
     chemical, 149-150
     mechanical, 149-150
   carcass joints, 169
   carpenter's, 149-152
   edge banding, 137
   end grain, 151
   epoxy resins, 153-154
   finger joints, 172-173
   Gougeon Brothers' West
     System, 153
   grain directions, 168
   hide, 154
   long grain, 151
   plastic resins, 152-153
   polyurethane, 155
   selecting, 151-155
Gougeon Brothers' West
  System, glues, 153
gouges, carving, 9
grades
   bolts, 187-188
   plywood, 136
   sandpaper, 305-306
   wood, 125-126

grain
   adhesives, 151
   direction, 130-131, 168
     long, 168
     particle board, 169
     plywood, 169
   log cutting, 123
   patterns, 106
     aberrations, 108-109
     flat-sawn, 106-108
     plain-sawn, 106-108
     quarter-sawn, 106-108
     rift-sawn, 106-108
   wood, 104-105
Greek moldings, 213-214
grinders, 92-94
grips
   length, 187-188
   vise, 8
grits
   sandpaper, 304-306
   sharpening stones, 91-92
grooves, 164
guides, 204-207
guns
   nail, 9, 69-70
   screw, 9, 62-63

H

Hafele America Co., 337
hair, 300
half-blind dovetails, 174-175
half-blind multiple spline
  joints, 173-174
half-overlay doors, 195-196
hammers, 188-189
   claw, 53
   finish, 7
hand scrapers, 309-310
hand tools, safety, 44-45
handles, chisels, 39
handsaws, 40-41
hard maple, 113
hardboard, 131-132
hardwares
   flush-mounted, 200
   surface-mounted, 200

hardwood stores, 115-116
    buying hardwoods, 116-117
    getting your wood home, 119
    measuring, 117-118
hardwoods. *See* wood
haunched mortise and tenon, 160
haunches, 160
heartwood, 103-105
hex bolts, 187-188
hex drive heads, 184
hex keys, 55
hide glues, 154
hinges, 197-199
    brass, 197
    butt, 194-198
    cast iron, 197
    cups, 198-199
    European cabinets, 198-199
    off-set knife, 199
    steel, 197
    strap, 197
holes
    counter bore, 186
    countersink, 182-183, 186
    free, 176-177, 186
    pilot, 176-177, 186
Honduran mahogany wood, 113
Hunnibel, Ken, 182

I

import woods, 113-114
Impractical Cabinetmaker, The, 341
in-feed tables, 76-77
Indian rosewood, 114
inset doors, 195-196
inswing doors, 193
interior moldings, 214
    baseboards, 217
    chair rails, 216
    coped corners, 218-219
    crown moldings, 215-216
    picture moldings, 216
Internet, tools, 10

J

jack planes, 8, 42-43
Japanese
    Dozuki saws, 8
    electric water stones, 98
    sharpening stones, 91
    tools, 43-44
Japanese Woodworking Tools: Their Tradition, Spirit and Use, 341
jigs, 30
jigsaws, 8, 64
jointer planes, 42-43
jointers, 15, 76-77
joints, 158, 164
    biscuit joints, 9, 68-69, 162-163, 167-168, 208
    bridal joints, 161
    carcass, 158, 167-168
        biscuit joints, 171-172
        dovetails, 174-175
        finger joints, 172-173
        glues, 169
        grain patterns, 168
        multiple spline joints, 173-174
        plywood, 169
        screws, 176-177
        single spline joints, 170
        tongue-and groove joints, 171
    carcass structures, 177
        blanket chest, 179
        chest of drawers, 177-178
        kitchen cabinets, 177
    chairs, 165-166
    coped corners, 218-219
    dining tables, 164
    dowels, 161-162
    drawers, 206
    finger, 168
    frame joints, 158-161
    lap joints, 161
    miters, 163
    screws, 186
    sliding dovetails, 205-206
    spline joints, 161
    tongue-and-groove, 208

K

kerf, saw, 123, 127
keyhole saws, 8
keys
    Allen, 55
    Hex, 55
kickers, 204, 207-210
kiln-dried wood, 124-125
kits, woodworking, 12
knives
    cope-and-stick cutters, 194-195
    marking, 8, 50-51
knobs, 200

L

lac beetles, shellacs, 282, 294-295
lacquers, 280-286
    acrylic, 285
    catalyzed, 285-286
    Chinese, 283-284
    nitocellulose, 297
    nitrocellulose-based, 285
    spray, 284-285
    thinners, 297
lag bolts, 187-188
laminate trimmers, 67-68
laminations, plywood edges, 137
lap joints, 161
latches, touch, 200-201
lathes, 15
left-hand opening doors, 193
levels, 8, 56
Lexan, 193-194
lights, 193-194
lines, chalk, 8
linseed oils, 15, 281-282, 292-293
lists
    project planning, 343-348
    tools, 7-9
lock washers, 188
lockable casters, 28
locks, 200-201

logs
    carriages, 122
    cutting, 122-123
    drying, 124
        air-drying, 124-125
        kiln-drying, 125
long grain, 151, 168
long oil varnishes, 296
long straightedge, 50
Luan mahogany, 114,
    132-133
lubricants, 184
    sandpaper, 305-306
    sharpening stones, 91-92
Lufkin, tape measures, 50
Lufkin Red End, folding rules,
    50
lumber, 103-104,112. *See also*
    wood
    103-104, 112
    dressed, 126
    drying, 124-125, 140-142
        air-drying, 124-125
        kiln-drying, 125
    firsts, 126
    grading, 125-126
    milling, 6-7
    moisture, 109-110, 142-143
    No. 1 Common, 126
    No. 2 Common, 126
    No. 3A Common, 126
    No. 3B Common, 126
    precut, storage, 143
    purchasing, 347-348
    quarter-sawn, 207
    racks, 144
    rough, 126
    seconds, 126
    selects, 126
    storage, 18-19, 139-142
    stores, 114-119
    surfaced, 126
    veneer-core, 131
    waney-edged, 122-123
lumber-core, 133
lumberyards, 114-116
    buying hardwoods, 116-117
        getting your wood
            home, 119
        measuring, 117-118
    moldings, 220

M

machines, 15
    bolts, 187-188
    dovetails, 206
    sanding, 304-305
    setting up, 18-19
    stationary, 74
        band saws, 81
        belt sanders, 84-85
        chop saws, 82
        disk sanders, 84-85
        drill presses, 84
        dust collectors, 85
        jointers, 76-77
        planers, 77-78
        radial arm saws, 82
        router tables, 83
        safety, 75
        table saws, 78-81
    tooling accessories, 29
    wheels, 16
mahogany
    Honduran, 113
    Luan, 114, 132-133
mallets, 7
    butt chisels, 36-37
    dead blow, 9
    synthetic, 54
manufacturers
    planing mills, 126
    sawmills
        cutting logs, 122-123
        drying lumber, 124-125
        lumber grading, 125-126
    veneer mills, 127
        rotary-cut veneers, 127
        sliced veneers, 128
maple, hard and soft, 113
markets (flea), tools, 10
marking
    gauges, 8
    knives, 8
    tools, 50
        chalk, 52
        gauges, 51-52
        knives, 50-51
marks, milling, 308
masks, dust, 64, 75

masonite, 131-132
materials
    nails, 188
        pneumatic nailers, 189
        power nailers, 189
    nuts and bolts, 187-188
    screws, 182
        Allen drive heads, 184
        bugle head, 182-183
        button head, 182-183
        contents, 184-185
        flathead, 182-183
        hex drive heads, 184
        ordering, 185
        oval head, 182-183
        pan head, 182-183
        Phillips drive heads, 184
        roundhead, 182-183
        sizes, 185
        slotted drive heads, 184
        square drive heads, 184
    washers, 188
    wood, 102
mauls, 7, 53
MDF (medium-density fiber-
    board), 131-133
measuring
    board/foot system, 117-118
    plywood, 134-135
    thickness of wood, 118
measuring tools, 47-48
    bevel gauges, 49
    combination squares, 48
    folding rule, 50
    framing squares, 49
    long straightedge, 50
    six-inch engineer's squares,
        49
    six-inch rule, 48
    tape measure, 7, 50
mechanical tracks, 196
mechanically bonding adhe-
    sives, 149-150
medium-density fiberboard.
    See MDF
metal
    hinges, 197
    screws, 184-185

meters, moisture, 9, 125, 142-143
methylane chloride, 13, 311-312
metric wrenches, 55
milling, 6-7
  lumber, moldings, 220-221
  lumberyards, 115-117
  marks, 308
  planing, 126
  veneers, 127
    rotary-cut veneers, 127
    sliced veneers, 128
miters, 163
  box, 8
  joints, 170-172
  saws, compound, 9
mitered biscuit joints, 171-172
mitered single spline joint, 170
moisture
  lumber, 109-110
  meters, 9, 125, 142-143
  wood, 109-110, 124-125
moldings, 126, 213-214, 220-221
  baseboards, 217
  buying, 220
  cabinets, 219
  chair rail, 216
  coped corners, 218-219
  crown, 215-216
  dental, 215-216
  furniture, 219
  Greek, 213-214
  interior, 214
    baseboards, 217
    chair rail, 216
    coped corners, 218-219
    crown moldings, 215-216
    picture moldings, 216
  picture, 216
  Roman, 213-214
money (budgeting), woodworking, 5-6
mortises, 36, 159-161, 164-166
mullions, 193-194
multiple spline joints, 168, 173-174
multispur bits, 62
mythology, finishes, 289-290

N

naguras, 96-97
nails, 188
  guns, 9, 69-70
  pneumatic nailers, 189
  power nailers, 189
  sizing, 188
National Hardwood Lumber Association. *See* NHLA
natural resins, 283
NGR (non-grain-raising) stains, 300
NHLA (National Hardwood Lumber Association), 126
nitrocellulose-based lacquers, 285, 297
No. 1 Common, lumber, 126
No. 2 Common, lumber, 126
No. 3A Common, lumber, 126
No. 3B Common, lumber, 126
nominal thickness, 118
non-grain-raising stains. *See* NGR stains
Northern European benches, 23
Norton Adalox sandpaper, 305
nuts, 187-188

O

oak, red and white, 113
Occupational Safety and Health Administration. *See* OSHA
off-set knife hinges, 199
oil-based stains, 300
oils, 280-282, 290-292
  Danish, 15, 293
  flammable, 293
  linseed, 15, 281-282, 292-293
  pros and cons, 294
  tung, 281-282, 292-293
oilstones, 91-92
open-coat sandpaper, 305-306
orbital pad sanders, 8, 66
ordering, screws, 185

organizing
  projects, 343-348
  woodworking, 343-348
oriented strand board, *See* OSB
OSB (oriented strand board), 131-132
OSHA (Occupational Safety and Health Administration), 19
out-feed tables, 76-77
outswing doors, 193
oval head screws, 182-183
overextensions, 209-210
overseas, tools, 9

P

padauk, 112-114
pan head screws, 182-183
panel saws, 40-41
panels, 193-194
  floating, 158
  glass, 193-194
  plywood, 193-194
  wood, 193-194
papers, flint, 305
parameters, woodworking, 5
paring chisels, 8, 36-38
  beveling, 38
  chamfering, 38
  cranked-neck, 38
partial extensions, 209-210
particle board, 131-132, 169
patterns, grain, 106
  aberrations, 108-109
  flat-sawn, 106-108
  plain-sawn, 106-108
  quarter-sawn, 106-108
  rift-sawn, 106-108
pearwood, Swiss, 114
penetrating finishes, 280-281, 303-304
  oils, 281-282
  waxes, 281-282
phenolic resins, 296-297
Phillips
  drive heads, 184
  screwdrivers, 54-55, 183
  screws, 184

photosynthesis, 102
picture moldings, 216
pigments, stains, 298-299
pilot holes, 176-177, 186
pin nailers, 189
pine, 113
plain-sawn grain patterns, 106-108
planers, 15, 77-78
planes, 9, 42-43, 67
    benches, 42-43
        jack, 42-43
        jointer, 42-43
        smoothing, 42-43
    blocks, 8, 42-43
    bullnose, 9
    compass, 9
    cutting edges
        aiming, 88
        angles, 90
        sharpness, 89-90
    flattening, 42-43
    jack, 8
    rabbet, 8, 42-43
    Record, 43
    smoothing, 8
    Stanley, 43
    straightening, 42-43
    trimming, 42-43
planing mills, 126
planning projects, 5-6, 343-348
plastic resins, 152-153, 285-286
platens, 66
plates, throat, 81
platform stock, 133
Plexiglass, 193-194
pliers, 7, 55-56, 187
plugs, 186
plumb bob, 9
plunge routers, 67-68
plywood, 104-105, 127-132, 167-168
    buying, 136
    cabinet doors, 194-195
    carcass joints, 169
        biscuit joints, 171-172
        dovetails, 174-175

multiple spline joints, 173-174
    screws, 176-177
    single spline joints, 170
    tongue-and-groove joints, 171
core-veneers, 132-133
decorative, 133
    book-matching, 134
    flitches, 134
    slip-matching, 134
    veneers, 133
dimensions, 134-135
dovetails, 206
drawers, 204
    constucting, 208
    fitting, 206, 208
    sliding dovetails, 205-206
edges, 137
grading, 136
lumber-core, 130-133
panels, 193-194
platform stock, 133
storage, 145
pneumatic tools, 69
    compressors, 69-70
    nail guns, 9, 70
polishing, French, 279-282, 294-295, 303-304
polycarbonate windows, 193-194
polyesters, 285-286
polyurethanes, 285-286
    glues, 155
    varnishes, 296-297
polyvinyl acetate emulsion. *See* PVA
poplar, 113, 132-133
portable chop saws, 82
power tools, 60
    biscuit joiners, 68-69
    compressors, 69-70
    drills, 61
        bits, 62
        chucks, 61-62
        speed, 62
    nail guns, 69-70
    planes, 67
    pneumatic tools, 69-70
    routers, 67-68
    safety, 60-61

sanders, 65, 309
    belt, 65-66
    disk, 65
    orbital pad, 66
    random orbit, 67
saws, 63
    circular, 63-64
    jigsaws, 64
screw guns, 62-63
presses, drills, 15, 84
problems, finishes, 289-290
procedure lists, project planning, 343-348
professional shops
    space, 17
        electrical service, 17-18
        setting up, 18-19
    woodworking, 17
        electrical service, 17-18
        setting up, 18-19
    workspace, 17
        electrical service, 17-18
        setting up, 18-19
projects
    organizing, 343-348
    planning, 5-6, 343-348
pulls, 200, 211
purple heart wood, 114
push sticks, 29
putty, 218-219
PVA (polyvinyl acetate emulsion), 152

Q

quarter-sawn
    boards, 123
    grain patterns, 106-108
    lumber, 207
quick-release couplings, 69-70

R

rabbet planes, 8, 42-43
racks, lumber, 144
radial arm saws, 82
rags, oil, 293
rails, 158
raising the grain, 300

random orbit sanders, 67
random-matching, 133
rasps, 8, 39-40
ratchet socket wrenches, 55
raw linseed oil, 292-293
Record, planes, 43
red oak, 113
reduced shanks, drills, 62
referencing, 162
refinishing, 311-312
rented shops
    woodworking, 17
        electrical service, 17-18
        setting up, 18-19
    workspace, 17
        electrical service, 17-18
        setting up, 18-19
resins
    alkyd, 296-297
    glues
        epoxies, 153-154
        plastic, 152-153
    natural, 283
    phenolic, 296-297
    plastic, 285-286
    synthetic, 283, 296-297
    Urashi, 283-284
resorcinol-formaldehyde
    glues, 152-153
resources, woodworking sup-
    plies, 335-341
rift-sawn boards, 123
rift-sawn grain patterns,
    106-108
right-hand opening doors,
    193
rings, tree trunks, 103-106
ripping, table saws, 78-79
ripsaws, 40-41
rolling carts, 28
rolling tool cabinets, 27-28
Roman moldings, 213-214
root diameter, 186
rosewood
    Brazilian, 114
    Indian, 114
rough lumber, 126
rough-milled boards, 116-117
roundhead screws, 182-183
Router Table Book, The, 340

routers, 8, 60, 67-68, 171
    multiple spline joints,
        173-174
    tables, 15, 83
rules, 8
    folding, 50
    six-inch, 48
runner-kicker drawer systems,
    204, 208-210
runners, 204-210

S

S1S (surfaced one side), 116,
    126
S2S (surfaced two sides), 116,
    126
S4S (surfaced four sides), 126
safety
    band saws, 81
    chop saws, 82
    drill presses, 84
    ear protection, 64, 75
    eye protection, 64, 75
    glasses, 8, 193-194
    power tools, 60-61
    radial arm saws, 82
    router tables, 83
    sanders, 65-67
    saws, 63-64
    stationary machines, 75
    table saws, 80-81
    tools, 44-45
sanders, 65
    belt, 9, 65-66
    disk, 65, 84-85
    orbital pad, 8, 66
    random orbit, 67
    stationary belt, 84-85
sanding, 303-308
    blocks, 8
    cork blocks, 307-308
    edges, 309
    machines, 304-305
    milling marks, 308
    power sanders, 309
sandpaper, 53, 91-92, 304-305
    aluminum oxide, 305
    flint paper, 305
    garnet, 305

    grades, 305-306
    Norton Adalox, 305
    silicon carbide, 305
sapwood, tree trunks, 104
saw kerf, 123, 127, 135
sawhorses, 25-26
sawmills
    buying hardwoods, 120
    cutting logs, 122-123
    drying lumber, 124
        air-drying, 124-125
        kiln-drying, 125
    lumber grading, 125-126
saws, 8, 63
    back, 40-41
    band, 15, 81, 122
    bow, 40-41
    chop, 82
    circular, 9, 63-64, 122
    crosscut, 40-41
    jigsaws, 64
    keyhole, 8
    miter, compound, 9
    panel, 40-41
    radial arm, 82
    rip, 40-41
    sharpening, 98
    table, 15, 78, 171
        blades, 80
        crosscutting, 79
        multiple spline joints,
            173-174
        ripping, 78-79
        safety, 80-81
scales, 4
Scotch-Brite pads, 306
scrapers, 8, 309-310
screwdrivers, 7, 54-55, 183
screws, 176-177, 186
    Allen drive heads, 184
    brass, 184-185
    bugle heads, 182-183
    button heads, 182-183
    characteristics, 182
    contents, 184-185
    flatheads, 182-183
    galvanized, 184-185
    guns, 9, 62-63
    hex drive heads, 184
    joints, 186
    ordering, 185

oval heads, 182-183
pan heads, 182-183
Phillips drive heads, 184
roundhead, 182-183
sheet metel, 184-185
Sheetheads, 183
silicone bronze, 184-185
sizes, 185
slotted, 198
slotted drive heads, 184, 198
square drive heads, 184
steel pot metal, 184-185
washers, 188
zinc-plated, 184-185
scribing, 218-219
seconds, lumber, 126
selects, lumber, 126
services (electrical), three-phase power, 17-18
setting up
    commercial shops, 18-19
    woodworking shops, 22
        beams, 26
        jigs, 30
        push sticks, 29
        rolling carts, 28
        sawhorses, 25-26
        storage, 30-31
        tool cabinets, 27-28
        tooling accessories, 29
        workbenches, 22-25
shanks, 62, 186
sharpening, 92, 98
    burning the blade, 94-96
    chisels, 97
        finishing stones, 96-97
        grinders, 92-94
    saws, 98
    stones, 8, 91-98
    whetstones, 95-96
sharpness, cutting edges, 89-90
sheds, drying, 142
sheet metal screws, 184-185
Sheetrock screws, 19, 183
Sheffield chisels, steel, 39
shellacs, 279-283, 294-295
shelves, storage, 15-16, 30-31
shoes, circular saws, 63-64

shops
    apartments, 12-14
    basements, 15-16
        machines, 15
        storage, 15-16
    commercial, 17
        electrical service, 17-18
        setting up, 18-19
    garages, 15-16
        machines, 15
        storage, 15-16
    professional, 17
        electrical service, 17-18
        setting up, 18-19
    rented, 17-19
        electrical service, 17-19
        setting up, 18-19
short oil varnishes, 296
shoulders, 160
side chairs, 165-166
side-mounts, 208-210
silicone
    bronze screws, 184-185
    carbide sandpaper, 305
single spline joints, 170
six-inch engineer's squares, 49
six-inch rule, 48
sizes
    nails, 188
    plywood, 134-135
sleds, 79
sliced veneers, 133
slides, drawers, 208-210
    extensions, 210
    finishes, 211
sliding door cabinets, 196
sliding dovetails, 205-206
slip-matching, 133-134
slotted screws, 184-185, 198
slurry, 95-97, 131-132
smoothing planes, 8, 42-43
socket wrenches, 55
soft maple, 113
Solingen chisels, steel, 39
solvents, stains, 299
space
    apartments, 12-14
    basements, 15-16
        machines, 15
        storage, 15-16

commercial space, 17
    electrical service, 17-18
    setting up, 18-19
garages, 15-16
    machines, 15
    storage, 15-16
professional shops, 17
    electrical service, 17-18
    setting up, 18-19
rented shops, 17
    electrical service, 17-18
    setting up, 18-19
woodworking, 6-7
spacers, tooling accessories, 29
spade bits, 9
spar varnishes, 296
speed drills, 62
spikes, 188
splines, 162-163, 167-168
    joints, 161
        butted, 170
        mitered, 170
        multiple, 173-174
    multiple, 168
    single joints, 170
    stopped, 170
    through, 170
Spray Finishing, 340
spray sprays
    finishes, 291
    lacquers, 284-285
    nitrocellulose lacquers, 297
square drive heads, 184
squares
    combination, 7, 48
    engineer, 8
    framing, 8, 49
    six-inch engineer's, 49
stainless-steel screws, 184-185
stains, 298
    alcohol-based aniline dyes, 300
    binders and solvents, 299
    gels, 300
    NGR, 300
    oil-based, 300
    water-based, 299

Stanley
chisels, steel, 39
planes, 43
tape meausres, 50
Starrett
tape measures, 50
tools, 48
starter tools, 7-9
stationary machines, 74
band saws, 81
belt sanders, 84-85
chop saws, 82
disk sanders, 84-85
drill presses, 84
dust collectors, 85
jointers, 76-77
planers, 77-78
radial arm saws, 82
router tables, 83
safety, 75
stationary belt sanders, 84-85
table saws, 78
blades, 80
crosscutting, 79
ripping, 78-79
safety, 80-81
stearated sandpaper, 305-306
steel
chisels, 39
hinges, 197
wool, 306
steel pot metal, screws, 184-185
stickers, drying lumber, 124-125, 140-142
sticks, push, 29
stones, sharpening, 8, 91-92
stopped splines, 170
storage, 15-16
closets, 13-14
lumber, 18-19, 139-142
lumber racks, 144
plywood, 145
precut lumber, 143
shelves, 30-31
tools, 56-57
wood, 139-142

stores
hardwood, 115-119
lumber, 114-119
straightedges, 9, 50, 56
straightening planes, 42-43
strap hinges, 197
stretchers, 158, 165-166
striking tools, 52
hammers, claw, 53
synthetic mallets, 54
wooden mauls, 53
stripping, 311-312
chemicals, 13
furniture, 13
wood, 311-312
structures
carcass, 177
blanket chest, 179
chest of drawers, 177-178
kitchen cabinets, 177
frame, 164
chairs, 165-166
dining tables, 164
stub tenons, 194-195
suppliers, woodworking, 335-340
surface-mounted hardware, 200
surfaced boards, 116-117
surfaced four sides. *See* S4S
surfaced lumber, 116, 126
surfaced one side. *See* S1S
surfaced two sides. *See* S2S
surveying, drawer slides, 208-210
swinging doors, 193
Swiss pearwood, 114
swiveling casters, 27
synthetics
mallets, 54
resins, 283, 296-297
varnishes, 296-297
systems
measuring, 117-118
trees, 102-105

T

table saws, 15, 78, 171
blades, 80
crosscutting, 79
multiple spline joints, 173-174
ripping, 78-79
safety, 80-81
tables, 74
dining, 164
in-feed, 76-77
out-feed, 76-77
routers, 15, 83
tabletop varnishes, 296
Tage Frid Teaches Woodworking Books 1 & 2 & 3, 340
tampons, 279-282, 294-295
tape
measures, 7, 50
veneers, 137, 194-195
tarps, 14
Taunton Press Web site, 341
tearout, 40-43, 309-311
tempered masonite, 131-132
tenons, 159-166, 194-195
thickness
measuring wood, 118
planers, 77-78
plywood, 134-135
thinners, lacquers, 297
three-phase power, 17-18
throat plates, 81
through dovetails, 174-175
through splines, 170
through tenon, 160
through-and-through cutting, 122-123
tiger grain, 108-109
tongue-and-groove joints, 171, 208
Toolbox Book, The, 341
toolboxes, 8, 54
tooling accessories, 29
tools, 7-9, 54
adjustable wrenches, 55-56
Allen keys, 55
American, 9
auctions, 10
cabinets, 27-28, 57

chisels, 36
    butt, 36-37
    choosing, 39
    cranked-neck paring, 38
    paring, 38
collecting, 9-10
files, 39-40
flea markets, 10
hammers, 189
handsaws, 40-41
Hex keys, 55
Japanese, 43-44
levels, 56
marking, 50
    chalk, 52
    gauges, 51-52
    knives, 50-51
measuring, 47-48
    bevel gauges, 49
    combination squares, 48
    folding rule, 50
    framing squares, 49
    long straightedge, 50
    six-inch engineer's
      squares, 49
    six-inch rule, 48
    tape measure, 50
overseas, 9
pin nailers, 189
planes, 42-43
pliers, 55-56
pneumatic nailers, 189
power, 60
    biscuit joiners, 68-69
    drills, 61-62
    nail guns, 69-70
    nailers, 189
    planes, 67
    pneumatic tools, 69-70
    routers, 67-68
    safety, 60-61
    sanders, 65-67, 309
    saws, 63-64
    screw guns, 62-63
rasps, 39-40
ratchet socket wrenches, 55
safety, 44-45
screwdrivers, 54-55, 183
Starret, 48

storage, 30-31, 56-57
striking, 52
    claw hammers, 53
    synthetic mallets, 54
    wooden mauls, 53
tweezers, 55-56
vise grips, 55-56
want ads, 10
woodworking, 5-6
Tools and Their Uses, 341
touch latches, 200-201
tracks
    mechanical, 196
    sliding doors, 196
transporting wood, 119
trees, 102
    fibers, 103-104
    trunks, 102
        fibers, 104-105
        heartwood, 103-104
        sapwood, 104
trimming
    paring chisels, 38
    planes, 42-43
trunks, 102
    cambium layers, 103-104
    fibers, 104-105
    heartwood, 103-104
    sapwood, 104
tung oils, 281-282, 292-293
tweezers, 55-56
twist drills, 62

U

under-mounts, 208-210
Understanding Wood, 340
Understanding Wood Finishing,
    340
unstearated sandpaper, 305-306
Urashi, resins, 283-284
urea-formaldehyde glues,
    152-153

V

varnishes, 280-283, 286,
    296-297
    conversion, 285-286
    long oil, 296
    polyurethane, 296-297
    short oil, 296
    spar, 296
    synthetic, 296-297
    tabletop, 296
veneers, 127-132
    backing, 134-135
    core, 130
    decorative, 133
    face, 130-133, 169
        book-matching, 134
        flitches, 134
        slip-matching, 134
    flitches, 134
    lumber-core plywood,
        130-131
    mills, 127
        rotary-cut veneers, 127
        sliced veneers, 128
    plywood, cabinet doors,
        194-195
    rotary-cut veneers, 127
    sliced, 128-133
    tape, 137, 194-195
veneer-core plywood, 131
ventilation, 17-18
videos, woodworking, 340-341
vise grips, 8, 55-56, 187
vises, 7, 14, 23-25
voids, 132

W–X

walnut wood, 113
waney-edges, 122-123
want ads, tools, 10
washers, 188
water
    stones, 91-98
    wood, 109-110
water-based finishes, 286,
    292, 297-298
water-based stains, 299

waxes, 294
Web sites
    Taunton Press, 341
    Woodworking, 341
    Woodzone, 341
wedged-through tenons, 160
weight, chisels, 39
wenge wood, 114
Western back saws, 8
wet-sanding, 304-306
wheels
    lockable casters, 28
    machines, 16
    rolling carts, 28
    swiveling casters, 27
    tool cabinets, 27-28
whetstones, 91-92, 95-97
white carpenter's glue, 149-152
White Chapel Brasses, mark-
    ing knives, 51
white glues, 152
white oak, 113
windows
    acrylic plastic, 193-194
    polycarbonate, 193-194
wood, 102, 112. *See also* lum-
    ber
    abrasives, 306
        bronze wool, 306-307
        sandpaper, 304-306
        steel wool, 306
    ash, 113
    aspen, 132-133
    birch, 113
    Brazilian rosewood, 114
    buying, 116-117
    cabinet doors, 194-195
    carcass joints
        biscuit joints, 171-172
        dovetails, 174-175
        finger joints, 172-173
        multiple spline joints,
            173-174
        screws, 176-177
        single spline joints, 170
        tongue-and-groove
            joints, 171
    cherry, 113
    domestic, 113
    dovetails, 206

drawers, 204
    fitting, 206-208
    sliding dovetails, 205-206
drying, 124, 140-142
    air-drying, 124-125
    kiln-drying, 125
exotic, 112
figured, 108-109, 311
finishes, 279-281, 303-304
    conversion, 285-286
    French polishing, 282
    lacquers, 283-285, 297
    lasting, 292
    oils, 281-282, 290-294
    shellacs, 282-283,
        294-295
    spray, 291
    varnishes, 283, 296-297
    water-based, 286,
        297-298
    waxes, 281-282, 294
fir, 132-133
gaboon ebony, 114
glues, 152
grading, 125-126
grain patterns, 104-106
    aberrations, 108-109
    flat-sawn, 106-108
    plain-sawn, 106-108
    quarter-sawn, 106-108
    rift-sawn, 106-108
Honduran mahogany, 113
imports, 113-114
Indian rosewood, 114
knots, 102
Luan mahogany, 114,
    132-133
maple, hard and soft, 113
measuring
    board/foot system,
        117-118
    thickness, 118
moisture, 109-110
moisture meters, 142-143
oak, red and white, 113
padauk, 112, 114
panels, 193-194
pine, 113
plywood, 130-132
    lumber-core, 130-131
    veneer-core, 131

poplar, 113, 132-133
purple heart, 114
refinishing, 311-312
sawmills, 120
scrapers, 309-310
screws, 182
    Allen drive heads, 184
    bugle head, 182-183
    button head, 182-183
    contents, 184-185
    flathead, 182-183
    hex drive heads, 184
    oval head, 182-183
    pan head, 182-183
    Phillips drive heads, 184
    roundhead, 182-183
    slotted drive heads, 184
    square drive heads, 184
stains, 298
    alcohol-based aniline
        dyes, 300
    binders and solvents,
        299
    gels, 300
    NGR, 300
    oil-based, 300
    water-based, 299
storage, 139-142
Swiss pearwood, 114
transporting, 119
walnut, 113
water, 109-110
wenge, 114
zebra, 114
wooden mallets, butt chisels,
    36-37
wooden mauls, 53
woodshops, 10
woodworking
    abrasives, 306
        bronze wool, 306-307
        sandpaper, 304-306
        steel wool, 306
    apartments, 12-14
    basements, 15-16
    books, 340-341
    budgeting, 5-6
    commercial shops, 17-19
    cutting edges, 88
        aiming, 88
        angles, 90
        sharpness, 89-90

doors, 191-192
  cabinets, 194-195
  full-overlay, 195-196
  half-overlay, 195-196
  hardware, 200-201
  hinges, 197-199
  inset, 195-196
  panels, 193-194
  sliding, 196
  swinging, 193
dovetails, 206
drawers, 204
  bottoms, 211-212
  constructing, 208
  fitting, 206, 208
  fronts, 211
  slides, 208-211
  sliding dovetails, 205-206
evaluating, 4
finesse, 5
finishes, 279-281, 303-304
  lacquers, 297
  lasting, 292
  oils, 290-294
  shellacs, 294-295
  spray, 291
  varnishes, 296-297
  water-based, 297-298
  waxes, 294
French polishing, 282
  conversion, 285-286
  lacquers, 283-285
  oils, 281-282
  shellacs, 282-283
  varnishes, 283
  water-based, 286
  waxes, 281-282
fixtures, 22
  beams, 26
  jigs, 30
  push sticks, 29
  rolling carts, 28
  sawhorses, 25-26
  storage, 30-31
  tool cabinets, 27-28
  tooling accessories, 29
  workbenches, 22-25
garages, 15-16
joints, 158, 164, 177
  biscuit joints, 162-163
  blanket chest, 179

bridal joints, 161
carcass joints, 158,
  167-177
chairs, 165-166
chest of drawers, 177-178
dining tables, 164
dowels, 161-162
frame joints, 158-161
kitchen cabinets, 177
lap joints, 161
miters, 163
spline joints, 161
kits, 12
machines, stationary, 74-85
marking tools, 50-52
measuring tools, 47-48
  bevel gauges, 49
  combination squares, 48
  folding rule, 50
  framing squares, 49
  long straightedge, 50
  six-inch engineer's
    squares, 49
  six-inch rule, 48
  tape measure, 50
moldings, 213-214, 220-221
  buying, 220
  cabinets, 219
  furniture, 219
  interior, 214-219
organizing, 343, 346-348
parameters, 5
power tools, 60
  biscuit joiners, 68-69
  drills, 61-62
  nail guns, 69-70
  planes, 67
  pneumatic tools, 69-70
  routers, 67-68
  safety, 60-61
  sanders, 65-67
  saws, 63-64
  screw guns, 62-63
professional shops, 17-19
rented shops, 17-19
resources, supplies, 335-341
scrapers, 309-310
sharpening, 92, 98
  chisels, 92-97
  saws, 98

sharpening stones, 91-92
stains, 298
  alcohol-based aniline
    dyes, 300
  binders and solvents,
    299
  gels, 300
  NGR, 300
  oil-based, 300
  water-based, 299
striking tools, 52
  claw hammers, 53
  synthetic mallets, 54
  wooden mauls, 53
suppliers, 335-340
tools, 5-9, 54
  adjustable wrenches,
    55-56
  Allen keys, 55
  chisels, 36-39
  collecting, 9-10
  files, 39-40
  handsaws, 40-41
  hex keys, 55
  Japanese, 43-44
  levels, 56
  planes, 42-43
  pliers, 55-56
  rasps, 39-40
  ratchet socket wrenches,
    55
  safety, 44-45
  screwdrivers, 54-55
  tweezers, 55-56
  vise grips, 55-56
videos, 340-341
workspace, 6-7
Woodworking Web site, 341
Woodzone Web site, 341
wool
  bronze, 306-307
  steel, 306
Workbench Book, The, 341
workbenches, 6-7, 14, 22-25
Workshop Book, The, 341
workspaces
  apartments, 12-14
  basements, 15-16
    machines, 15
    storage, 15-16

363

commercial shops, 17
    electrical service, 17-18
    setting up, 18-19
garages, 15-16
    machines, 15
    storage, 15-16
professional shops, 17
    electrical service, 17-18
    setting up, 18-19
rented shops, 17
    electrical service, 17-18
    setting up, 18-19
woodworking, 6-7
wrenches
    adjustable, 55-56
    Allen, 55
    fractional, 55
    hex, 55
    metric, 55
    ratchet socket, 55
    tooling accessories, 29

Y–Z

yellow carpenter's glues,
  149-152

zebra wood, 114
zinc-plated screws, 184-185